PROHIBITED FORCE

Prohibited 'use of force' under article 2(4) of the UN Charter and customary international law has until now not been clearly defined, despite its central importance in the international legal order and for international peace and security. This book accordingly offers an original framework to identify prohibited uses of force, including those that use emerging technology or take place in newer military domains such as outer space. In doing so, Erin Pobjie explains the emergence of the customary prohibition of the use of force and its relationship with article 2(4) and identifies the elements of a prohibited 'use of force'. In a major contribution to the scholarship, the book proposes a framework that defines a 'use of force' in international law and applies this framework to illustrative case studies to demonstrate its usefulness as a tool for legal scholars, practitioners and students. This title is also available as Open Access on Cambridge Core.

ERIN POBJIE is Assistant Professor at the University of Essex and a Senior Research Affiliate at the Max Planck Institute for Comparative Public Law and International Law. She is co-Rapporteur of the International Law Association's Committee on the Use of Force.

Prohibited Force

THE MEANING OF 'USE OF FORCE' IN INTERNATIONAL LAW

ERIN POBJIE
University of Essex

CAMBRIDGE
UNIVERSITY PRESS

CAMBRIDGE
UNIVERSITY PRESS

Shaftesbury Road, Cambridge CB2 8EA, United Kingdom

One Liberty Plaza, 20th Floor, New York, NY 10006, USA

477 Williamstown Road, Port Melbourne, VIC 3207, Australia

314–321, 3rd Floor, Plot 3, Splendor Forum, Jasola District Centre, New Delhi – 110025, India

103 Penang Road, #05-06/07, Visioncrest Commercial, Singapore 238467

Cambridge University Press is part of Cambridge University Press & Assessment, a department of the University of Cambridge.

We share the University's mission to contribute to society through the pursuit of education, learning and research at the highest international levels of excellence.

www.cambridge.org
Information on this title: www.cambridge.org/9781316516973

DOI: 10.1017/9781009022897

First published 2024

A catalogue record for this publication is available from the British Library

Library of Congress Cataloging-in-Publication Data
NAMES: Pobjie, Erin, 1985- author.
TITLE: Prohibited force : the meaning of 'use of force' in international law / Erin Pobjie, University of Essex.
DESCRIPTION: Cambridge, United Kingdom ; New York, NY : Cambridge University Press, 2024. | Includes bibliographical references and index.
IDENTIFIERS: LCCN 2023035028 (print) | LCCN 2023035029 (ebook) | ISBN 9781316516973 (hardback) | ISBN 9781009016537 (paperback) | ISBN 9781009022897 (ebook)
SUBJECTS: LCSH: Intervention (International law) | Aggression (International law)
CLASSIFICATION: LCC KZ6374 .P63 2024 (print) | LCC KZ6374 (ebook) | DDC 341.5/84–dc23/eng/20231003
LC record available at https://lccn.loc.gov/2023035028
LC ebook record available at https://lccn.loc.gov/2023035029

ISBN 978-1-316-51697-3 Hardback

To my mother, Tessie

Contents

Foreword *Claus Kreß*	xi
Acknowledgements	xiii
Introduction	1
The Research Question	5
Why Does It Matter?	6
Aims and Contribution of Work	11
Outline of Book	13
PART I TREATY VERSUS CUSTOM	
Introduction	15
1 **How and When Did the Customary Prohibition of the Use of Force Emerge? The Status of the Customary Norm Pre-1945**	17
Introduction	17
The *Nicaragua* Case	18
How and When Did the Customary Prohibition of the Use of Force Emerge?	21
The Status of the Customary Norm Pre-1945	21
Conclusion	29
2 **Baxter's Paradox and the Customary Prohibition of the Use of Force**	30
Introduction	30
Challenges of the Two-Element Approach	30

The 'Own Impact' of Article 2(4) 51
Conclusions: Are the Charter and Customary Prohibitions of the Use of Force Identical? 56

3 **The Relationship between the Customary Prohibition of the Use of Force and Article 2(4) of the UN Charter** 59
Introduction 59
Effect of Customary Prohibition on the Interpretation of Article 2(4) 60
Evolutive Interpretation of Article 2(4) 66
Jus Cogens and the Prohibition of the Use of Force 70
Conclusion: Which Source to Interpret or Apply? 77

PART II ELEMENTS OF PROHIBITED FORCE
Introduction 81

4 **Contextual Elements of a Prohibited 'Use of Force': International Relations** 85
Introduction 85
'All Members' 85
'Shall refrain . . . from' 87
'in their international relations' 87
'against the territorial integrity or political independence of any state or in any other manner inconsistent with the Purposes of the United Nations' 101
Conclusion 104

5 **Elements of 'Use of Force': Means** 106
Introduction 106
Subsequent Agreements Regarding Article 2(4) 106
Ordinary Meaning 115
Means 116
Conclusion 131

6 **Elements of 'Use of Force': Effects, Gravity and Intention** 132
Introduction 132
Effects 132
Gravity 138
Intention 145
Conclusion 157

PART III DEFINING PROHIBITED FORCE

7 **Anomalous Examples of 'Use of Force' and Non-'Use of Force' under Article 2(4) of the UN Charter** 161
Introduction 161
Anomalous Examples of 'Use of Force' 161
Anomalous Examples of Non-'Use of Force' 176
Possible Explanations 186

8 **The Meaning of Prohibited 'Use of Force' in International Law** 190
Introduction 190
What Is a Type? 190
Type Theory and 'Use of Force' 194
Applying Type Theory to Anomalous Examples of 'Use of Force' 199
Illustrative Examples of Balancing the Elements of a 'Use of Force' 201
Case Study: The Attempted Killing of Sergei Skripal 212
Case Study: Use of Force in Outer Space 216
Reflections 227

Conclusion: A Definition of Prohibited 'Use of Force' 229

Bibliography 233
Index 259

Foreword

Despite the central importance of this provision in the international legal order, there remains genuine uncertainty among States, scholars and jurists about the meaning of a prohibited 'use of force' under article 2(4) of the UN Charter and customary international law.

It is difficult to disagree with this starting point of Dr Erin Pobjie's analysis if one only considers the present uncertainty about the right answers to be given to questions such as whether the use of force within the meaning of the prohibition must pass a certain gravity threshold, whether such a use of force presupposes a physical effect or at least the potential of a physical effect, what level of directness between the means employed and the (potential physical) effects is required, whether there is a need to distinguish the use of force within the meaning of the prohibition from forcible police measures or whether the term 'use of force' implies an element of intentionality. This state of affairs leaves much to be desired not only because the prohibition of the use of force, in the words of the International Court of Justice, constitutes a 'cornerstone of the United Nations Charter' but also because of the fact that the existence of a use of force entails distinct legal consequences. Hence, one cannot but agree with the author's conviction that 'for such a foundational rule of the international legal system, it is not satisfactory to apply vague, ad hoc standards' to determine whether or not potentially forcible incidents fall within the scope of the prohibition of the use of force. Dr Pobjie is therefore to be commended for having produced a book which applies both impressive doctrinal rigour and remarkable intellectual creativity to the clarification of the meaning of a core concept of the existing international legal order. In my humble view, the central contribution of this elegantly written study consists of the suggestion to treat the term 'use of force' as a *type* rather than a *concept* and to identify a basket of elements which, while not all having to be present, must be weighed and balanced to determine whether the threshold for the definition is met. It is by no means a weakness, but it rather testifies to the author's unfailing scholarly spirit that she does not pretend to be able to apply her innovative approach to all conceivable questions of delineation in a work that she has thankfully kept to an accessible size. Instead, the author has carefully chosen a number of illustrative case studies in order to demonstrate by way of examples the work her new methodology is capable of doing. Apart from making for enjoyable and stimulating reading, these practical applications put the author's approach to the reader's test in all due concreteness and transparency. Dr Pobjie does not make the bold assertion that the use of her methodology will yield incontrovertible results in all possible instances. More modestly, but probably more realistically, she claims that it provides a shared language and coherent framework for legal analysis and scholarly debate regarding the content of a prohibited 'use of force' between States under international law. In that vein, her thoughtfully worded conclusion reads as follows:

> The framework of type theory has the potential to facilitate clearer analysis of 'uses of force' between States. It is hoped that this clarity will in turn lead to greater compliance with the prohibition of the use of force between States in their international relations and contribute to our shared endeavour of international peace and security.

Such new potential would indeed constitute a significant advance in strengthening the international legal order in one of its core components. For this reason alone, Erin Pobjie's book deserves the closest attention of international lawyers worldwide. At the very least, *Prohibited Force: The Meaning of 'Use of Force' in International Law* will move the conversation about the prohibition of the use of force to a higher level of analytical clarity. This is no small achievement.

Claus Kreß
Cologne

Acknowledgements

This book began as my PhD thesis and has accompanied me along the way from Zürich to Cologne, Heidelberg and, finally, Colchester. I'm very grateful for the support of everyone who helped me on my journey, starting with Noam Lubell, who sparked my interest in *jus contra bellum* in an inspiring first lecture on the law of armed conflict during my LLM degree at the University of Essex and who encouraged me to pursue a PhD. It is a privilege to now be his colleague and to teach that very same module alongside him. Noam was the one who introduced me to my future PhD supervisor, Claus Kreß, during a meeting in Cambridge of the International Law Association's Committee on the Use of Force. During that Committee meeting, which I attended as a research assistant to the Rapporteur during my LLM, it was inspiring to listen to the experts whose books I had read and to discuss international law with them during the breaks – scholars whose work I have drawn on extensively in this book, including Claus, Michael Wood, Tom Ruys, James Green and Christian Henderson. It is a great honour to now be co-Rapporteur of the ILA Committee on the Use of Force and to continue these conversations and contribute to the discussion.

In German, a PhD supervisor is called a *Doktorvater* (or *Doktormutter*) and in the case of Claus Kreß, this expression captures the sense of academic family that he created at the Institute for International Peace and Security Law at the University of Cologne. Claus is an incisive and brilliant scholar, inspiring mentor and now friend, and this book would not have been possible without the opportunities he gave me and his invaluable guidance and support.

I also wish to thank the many scholars who have generously given feedback on early drafts and discussed my thoughts and ideas, including Christine Gray, Sarah Nouwen, Anne Peters, Christian Marxsen, Michael Byers, Gus Waschefort and Noam Lubell, as well as my friends and colleagues at the

Institute for International Peace and Security Law at the University of Cologne, the Lauterpacht Centre for International Law at the University of Cambridge, the Max Planck Institute for Comparative Public Law and International Law in Heidelberg (in particular, the Max Planck research group Shades of Illegality in International Peace and Security Law) and at Essex Law School. During the writing process, I benefited from the generous support of the German Academic Exchange Service (DAAD), which funded my research fellowship at the Lauterpacht Centre in Cambridge, and the Max-Planck-Förderstiftung, which granted me a fellowship to spend one summer writing this book from the ancient farmhouse of the scientist Max Planck overlooking Lake Tegern and the Bavarian Alps. I would also like to thank the University of Essex for generously supporting the open access publication of this book.

Family and friends supported, encouraged and inspired me throughout the PhD. I am particularly grateful to my mother, Tessie, and to Tim Sykes, who sprinkled in many adventures along the way. The writing of the book was also marked by sadness, as my father Warren passed away one day before my viva. The day I was awarded the PhD was one of the saddest and happiest of my life, and I am grateful for the support of my family, friends, Claus and my colleagues in Cologne, who surrounded me during those moments and beyond.

Finally, I would like to thank the editorial team at Cambridge University Press, especially Tom Randall and Marianne Nield, for their capable efforts in bringing this book to life.

Introduction

Recent events such as Russia's illegal invasion of Ukraine on 24 February 2022 have drawn renewed attention to the international law prohibiting the use of force between States. The prohibition is enshrined in article 2(4) of the UN Charter[1] and customary international law and is considered a 'cornerstone' of the modern international legal system.[2] Article 2(4) of the UN Charter provides as follows:

> All Members shall refrain in their international relations from the threat or use of force against the territorial integrity or political independence of any state, or in any other manner inconsistent with the Purposes of the United Nations.

This legal framework – the *jus contra bellum* – introduced in the aftermath of World War II to 'save succeeding generations from the scourge of war',[3] clearly did not prevent the use of force in this instance. But it is not irrelevant; to the contrary, such egregious violations highlight the urgent need to bolster the existing rules aimed at preventing the use of force in international relations. Indeed, the continued salience of these rules was affirmed by the outrage and strong response of the international community to Russia's

[1] *Charter of the United Nations* 1945 (adopted 26 June 1945, entered into force 24 October 1945), 1 UNTS 16 ('UN Charter').

[2] *Case concerning Military and Paramilitary Activities in and against Nicaragua (Nicaragua v United States of America), Merits, Judgment* (1986) ICJ Reports 14 ('*Nicaragua* case'), Separate Opinion of President Nagendra Singh, 153; *Oil Platforms (Islamic Republic of Iran v United States of America), Judgment* (2003) ICJ Reports 161 ('*Oil Platforms* case'), Dissenting Opinion of Judge Elarby, para. 1.1; *Armed Activities on the Territory of the Congo (Democratic Republic of the Congo v Uganda)* (2005) ICJ Reports 168 ('*Armed Activities* case'), para. 148.

[3] UN Charter, n. 1, preamble.

aggression, which explicitly condemned the invasion as a violation of the prohibition of the use of force and an act of aggression.[4]

Although large-scale violations of the prohibition of the use of force garner significant international attention, it is in fact violations at the lower end of the intensity spectrum which occur more frequently and over which uncertainty reigns. The international reaction to and scholarly analysis of incidents such as North Korea's ballistic missile tests over Japan on 28 August and 15 September 2017;[5] the attempted assassination of the former Russian spy Sergei Skripal in Salisbury, United Kingdom, on 4 March 2018;[6] and the major US cyber attack on Iran on 20 June 2019 in response to Iran's targeting of oil tankers[7] demonstrate the lack of a shared analytical framework to determine if they violate the prohibition of the use of force. In addition, new forms and applications of technology with potential military effects (such as cyber operations[8] and counter-space capabilities in outer space[9]) present increasingly significant security threats and defy clear legal categorisation under the *jus contra bellum*.

Notwithstanding the central importance of the prohibition of the use of force in the international legal order, there remains genuine uncertainty among States, scholars and jurists about the meaning of prohibited force. As Andrea Bianchi notes, 'despite the rhetorical commitment to the Charter, the interpretation of its provisions, particularly Article 2(4) and Article 51, has become highly controversial. In other words, the social consensus on the centrality of the Charter regulatory framework to the use of force evaporates

4 UN General Assembly Resolution on Aggression against Ukraine, UN Doc A/RES/ES-11/1 (2 March 2022), adopted by a vote of 141 in favour to 5 against with 35 abstentions. In the resolution, the UN General Assembly '[d]eplores in the strongest terms the aggression by the Russian Federation against Ukraine in violation of Article 2 (4) of the Charter' (para. 2).

5 Arms Control Association, 'Chronology of US-North Korean Nuclear and Missile Diplomacy' (2022), www.armscontrol.org/factsheets/dprkchron.

6 'Russian Spy: What Happened to the Skripals?' *BBC News* (18 April 2018), www.bbc.com/news/uk-43643025.

7 Julian E Barnes, 'U.S. Cyberattack Hurt Iran's Ability to Target Oil Tankers, Officials Say', *New York Times* (28 August 2019) www.nytimes.com/2019/08/28/us/politics/us-iran-cyber-attack.html.

8 For instance, in 2016 NATO declared cyber space as an operational domain, and in October 2018 it established a Cyberspace Operations Centre: Laura Brent, 'NATO's Role in Cyberspace', *NATO Review* (12 February 2019) www.nato.int/docu/review/2019/Also-in-2019/natos-role-in-cyberspace-alliance-defence/EN/index.htm.

9 NATO declared outer space as an operational domain in 2019: NATO, 'NATO's Approach to Space' (2 December 2021) www.nato.int/cps/en/natohq/topics_175419.htm. Space security and the use of force is discussed in Chapter 8 of this book.

when it comes to interpreting the content and scope of application of its most fundamental provisions.'[10]

The International Court of Justice (ICJ) has made scant contribution to clarifying the meaning of a prohibited 'use of force'. The ICJ first considered the interpretation and application of article 2(4) in its earliest decision in the *Corfu Channel* case in 1949.[11] Since then, it has had occasion to consider the interpretation and application of article 2(4) either directly or indirectly in a number of cases, including the 1974 *Fisheries Jurisdiction* case *(Federal Republic of Germany v Iceland)*;[12] the 1980 *Tehran Hostages* case;[13] the 1986 *Nicaragua* case;[14] the 1995 *Fisheries Jurisdiction* case *(Spain v Canada)*;[15] the 1996 *Nuclear Weapons Advisory Opinion*;[16] the 2003 *Oil Platforms* case;[17] the 2004 *Wall Advisory Opinion*[18] and the 2005 *Armed Activities* case.[19] Of these, the *Nicaragua* case and the *Armed Activities* case are the most relevant to the meaning of a prohibited 'use of force'. These cases are discussed in further detail in the relevant sections of this work.

Similarly, few scholars have examined the question directly.[20] As early as 1963, Ian Brownlie noted:

[10] Andrea Bianchi, 'The International Regulation of the Use of Force: The Politics of Interpretive Method' (2009) 22 *Leiden Journal of International Law* 651, 659.

[11] *Corfu Channel Case (UK v Albenia), Merits, Judgment* (1949) ICJ Reports 4.

[12] *Fisheries Jurisdiction Case (Federal Republic of Germany v Iceland), Merits, Judgment* (1974) ICJ Reports 175.

[13] *United States Diplomatic and Consular Staff in Tehran (USA v Iran), Judgment* (1980) ICJ Reports 3.

[14] *Nicaragua* case, n. 2.

[15] *Fisheries Jurisdiction Case (Spain v Canada), Jurisdiction of the Court, Judgment* (1998) ICJ Reports 432.

[16] *Legality of the Threat or Use of Nuclear Weapons, Advisory Opinion* (1996) ICJ Reports 226.

[17] *Oil Platforms (Islamic Republic of Iran v United States of America), Judgment* (2003) ICJ Reports 161.

[18] *Legal Consequences of the Construction of a Wall in the Occupied Palestinian Territory (Advisory Opinion)* (2004) ICJ Reports 136.

[19] *Armed Activities* case, n. 2.

[20] Scholars who have analysed the meaning of 'use of force' include Olivier Corten, *The Law against War: The Prohibition on the Use of Force in Contemporary International Law* (Hart Publishing, 2021), chapter 2; Mary Ellen O'Connell, 'The Prohibition of the Use of Force' in Nigel D White and Christian Henderson (eds), *Research Handbook on International Conflict and Security Law:* Jus ad Bellum, Jus in Bello *and* Jus post Bellum (Elgar, 2013), 89; Tom Ruys, 'The Meaning of "Force" and the Boundaries of the *Jus Ad Bellum*: Are "Minimal" Uses of Force Excluded from UN Charter Article 2 (4)?' (2014) 108(2) *American Journal of International Law* 159; Christian Henderson, *The Use of Force and International Law* (Cambridge University Press, 2018), chapter 2.

> Although the terms 'use of force' and 'resort to force' are frequently employed by writers they have not been the subject of detailed consideration. There can be little doubt that 'use of force' is commonly understood to imply a military attack, an 'armed attack', by the organized military, naval, or air forces of a state; but the concept in practice and principle has a wider significance.[21]

Most of the scholarly attention to date has instead been on clarifying the meaning of 'armed attack' under article 51 and the definition of aggression. Defining aggression has been an international law project of central importance for various reasons including its connection to crimes against peace (and more recently the crime of aggression under the Rome Statute of the International Criminal Court (ICC)) and its triggering of UN Security Council enforcement powers and international State responsibility.[22] It is also significant because it is seen as the other side of the coin to self-defence and hence connected to protecting the territorial integrity of the State.[23] As a major exception to the general prohibition of the use of force, the right to self-defence is not only an essential bastion of security and survival of the State but also a key source of insecurity due to its potential for abuse. The meaning of 'force' has to date received significantly less attention, though it is also (though perhaps less obviously) of fundamental importance for the reasons that follow further below.

Thus far, scholarly analysis of the meaning of an unlawful 'use of force' leaves unclear the actual content and meaning of a prohibited 'use of force', namely, its elements, the relationship between those elements, and the lower threshold of prohibited force. Generally, scholars are more comfortable analysing and arguing about 'armed attack' because it has more substance; it is at least clear what precisely we are arguing about. In contrast, since the criteria for an act to fall within the scope of the *jus contra bellum* are less clear, there is no shared language to talk about international incidents in terms of the prohibition of the use of force. The concept of a 'use of force' thus appears inchoate, even if there is an emergent language developing with respect to a *de minimis* gravity threshold and hostile intent.[24]

Clearly, this situation is unsatisfactory for a norm of fundamental importance to the international legal system and one that is said to be a primary

[21] Ian Brownlie, *International Law and the Use of Force by States* (Clarendon, 1963), 361, footnote omitted.

[22] See Dapo Akande and Antonios Tzanakopoulos, 'The International Court of Justice and the Concept of Aggression' in Claus Kreß and Stefan Barriga (eds), *The Crime of Aggression: A Commentary* (Cambridge University Press, 2017), 214.

[23] Brownlie, n. 21, 351–2.

[24] See Chapter 6.

example of *jus cogens*.[25] For these reasons, setting out the scope of the prohibition of the use of force and identifying its criteria is essential – at the very least, even if the criteria themselves are debated, it provides a framework for analysing and discussing these issues using a shared language, leading to a clearer understanding of the law and ultimately increasing its compliance pull.

THE RESEARCH QUESTION

This book addresses the fundamental question: what is the meaning of a prohibited 'use of force' between States under international law? The focus is on the interpretation of the term 'use of force' as such in *jus contra bellum*. Some of the fundamental grey areas regarding the meaning of 'use of force' that will be addressed include the following:

- Does 'force' mean physical/armed force only, and are kinetic means or the use of particular weapons required?
- Is a (potential) physical effect required? What is the required nature of such effects: must they be permanent, what object or target must experience the effect and what is the required level of directness between the means employed and these effects?
- Is there a gravity threshold below which a forcible act violates international law but does not violate the prohibition of the use of force in article 2(4) of the UN Charter? If there is such a threshold, how low is it? Does mere unauthorised presence of a State's armed forces in the territory of another State suffice?
- Is a coercive intent required in order for conduct to qualify as a prohibited 'use of force'? Or are forcible acts which are unintentional, mistaken or with a limited purpose also prohibited by article 2(4)?
- Does the *jus contra bellum* govern a State using force in response to a small-scale incursion within its territory, such as a small troop of soldiers crossing the border, unauthorised overflight of a military aircraft, or a submerged submarine passing through its territorial waters? States have the right to respond to such incursions but on what legal basis?
- What distinguishes a prohibited 'use of force' under article 2(4) from police measures against civil aircraft or merchant vessels registered to another State, either within a State's own territory or outside its territory (e.g. within the territory of another State, or beyond)? When does the

[25] See Chapter 3 for a discussion of the prohibition of the use of force and *jus cogens*.

exercising by a State of its sovereign rights within its own jurisdiction become a prohibited use of force?

The main focus of the book is on the meaning of a 'use of force' but necessarily also covers contextual elements which bring a 'use of force' within the scope of the *jus contra bellum* in the first place, in particular, the meaning of a use of force 'in international relations'. It does not examine the scope of exceptions to the prohibition of the use of force, such as the right to self-defence under article 51 and customary international law or uses of force authorised by the UN Security Council acting under Chapter VII of the UN Charter, as these do not affect whether an act meets the definition of a 'use of force' falling within the scope of the *jus contra bellum*.

WHY DOES IT MATTER?

It is important to determine the meaning of a prohibited 'use of force' between States because it has significant practical implications for contemporary challenges States face as well as international legal consequences. Significantly, the definition of prohibited force and its lower threshold have direct relevance for the right to self-defence and the lawful responses available to States to security threats. Under article 51 of the UN Charter and customary international law, States are only permitted to use force in self-defence in response to prohibited uses of force rising to the level of an 'armed attack'. In the *Nicaragua* case, the ICJ distinguished 'the most grave forms of the use of force (those constituting an armed attack) from other less grave forms'.[26] There is some controversy over this distinction between 'use of force' and 'armed attack', with some States such as the United States taking the view that there is no gap between the gravity thresholds of the two.[27] However, the International Law Association Committee on the Use of Force noted in its report on aggression that '[d]epending upon the interpretations given to the thresholds of "use of force" and "armed attack", conflation of the two terms may have dangerous implications'.[28]

[26] *Nicaragua* case, n. 2, para. 191.

[27] For example, remarks by then-Legal Adviser to the US Department of State, Harold Hongju Koh, 'International Law in Cyberspace' (at the USCYBERCOM Inter-Agency Legal Conference, Ft. Meade, MD, 18 September 2012) https://2009-2017.state.gov/s/l/releases/remarks/197924.htm.

[28] ILA Committee on the Use of Force, 'Final Report on Aggression and the Use of Force' (2018), 5. The ILA committee took the position that

The lower threshold of a prohibited use of force affects the size of the gap between prohibited force under article 2(4) and an armed attack giving rise to a right of self-defence under article 51 by making the gap larger (if article 2(4) has a low threshold) or smaller (if article 2(4) has a high threshold). If one holds that there is a large gap between 'use of force' and 'armed attack', this reduces the scope for States to take forcible measures in response to acts falling within the gap since a higher article 2(4) threshold means that a State that is a victim of 'gap' measures cannot itself use measures falling above the threshold of article 2(4) in response since it is prohibited unless it is the victim of an 'armed attack'. For instance, if a particular cyber operation is characterised as a 'use of force' but does not rise to the level of an armed attack, this raises the problem of the inability of the victim State to lawfully respond with in-kind countermeasures. Conversely, if one holds that there is a small gap between 'use of force' and 'armed attack' due to a high threshold of the former, this results in greater permissibility for States to have recourse to forcible measures which fall short of that threshold.

More often, forcible incidents fall within the category of 'use of force' under article 2(4) and do not reach the threshold of an 'armed attack' giving rise to a right of self-defence under article 51 of the UN Charter – for example, cyber operations. Despite this, there is an imbalance in scholarly attention between these two categories, leaving the lower threshold of the *jus contra bellum* unclear. It is therefore useful for States to be able to determine whether an act constitutes prohibited force. This provides legal certainty to States about the range of measures they may lawfully use to address modern security threats outside of self-defence or UN Security Council authorisation. This is increasingly important with respect to law enforcement, counter-terrorism and counter-proliferation measures.

The existing legal uncertainty over the interpretation of prohibited force is open to exploitation by States, in so-called grey zone operations, which are designed to take advantage of ambiguity in the law or to remain below legal thresholds for armed response.[29] It is surmised that there is increased instability at the lower boundary of the *jus contra bellum* ('use of force') due to

> [o]verall, it would appear that the determining criteria would more appropriately be centred upon questions of scale and effects of the attack. Moreover, in practice it appears that the gravity threshold attached to armed attacks is not markedly high, and would include most uses of force likely to cause casualties or significant property damage. As such, if there is a gap between 'use of force' and 'armed attack', it would be relatively narrow.

[29] Scott W Harold et al (eds), *The U.S.-Japan Alliance and Deterring Gray Zone Coercion in the Maritime, Cyber, and Space Domains* (RAND Corporation 2017), introduction, fn1, 1.

increased stability at the higher end ('armed attack'), resulting in more frequent 'grey zone challenges' at the lower end of the spectrum.[30] Such grey zone operations include the use of maritime militia in disputed zones of the South China Sea.[31] The US cyber attack on Iran in September 2019 was also reportedly 'calibrated to stay well below the threshold of war'.[32] In the face of these modern security threats and the increasingly bellicose geopolitical stance in regions such as the Middle East and the South and East China Seas, it is more important than ever to increase legal certainty over the interpretation of the applicable norms and, in particular, the meaning of prohibited force between States. Strengthening international norms can play a role in deterring or reducing incentives for grey zone activities and responds to the changing nature of conflict.[33]

The meaning of a prohibited 'use of force' also matters because acts which meet the threshold give rise to distinct legal consequences for States under both the UN Charter and customary international law. Under the UN Charter, the concept of a 'use of force' is important for delineating between articles 41 and 42. These two articles set out the measures that the Security Council may decide shall be taken to maintain or restore international peace and security once it has determined the existence of a threat to the peace, breach of the peace or act of aggression under Chapter VII of the Charter.[34] Articles 41 and 42 distinguish between forcible and non-forcible coercive

[30] Junichi Fukuda, 'A Japanese Perspective on the Role of the U.S.-Japan Alliance in Deterring – Or, If Necessary, Defeating – Maritime Gray Zone Coercion' (RAND Corporation, 2017), 23, 30, citing the 'stability-instability paradox' discussed by Glenn Snyder in relation to nuclear and conventional weapons, in 'The Balance of Power and the Balance of Terror', in Paul Seabury (ed), *The Balance of Power* (Chandler, 1965).

[31] James Kraska, 'China's Maritime Militia Upends Rules on Naval Warfare' *The Diplomat* (10 August 2015), https://thediplomat.com/2015/08/chinas-maritime-militia-upends-rules-on-naval-warfare/.

[32] Barnes, n. 7.

[33] See further Michael J Mazarr, *Mastering the Gray Zone: Understanding a Changing Era of Conflict* (United States Army War College Press, December 2015), who argues that large-scale grey zone operations will be the 'dominant form of state-to-state rivalry in the coming decades' (p. 2). According to Mazarr, grey zone conflict is not a new phenomenon but is becoming increasingly important for three reasons: increased reliance on these techniques by Russia, China and Iran; global economic interdependence and high costs of outright military aggression incentivise grey zone conflict; and new tools (such as cyber; new forms of information campaigns and new forms of State force such as coastguards) intensify grey zone conflict (p. 3). The overall idea is that strategic gradualism (through salami-slicing and series of small fait accompli) (p. 34) is being combined with grey zone actions (including with new tools) to pursue revisionist intent.

[34] Article 39 of the UN Charter, n. 1.

measures.[35] Under article 41, the UN Security Council may call on States to take certain coercive measures not involving the use of armed force to give effect to its decisions. In contrast, the Security Council may only 'take such action by air, sea, or land forces as may be necessary to maintain or restore international peace and security' if it considers that 'measures provided for in Article 41 would be inadequate or have proved to be inadequate'. Therefore, the definition of a 'use of force' may be relevant to whether, for example, certain types of cyber operations,[36] maritime interdictions[37] and peace operations[38] may be authorised under article 42 of the UN Charter without a need to establish that non-forcible measures are inadequate.[39]

Under customary international law, a prohibited use of force gives rise to international State responsibility and the obligation to cease the unlawful act,[40] make reparation[41] and the right of the victim State to take non-forcible countermeasures.[42] There are additional consequences if a use of force in violation of article 2(4) is considered to be a serious breach of a peremptory norm,[43] namely, that other States shall co-operate using lawful means to bring the violation to an end, shall not recognise the situation as lawful and shall not render aid or assistance in maintaining the situation,[44] and that the prohibition cannot be overridden by inconsistent treaty. In addition, under article

[35] See Nico Krisch, 'Chapter VII Powers: The General Framework. Articles 39 to 43' in Bruno Simma et al (eds), *The Charter of the United Nations: A Commentary* (Oxford University Press, 3rd ed, 2012), vol. I, 1237.

[36] See Michael N Schmitt, 'The Use of Cyber Force and International Law' in Marc Weller (ed), *The Oxford Handbook of the Use of Force in International Law* (Oxford University Press, 2015), 1110, 1118.

[37] Douglas Guilfoyle, 'Interdicting Vessels to Enforce the Common Interest: Maritime Countermeasures and the Use of Force' (2007) 56(1) *The International and Comparative Law Quarterly* 69.

[38] See James Sloan, *The Militarisation of Peacekeeping in the Twenty-First Century* (Hart Publishing, 2011), 256 who notes that the legal basis for use of force by peacekeepers going beyond self-defence could be based on article 40 or 41 of the UN Charter rather than article 42 if it is sufficiently limited.

[39] Although this may be of little practical relevance as the general practice of the Security Council is to just refer to Chapter VII: see Niels Blokker, 'Outsourcing the Use of Force: Towards More Security Council Control of Authorized Operations?' in Marc Weller (ed), *The Oxford Handbook of the Use of Force in International Law* (Oxford University Press, 2015), 202, 209.

[40] ILC Draft Articles, n. 46, art. 30.

[41] *Ibid.*, art. 31.

[42] *Ibid.*, art. 22.

[43] See discussion in Chapter 3.

[44] ILC, 'Draft Articles on Responsibility of States for Internationally Wrongful Acts, with Commentaries, in Report of the International Law Commission on the Work of Its Fifty-Third Session' UN Doc A/56/10 (2001) ('ILC Draft Articles'), art. 41.

52 of the Vienna Convention on the Law of Treaties (VCLT), '[a] treaty is void if its conclusion has been procured by the threat or use of force in violation of the principles of international law embodied in the Charter of the United Nations'. This was held by the ICJ in the *Fisheries Jurisdiction case (UK v Iceland)* to reflect customary international law: 'There can be little doubt, as is implied in the Charter of the United Nations and recognized in Article 52 of the Vienna Convention on the Law of Treaties, that under contemporary international law an agreement concluded under the threat or use of force is void.'[45]

Furthermore, the threshold for a prohibited use of force under article 2(4) determines the availability of circumstances precluding wrongfulness: acts falling below the threshold could be legally justified by necessity, *force majeure*, distress and countermeasures, whereas acts falling above it may only be lawfully justified by an accepted exception to the prohibition, namely, self-defence or UN Security Council authorisation. The justification is necessary to the extent that those acts violate other rules of international law, such as the non-intervention principle. For instance, how far can countermeasures go before violating the prohibition in article 2(4)?[46]

Further legal consequences of whether an act is a 'use of force' or not are that it may constitute a breach of an *erga omnes* norm, which could permit third States to take (non-armed) countermeasures against the breaching State under customary international law[47] and that it may bring into effect an international armed conflict between the two States concerned,[48] thus making the international law of armed conflict applicable (though any further use of

45 *Fisheries Jurisdiction (UK v Iceland), Jurisdiction* (1973) ICJ Reports 3, para. 14; see further 1966 ILC Yearbook, vol. II, 246, draft article 49 of the Draft Convention on the Law of Treaties with commentary, reprinted in ILC, 'Report of the International Law Commission on the Work of Its Eighteenth Session' 4 May–19 July 1966, Official Records of the General Assembly, Twenty-First Session, Supplement No. 9, UN Doc A/CN.4/191, UN Doc A/6309/ Rev.1 (1966), chapter II Law of Treaties.

46 ILC Draft Articles, n. 44, art. 49. Article 50 (1)(a) of the ILC Draft Articles provides that '[c]ountermeasures shall not affect the obligation to refrain from the threat or use of force as embodied in the Charter of the United Nations'.

47 The commentary to article 54 of the ILC Draft Articles notes (para. 6) that

> the current state of international law on countermeasures taken in the general or collective interest is uncertain. State practice is sparse and involves a limited number of States. At present, there appears to be no clearly recognized entitlement of States referred to in article 48 to take countermeasures in the collective interest. . . . chapter II includes a saving clause which reserves the position and leaves the resolution of the matter to the further development of international law.

48 Although it is uncertain whether a 'use of force' under *jus contra bellum* has the same meaning as for an international armed conflict under *jus in bello*. See further discussion in Chapter 8 in

force e.g. in self-defence remains subject to the rules of the *jus contra bellum*).[49] An additional consequence of this is the possibility of prosecuting certain acts as a war crime either before an international tribunal (such as the ICC) or before domestic courts, subject to issues of immunity *ratione materiae*.[50] Uses of force reaching the threshold of aggression may also give rise to international criminal responsibility for the individuals responsible and be prosecuted as the crime of aggression.

Often States' reactions to a particular incident are unclear in legal terms, or an incident does not provoke a widespread reaction or debate among States at all. Legal practitioners and scholars need tools apart from relying solely on ex-post-facto State assessments of a particular incident to determine if it is a prohibited use of force. It is also important for a State considering deploying a potential use of force to be able to make a legal assessment of whether the act would violate the *jus contra bellum*. Defining the meaning of prohibited force under international law provides legal certainty for States, their legal advisers and international adjudicators as to when an act falls within the scope of the prohibition. Legal certainty increases the 'compliance pull' of the norm and makes it harder to justify acts which are prohibited by the rule.[51] Setting out the meaning of prohibited force is essential to clarify the scope and content of a cardinal rule of public international law.

AIMS AND CONTRIBUTION OF WORK

This book sets out to provide a framework for identifying a prohibited 'use of force' under article 2(4) of the UN Charter; in other words, when an act falls within the scope of the prohibition of the use of force set out in that article. In doing so, it makes the following original contributions:

Firstly, it explains the emergence of the customary prohibition of the use of force and its relationship with article 2(4) of the UN Charter. Surprisingly, it is not known how or precisely when the customary prohibition of the use of

relation to classification of international armed conflict and 'use of force' under *jus contra bellum*.

49 Dapo Akande, 'The Use of Nerve Agents in Salisbury: Why Does It Matter Whether It Amounts to a Use of Force in International Law?' *EJIL: Talk!* (17 March 2018) www.ejiltalk.org/the-use-of-nerve-agents-in-salisbury-why-does-it-matter-whether-it-amounts-to-a-use-of-force-in-international-law/.

50 *Ibid.*

51 Thomas M Franck, 'Legitimacy in the International System' (1988) 82(4) *American Journal of International Law* 705, 713.

force arose, a question made more complex by Baxter's paradox.[52] The answer has profound implications for the relationship between the prohibition under article 2(4) of the UN Charter and custom, including which source to interpret or apply in order to ascertain the meaning of a prohibited use of force under international law and how the norm may change over time. In delving into this complex question, this book untangles the intricate relationship between the treaty and customary prohibition of the use of force and answers the question of which source to interpret or apply to discover the meaning of prohibited force.

Secondly, it identifies the elements of a prohibited 'use of force' and their content. In stark contrast to the concept of 'armed attack' in article 51 of the UN Charter with respect to the right of self-defence, in the analysis and discussion among States and legal scholars of lower-level forcible incidents falling below this threshold, so far there is no established criteria for determining whether an act violates the prohibition of the use of force in article 2(4). While some elements of prohibited force have been identified and debated (such as whether 'force' means armed/physical force only,[53] if there is a *de minimis* gravity threshold and if or what kind of intent is required[54]), thus far there are few examples of a detailed and systematic analysis of which elements form part of a prohibited 'use of force' and, especially, how these elements interrelate with one another.[55]

Thirdly, this book proposes a definition of prohibited force and offers an original framework – type theory – to identify unlawful uses of force, particularly those which are at the lower end of the gravity spectrum, use emerging technology or take place in newer military domains. Its major contribution is to propose the idea that an unlawful 'use of force' is not a concept (with a checklist of necessary elements) but rather a type, characterised by a basket of elements which must not all be present and which must be weighed and balanced to determine whether the threshold for the definition is met and an act is an unlawful 'use of force' under article 2(4) of the UN Charter.

52 RR Baxter, 'Treaties and Custom' (1970) 129 *Recueil des cours: Collected Courses of the Hague Academy of International Law* 25, 64. The 'paradox' relates to the challenges of separately adducing the content of the parallel customary prohibition in the presence of the parallel near-universal treaty obligation. Baxter's paradox and the prohibition of the use of force is discussed in Chapter 2.

53 See Chapter 6.

54 See Chapter 7.

55 Some examples that do discuss the elements of a prohibited 'use of force' include Corten, n. 20, —chapter two; Ruys, n. 20; Marco Roscini, *Cyber Operations and the Use of Force in International Law* (Oxford University Press, 2014), 45–67 in relation to cyber operations; Henderson, n. 20, 50–80.

A framework for defining a 'use of force' under article 2(4), bringing together each of the elements of that provision, is set out in the Conclusion.

Through these contributions, this book aims to enable a meaningful discussion and debate of the lawfulness of specific incidents using a shared language. This will be practically useful to States, legal advisers and scholars and lead to a clearer understanding of the law. The ultimate aim of this book is to thereby increase the compliance pull of the international legal prohibition of the use of force between States and indirectly contribute to international peace and security.

OUTLINE OF BOOK

Part I deals with how to determine the meaning of a prohibited 'use of force' between States under international law. Since the prohibition of the use of force is found in both treaty (the UN Charter) and customary international law, this part examines whether its content is identical under both sources and which one to interpret or apply. It argues that the customary rule emerged as a result of article 2(4) and that due to the relationship between the two sources, we should focus on interpreting the UN Charter to determine the meaning of prohibited force. Part I is divided into three chapters. Chapters 1 and 2 analyse how and when the customary norm arose, with Chapter 1 focusing on the status of the norm pre-UN Charter and Chapter 2 then analysing the emergence of the norm after the entry into force of the UN Charter in 1945. This chapter grapples with the challenges raised by Baxter's paradox for analysing the emergence and content of the customary norm using the standard two-element approach of State practice and *opinio juris* and proposes an alternative approach. Chapter 3 then examines the current relationship between the treaty and customary international law prohibitions, the possibilities for the norm to change over time (including the constraints on this posed by the peremptory nature of the prohibition), and argues in favour of interpreting and applying article 2(4) to discover the meaning of prohibited force.

Part II applies treaty interpretation to article 2(4) of the UN Charter, looking at all of the terms of that provision. Chapter 4 sets out the contextual elements that must be present for a 'use of force' to fall within the scope of article 2(4), including the requirement that the 'use of force' be in 'international relations'. Chapters 5 and 6 identify the elements of a 'use of force' under article 2(4) and their content. Chapter 5 examines the ordinary meaning of this term, before delving into the element of means. In particular, it examines whether 'use of force' refers to physical/armed force only and if kinetic means or the use of particular type of weapon is required. Chapter 6 continues the analysis of the elements of a prohibited 'use of force' by examining its required effects, the object or target of a 'use of force', gravity and intention. This chapter discusses the type of effects that may be relevant to the characterisation of an act as a 'use of force' under article 2(4), namely, whether a (potential) physical effect is required; if such effect should be permanent; the required object or target that must experience the effect; the required level of directness between the means employed and these effects; if a hostile intent is required and if there is a lower threshold of gravity of effects below which a forcible act will not fall within the scope of article 2(4) of the UN Charter.

Part III challenges the previously accepted paradigm of a 'use of force' as a coherent concept and proposes an original framework for defining an unlawful 'use of force' under article 2(4), bringing together each of the elements of that provision. Chapter 7 considers anomalous examples of 'use of force' in the subsequent agreement and subsequent practice of States that do not conform with the usual understanding of this term because they do not display one or more of the elements discussed in Part II. It also discusses anomalous examples of non-'use of force', namely, acts which appear to meet the criteria for an unlawful 'use of force' but are not characterised as such by States. Chapter 8 then puts forward a hypothesis that explains these anomalous examples and proposes a definitional framework for prohibited force. In contrast to the prevailing view, this book argues that none of the elements of a 'use of force' – including physical means or physical effects – is strictly necessary for the definition to be met. Rather, it proposes that a 'use of force' is a 'type', meaning that its elements must be weighed and balanced to reach a certain threshold. It proposes an original framework for defining an unlawful 'use of force' under article 2(4), bringing together each of the elements of that provision. This final chapter applies the proposed framework to concrete case studies in State practice and to the rapidly developing field of outer space security to demonstrate the potential value of this theory as a tool for legal scholars and practitioners.

PART I

Treaty versus Custom

INTRODUCTION

Disagreements about the content of international law, particularly in the field of *jus contra bellum*, often begin due to differently held assumptions about the legitimate process for identifying the content of the law.[1] 'Method, far from being a theoretical preoccupation, lays down the framework in which practice takes place.'[2] This part sets out the theoretical foundation and method for determining the meaning of a prohibited 'use of force' between States in international law. The prohibition of the use of force exists under two main sources of law: customary international law[3] and treaty (article 2(4) of the UN Charter). It is

1 See Andrea Bianchi, 'The International Regulation of the Use of Force: The Politics of Interpretive Method' (2009) 22(4) *Leiden Journal of International Law* 651–76, 653 ff, who argues: 'The fundamental contention is that to agree on method could cure much of the current divergence of views about the content and scope of application of some of the international rules regulating the use of force.' See also Olivier Corten, 'Chapter 1: Methodological Approach', in *The Law against War: The Prohibition on the Use of Force in Contemporary International Law* (Hart Publishing, 2010).

2 Bianchi, n. 1, 676.

3 Customary international law is referred to in article 38(1)(b) of the Statute of the International Court of Justice (ICJ) as 'evidence of a general practice accepted as law'. Although this definition is for the purposes of setting out the sources of international law that the ICJ shall apply, it has come to be widely accepted as a general definition of this legal concept. Michael Wood, 'First Report on Formation and Evidence of Customary International Law' UN Doc A/CN.4/663 (ILC, 17 May 2013), 96. Unlike treaty rules, which govern only the parties to the treaty in their mutual relations, rules of customary international law are binding on all States except persistent objectors (States that have 'objected to a rule of customary law while that rule was in the process of formation', and have clearly expressed the objection to other States and maintained it persistently) (Michael Wood, 'Third Report on Identification of Customary International Law' UN Doc A/CN.4/682 (ILC, 27 March 2015), 70, draft conclusion 15) and particular customary international law rules which apply only between a limited number of States. See also International Law Commission ('ILC'), draft conclusion 16(1). Although the UN Charter is almost universally ratified, the parallel existence of the customary prohibition of the use of force remains relevant – for example, in the event that an international tribunal does not have jurisdiction to apply the UN Charter but does have jurisdiction to apply customary international law (as in the *Nicaragua* case).

practically axiomatic that the prohibition of the use of force has an identical scope and content under both article 2(4) of the UN Charter and customary international law. Already in 1966, Sir Humphrey Waldock observed: 'Whatever may be their opinions about the state of the law prior to the establishment of the United Nations, the great majority of international lawyers consider that Article 2, paragraph 4, together with other provisions of the Charter, authoritatively declares the modern customary law regarding the threat or use of force.'[4]

If the scope and content of the prohibition of the use of force under article 2 (4) and custom are identical, which source of law should one interpret or apply to determine the meaning of a prohibited 'use of force' between States under international law: article 2(4), customary international law, or both? This question raises several fundamental issues. Firstly, are the scope and content of the prohibition of the use of force under article 2(4) of the UN Charter and customary international law really identical? Secondly, is it even possible to adduce the content of the customary rule separately to the treaty rule? The novel contribution of this part is to analyse how the customary prohibition of the use of force arose, and its relationship to article 2(4) of the UN Charter. It argues that the customary rule reflects the pre-existing treaty rule and that due to the relationship between them, the preferable approach is to focus on interpreting the UN Charter to determine the meaning of a prohibited 'use of force' under international law.

4 ILC, 'Report of the International Law Commission on the Work of Its Eighteenth Session' (4 May–19 July 1966) UN Doc A/CN.4/191, UN Doc A/6309/Rev.1, Chapter II Law of Treaties, 20, para. 7. See also ILC, 'Yearbook of the International Law Commission 1966, Vol. II' UN Doc A/CN.4/SER.A/1966/Add.l (1966), 247; Tom Ruys, *'Armed Attack' and Article 51 of the UN Charter* (Cambridge University Press, 2010), 18 with further citations.

1

How and When Did the Customary Prohibition of the Use of Force Emerge?

The Status of the Customary Norm Pre-1945

INTRODUCTION

The question of whether the prohibition of the use of force is identical under the UN Charter and customary international law is fundamental to deciding the approach to take to discover the meaning of prohibited force under international law. If they differ in some way, then it would be necessary to adduce the content under each source separately. Even if the customary and treaty prohibitions of the use of force are presently identical in scope and content, the current relationship between the two is especially relevant to potential future changes in the prohibition under both treaty and custom,[1] as we shall see later in Chapter 3. In particular, there are significant differences in the way that the rule may evolve through subsequent practice in the application of the treaty versus evolution of custom, as well as limits to such changes including the constraints of informal treaty modification and the peremptory nature of the prohibition. For these reasons, it is essential to commence our enquiry by examining the relationship between the treaty (UN Charter) and customary prohibitions of the use of force: are they indeed identical, what is their present relationship, and which should we interpret or apply to discover the meaning of prohibited force under international law? The starting point for this enquiry is the origin of the customary rule: how and

[1] ILC Rapporteurs Sir Michael Wood and Georg Nolte delineate the effect of treaties on the formation of customary international law (as part of the topic of identification of customary international law) from the role of customary international law in the interpretation of treaties (as part of the topic of subsequent agreement and subsequent practice in relation to interpretation of treaties): Georg Nolte, 'First Report on Subsequent Agreements and Subsequent Practice in Relation to Treaty Interpretation' UN Doc A/CN.4/660 (19 March 2013), para. 7.

when did it actually emerge, and what is its relationship to article 2(4) of the UN Charter?

THE *NICARAGUA* CASE

Before we continue, let us first address and dispense with the case that is often proffered as the answer to these questions: the *Nicaragua* case. Certainly, the International Court of Justice (ICJ) in the *Nicaragua* case affirmed that there is a customary prohibition of the use of force.[2] However, as we shall see, the Court did not actually hold that the content of the customary prohibition is identical to the prohibition in article 2(4), and its assertion of how and when the customary norm emerged is problematic.

In the *Nicaragua* case, the ICJ found that it had jurisdiction to determine the dispute on the basis of customary international law only, and not the UN Charter due to the US reservation to the Court's jurisdiction.[3] In its judgment on the merits, the Court indicated its view that the principles of the non-use of force and of the right to self-defence were already present in customary international law before the Charter and that these parallel (and largely identical) customary rules 'developed under the influence of the Charter'. The Court held:

> [S]o far from having constituted a marked departure from a customary international law which still exists unmodified, the Charter gave expression in this field to principles already present in customary international law, and that law has in the subsequent four decades developed under the influence of the Charter, to such an extent that a number of rules contained in the Charter have acquired a status independent of it. The essential consideration is that both the Charter and the customary international law flow from a common fundamental principle outlawing the use of force in international relations.[4]

2 *Case concerning Military and Paramilitary Activities in and against Nicaragua (Nicaragua v United States of America), Jurisdiction and Admissibility, Judgment* (1984) ICJ Reports 392, para. 73.

3 *Ibid.*: 'Principles such as those of the non-use of force, non-intervention, respect for the independence and territorial integrity of States, and the freedom of navigation, continue to be binding as part of customary international law, despite the operation of provisions of conventional law in which they have been incorporated.'

4 *Case Concerning Military and Paramilitary Activities in and against Nicaragua (Nicaragua v United States of America), Merits, Judgment* (1986) ICJ Reports 14 ('*Nicaragua* case (Merits)'), para. 181. Judge Schwebel in his Dissenting Opinion also acknowledged that 'it is generally accepted . . . that Charter restrictions on the use of force have been incorporated into the body of customary international law, so that such States as Switzerland, the Koreas, and diminutive

However, the ICJ did not explicitly hold that the prohibition under each source of law was identical, and its analysis in identifying the parallel customary rule has been rightly criticised. The Court was rather obtuse about whether the prohibition of the use of force in article 2(4) is exactly the same in customary international law. It stated:

> The Court does not consider that, in the areas of law relevant to the present dispute, it can be claimed that all the customary rules which may be invoked have a content exactly identical to that of the rules contained in the treaties which cannot be applied by virtue of the United States reservation. On a number of points, the areas governed by the two sources of law do not exactly overlap, and the substantive rules in which they are framed are not identical in content.[5]

The Court re-states this point in the following paragraph, holding that '[t]he areas governed by the two sources of law thus do not overlap exactly, and the rules do not have the same content'.[6] Claus Kreß argues that despite the ICJ's statements, subsequent parts of the judgment show that it has interpreted customary international law and article 2(4) 'in a largely identical manner'.[7] Furthermore, since in the *Armed Activities* case, the ICJ referred to the 'principle' of the non-use of force in international relations without citing its source,[8] Kreß concludes that it is based on 'essentially identical rules of treaty and customary law existing alongside each other'.[9] However, this finding was far from explicit, and other scholars have noted that the ICJ seems to treat the two as identical in substance without much analysis.[10]

States are bound by the principles of Article 2 of the Charter even though they are non-members' (para. 95), although he disagreed with the position that Member States of the UN should be treated as being bound only by customary international law when in fact the UN Charter applied between them.

5 *Ibid.*, para. 175.

6 *Ibid.*, para. 176.

7 Claus Kreß, 'The International Court of Justice and the Non-Use of Force' in Marc Weller (ed), *The Oxford Handbook of the Use of Force in International Law* (Oxford University Press, 2015), 561, 568, citing the *Nicaragua* case, paras. 181, 188.

8 *Armed Activities on the Territory of the Congo (Democratic Republic of the Congo v Uganda)* (2005) ICJ Reports 168, para. 345(1).

9 Kreß, n. 7, 569, though he notes the Dissenting Opinion of Judge Jennings in the *Nicaragua* case, which disputes this view.

10 See, for example, Albrecht Randelzhofer and Oliver Dörr, 'Article 2(4)' in Bruno Simma et al. (eds), *The Charter of the United Nations: A Commentary* (Oxford University Press, 3rd ed, 2012), 200, 230 MN65.

The ICJ has also been criticised for its reasoning in identifying the parallel customary prohibition of the use of force. Despite its frequent references to the need to evaluate the existence of a general practice accepted as law in order to identify a rule of customary international law and its holding that '[t]he Court must satisfy itself that the existence of the rule in the *opinio juris* of States is confirmed by practice',[11] Christine Gray notes that '[the Court] was criticized for inferring *opinio juris* from General Assembly resolutions and for not undertaking a wide survey of practice'.[12] The Court also failed to clearly distinguish between practice in the application of the treaty and State practice and *opinio juris* under customary international law. It noted that Nicaragua and the USA 'accept a treaty-law obligation to refrain in their international relations from the threat or use of force against the territorial integrity or political independence of any State, or in any other manner inconsistent with the purposes of the United Nations'.[13] The Court correctly held that it 'has however to be satisfied that there exists in customary international law an *opinio juris* as to the binding character of such abstention'.[14] Oscar Schachter observes that '[j]ust how the Court could tell whether practice since 1945 by the treaty parties relative to the use of force was "customary" rather than treaty is not made clear.'[15] The Court also relied on multilateral conventions such as the UN Charter and the Charter of the Organization of American States to ascertain the content of the customary rule without further explanation.[16]

These deficiencies in the judgment and the fact that the Court left open whether the customary and UN Charter prohibitions of the use of force are actually identical mean that the *Nicaragua* case is not the end of the road in our quest to discover whether the prohibition is identical under each source of law, and their present relationship. The rest of Part I will examine this question afresh.

[11] Nicaragua case (Merits), n. 4, para. 184.

[12] Christine Gray, *International Law and the Use of Force* (Oxford University Press, 3rd ed, 2008), 8–9, footnote 30. However, she notes that 'as the Court said, the parties were in agreement that Article 2(4) was customary law. It was not surprising that the Court's inquiry into customary international law was relatively brief'.

[13] *Nicaragua* case (Merits), n. 4, para. 188.

[14] *Ibid.*

[15] Oscar Schachter, 'Entangled Treaty and Custom' in Yoram Dinstein (ed), *International Law at a Time of Perplexity: Essays in Honour of Shabtai Rosenne* (Martinus Nijhoff Publishers, 1989), 717, 719.

[16] *Nicaragua* case (Merits), n. 4, para. 183.

HOW AND WHEN DID THE CUSTOMARY PROHIBITION OF THE USE OF FORCE EMERGE?

There are four possibilities for how and when the current customary prohibition of the use of force between States arose.[17] The first possibility is that the customary rule developed prior to the UN Charter and that article 2(4) was declaratory of that pre-existing custom. The second possibility is that article 2 (4) crystallised a rule of customary international law that was by 1945 already in the process of formation. The third possibility is that article 2(4) gave rise to a new rule of customary international law in the usual way, that is, through subsequent State practice and *opinio juris* (the two-element approach). The fourth possibility is that article 2(4) gave rise to a new customary rule from its own impact, due to its 'fundamentally norm-creating character' 'accepted as such by the opinio juris' and a sufficient number of ratifications and accessions to imply a 'positive acceptance of its principles' and 'extensive and virtually uniform' State practice.[18] The following discussion will canvass the first of these two possibilities and examine the status of the customary norm prior to 1945. Chapter 2 will then focus on the status of the customary norm in the UN Charter era and whether it is currently identical to the rule in article 2(4) of the Charter.

THE STATUS OF THE CUSTOMARY NORM PRE-1945

Article 2(4) as Declaratory of Pre-existing Customary International Law?

The first possibility is that article 2(4) was declaratory of a customary international law rule prohibiting the use of force between States that pre-dated the 1945 UN Charter. If article 2(4) was merely declaratory of such a customary rule, then the customary rule would continue to be in force alongside the Charter. For a pre-existing rule of customary international law prohibiting the use of force in the same terms as article 2(4) to have arisen prior to 1945, the requirements of a general practice accepted as law must have been present prior to that date. This was not the case. Rather, article 2(4) of the UN Charter was a significant new legal development.

[17] This work takes the position that any pre-existing custom that was inconsistent with the later treaty provision in article 2(4) of the UN Charter was thereby superseded, at least with respect to the parties to that treaty, which in this case, is nearly all States.

[18] *North Sea Continental Shelf (Federal Republic of Germany/Denmark; Federal Republic of Germany/Netherlands) Judgment* (1969) ICJ Reports 3 ('*North Sea Continental Shelf Cases*').

Pre-Charter Era

Prior to 1945, there were legal developments restricting the right to resort to war between States, but this fell short of outlawing 'use of force'. The historical trajectory of the prohibition of the use of force has, broadly speaking, traced a liberal attitude towards war, in which rulers were absolutely free to resort to war, to the development of a moral discourse on war in the form of just war theory, which gave an account of the conditions under which resort to war was righteous.[19] Just war doctrine has its roots in Roman law and the early writings of Saint Augustine, and came to fruition during the Middle Ages.[20] Prior to the twentieth century, there was no international legal regulation of the use of force between States.[21] The Hague Peace Conferences of 1899 and 1907 were the first attempts to restrict such freedom to resort to force and included modest restrictions.[22]

During the inter-war period (November 1918 to September 1939), efforts to restrict legal resort to war between States intensified. The two most notable international instruments during this period were the Covenant of the League of Nations,[23] and the 1928 Kellogg–Briand Pact (General Treaty for Renunciation of War as an Instrument of National Policy).[24] The Covenant of the League of Nations required peaceful dispute settlement between States and provided for a system of collective security and sanctions.[25] The League Covenant of 1919 contained exceptional qualifications on the right to resort to war. 'Resort to war in violation of the Covenant was illegal but the content of the illegality was *prima facie* the violation of a treaty obligation.'[26] However, the Covenant did not prohibit war if dispute settlement was unsuccessful, after

[19] For an early comprehensive account of the prohibition of the use of force, see Ian Brownlie, *International Law and the Use of Force by States* (Clarendon, 1963). For a concise overview of the historical development of the outlawing of war, critiquing the overly simplified treatment of this development by many scholars, see Randall Lesaffer, 'Too Much History: From War as Sanction to the Sanctioning of War' in Marc Weller (ed), *The Oxford Handbook of the Use of Force in International Law* (Oxford University Press, 2015), 35, who argues that the just war tradition continued to influence the law in the modern era and explains how many features of the current *jus contra bellum* have a basis in this tradition.

[20] Lesaffer, n. 19, 37.

[21] Randelzhofer and Dörr, n. 10, 204, MN4.

[22] *Ibid.*, 204, MN5.

[23] *Covenant of the League of Nations* 1919 (adopted 28 April 1919, entered into force 10 January 1920).

[24] *Treaty between the United States and Other Powers Providing for the Renunciation of War as an Instrument of National Policy* (concluded 27 August 1929, entered into force 24 July 1929) 94 LNTS 57 (*'Kellogg–Briand Pact'*).

[25] Articles 10, 12, 13 and 15.

[26] Brownlie, n. 19, 66.

a cooling-off period, and 'it did not restrict use of force other than war and aggression'.[27] From 1919, there were a number of international instruments variously declaring aggressive war/wars of aggression as an international crime (e.g. the Draft Treaty of Mutual Assistance, which never entered into force; the 1925 Sixth Assembly resolution: 'war of aggression' is 'an international crime'; the 1927 Eighth Assembly resolution: 'wars of aggression are ... prohibited'). But this 'just affirmed existing international law' and 'did not go beyond the [League] Covenant'.[28] The 1928 Resolution of the Sixth International Conference of American States also considered and resolved that aggression is 'illicit and as such declared as prohibited', but there remained the problem of a lack of definition.

The turning point which galvanised the emerging international law prohibiting recourse to war was the 1928 Kellogg–Briand Pact: the General Treaty for Renunciation of War. The parties to the Pact 'condemne[d] recourse to war for the solution of international controversies, and renounce [d] it, as an instrument of national policy in their relations with one another'.[29] '[W]ar in violation of the Paris Pact was equated to aggression, triggering the obligations of third states under Article 10 of the Covenant.'[30] The Pact did not provide for sanctions, though violation did have consequences, for example, liability for damages, a right of intervention and no rights arising from a war in violation of the Pact.[31] Ian Brownlie notes, '[t]he treaty was of almost universal obligation since only four states in international society as it existed before the Second World War were not bound by its provisions'.[32]

It is controversial whether these legal developments amounted to the creation of a customary rule prohibiting force that was merely replicated later in article 2(4) of the UN Charter. Brownlie took the position that these multilateral treaties – together with a multitude of bilateral treaties during this time period reflecting similar provisions, various statements by States demonstrating an acceptance of the legal nature of the obligation to refrain from recourse to force in international relations (though it seems that these

[27] Lesaffer, n. 19, 52 with extensive footnotes. See also Hans Kelsen, *The Law of the United Nations: A Critical Analysis of Its Fundamental Problems* (Stevens, 1950), 708: 'The Covenant of the League of Nations did not forbid war under all circumstances. The Members of the League were allowed to resort to war against one another under certain circumstances, but only "for the maintenance of right and justice."'

[28] Brownlie, n. 19, 73.

[29] Article 1.

[30] Lesaffer, n. 19, 53, footnote omitted.

[31] *Ibid.*, 52, citing Neff.

[32] Lesaffer, n. 19, 75, footnote omitted.

statements really emphasise that the legal obligation stems from the Pact and the League Covenant) and State practice – support the conclusion that at least by 1939, resort to war was illegal unless in self-defence.[33] However, he acknowledges that '[t]here was no general agreement on the precise meaning of the terms used in instruments and diplomatic practice relating to the use of force. This still creates serious difficulty but it is absurd to suggest that because there is a certain degree of controversy the basic obligation does not apply to the more obvious instances of illegality.'[34]

Many of the legal developments referred to earlier in the chapter did not explicitly prohibit 'force', but 'war', which may have been a broader term. 'Whether "war" in the Pact was used in its technical meaning and all other uses of force were excluded was and remains a matter of contention among international lawyers.'[35] Brownlie argues that '[t]he subsequent practice of parties to the Kellogg-Briand Pact leaves little room for doubt that it was understood to prohibit *any substantial use of armed force*'.[36] Randall Lesaffer believes that Brownlie's view is too 'rosy' a picture, since State practice post-World War II 'indicates that states still considered themselves to have a right to resort to war and formally declare war in the case of prior aggression by an enemy. Moreover, the Covenant and the [Kellogg–Briand] Pact had left the door wide open for an alternative strategy to resort to force rather than war, primarily in the guise of self-defence.'[37]

The UN Charter Era

After the conclusion of World War II, a new era of international law was ushered in with the advent of the UN Charter in 1945, and, in particular, its cornerstone provision in article 2(4) prohibiting the 'use of force' between States. As Hans Kelsen notes, '[t]he Charter of the United Nations goes much

33 Brownlie, n. 19, 110.

34 *Ibid.*, 111.

35 Lesaffer, n. 19, 53, citing Brownlie, n. 19, 84–92. See Carrie McDougall, 'The Crimes against Peace Precedent' in Claus Kreß and Stefan Barriga (eds), *The Crime of Aggression: A Commentary* (Cambridge University Press, 2017), 49, 55–58 for a discussion of the pre-World War II legal understanding of 'war' according to Brownlie, and an analysis of the interpretation of 'war of aggression' by the Nuremberg and Tokyo Tribunals: 'at the very least it can be said that in the pre-war era there were multiple meanings of the term "war", not all of which had an agreed definition.'

36 Brownlie, n. 19, 88, emphasis added and footnote omitted. Cf Kelsen, n. 27, 708, who argued that 'The Briand-Kellogg Pact outlawed war as an instrument of national policy; consequently, war as an instrument of international policy and especially a war waged by one state against a state which has violated the Pact was not forbidden'.

37 Lesaffer, n. 19, 53–4.

farther than its predecessors. It obligates the Members of the United Nations not only not to resort to war against each other but to refrain from the threat or use of force and to settle their disputes by peaceful means (Article 2, paragraphs 3 and 4).'[38] The prohibition of a 'use of force' in article 2(4) was therefore a significant legal development in comparison to earlier international law existing at that time, which prohibited resort to 'war'.[39]

This view is also supported by statements made during the drafting of the Vienna Convention on the Law of Treaties, with respect to draft article 36. The draft article, entitled 'coercion of a State by the threat or use of force', provided that '[a] treaty is void if its conclusion has been procured by the threat or use of force in violation of the principles of the Charter of the United Nations.' In the discussion of the draft provision, the Netherlands and the United States raised the question of its retroactive applicability. The United States noted that:

> The traditional doctrine prior to the League Covenant was that the validity of a treaty was not affected by the fact that it had been entered into under the threat or use of force. With the Covenant and the Pact of Paris, this traditional doctrine came under attack; with the Charter it was overturned. In the view of the United States Government, *it was therefore only with the coming into effect of the Charter* that the concept of the illegitimacy of threats or uses of force in violation of the territorial integrity or political independence of any State, or in any other manner inconsistent with the purposes of the United Nations, was accepted.[40]

This view was affirmed by Sir Humphrey Waldock and cited by Judge Jennings in the *Nicaragua* case: 'The illegality of recourse to armed reprisals or other forms of armed intervention not amounting to war was not established beyond all doubt by the law of the League, or by the Nuremberg and Tokyo Trials. That was brought about by the law of the Charter.'[41]

[38] Kelsen, n. 27, 708.

[39] Judge Jennings took this position in his Dissenting Opinion in the *Nicaragua* case (Merits), n. 4, 520:

> It could hardly be contended that these provisions of the Charter [articles 2(4) and 51] were merely a codification of the existing customary law. The literature is replete with statements that Article 2, paragraph 4, – for example in speaking of 'force' rather than war, and providing that even a 'threat of force' may be unlawful – represented an important innovation in the law.

[40] International Law Commission, 'Yearbook of the International Law Commission 1966, Vol. II' (1966), A/CN.4/SER.A/1966/Add.l, Observations and Proposals of the Special Rapporteur, 16.

[41] Dissenting Opinion, *Nicaragua* case (Merits), n. 4, 520, citing Waldock, 106 *Collected Courses, Academy of International Law* (The Hague, 1962-II), 231.

Conclusion

Article 2(4) of the UN Charter did not merely codify an existing customary prohibition of the use of force but was rather a significant legal development which went beyond the existing laws of the time in order to found a new international legal order in the aftermath of World War II. In terms of how this position squares with the pronouncements of the majority judgment in the *Nicaragua* case, it must be recalled that the Court did not state that a rule of customary international law pre-existed the Charter but rather that the customary international law *principle* pre-existed the Charter and subsequently developed into a rule of customary international law under the Charter's influence. Although it is not clear what legal meaning a customary international law 'principle' has given that this category is not recognised in article 38(1) of the Statute of the International Court of Justice, if it is understood as meaning that a legal zeitgeist was developing towards a stricter regulation of the use of force between States culminating in the prohibition set out in article 2(4) of the UN Charter, this is consistent with the historical narrative of the inter-war period outlined earlier in the chapter.

Article 2(4) as Crystallising a Rule of Customary International Law in the Process of Formation?

Another possibility for the formation of the customary prohibition of the use of force is that it was starting to emerge prior to the UN Charter and crystallised *as a result* of the negotiation and drafting of article 2(4). The process of crystallisation of a customary rule occurs when 'the law evolve[s] through the practice of States on the basis of the debates and near-agreements' revealing 'general consensus' during the treaty negotiation process that the rule in question is of a customary nature.[42] This process of 'State practice ... developing in parallel with the drafting of the treaty' is more likely to occur when the treaty negotiations and drafting take place over a long period of time,[43] as occurred with the new concept of the exclusive economic zone developed during the Third United Nations Conference on the Law of the Sea (1973–1982) and its acceptance by States as customary international law

[42] *Fisheries Jurisdiction (UK v Iceland), Merits, Judgment* (1974) ICJ Reports 3, para. 52.

[43] International Law Association Committee on Formation of Customary (General) International Law, 'Final Report of the Committee: Statement of Principles Applicable to the Formation of General Customary International Law' (ILA, 2000), 49.

prior to the adoption and entry into force of the 1982 UN Convention on the Law of the Sea in 1994.[44]

However, article 2(4) of the Charter arguably did not 'crystallise' a rule of customary international law in the process of formation, because any pre-existing customary limitations on recourse to force were significantly broadened by the advent of article 2(4), and the process of drafting was not accompanied by meaningful State practice 'developing in parallel with' this radical change in the law. First of all, the relevant period for crystallisation of a customary rule – the period of treaty negotiation and drafting prior to signing of the UN Charter – was extremely brief 'due to the special circumstances occasioned by the war'.[45] 'The constitutive instrument of the UN was conceived, negotiated, drafted, signed, and ratified in four phases, corresponding closely with events of the war . . . it was only towards the end of the first phase and at the beginning of the second phase [the summer of 1944] that a diplomatic exchange of ideas was set in motion.'[46] The UN Charter was then adopted on 25 June 1945 and entered into force on 24 October of the same year.

Furthermore, the term 'use of force' in article 2(4) was deliberately chosen by the drafters of the UN Charter to go beyond the earlier (failed) attempts to outlaw 'war' in the League Covenant and the Kellogg–Briand Pact, which had left open the possibility for States to claim that no war had been formally declared or officially recognised and that forcible measures fell short of war and were therefore permissible.[47] Of course, this gap between the pre-Charter prohibition of war and the prohibition of 'use of force' in article 2(4) is not itself an obstacle to crystallisation of any nascent customary prohibition, but it brings into stark relief that State practice (i.e. 'the reactions of Governments to the negotiations and consultations during the work in progress'[48] or 'repeated

44 Michael Wood, 'Third Report on Identification of Customary International Law' UN Doc A/CN.4/682 (ILC, 27 March 2015) ('Wood Third Report'), para. 38. In the *Continental Shelf (Libyan Arab Jamahiriya/Malta), Judgment* (1985) ICJ Reports 13, para. 34, the ICJ recognised that 'the institution of the exclusive economic zone, with its rule on entitlement by reason of distance, is shown by the practice of States to have become a part of customary law'.

45 Wilhelm G Grewe and Daniel-Erasmus Khan, 'Drafting History' in Bruno Simma et al. (eds), *The Charter of the United Nations: A Commentary* (Oxford University Press, 2nd ed, 2002), vol. I, 1, MN 3.

46 *Ibid.*, MN3, 4 and 6.

47 See Robert C Hilderbrand, *Dumbarton Oaks: The Origins of the United Nations and the Search for Postwar Security* (University of North Carolina Press, 1990) regarding the intention of Charter drafters to 'settle the discussion on the extent of the prohibition of "war"' by changing the term 'resort to war' to threat or use of force, cited in Lesaffer, n. 19, 54.

48 Yoram Dinstein, 'The Interaction between Customary International Law and Treaties' (2006) 322 *Recueil des cours: Collected Courses of the Hague Academy of International Law* 243, 358.

practice by the States concerned'[49]) did not parallel this radical legal development in the treaty during the brief negotiation process.

In particular, the reaction of States to article 2(6) of the UN Charter during the drafting process clearly illustrates that they did not already accept the rule in article 2(4) as a binding rule of customary international law during the period of drafting and negotiation. Article 2(6) provides that the United Nations 'shall ensure that states which are not Members of the United Nations act in accordance with [the Principles in article 2] so far as may be necessary for the maintenance of international peace and security'. The *travaux préparatoires* for this provision indicate that the delegates did not believe that they were imposing a customary obligation onto non-Members but rather that they were seeking a way to impose *treaty* obligations on non-treaty parties for the purpose of maintaining international peace and security as part of the new international order. The Report of the Rapporteur of the relevant Subcommittee of the San Francisco Conference stated:

> The vote was taken on the understanding that the association of the United Nations, representing the major expression of the international legal community, is entitled to act in a manner which will insure the effective co-operation of non-Member states with it, so far as that is necessary for the maintenance of international peace and security.[50]

Furthermore, as Kelsen highlights:

> In the discussion of this paragraph at the 12th meeting of Committee I/I (U.N.C.I.O. Doc. 810, I/I/30, p.7) 'The Delegate of Uruguay asked for a clarification of the meaning of this paragraph. He asked how a non-Member could be brought within the sphere of the Organisation and how the Organisation could impose duties upon non-Members. The Rapporteur replied that the paragraph was intended to provide a justification for extending the power of the Organisation to apply to the actions of non-Members, but that the wording might have to be reconsidered if it were not clear. ... The Australian Delegate agreed that this was a difficult

[49] *Continental Shelf (Tunisia/Libyan Arab Jamahiriya), Judgment* (1982) ICJ Reports 18, Dissenting Opinion of Judge Oda, para. 23: 'It is however possible that, before the draft of a multilateral treaty becomes effective and binding upon the States Parties in accordance with its final clause, some of its provisions will have become customary international law through repeated practice by the States concerned.' But note the caution in the *North Sea Continental Shelf Cases*, n. 18, para. 76, that practice consistent with a treaty by States parties before a treaty enters into effect is not necessarily evidence that the rule in question is a customary norm, since those States are presumably 'acting actually or potentially in the application of the Convention'. Further on this point, see the discussion in Chapter 2.

[50] Report of Rapporteur of Subcommittee I/I/A to Committee I/I of the San Francisco Conference (U.N.C.I.O. Doc 739, I/I/A/19 (a), p. 6), cited in Kelsen, n. 27, 110, footnote 9.

provision to enforce but that it was an essential one. The Organisation would have to see that everything possible would be done to suppress an aggressor.'[51]

During the discussions regarding article 2(6), States did not refer to a customary obligation to refrain from the use of force but, to the contrary, showed consternation about the legal basis for imposing this obligation in the UN Charter onto non-Member States. This could only be the case if States did not already accept that it was a binding rule of customary international law at the time of drafting the UN Charter. This weighs strongly against any crystallisation of a customary prohibition of the use of force *in statu nascendi* during the drafting and conclusion of article 2(4) of the UN Charter. Although the *travaux préparatoires* relating to article 2(6) are evidence that at the time of drafting and negotiation of the UN Charter, the prohibition of the use of force in article 2(4) was not accepted as a customary rule by States, it is evidence that States sought to establish a *new* customary rule *through the impact of the UN Charter*. This nuanced distinction illustrates that although crystallisation of an emerging customary rule and the development of a new customary rule triggered by a new treaty rule are 'distinct processes, in a given case, they may shade into one another'.[52] The significance of article 2(6) for the generation of the customary prohibition of the use of force is discussed further in Chapter 2.

CONCLUSION

Since article 2(4) of the UN Charter was more restrictive than pre-existing customary international law, it was not declaratory of pre-existing customary international law. For the reasons set out earlier, nor did it crystallise customary international law in the process of formation. Therefore, the customary rule prohibiting recourse to force between States must have arisen *after* the Charter entered into force. This is consistent with the finding of the ICJ in the *Nicaragua* case, as the Court did not posit that article 2(4) was declaratory of pre-existing customary international law but that the principle of the prohibition already existed under customary international law and subsequently developed under the influence of the Charter. There are two possibilities for the way this process occurred: either the new rule of customary international law developed in the usual way (State practice accompanied by an *opinio juris*), or article 2(4) gave rise to a new rule of customary international law through its own impact. These possibilities are discussed in Chapter 2.

[51] *Ibid.*

[52] Wood Third Report, n. 44, para. 35.

2

Baxter's Paradox and the Customary Prohibition of the Use of Force

INTRODUCTION

As we excluded in Chapter 1 the first two possibilities for the emergence of the customary prohibition of the use of force (pre-existing custom and crystallisation), let us now turn to the remaining two options for how the customary norm emerged after the advent of the UN Charter in 1945. This brings us into the realm of Baxter's paradox and the imaginative alternative proposed by the International Court of Justice (ICJ) in the *North Sea Continental Shelf Cases*. This chapter accordingly explores the challenges of separately adducing the content of the parallel customary prohibition of the use of force in the presence of the parallel near-universal treaty obligation in article 2(4). Delving into these theoretical issues is not only an intriguing intellectual exercise but, as we saw in Chapter 1, fundamental to discerning the relationship between the customary and Charter prohibitions of the use of force, and in turn, the appropriate method for interpreting the meaning of prohibited force under international law (i.e. whether to focus on custom, the treaty or some combination of the two). The conclusions drawn from this chapter lay the foundation for the method that will be applied in the rest of the book to uncover the meaning of prohibited force in international law.

CHALLENGES OF THE TWO-ELEMENT APPROACH

The third option for how the customary prohibition of the use of force emerged is also the mainstream approach[1] to establishing the existence and

[1] Alternative approaches to the identification of custom have been proposed, for example, a sliding scale of State practice and *opinio juris*, such that 'a clearly demonstrated and strong *opinio juris* reduces (or even eliminates) the need to show general practice'. Oscar Schachter, 'Entangled Treaty and Custom' in Yoram Dinstein (ed), *International Law at a Time of*

content of a rule of customary international law, namely, the two constituent element approach: a general practice that is accepted as law.[2] This was the approach of the ICJ in the *North Sea Continental Shelf Cases*, when it held:

> [T]wo conditions must be fulfilled. Not only must the acts concerned amount to a settled practice, but they must also be such, or be carried out in such a way, as to be evidence of a belief that this practice is rendered obligatory by the existence of a rule of law requiring it. The need for such a belief, i.e., the existence of a subjective element, is implicit in the very notion of the *opinio juris sive necessitatis*. The States concerned must therefore feel that they are conforming to what amounts to a legal obligation.[3]

The two-element approach has been adopted by the International Law Commission (ILC) Committee on the Identification of Customary International Law.[4] The ILC Committee stated that each element must be separately ascertained by assessing the evidence for each element.[5] The ILC Committee Special Rapporteur clarified that 'the existence of one element cannot be deduced from the existence of the other'.[6]

Although this is the widely accepted approach to the identification of customary international law, it is uniquely difficult to apply to the customary

Perplexity: Essays in Honour of Shabtai Rosenne (Martinus Nijhoff Publishers, 1989), 717, 733. In relation to lack of uniform State practice and frequent violations of the prohibition of the use of force, Schachter argues that the higher normative status of the rule explains the continuity of the rule as custom and that since this is an area of international law where breach is likely, this is a reason to lower the requirements of uniform practice (732–5). A related argument is set forward by Anthea Roberts, 'Traditional and Modern Approaches to Customary International Law: A Reconciliation' (2001) 95(4) *American Journal of International Law* 757, referring to a sliding scale that takes into consideration the moral importance of the norm. See also Bin Cheng's argument that 'international customary law has in reality only one constitutive element, the *opinio juris*': 'United Nations Resolutions on Outer Space: "Instant" International Customary Law?' (1965) 5 *Indian Journal of International Law* 36.

2 See Michael Wood, 'Fourth Report on Identification of Customary International Law' UN Doc A/CN.4/695 (ILC, 6 March 2016) ('Wood Fourth Report'), 5, para. 15.

3 *North Sea Continental Shelf (Federal Republic of Germany/Denmark; Federal Republic of Germany/Netherlands) Judgment* (1969) ICJ Reports 3, para. 77; affirmed in *Case concerning Military and Paramilitary Activities in and against Nicaragua (Nicaragua v United States of America), Merits, Judgment* 1986 ICJ Reports 14 ('*Nicaragua* case'), para. 207.

4 International Law Commission, *Draft Conclusions on Identification of Customary International Law, with Commentaries*, Yearbook of the International Law Commission (2018), vol. II, Part Two, UN Doc A/73/10, draft conclusion 2 ('ILC Draft Conclusions on Identification of Customary International Law').

5 *Ibid.*, draft conclusion 3(2).

6 International Law Commission, 'Identification of Customary International Law: Statement of the Chair of the Drafting Committee, Mr. Mathias Forteau' (ILC, 29 July 2015) (2015 Statement of Chair), 3.

prohibition of the use of force due to the presence of the parallel and near-universal treaty obligation in article 2(4) of the UN Charter. The main issue is that it is difficult to identify sufficient relevant State practice and *opinio juris* outside the treaty. Whether such practice and *opinio juris* 'counts' depends primarily on the extent to which conduct connected with a treaty is considered as relevant State practice or serves as evidence of an *opinio juris*. It also depends on the significance of verbal acts (including silence) and inaction as 'practice', and of UN General Assembly resolutions as evidence of *opinio juris*. Finally, it depends on the relative weight to be given to practice versus *opinio juris*. Establishing evidence of the customary rule and its content thus depends on a number of theoretical issues that remain unsettled or over which significant controversy exists. These factors taken together render it a highly fraught and complicated exercise to determine exactly when the customary prohibition of the use of force arose, as well as to identify the scope of the customary prohibition in a process distinct from the application and interpretation of article 2(4) of the UN Charter.

Non-treaty Practice

The first challenge in determining the scope of the customary prohibition of the use of force is that there is insufficient relevant State practice outside the UN Charter. Although usually 'the conduct of parties to a treaty in relation to *non-parties* is not practice under the treaty, and therefore counts towards the formation of customary law',[7] article 2(4) of the UN Charter prohibits Member States of the United Nations from using force not only against each other but against any State, including non-Member States. This means that the only relevant practice outside the UN Charter is that of non-UN Member States.[8]

7 International Law Association Committee on Formation of Customary (General) International Law, 'Final Report of the Committee: Statement of Principles Applicable to the Formation of General Customary International Law' (ILA, 2000) ('ILA 2000 Report'), 47, commentary to section 24. See also Michael Wood, 'Third Report on Identification of Customary International Law' UN Doc A/CN.4/682 (ILC, 27 March 2015) ('Wood Third Report'), para. 41.

8 The International Law Association Committee on Formation of Customary (General) International Law suggests that new customary international law was generated through extension via replication in the practice of *non*-States parties of the treaty obligations in articles 2(4) and 51 of the UN Charter. However, this seems to contradict what it wrote elsewhere in the same report about the customary rule arising out of the impact of the Charter, and the report does not state what that practice outside the treaty consisted of. ILA 2000 Report, n. 7, 46, commentary (a) to section 24.

It is true that there is some potentially relevant practice by non-UN Member States. For instance, prior to becoming Members of the United Nations (i.e. before the UN Charter became directly binding on them), some States have declared their acceptance of the principles of the UN Charter including the prohibition of the use of force in article 2(4). In 1951, prior to becoming a Member of the United Nations in 1956, Japan 'declar[ed] its intention ... in all circumstances to conform to the principles of the Charter of the United Nations' and 'accept[ed] the obligations set forth in Article 2 of the Charter of the United Nations, in particular the obligations ... to refrain in its international relations from the threat or use of force against the territorial integrity or political independence of any State or in any other manner inconsistent with the Purposes of the United Nations'.[9] Prior to their membership of the United Nations, the Federal Republic of Germany and the German Democratic Republic also both agreed to settle their disputes exclusively by peaceful means and to refrain from the threat or use of force in accordance with the UN Charter.[10] Similarly, Switzerland accepted the obligations in the UN Charter prior to becoming a Member of the United Nations in September 2002.[11] To this may be added instances of non-UN Member States refraining from the threat or use of force. The legal relevance of silence and inaction to the identification of a customary rule is discussed later in this chapter.

However, there are two problems with concluding that the conduct of non-States parties to the UN Charter (i.e. States that are not Members of the United Nations) that is consistent with the obligation in article 2(4) is evidence of the existence of the rule in customary international law. First, such conduct must still be accompanied by an *opinio juris*. The ICJ in the *North Sea Continental Shelf Cases* held that no inference could be drawn from State practice by non-parties to a convention which was consistent with a principle set out in it, since it did not *in itself* constitute evidence of an *opinio juris*.[12] But the second and main problem is that there is hardly any such relevant

[9] *Treaty of Peace with Japan* (signed at San Francisco on 8 September 1951, entered into force 28 April 1952), 1952 UNTS 46, preamble and art. 5(ii).

[10] *Treaty on the Basis of Relations between the Federal Republic of Germany and the German Democratic Republic* (*Grundlagenvertrag*) *and Supplementary Documents* (signed at Berlin on 21 December 1972), art. 3.

[11] Letter dated 20 June 2002 from the President and the Chancellor of the Swiss Confederation on behalf of the Swiss Federal Council addressed to the Secretary-General, UN Doc A/56/1009–S/2002/801 (24 July 2002). Switzerland accepted these obligations a few months before joining the United Nations.

[12] *North Sea Continental Shelf Cases*, n. 3, para. 76.

practice due to the nearly universal nature of the UN Charter. This renders difficult the identification of relevant practice by non-parties to the UN Charter, which in any case due to their relatively small number could hardly be described as a 'general practice'. Since UN membership has grown over time, there have been periods in which a considerable number of States (including newly independent States) were not yet Members.[13] But it is not their practice that is usually cited in support of the argument that the prohibition has formed a rule of customary international law due to widespread practice and *opinio juris*. As noted by Judge Sir Robert Jennings in his dissenting opinion in the *Nicaragua* case:

> [T]here are obvious difficulties about extracting even a scintilla of relevant 'practice' on these matters from the behaviour of those few States which are not parties to the Charter; and the behaviour of all the rest, and the *opinio juris* which it might otherwise evidence, is surely explained by their being bound by the Charter itself.[14]

This was the paradox identified by RR Baxter:

> [T]he proof of a consistent pattern of conduct by non-parties becomes more difficult as the number of parties to the instrument increases. The number of participants in the process of creating customary law may become so small that the evidence of their practice will be minimal or altogether lacking. Hence the paradox that as the number of parties to a treaty increases, it becomes more difficult to demonstrate what is the state of customary international law dehors the treaty.[15]

Clearly, the ICJ in the *Nicaragua* case (decided subsequent to Baxter's famous pronouncement) 'did not accept this reasoning, although it did not indicate how conduct relating to a treaty rule and to an identical customary law rule can be differentiated'.[16] James Crawford also noted that 'State practice requires that the Baxter paradox hold – that is, that treaty participation is not enough. Custom is more than treaty, more even than a generally accepted treaty . . . [yet] the coexistence of custom and treaty suggests that the Baxter paradox is not actually a genuine paradox.'[17] Hugh Thirlway also argues that Baxter's paradox is not really a paradox but

[13] See www.un.org/en/about-us/growth-in-un-membership.
[14] *Nicaragua* case, n. 3, 532, footnote omitted.
[15] RR Baxter, 'Treaties and Custom' (1970) 129 *Recueil des cours: Collected Courses of the Hague Academy of International Law* 25, 64.
[16] Schachter, n. 1, 726–7.
[17] James Crawford, *Chance, Order, Change* (Martinus Nijhoff Publishers, 2013), 107, 110.

> [i]t has merely a counter-intuitive element: one would expect that the more States show allegiance to a developing rule of law, by ratifying a treaty embodying it, the more easily it could be shown to have become a general customary rule. It states, or represents, in dramatic form a fact which is inconvenient for the development of international law, and its consistent application. There is no need to seek a 'solution' to the paradox, but rather a way of palliating that inconvenience.[18]

There are proposals to address this *de lege ferenda*,[19] but *de lege lata*, it remains unclear how one can identify the scope of the parallel customary prohibition separately to article 2(4) of the UN Charter. It squarely raises the question of how post-treaty practice (such as treaty ratification, frequent repetition of a rule in multiple treaties and conduct by States parties to a treaty consistent with their treaty obligations) is to be taken into account in the formation of the customary rule. These issues are examined later.

Conduct Referable to the Treaty

Since there is virtually no potentially relevant State practice with respect to the prohibition of the use of force completely outside the UN Charter (essentially, only the practice of non-UN Member States, which we have seen earlier is extremely limited), the next questions are, first, whether State practice in compliance with a treaty obligation may count as relevant practice for the purpose of identifying a rule of customary international law; and second, whether and how we can determine if such practice in compliance with a treaty obligation is motivated by a belief in a legal obligation outside the treaty.

Does Conduct Consistent with Treaty Obligations Count as Practice?

The ICJ in the *North Sea Continental Shelf Cases*[20] confirmed that State practice consistent with the treaty by States parties should not be given weight for the purpose of identifying a customary rule. In that case, the ICJ

[18] Hugh WA Thirlway, 'Professor Baxter's Legacy: Still Paradoxical?' (2017) 6(3) *ESIL Reflection* 1.

[19] For example, Thirlway suggests that

> one may introduce some adjustments into the classic analysis of custom-making: thus Crawford proposes, as we have seen, the adoption of a presumption of *opinio juris* from the simple fact of widespread participation in a law-making convention, and that account be taken of the attitude towards the relevant rule adopted by States who are committed to it in its convention form.
>
> (*Ibid.*)

[20] *North Sea Continental Shelf Cases*, n. 3, para. 76.

discounted practice consistent with the treaty by States parties, even before the treaty entered into effect, since they were presumably 'acting actually or potentially in the application of the Convention'. With respect to State practice consistent with treaty obligations, '[c]onduct which is wholly referable to the treaty itself does not count for this purpose as practice';[21] 'in principle ... what States do in pursuance of their treaty obligations is *prima facie* referable only to the *treaty*, and therefore does not count towards the formation of a *customary* rule'.[22] Conduct referable to the treaty is not relevant 'practice' unless accompanied by an *opinio juris* outside the treaty, since on its own it does not provide evidence that a State is applying customary international law. It will require something additional to show that the conduct is not merely referable to the treaty but indicates that State's belief about a customary legal obligation; this would usually require a verbal statement to show the State was not merely applying the treaty.

Are Acts in Compliance with Treaty Obligations Evidence of *Opinio Juris*?
Treating conduct of States parties to a treaty consistent with their treaty obligations as evidence of *opinio juris* for the existence of a customary rule is also problematic for the same reason explained earlier: on its own, State conduct in compliance with a treaty obligation is not evidence of a belief that the conduct is required by customary international law since the conduct is referable to the treaty.

Treaty Ratification and Repetition of a Rule in Multiple Treaties

In addition to the forms of practice described earlier, a plethora of multilateral treaties affirm the obligation to refrain from the threat or use of force, such as the UN Convention on the Law of the Sea, which provides in article 301 that '[i]n exercising their rights and performing their duties under this Convention, States Parties shall refrain from any threat or use of force against the territorial integrity or political independence of any State, or in any other manner inconsistent with the principles of international law embodied in the Charter of the United Nations'.[23] Do these treaty ratifications and repetition of the rule in multiple treaties count as *opinio juris*? The ILC 'has found that the frequent enunciation of a provision in international treaties did not

[21] ILA 2000 Report, n. 7, 46.
[22] *Ibid.* See also Wood Third Report, n. 7, para. 41 with further references.
[23] *United Nations Convention on the Law of the Sea* 1982 (adopted 10 December 1982, entered into force 16 November 1994) 1833 UNTS 397 ('UNCLOS').

necessarily indicate that the provision had developed into a rule of customary international law'.[24] Similarly, draft conclusion 11, paragraph 2 of the ILC Committee on the Identification of Customary International Law provides that '[t]he fact that a rule is set forth in a number of treaties may, but does not necessarily, indicate that the treaty rule reflects a rule of customary international law'.[25] However, 'in some cases it may be that frequent repetition in widely accepted treaties evinces a recognition by the international community as a whole that a rule is one of general, and not just particular, law. . . . But the test remains qualitative rather than quantitative.'[26] The ILC has previously relied upon treaty practice in assessing *opinio juris* for the purpose of identifying a rule of customary international law,[27] including with respect to the prohibition of the use of force, by referring to paragraphs (1) and (5) of the commentary to draft article 49 on the law of treaties (which mention the prohibition of the use of force in article 2(4) of the UN Charter).[28]

Christian Tams notes that '[a]s regards the context, the Court has been unwilling to compartmentalise State conduct as belonging to one particular source of law only. Notably . . . it has regularly relied on the participation of States in treaties.'[29] Tams notes that '[a]ccording to Pellet, this in fact "might be the most important and frequent aspect of practice"'.[30] The Court in the *Nicaragua* case considered the actual treaty commitments to a rule prohibiting the use of force as themselves evidence of the parties expressing recognition of the validity of the rule as binding under customary international law:

> In the present dispute, the Court, while exercising its jurisdiction only in respect of the application of the customary rules of non-use of force and non-intervention, cannot disregard the fact that the Parties are bound by these rules as a matter of treaty law and of customary international law. Furthermore, in the present case, *apart from the treaty commitments binding the Parties to the rules in question*, there are various instances of their having

[24] *Ibid.*, 33–4, footnote omitted. See also ILA 2000 Report, n. 7, principle 25.

[25] ILC Draft Conclusions on Identification of Customary International Law, n. 4.

[26] ILA 2000 Report, n. 7, 48, commentary to section 25.

[27] See International Law Commission, 'Formation and Evidence of Customary International Law – Elements in the Previous Work of the International Law Commission That Could Be Particularly Relevant to the Topic – Memorandum by the Secretariat' UN Doc A/CN.4/659 (14 March 2013), 14, commentary to Observation 7, para. 23, and 21–2, commentary to Observation 12, para. 29, with extensive examples cited in footnotes.

[28] ILC, 'Yearbook of the International Law Commission 1966, Vol. II' UN Doc A/CN.4/SER.A/1966/Add.l (1966), p. 246, cited in footnote 85 of ILC Secretariat Memorandum, *ibid.*, 22.

[29] Christian J Tams, 'Meta-Custom and the Court: A Study in Judicial Law-Making' (2015) 14(1) *The Law and Practice of International Courts and Tribunals* 51, 68, footnote omitted.

[30] *Ibid.*, 68, footnote 90.

> expressed recognition of the validity thereof as customary international law *in other ways*.[31]

For instance, the Court held that the US ratification of the 1933 Montevideo Convention on Rights and Duties of States, 'Article 11 of which imposes the obligation not to recognize territorial acquisitions or special advantages which have been obtained by force' was evidence of the US *opinio juris*.[32] In other words, the Court viewed the ratification of a treaty containing the obligation to refrain from the use of force in international relations as evidence that the ratifying State accepted that such obligations in the treaty were already binding as a matter of customary international law.

However, to classify treaty ratification or the repetition of a treaty provision in a number of treaties as evidence of *opinio juris* regarding the existence of a customary rule requires further evidence that the States parties to the treaty believe that the treaty provision is also a customary rule; by ratifying a treaty, the parties to the treaty arguably intend to accept a *treaty* obligation.[33]

Verbal Acts

Verbal Acts as Practice

Although acts connected with a treaty when carried out by States parties to that treaty do not necessarily carry weight as State practice for the purpose of identifying a rule of customary international law, verbal acts by States may in some cases constitute 'general practice'. This is particularly relevant to our enquiry because most forms of practice with respect to the prohibition of the use of force between States in international law are verbal acts – statements, declarations, exchanges of claims and counter-claims – rather than physical acts such as the actual employment of inter-State force.[34] Unlike physical acts, many verbal acts explicitly refer to the customary nature of the rule. For example:

- UN General Assembly resolutions such as the 1970 Friendly Relations Declaration (discussed further below) and 1987 General Assembly Resolution 42/22. The latter resolution held that

[31] See *Nicaragua* case, n. 3, para. 185, emphasis added.

[32] *Ibid.*, para. 189.

[33] For scholarly views for and against this position, see Michael Wood, 'Second Report on Identification of Customary International Law' UN Doc A/CN.4/672 (22 May 2014) ('Wood Second Report'), 25.

[34] This point is also made by the ILA Committee in general about customary international law: ILA 2000 Report, n. 7, 14.

> *[e]very State* has the duty to refrain in its international relations from the threat or use of force against the territorial integrity or political independence of any State, or from acting in any other manner inconsistent with the purposes of the United Nations. Such a threat or use of force constitutes a violation of international law *and* of the Charter of the United Nations and entails international responsibility.[35]

The final sentence implies that the prohibition is a rule of customary international law in addition to a treaty rule in the Charter. The resolution went on to declare that '[t]he principle of refraining from the threat or use of force in international relations is universal in character and is binding, regardless of each State's political, economic, social or cultural system or relations of alliance'.[36] The significance of UN General Assembly resolutions as verbal acts is discussed further below.

- 1975 Helsinki Final Act (declaration on principles governing the mutual relations of States participating in the Conference on Security and Co-operation in Europe). The ICJ in the *Nicaragua* case described the effects of the Act as follows: 'the participating States undertake to "refrain in their mutual relations, as well as in their international relations in general," ... from the threat or use of force. Acceptance of a text in these terms confirms the existence of an *opinio juris* of the participating States prohibiting the use of force in international relations.'[37] The Pact of Bogota (the American Treaty on Pacific Settlement) also requires the contracting parties to 'refrain from the threat or the use of force, or from any other means of coercion for the settlement of their controversies';[38]
- State representations before the ICJ have asserted the customary international law nature of the prohibition, notably, for example, Nicaragua and the United States in the *Nicaragua* case;[39]
- In the 1990 Charter of Paris for a New Europe, participating countries, '[i]n accordance with [their] obligations under the Charter of the United Nations and commitments under the Helsinki Final Act, ... renew[ed] [their] pledge to refrain from the threat or use of force against the

[35] UN General Assembly, *Resolution 42/22: Declaration on the Enhancement of the Effectiveness of the Principle of Refraining from the Threat or Use of Force in International Relations*, UN Doc A/Res/42/22 (18 November 1987) (adopted without a vote), para. 1, emphasis added.

[36] *Ibid.*, para. 2.

[37] *Nicaragua* case, n. 3, para. 189.

[38] Cited in Dissenting Opinion of Judge Weeramantry in *Legality of the Threat or Use of Nuclear Weapons, Advisory Opinion* (1996) ICJ Reports 226 ('*Nuclear Weapons* Advisory Opinion'), 525.

[39] *Nicaragua* case, n. 3, paras. 187–8.

> territorial integrity or political independence of any State, or from acting in any other manner inconsistent with the principles or purposes of those documents'.[40]

Despite early debates about whether verbal acts count as State practice as well as physical acts,[41] it is the dominant view in scholarship and jurisprudence that verbal acts do indeed count as State practice.[42] The ILC acknowledges that '[p]ractice may take a wide range of forms. It includes both physical and verbal acts'[43] including 'conduct in connection with resolutions adopted by an international organization or at an intergovernmental conference'.[44]

The ILA Committee on Formation of Customary (General) International Law in its 2000 report also acknowledged that '[v]erbal acts, and not only physical acts, of States count as State practice'.[45] The ILA Committee argued that '[t]here is no inherent reason why verbal acts should not count as practice, whilst physical acts (such as arresting individuals or ships) should. For voluntarists, this must necessarily be so: both forms of conduct are manifestations of State will'.[46] Verbal acts recognised by the ILA Committee as forms of State practice were extensive:

> Diplomatic statements (including protests), policy statements, press releases, official manuals (e.g. on military law), instructions to armed forces, comments by governments on draft treaties, legislation, decisions of national courts and executive authorities, pleadings before international tribunals, statements in international organizations and the resolutions these bodies adopt – all of which are frequently cited as examples of State practice – are all forms of speech-act.[47]

Although it is recognised that verbal acts constitute a form of State practice, it is still 'necessary to take account of the distinction between what conduct counts as State practice, and the weight to be given to it'.[48] Some argue that verbal acts carry more weight (e.g. the position explained by ILA), while others

40 *Charter of Paris for a New Europe* 1990, Organization for Security and Co-operation in Europe, 21 November 1990, 5.

41 See Wood Second Report, n. 33, 19, footnote 84 for extensive references to scholarship.

42 *Ibid.*, 20.

43 'ILC Draft Conclusions on Identification of Customary International Law', n. 4, draft conclusion 6, para. 1.

44 *Ibid.*

45 ILA 2000 Report, n. 7, 14.

46 *Ibid.*, 14, citation omitted.

47 *Ibid.*, 14, footnote omitted.

48 *Ibid.*, 13.

argue that physical acts carry more weight ('talk is cheap').[49] The weight to be given to verbal versus physical acts will depend on the circumstances of the case. Furthermore, the weight to be given to any particular conduct, whether verbal or physical, is arguably less a matter of weight in terms of the objective element of customary international law but goes towards the strength of evidence of an accompanying *opinio juris*. This is the underlying objection to accepting verbal acts as State practice, because verbal acts may not demonstrate the same commitment of the State to a position regarding the legality of an act under customary international law – a matter of *opinio juris*.

There is some debate as to whether double counting of verbal practice is permitted – that is, whether the same verbal acts may count as both State practice and evidence of *opinio juris*[50] – but it is widely accepted that this is permitted so long as both elements (State practice and *opinio juris*) are found to be present.[51] This approach is advantageous, since 'verbal acts generally provide explicit evidence of *opinio juris* unlike physical acts',[52] given that a belief underlying a physical act may need to be inferred.[53] 'It cannot be assumed that the implication of a state's physical acts is a belief that the act is lawful.'[54] Since verbal acts may be intended to promote a State's preferred direction of legal developments (*lex ferenda*) rather than reflect its belief as to the actual state of the law (*lex lata*), caution is required when assessing verbal acts as evidence of an *opinio juris*.[55]

Do UN General Assembly Resolutions Count as Evidence of *Opinio Juris*?
One form of verbal act has particular relevance for our enquiry into the customary international law status of the prohibition of the use of force and its scope: UN General Assembly resolutions. UN General Assembly resolutions and other 'resolution[s] adopted by an international organization or at an intergovernmental conference may provide evidence for determining the

49 *Ibid.*, for a discussion and critique of this view.
50 See, for example, Roberts, n. 1.
51 2015 Statement of Chair, n. 6, 4. For a different view, see the ILA 2000 Report, n. 7, 7; Mary Ellen O'Connell, 'Taking *Opinio Juris* Seriously: A Classical Approach to International Law on the Use of Force' in Enzo Cannizzaro and Paolo Palchetti (eds), *Customary International Law on the Use of Force: A Methodological Approach* (Martinus Nijhoff Publishers, 2005), 9, 16.
52 O'Connell, *ibid.*, 15.
53 ILA 2000 Report, n. 7, 14.
54 O'Connell, n. 51, 15.
55 *Ibid.*, 16.

existence and content of a rule of customary international law, or contribute to its development'.[56]

In the *Nicaragua* case, the sources that the Court considered to be evidence of an *opinio juris* that the prohibition of the use of force is a rule of customary international law were primarily General Assembly resolutions, and in particular the 1970 Friendly Relations Declaration:

> The effect of consent to the text of such resolutions cannot be understood as merely that of a 'reiteration or elucidation' of the treaty commitment undertaken in the Charter. On the contrary, it may be understood as an acceptance of the validity of the rule or set of rules declared by the resolution by themselves. The principle of non-use of force, for example, may thus be regarded as a principle of customary international law, not as such conditioned by provisions relating to collective security, or to the facilities or armed contingents to be provided under Article 43 of the Charter. It would therefore seem apparent that the attitude referred to expresses an *opinio juris* respecting such rule (or set of rules), to be thenceforth treated separately from the provisions, especially those of an institutional kind, to which it is subject on the treaty-law plane of the Charter.[57]

However, Judge Roberto Ago in that case criticised the Court's approach to identification of customary international law, stating:

> There are, similarly, doubts which I feel bound to express regarding the idea which occasionally surfaces in the Judgment (paras. 191, 192, 202 and 203) that the acceptance of certain resolutions or declarations drawn up in the framework of the United Nations or the Organization of American States, as well as in another context, can be seen as proof conclusive of the existence among the States concerned of a concordant *opinio juris* possessing all the force of a rule of customary international law.[58]

In the *Nuclear Weapons* Advisory Opinion, the Court noted the necessity of examining whether an *opinio juris* exists with respect to the normative character of the resolution:

56 ILC Committee provisionally adopted conclusions, draft conclusion 12(2). The ILA Committee in its 2000 Report, n. 7, 55, para. 28 also takes the position that 'resolutions of the United Nations General Assembly may in some instances constitute evidence of the existence of customary international law; help to crystallize emerging customary law; or contribute to the formation of new customary law. But as a general rule, and subject to Section 32, they do not ipso facto create new rules of customary law'.

57 *Nicaragua* case, n. 3, para. 188.

58 *Ibid.*, Separate Opinion of Judge Ago, para. 7.

> General Assembly resolutions, even if they are not binding, may sometimes have normative value. They can, in certain circumstances, provide evidence important for establishing the existence of a rule or the emergence of an *opinio juris*. To establish whether this is true of a given General Assembly resolution, it is necessary to look at its content and the conditions of its adoption; it is also necessary to see whether an *opinio juris* exists as to its normative character. Or a series of resolutions may show the gradual evolution of the *opinio juris* required for the establishment of a new rule.[59]

This highlights that there is no automatic equating a State voting in favour of a resolution with that State's belief in the normative character of the resolution. States may have other (especially political) reasons for voting the way that they do. 'Importantly, "[a]s with any declaration by a state, it is always necessary to consider what states actually mean when they vote for or against certain resolutions in international fora". As States themselves often stress, the General Assembly is a political organ in which it is often far from clear that their acts carry juridical significance.'[60]

Furthermore, it is important to take into account that unless the language of the resolution makes clear otherwise, such resolutions are usually non-binding.[61] However, with the appropriate caution, UN General Assembly resolutions may indeed provide important evidence of *opinio juris* when the context, content and language of the resolution justify such a conclusion. Especially since the General Assembly is 'a forum of near universal participation',[62] resolutions that are unanimous or passed by consensus are a particularly important source of evidence of *opinio juris* regarding the state of international law on a given topic, provided that they are not merely taken at face value but analysed with due care to identify whether the reasons for voting reflect a belief in the normative character of the resolution.

One particular example of a UN General Assembly resolution that serves as strong evidence of *opinio juris* that the content of the customary prohibition of the use of force is identical to article 2(4) of the UN Charter is Resolution 2625 (XXV), the Declaration on Principles of International Law concerning Friendly Relations and Co-operation among States in accordance with the Charter of the United Nations ('Friendly Relations Declaration'). The UN

[59] *Nuclear Weapons* Advisory Opinion, n. 38, para. 70.
[60] Wood Third Report, n. 7, 33, footnotes with extensive citations omitted.
[61] See, for example, Martti Koskenniemi, *From Apology to Utopia: The Structure of International Legal Argument* (Cambridge University Press, 2005), 434–5, cited in Wood Third Report, n. 7, footnote 117.
[62] See, for example, Wood Third Report, n. 7, 9, para. 25, noting that this was suggested in the Sixth Committee and concurring.

General Assembly adopted this resolution by consensus on 24 October 1970 on the occasion of the twenty-fifth anniversary of the United Nations.

In the Friendly Relations Declaration, the UN General Assembly proclaimed:

> Every State has the duty to refrain in its international relations from the threat or use of force against the territorial integrity or political independence of any State, or in any other manner inconsistent with the purposes of the United Nations. Such a threat or use of force constitutes a violation of international law and the Charter of the United Nations and shall never be employed as a means of settling international issues.[63]

Principle 1 of the Declaration proclaims:

> The principle that States shall refrain in their international relations from the threat or use of force against the territorial integrity or political independence of any State, or in any other manner inconsistent with the purposes of the United Nations.

In addition to comprising a subsequent agreement of UN Member States on the interpretation of article 2(4), the ICJ relied on the Friendly Relations Declaration in the *Nicaragua* case as an indication of States' *opinio juris* on the existence and content of the customary prohibition of the use of force[64] due to its references to 'all States',[65] 'principle',[66] 'every State',[67] 'a violation of international law and the Charter'[68] and the statement that '[t]he principles of the Charter which are embodied in this Declaration constitute basic principles of international law'.[69]

The 1970 Friendly Relations Declaration is therefore strong evidence of *opinio juris* regarding the customary prohibition of the use of force and its content. However, although the Declaration and the other verbal acts set out earlier in the chapter refer to and confirm the customary nature of the prohibition of the use of force, they are less useful for identifying the precise scope of the customary rule and if it is identical to article 2(4) of the UN Charter. This is because these types of verbal acts that refer explicitly to

63 Friendly Relations Declaration, para. 1(1).
64 *Nicaragua* case, n. 3, para. 191.
65 Friendly Relations Declaration, 10th preambular paragraph.
66 *Ibid.*, Principle 1.
67 *Ibid.*
68 *Ibid.*, Principle 1, para. 1.
69 *Ibid.*, para. 3.

customary international law are by their nature general and abstract rather than in response to specific incidents.

Silence and Inaction as State Practice and Evidence of Opinio Juris

A final category of potentially relevant practice for the identification of the scope and content of a customary international law rule prohibiting the use of force is silence and inaction, which presents further challenges. Much State practice that may be relevant is that of omission: refraining from the use of force in particular situations, refraining from characterising an act by another State as a use of force, and lack of protest. This section will look at the significance of silence and inaction for the identification of a rule of customary international law: is it relevant that States seem to refrain from making claims about 'marginal' forcible actions under the *jus contra bellum* framework? Is it enough that States generally refrain from using force against each other (inaction as relevant practice), coupled with an *opinio juris*?

This work uses the overarching category of 'omission' to describe both inaction and silence.[70] Within this broad category, one may distil two different types of omission. The first type is omission which may constitute *State practice*. The second type is omission in response to another State's conduct, which may constitute evidence of *opinio juris* regarding the legality of the other State's conduct through acquiescence. Collecting examples of inaction is senseless without an idea of what type of conduct is in fact being abstained from, and the categories of inaction are limited only by the imagination of the person identifying such examples. As such, to narrow the universe of all forms of State inaction to something meaningful for a legal analysis, the types of inaction that may be relevant to State practice fall into the following categories: inaction accompanied by explicit verbal statements that such conduct would be unlawful; abstention from types of forcible conduct whose legality is disputed; and inaction in circumstances where the expectation or possibility is raised for a particular State to act, such as where it is called on to do so or has previously asserted a right to so act, or where some States have taken that type

[70] A note on terminology: Tom Ruys refers to 'omission' (Tom Ruys, 'The Meaning of "Force" and the Boundaries of the *Jus Ad Bellum*: Are "Minimal" Uses of Force Excluded from UN Charter Article 2 (4)?' (2014) 108(2) *American Journal of International Law* 159, 167–71); Olivier Corten discusses the significance of 'silence' (Olivier Corten, *The Law against War: The Prohibition on the Use of Force in Contemporary International Law* (Hart Publishing, 2010), 35–8.) and Sir Michael Wood uses the term 'inaction' in his reports but notes that inaction is 'also referred to as passive practice, abstention from acting, silence or omission' (Wood Third Report, n. 7, para. 19.).

of action but similar conduct is not adopted by other States. Collecting data relating to omission as potential evidence of *opinio juris* regarding the prohibition of the use of force under customary international law is more straightforward, since such silence or inaction will be in response to conduct of another State – either through a potential or actual threat or use of force, or official claims regarding the legality of certain conduct. For this category, one would need to identify forcible acts by States as well as verbal practice asserting the legality of forcible conduct and examine the response (or non-response) of third States. Under certain circumstances discussed in this section, inaction and silence may constitute State practice and evidence of *opinio juris* for the purposes of identifying a rule of customary international law. However, due to the nature of inaction and silence, they are often ambiguous and will require something more in order to be construed as evidence of such. In assessing whether inaction or silence in the face of forcible conduct or legal claims is evidence of an *opinio juris* regarding the legality of the conduct in question, one should consider whether the silent/inactive State had knowledge of the conduct, the capacity to respond, whether its interests are affected and if there is any evidence regarding the reasons for its silence or inaction.[71]

Omission as State Practice

Omission may count as State practice when inaction comprises abstention from conduct (such as the use of force) or silence in the form of refraining from asserting legal claims. According to Wood, this is a form of relevant State practice for the purpose of identifying a rule of customary international law, as long as it is accompanied by an *opinio juris*.[72] Omission as State practice is distinguished from omission as evidence of *opinio juris* in that the former comprises abstention from asserting original legal claims to act in a particular manner under customary international law, whereas the latter is in response to another State's conduct and may be interpreted as acquiescence in the legality of such.

Inaction as Practice

Inaction (in the sense of abstaining from physical action) has been variously characterised as a potential form of State practice, or as evidence of *opinio juris*.[73] For inaction to count as relevant State practice giving rise to a rule of

[71] 2015 Statement of Chair, n. 6, 10; Wood Third Report, n. 7, 8, para. 22.
[72] Wood Third Report, n. 7, para. 20.
[73] Wood Second Report, n. 33, para. 42 (with extensive further references at footnote 124); ILA 2000 Report, n. 7, 15.

customary international law, it must be general and accompanied by an *opinio juris*.[74] Examples of inaction that have been accepted as State practice include 'refraining from exercising protection in favour of certain naturalized persons; abstaining from the threat or use of force against the territorial integrity or political independence of any State; and abstaining from instituting criminal proceedings in certain circumstances'.[75]

In the *North Sea Continental Shelf Cases*, the ICJ cited and followed the *Lotus* case,[76] in which the Permanent Court of International Justice (PCIJ) held:

> Even if the rarity of the judicial decisions to be found ... were sufficient to prove ... the circumstance alleged ..., it would merely show that States had often, in practice, abstained from instituting criminal proceedings, and not that they recognized themselves as being obliged to do so; for only if such abstention were based on their being conscious of having a duty to abstain would it be possible to speak of an international custom. The alleged fact does not allow one to infer that States have been conscious of having such a duty; on the other hand, ... there are other circumstances calculated to show that the contrary is true.[77]

The clear problem is that in certain cases (such as the PCIJ *Lotus* decision), mere abstention can be too ambiguous to be treated as 'a precedent capable of contributing to the formation of a customary rule'.[78] The ILA Committee states in its commentary that when conduct 'is not clearly referable to an existing or potential legal rule' (such as ambiguous omission), it should not count as a precedent unless there is additional evidence explaining that it occurred due to an *opinio juris* that the conduct abstained from would be unlawful under customary international law (as distinguished from other reasons for a State to abstain from conduct such as 'lack of jurisdiction under municipal law; lack of interest; or a belief that a court of the flag State is a more convenient forum').[79]

Silence as Practice

Just as inaction may be a form of practice if accompanied by the required *opinio juris*, silence in certain circumstances can also be a form of State practice if it is 'general'. The forms of silence referred to here are those that

74 Wood Third Report, n. 7, para. 20.
75 *Ibid.*, para. 20, footnotes omitted.
76 *North Sea Continental Shelf Cases*, n. 3, paras. 77–8.
77 *SS Lotus Case (France v Turkey)* [1927] PCIJ Series A, No 10 (7 September 1927), 28.
78 ILA 2000 Report, n. 7, 15–16, section 17(iv).
79 *Ibid.*, 36–7.

are not in response to the acts or claims of other States, since that is rather evidence of *opinio juris* (see later in the chapter). One example is given in Wood's Second Report: that of the dissenting opinion of Judge Read in the *Interpretation of Peace Treaties* case ('The fact that no State has adopted this position [that a State party to a dispute may prevent its arbitration by the expedient of refraining from appointing a representative on the Commission] is the strongest confirmation of the international usage or practice in matters of arbitration which is set forth above')[80]; although Wood lists this as an example of inaction as evidence of *opinio juris*, it seems to in fact comprise an instance of State practice through omission, rather than acquiescence in the practice of other States.

Omission as *Opinio Juris*

The second type of omission is *inaction* in response to the conduct of another State, or *silence* in the form of lack of verbal protest (which could include a failure to invoke a violation of article 2(4) or a failure to invoke a right to use force in self-defence in response to the original act). Such silence may be evidence of an *opinio juris* that the act does not fall within the scope of the prohibition of the use of force, such as acquiescence in the legal claims made by another State through that other State's practice (including verbal practice). Wood goes so far as to note that '[i]naction by States may be central to the development and ascertainment of rules of customary international law, in particular when it qualifies (or is perceived) as acquiescence'.[81] Drawing this conclusion with respect to particular incidents requires the same caution as mentioned earlier, since silence in itself is also ambiguous. Hence, the often stated requirement of the State failing to act, or remaining silent, in the face of an expectation that it act or in other circumstances that indicate an *opinio juris*.

Inaction as *Opinio Juris*

The ILC's draft conclusion 10(3) on forms of evidence of acceptance as law (*opinio juris*) provides thus:

> Failure to react over time to a practice may serve as evidence of acceptance as law (*opinio juris*), provided that States were in a position to react and the circumstances called for some reaction.[82]

80 Wood Second Report, n. 33, footnote 279, citing *Interpretation of Peace Treaties (second phase), Advisory Opinion* (1950) ICJ Reports, 221, 242.
81 Wood Second Report, n. 33, para. 42, footnote omitted.
82 ILC Draft Conclusions on Identification of Customary International Law, n. 7.

The accompanying statement of the Committee Chair[83] explains as follows:

> The first condition is temporal. To be considered as expressing *opinio juris*, the failure to react needs to be maintained over a sufficient period of time, assessed in light of the particular circumstances. This condition is referred to by the expression 'over time'. Second, paragraph 3 indicates that, in order for inaction to qualify as acceptance as law, the State must be in a 'position to react'. This formulation is broad enough to cover the need for knowledge of the practice in question, but also other situations that might prevent a State from reacting, such as political pressures. Thirdly, it is also necessary that the circumstances called for some reaction. The Drafting Committee shared the view that States could not be expected to react to each instance of practice by other States. Attention is drawn to the circumstances surrounding the failure to react in order to establish that these circumstances indicate that the State choosing not to act considers such practice to be consistent with customary international law.

The main point is that inaction (failure to take action or to make verbal statements) in response to the acts of other States may be interpreted in certain circumstances as acquiescence in the practice of those other States – in other words, as giving rise to something similar to estoppel, so that the other States rely on the position apparently taken by the silent State vis-à-vis the act that it did not respond to. It is taken as given that the silent State has accepted the (implicit) assertion of legality of the acts taken by the first State, whose position may subsequently be relied on by that State as well as other States. This complies with the consent model of customary international law. Hence, the requirements that the silent State must have been aware of the conduct that it has not responded to and that there should be a reasonable expectation that it respond to that conduct, for example, that its interests are affected.

Silence as Evidence of *Opinio Juris*

Both inaction and silence through failure to respond to acts by other States may be a form of acquiescence. Under certain circumstances, silence in response to forcible acts by other States may be evidence of an *opinio juris* that those acts are not unlawful. There must either be evidence that the silence was actually motivated by an *opinio juris* or else the silence must have been in circumstances that give rise to an inference that the silent State acquiesces in the active State's legal claims/actions. In the former case (of an *opinio juris*), the question is whether the silent State had an *opinio juris* that

[83] 2015 Statement of Chair, n. 6, 10.

the relevant conduct was lawful. A factor that may indicate this is that the conduct affected its interests.[84] In the latter case (of acquiescence), it is relevant to ask: did the silent State act in a way calculated to or that does reasonably give rise to the perception that it was acquiescing in the relevant conduct?[85] In both cases, these factors will be relevant: first, the silent State must have knowledge of the conduct of the other State and, second, the silence must not be mainly motivated by extra-legal considerations.[86]

In sum, this section has espoused the following dichotomy: 'original' inaction or silence as State practice (i.e. not in direct response to conduct or claims by another State) if general and accompanied by an *opinio juris* that such inaction/silence is either required or not prohibited by customary international law as the case may be, and silence and inaction in response to acts of other States as evidence of an *opinio juris* that such acts are lawful, that is, acquiescence. Ultimately, just as with other (i.e. active) conduct with respect to the prohibition of the use of force, in the absence of an explicit statement that a State is applying the customary rule, it will be hard or even impossible to discern whether the silence or inaction is referable to article 2(4) of the UN Charter. In other words, even if one determines that a particular State's inaction (abstention from conduct including the assertion of legal claims) or silence (acquiescence in the conduct or legal claims of another State) has legal significance as practice with respect to the prohibition of the use of force, such conduct may be explained as compliance with the treaty obligation in article 2(4) of the UN Charter (and therefore relevant as subsequent practice in the application of the treaty) rather than evidence of the rule of custom or of an *opinio juris*. Therefore, on their own, silence and inaction, as well as active conduct that is in compliance with a State's obligations under article 2 (4) of the UN Charter, are insufficient to separately identify the existence and scope of the customary prohibition of the use of force.

84 Andrea Bianchi, 'The International Regulation of the Use of Force: The Politics of Interpretive Method' (2009) 22(4) *Leiden Journal of International Law*, 651, 664: 'It would be but logical to think that states would react to acts affecting their own interests. . . . All the more so in the light of the erga omnes character of the prohibition of the use of force.'

85 In his study of the prohibition of the threat of force, *The Threat of Force in International Law* (Cambridge University Press, 2009), Nikolas Stürchler does not treat silence as either approval or protest, since it could reflect 'indifference, neutrality or indecision' (110, footnote omitted). Stürchler argues that most States do not react by filing protests or conveying approval of potential violations of the UN Charter. 'It turns out that, at least in threat-related cases, the assumption that silence equals approval is empirically false' (257, footnote omitted).

86 See Ruys, n. 70, 167–71.

Conclusion

The main evidence that establishes the existence of the customary prohibition falls into the following categories: treaty-related practice (which may include inaction) and verbal acts, including UN General Assembly resolutions. In particular, the 1970 Friendly Relations Declaration is strong evidence of *opinio juris* regarding the customary prohibition of the use of force and its content. To determine whether such evidence 'counts' towards establishing a general practice established as law raises fundamental issues, which have been highlighted earlier in the chapter. This makes it challenging to identify not only how and when the customary prohibition emerged, but the same difficulties present themselves when attempting to identify the content of the customary prohibition instead of interpreting article 2(4) of the UN Charter.

THE 'OWN IMPACT' OF ARTICLE 2(4)

Given these challenges, the fourth way for the prohibition in article 2(4) to have given rise to a rule of customary international law – through the UN Charter's 'own impact'[87] – is both appealing and pragmatic. This process is an 'exceptional case' in which 'it may be possible for a multilateral treaty to give rise to new customary rules (or to assist in their creation) "of its own impact" if it is widely adopted by States and it is the clear intention of the parties to create new customary law'.[88] The ICJ in the *North Sea Continental Shelf Cases* considered the possibility for a rule of customary international law to arise from the 'own impact' of a treaty, noting:

> [I]t clearly involves treating that Article as a norm-creating provision which has *constituted* the foundation of, or has generated a rule which, while only conventional or contractual in its origin, has since passed into the general corpus of international law, and is now accepted as such by the *opinio juris*,

[87] Interestingly, Thirlway does not mention this 'own impact' argument: Hugh WA Thirlway, *The Sources of International Law* (Oxford University Press, 2014). The ILC's draft conclusions on the identification of a rule of customary international law also do not mention this possibility. The draft conclusions simply set out the two-element approach and merely state: 'A rule set forth in a treaty may reflect a rule of customary international law if it is established that the treaty rule ... has given rise to a general practice that is accepted as law (*opinio juris*), thus generating a new rule of customary international law' (ILC Draft Conclusions on Identification of Customary International Law, n. 7, draft conclusion 11(1)(c)). The accompanying commentary states that 'the words "may reflect" caution that, in and of themselves, treaties cannot create a rule of customary international law or conclusively attest to its existence or content' (para. 2).

[88] ILA 2000 Report, n. 7, 50, rule 27.

> so as to have become binding even for countries which have never, and do not, become parties to the Convention. There is no doubt that this process is a perfectly possible one and does from time to time occur: it constitutes indeed one of the recognized methods by which new rules of customary international law may be formed. At the same time this result is not lightly to be regarded as having been attained.[89]

The ILA Committee on Formation of Customary Law in its 2000 Report offered the following justification for the Court's pronouncement:

> [T]the consent of States to a rule of customary law, whilst not a necessary condition of their being bound, is a *sufficient condition*. In other words, if States indicate *by any means* that they intend to be bound as a matter of customary law, being bound will be the consequence, so long as their intention is clear. They can evince that intention by a public statement, for instance. That being so, there is no a priori reason why they cannot instead evince it through, in conjunction with, or subsequent to, the conclusion of a treaty, *provided that it is their clear intention to accept more than a merely convention norm.*[90]

This way of creating custom is to be distinguished from the ordinary customary process triggered by a new treaty rule, because the latter entails 'a gradual build-up of customary law through the "traditional" process whereby the pool of States engaging or acquiescing in a practice gradually widens',[91] whereas under the 'own impact' process, the treaty itself generates the customary rule because States manifest their clear intention for it to do so. This also overcomes the problems discussed earlier with treating conduct connected with the treaty as relevant State practice or evidence of an *opinio juris* for the purposes of the two-element approach to the identification of a customary rule. The ILA Committee 2000 Report states that the prohibition of the threat or use of force in article 2(4) is a rare example of a treaty giving rise to a new customary rule of its own impact.[92]

In the *North Sea Continental Shelf Cases*, the ICJ set out the following requirements for this process to occur. First, the treaty provision must be 'of a **fundamentally norm-creating character** such as could be regarded as forming the basis of a general rule of law'.[93] The prohibition in article 2(4) can clearly be considered to meet this requirement, given that it has been

89 *North Sea Continental Shelf Cases*, n. 3, para. 71.
90 ILA 2000 Report, n. 7, 51–2.
91 *Ibid.*, 53–4.
92 *Ibid.*, 52.
93 *North Sea Continental Shelf Cases*, n. 3, para. 72, emphasis added.

recognised as the 'cornerstone' of the international legal order and is widely regarded as a norm of *jus cogens* (discussed in Chapter 3). In the *North Sea Continental Shelf Cases*, the ICJ found that the article in question in that case was not of a fundamentally norm-creating character for three reasons, namely, that the rule was subject to a 'primary obligation'; that it was subject to a legally uncertain exception of 'special circumstances' and 'the very considerable, still unresolved controversies as to the exact meaning and scope of this notion, must raise further doubts as to the potentially norm-creating character of the rule'; and third, the treaty permitted reservations to the article in question.[94] The problems identified by the Court in that case apply somewhat to article 2(4): it is subject to an exception of article 51 self-defence and Chapter VII enforcement measures, and there are 'very considerable, still unresolved controversies as to the exact meaning and scope' of the prohibition and its exceptions.[95] However, unlike that provision, it is not permitted to make reservations to article 2(4) and it is not subject to other primary obligations. Furthermore, the UN Charter itself is designed as a fundamentally important legal document aimed at universal adherence, and article 2(4) holds a central place within it. The rule in article 2(4) can therefore be considered to meet this requirement.

Second, the treaty provision must be '**accepted as such by the opinio juris**' – that is, accepted that it is of a fundamentally norm-creating character. As set out earlier in the chapter, there is ample evidence of an *opinio juris* that the prohibition of the use of force set out in article 2(4) is binding on all States as a matter of customary international law. Article 2(6) of the UN Charter, which extends the obligations in article 2 to non-UN Member States, could also be viewed as evidence of an *opinio juris* that through article 2(4), States intended to create a *new* rule of customary international law binding on all States. Since the obligation in article 2(4) was not already a rule of customary international law at the time of the establishment of the UN Charter (as argued in Chapter 1), then article 2(6) appears to create a treaty obligation for non-parties.[96] Kelsen recognised this when he stated that '[f]rom the point of view of existing international law, the attempt of the Charter to apply to

94 *Ibid.*, para. 72. The Court stated that 'the faculty of making reservations to article 6, while it might not of itself prevent the equidistance principle being eventually received as general law, does add considerably to the difficulty of regarding this result as having been brought about (or being potentially possible) on the basis of the Convention'.

95 *Ibid.*

96 Interestingly, draft article 59 of 1966 draft VCLT (treaties providing for obligations for third States) does not mention article 2(6) of the UN Charter: International Law Commission, 'Yearbook of the International Law Commission 1966, Vol. II', n. 28, 68.

states which are not contracting parties to it must be characterised as revolutionary'.[97] Hence, '[i]n Article 2, paragraph 6, the Charter shows the tendency to be the law not only of the United Nations but also of the whole international community, that is to say, to be general, not only particular, international law'.[98]

Of course, it is problematic to take the position that treaty parties could create obligations for non-parties without their consent,[99] but as Stefan Talmon notes:

> The controversy has largely been mitigated by the fact that the principles enunciated in Art. 2(1) to (4) are today generally accepted as forming part of customary international law and some, such as the principle on the prohibition of the use of force in Art 2 (4), are even considered *ius cogens* and, as such, are binding on members and non-members alike.[100]

The controversy is also avoided if it is considered that rather than directly seeking to impose a treaty obligation on non-treaty parties, the inclusion of article 2(6) in the UN Charter may indicate that the parties wished to create more than a conventional obligation through the establishment of the UN Charter. This position holds that non-UN Member States are bound by the prohibition only indirectly through the UN Charter (since they could be subject to enforcement action/sanctions for failing to comply with the relevant principles), but the source of their legal obligation is customary international law. Regardless of the significance attributed to article 2(6) of the Charter, at any rate at least by the time of the 1970 Friendly Relations Declaration (which declared the obligation in article 2(4) as applying to all States), an *opinio juris* was shared among States that the prohibition of the use of force was a rule applicable to all States and not only to UN Member States, that is, as a matter of customary international law.

Third, there must be a **sufficient number of ratifications and accessions** to imply a 'positive acceptance of its principles': 'a very widespread and representative participation in the convention might suffice of itself, provided it

[97] Hans Kelsen, *The Law of the United Nations: A Critical Analysis of Its Fundamental Problems* (Stevens, 1950), 110. This was referred to by Judge Jennings in his Dissenting Opinion in the *Nicaragua* case (n. 3, 532, footnote omitted): 'Kelsen would hardly have used the word "revolutionary" if he had thought of it as depending upon a development of customary law.'

[98] Kelsen, n. 97, 109.

[99] See VCLT, arts. 34 and 35.

[100] Stefan Talmon, 'Article 2 (6)' in Bruno Simma et al. (eds), *The Charter of the United Nations: A Commentary* (Oxford University Press, 3rd ed, 2012), vol. I, 252, 255, MN6, footnote omitted.

included that of States whose interests were specially affected.'[101] This suggests that the Court views participation in the convention through ratifications and accessions as a form of State practice for the purpose of identifying a rule of customary international law, which appears problematic, since without more, the parties by ratifying or acceding to the treaty are only accepting a conventional obligation and it does not indicate a belief that the rules expressed in the treaty are legally binding under customary international law.[102] In any case, the UN Charter was signed by fifty-one founding Member States in 1945 and presently enjoys near-universal ratification, and accordingly meets this criterion.

Fourth, '**State practice**, including that of States whose interests are specially affected, should have been both **extensive and virtually uniform** in the sense of the provision invoked; – and should moreover have occurred in such a way as to show a general recognition that a rule of law or legal obligation is involved.'[103] This is also problematic because as explained in Chapter 1, mere compliance with a treaty obligation does not provide evidence of an *opinio juris* that the obligation is also one of customary international law. However, it appears that this requirement is directed at ensuring the practice is 'sufficiently widespread and representative'.[104] It is difficult to apply this criterion to an obligation to refrain from conduct (i.e. the 'use of force'), and it is unfortunately true that there have been many instances of States resorting to force against one another since 1945. However, States resorting to force in violation of article 2(4) do not usually acknowledge this but rather justify their conduct by appealing to exceptions such as the right of self-defence in article 51. As the ICJ recognised in the *Nicaragua* case, perfect compliance is unnecessary for a rule to be established as customary and that '[i]f a State acts in a way prima facie incompatible with a recognized rule, but defends its conduct by appealing to exceptions or justifications contained within the rule itself, then whether or not the State's conduct is in fact justifiable on that basis, the significance of that attitude is to confirm rather than to weaken the rule'.[105] Furthermore, as set out in Chapter 1, the obligation to refrain from the use of force has since been reproduced in many multilateral and bilateral treaties, resolutions of the UN General Assembly and other international organisations, accepted unilaterally by States which were not at the time Members of

[101] *North Sea Continental Shelf Cases*, n. 3, para. 73, emphasis added.
[102] See discussion in Chapter 1.
[103] *North Sea Continental Shelf Cases*, n. 3, para. 74.
[104] ILA 2000 Report, n. 7, 53–4 on the point regarding a treaty giving rise to customary international law of its own impact.
[105] *Nicaragua* case, n. 3, para. 186.

the United Nations and is frequently recognised as a cornerstone of the international legal system.

Therefore, the fundamentally norm-creating character of the treaty obligation in article 2(4), its acceptance as such in the *opinio juris* (including possibly due to the effect of article 2(6)), the near-universality of the UN Charter and the extensive and virtually uniform State practice with respect to the prohibition of the use of force set out in that article may be considered to fulfil the criteria set out by the ICJ in the *North Sea Continental Shelf Cases* for a treaty provision to give rise to a new rule of customary international law 'of its own impact.'

CONCLUSIONS: ARE THE CHARTER AND CUSTOMARY PROHIBITIONS OF THE USE OF FORCE IDENTICAL?

As the previous sections have argued, the customary prohibition of the use of force arose from article 2(4) of the UN Charter, either as a result of the normal process for the creation of a new rule of customary international law (with the challenges and caveats noted earlier) or exceptionally from the impact of the UN Charter. Due to the way the customary rule arose, it is likely to have been identical in content to the prohibition of the use of force in article 2(4) of the UN Charter at its inception and the two rules continue to exist in parallel.[106] States do not differentiate between the content or application of the prohibition under each source of law. Furthermore, States have not modified the customary prohibition by asserting claims that it is either narrower or broader than article 2(4). There are no statements to the effect that States differentiate between the application of the customary international law and article 2(4) treaty rules that this author is aware of. As a result, the content of the prohibition of the use of force under customary international law and article 2(4) of the UN Charter have not diverged from one another.

However, it is still possible that the scope and content of the prohibitions under each source of law could differ in some way due to the embedded nature of article 2(4) within the UN Charter and its explicit references to other

[106] In the *Nicaragua* case, the ICJ affirmed that when the content of treaty and customary rules are identical, they both continue to exist and apply. *Ibid.*, paras. 177 and 179. (Green notes: 'Given that the UN Charter has been almost universally ratified, it would be difficult to see an alternate customary regime concerning the use of force as *overriding* the Charter provisions, though it may help to interpret them or augment them with provisions not provided for in the document (such as the requirements of necessity and proportionality).' James A Green, *The International Court of Justice and Self-Defence in International Law* (Hart Publishing, 2009), 132–3, footnote omitted.

provisions which may contain requirements not applicable to the customary rule. For example, article 2(4) refers to the Purposes of the United Nations. The customary prohibition could be narrower if it does not contain an obligation to refrain from the threat or use of force *inconsistent with the Purposes of the United Nations*, except insofar as those purposes are also principles of customary international law or general international law (i.e. logically inherent to the international legal system itself). On the other hand, the Friendly Relations Declaration and other documents mentioned earlier regarding the prohibition constituting customary international law also mention the Principles and Purposes of the UN Charter, which seems to indicate that a use of force inconsistent with those Purposes and Principles is also a violation of customary international law. In any case, it is difficult to conceive of a use of force inconsistent with such Purposes but not against the territorial integrity or political independence of another State, rendering this possible difference moot.

Another way that the prohibition of the use of force in the UN Charter could be broader than the customary prohibition would be if the procedural limitations to the self-defence exception to the prohibition set out in article 51 do not apply (or do not apply to the same degree) under customary law. For example, it is possible that at least non-UN Member States have a right of self-defence under customary international law which is not procedurally curtailed by the UN Security Council reporting requirement and the limit imposed on the right to self-defence 'until the Security Council has taken measures necessary to maintain international peace and security' set out in article 51, with the result that there may be greater scope to use force under customary law than under the UN Charter. But this does not affect the finding that the content of the prohibition of the use of force under custom and article 2(4) of the UN Charter are identical, because the self-defence exception to the prohibition of the use of force (either under article 51 or custom) is better understood for this purpose, not as a carve-out clause that affects the scope of the prohibition itself but a circumstance precluding wrongfulness of acts that would otherwise fall within its scope.

Even if the content is identical, the *scope of application* of the customary prohibition could differ from article 2(4) in respect of the subjects of the rule. It has been argued by Albrecht Randelzhofer and Oliver Dörr that unlike article 2(4) of the UN Charter, which only applies between States, under customary international law, international organisations (IOs) capable of conducting military operations are also bound by the prohibition, such as NATO, the EU, ECOWAS and the United Nations, and that many IOs already state this in their own constituting documents and ad hoc declarations, although this does not extend to individuals or groups.[107] This author is not aware of any State practice that has adopted the interpretation that non-State entities are *directly* bound by the prohibition of the use of force under customary international law and article 2(4) of the UN Charter from such IO declarations, although it is not excluded that the law could in future develop in this direction.

In conclusion, the prohibition of the use of force in article 2(4) of the UN Charter and under customary international law are likely to be presently identical in scope, although the possibility remains for future divergence. Chapter 3 will examine the consequences of this for the relationship between the treaty and customary rule, and the appropriate method for ascertaining the meaning of prohibited force under international law.

[107] Albrecht Randelzhofer and Oliver Dörr, 'Article 2(4)' in Bruno Simma et al. (eds), *The Charter of the United Nations: A Commentary* (Oxford University Press, 3rd ed, 2012), 200, 213, MN30–31.

3

The Relationship between the Customary Prohibition of the Use of Force and Article 2(4) of the UN Charter

INTRODUCTION

Even if the content of the customary prohibition of the use of force and the prohibition of the use of force in article 2(4) of the UN Charter are currently identical, each source of law has a different method of interpretation and application. In order to determine which source to interpret or apply to discover the meaning of a prohibited 'use of force' between States under international law, this chapter will explore the current relationship between the treaty and customary prohibitions of the use of force (i.e. the effect of the parallel customary rule on the interpretation of article 2(4) and vice versa). The effect of article 2(4) on the customary international law prohibition after the emergence of the latter is more straightforward than the role of the customary rule in interpreting article 2(4). In essence, the scope of article 2(4) acts as a restraint on the contraction of the customary rule (i.e. it makes it more difficult to assert that the customary rule has changed to become more permissive/less prohibitive than the article 2(4) prohibition). This is because a State taking action that violates the prohibition of the use of force in article 2(4) and claiming that this action is not prohibited by the customary rule would still be violating its concurrent obligation under the UN Charter.

The current relationship between the Charter and customary prohibitions of the use of force is therefore best understood by looking at the way that the interpretation of the rule under article 2(4) of the UN Charter may change over time and the role that the customary rule can play in this process. In doing so, this chapter will examine the following related but distinct concepts: the use of pre-existing or subsequently developing custom to fill gaps in the treaty, the use of subsequently developing custom to informally modify the interpretation of the treaty, an evolutive interpretation of the UN Charter and informal treaty modification through subsequent practice.

This chapter will argue that since the rule in article 2(4) is the origin of the customary prohibition of the use of force, it is not appropriate to use pre-existing or subsequently developing customary international law to fill gaps in interpretation of article 2(4), nor to use subsequently developing customary international law to modify article 2(4). Accordingly, due to the present relationship between the customary and Charter prohibitions of the use of force, the preferable approach to determine the meaning of prohibited force under international law is to focus on interpreting the UN Charter.

EFFECT OF CUSTOMARY PROHIBITION ON THE INTERPRETATION OF ARTICLE 2(4)

In terms of the effect of custom on treaty interpretation, customary international law rules may be used to supplement treaty interpretation by filling in gaps in the treaty.[1] The legal basis for doing so is article 31(3)(c) of the Vienna Convention on the Law of Treaties (VCLT).[2] This rule provides that, together with the context, 'any relevant rules of international law applicable in the relations between the parties' 'shall be taken into account' in interpreting a treaty. Such relevant rules include customary international law and treaty.[3] The use of customary international law rules to supplement treaty interpretation may take the form of a static interpretation (using customary international law rules existing at the time the treaty entered into force) or dynamic interpretation (using subsequently developing customary international law rules). One may take into account subsequent legal developments when interpreting a treaty if it was the intention of the parties at the time of concluding the treaty, taking into account the text, object and purpose of the treaty and the *travaux préparatoires*.[4] There is a presumption that this is the case for certain texts where they are open-ended or set out general obligations. International Court of Justice (ICJ) jurisprudence also supports this.[5]

1 Michael Wood, 'First Report on Formation and Evidence of Customary International Law' UN Doc A/CN.4/663 (17 May 2013) ('Wood First Report'), para. 35, with further extensive references: 'Rules of customary international law may also fill possible lacunae in treaties, and assist in their interpretation.'

2 *Vienna Convention on the Law of Treaties* 1969 (adopted 22 May 1969, entered into force 27 January 1980) ('VCLT'), 1155 UNTS 331.

3 Tom Ruys, *'Armed Attack' and Article 51 of the UN Charter* (Cambridge University Press, 2010), 20.

4 *Ibid.*, 21.

5 *Ibid.*

Use of Pre-existing Customary International Law to Fill Gaps

Since a customary international law rule prohibiting force did not pre-exist the UN Charter but developed as a consequence of it and is currently identical to it, it is not sensible to fill gaps in the interpretation of article 2(4) such as the term 'use of force' by looking to custom. This is the key difference between the interpretation of articles 2(4) and 51 of the UN Charter and means that the reasoning behind turning to customary international law to supplement the interpretation of the provision does not apply in the same way to article 2(4) as it does to article 51. As pointed out by the ICJ in the *Nicaragua* case, since article 51 refers to an inherent right of self-defence, it must therefore be a pre-existing right under customary international law which arises when an 'armed attack' occurs. Although there is debate regarding whether article 51 of the UN Charter confers a treaty right or merely recognises the pre-existing customary right,[6] it is not controversial that a right to self-defence pre-existed the UN Charter. Accordingly, it is appropriate to look to the content of that right under customary international law to fill gaps in the interpretation of article 51, such as the requirements of necessity and proportionality.[7]

Unlike article 51, which refers to a pre-existing customary rule (the right to self-defence), article 2(4) introduced a new rule (the prohibition of the 'use of force', as opposed to the prohibition of recourse to war). As the previous chapters explained, the new rule enshrined in article 2(4), though influenced by the pre-existing broader customary prohibition of recourse to war as an instrument of national policy, led to the emergence of a *new* customary rule. The term 'use of force' was not a legal term of art enshrined in customary international law prior to the UN Charter. It therefore does not make sense to look to the content of the customary prohibition of the use of force in order to

6 *Legality of the Threat or Use of Nuclear Weapons, Advisory Opinion* (1996) ICJ Reports 226 ('*Nuclear Weapons* Advisory Opinion'), para. 40.

7 James A Green, *The International Court of Justice and Self-Defence in International Law* (Hart Publishing, 2009), 131. Green looks at the issue from the perspective of two 'conceptions' of the law of self-defence, on the one hand 'armed attack as a grave use of force', which comes from article 51, and on the other hand one based on necessity and proportionality, which comes from customary international law. He asks whether the law on self-defence therefore stems from two distinct 'conceptions' with roots in two different formal sources of international law (p. 129). He interprets the *Nicaragua* case as the Court perceiving two distinct conceptions of the law on self-defence deriving from different sources, which are not identical but which are merged (p. 130). The *Nuclear Weapons* Advisory Opinion, n. 6, also suggests in his view that 'both conventional and customary international law are required to understand the right' (p. 130), since the Court stated that some constraints on the resort to self-defence were inherent in the very concept of self-defence and others specified in article 51.

interpret the treaty rule, since unlike the case of the right to use force in self-defence, the treaty provision in article 2(4) is itself the origin of the customary rule.

Use of Subsequently Developing Customary International Law to Interpret Article 2(4)

Though currently identical in scope, it is of course possible for the customary and treaty rule to diverge in the future. This 'could result from different methods of interpretation and application appropriate for each category'.[8] Although it is possible, it is unlikely that divergence would occur in the case of quasi-universal treaties. The main reason is that '[i]t is most unlikely in these cases that practice and *opinio juris* among the same States would distinguish conduct under the treaty from conduct in implementation of an identical rule of customary law'.[9] Hugh Thirlway also notes that 'the way in which customary law is formed theoretically involves awareness of, and lack of objection to, developments in the field on the part of the whole international community'.[10]

For our purposes, this means that developments in the customary prohibition of the use of force are at least accepted implicitly by the whole international community, most of the members of which are parties to the UN Charter, and, accordingly, the customary international law rule is unlikely to develop in a way that would directly conflict with their Charter obligations. The assertion of a new customary rule would require that States explicitly refer to a customary law justification for their acts. But there does not seem to be any evidence that States have already done this; when States make any reference to a source of the prohibition in their direct practice (claims and counterclaims attaching to actual uses of force), it is invariably also to the UN Charter. It therefore appears that the most plausible way the prohibition could

8 Oscar Schachter, 'Entangled Treaty and Custom' in Yoram Dinstein (ed), *International Law at a Time of Perplexity: Essays in Honour of Shabtai Rosenne* (Martinus Nijhoff Publishers, 1989), 717, 728, footnote omitted.

9 *Ibid.*, 728, cf. Yoram Dinstein, *War, Aggression and Self-Defence* (Cambridge University Press, 5th ed, 2011), 100, footnotes omitted:

> Although present-day customary international law can be looked upon essentially as a replica of Article 2(4), it is hard to believe that the exact correlation of the two will 'freeze' indefinitely. ... Nonetheless, the present author cannot share the view that contemporary customary law has already changed – or is in the process of changing – to the point that the *jus ad bellum* is on the cusp of becoming 'protean' in nature.

10 Hugh WA Thirlway, *The Sources of International Law* (Oxford University Press, 2014), 140–1.

change under custom only and not the UN Charter is if the prohibition is *extended* in a way that is clearly not covered by the terms of article 2(4) – for example, to cover uses of force by non-State entities or uses of force by a State within its own territory in a civil war, because then that conduct and *opinio juris* cannot be referable to the treaty provision.

Albeit unlikely, if it does occur, divergence in the scope or content of the prohibition of the use of force under article 2(4) and customary international law would lead to three possible interpretive outcomes. Firstly, it would result in separate rules from different legal sources simultaneously binding States.[11] Secondly, the development of a *new* customary rule with respect to the prohibition of the use of force could be used as an element of *interpretation* of article 2(4). And thirdly, the subsequent emergence of a new customary rule could be used as an element *modifying* the operation of article 2(4).[12] As the following discussion illustrates, these latter two possibilities – interpretation and modification – are not appropriate with respect to the prohibition of the use of force in article 2(4) of the UN Charter.

Interpreting Article 2(4) through Subsequently Evolving Custom

If the customary international law rule *subsequently develops* in a way that diverges from the article 2(4) rule, then it could make sense for the new customary rule to be used to interpret article 2(4) as a 'relevant rule of international law applicable between the parties',[13] since it would be a rule of international law *with a distinct content from article 2(4)*. An example of this is examining 'the evolution of the rule through custom'.[14] For instance, Olivier Corten's approach is that 'reliance on a novel right (A), supposedly accepted by all other States (B), would be both a customary evolution of the rule and a practice subsequently followed by the parties to the UN Charter and indicative of their agreement on the interpretation of the text'.[15] James Green applies similar reasoning when he states:

[11] See Schachter, n. 8.

[12] See Observations and Proposals of the Special Rapporteur in International Law Commission, 'Yearbook of the International Law Commission 1966, Vol. II' UN Doc A/CN.4/SER.A/1966/Add.l (1966), 88, para. 1: 'the three matters in question – a subsequent treaty, a subsequent practice of the parties in the application of the treaty and the subsequent emergence of a new rule of customary law – may have effects either as elements of interpretation or as elements modifying the operation of a treaty.'

[13] VCLT, n. 2, art. 31(3)(c).

[14] Olivier Corten, *The Law against War: The Prohibition on the Use of Force in Contemporary International Law* (Hart Publishing, 2010), 29.

[15] *Ibid.*, footnotes omitted.

> It may well be that a new interpretation of the meaning of 'force' will evolve in the future to take into account the growing threat of cyberwarfare. Such a change would not require any alteration of Article 2(4), of course, just a reinterpretation of its terminology in customary international law, based on state practice and *opinio juris* in the usual way.[16]

However, one must be careful not to automatically conflate changes in the customary international law rule with changes in the interpretation of the treaty rule. As noted by Roberto Ago in the International Law Commission (ILC) debates on the 1966 draft Convention on the Law of Treaties, such an approach does not sufficiently distinguish between the distinct modes of interpretation and application of customary law and treaty law.[17] Ago's interventions on the ILC regarding the draft 1966 VCLT support the position that we must differentiate between these separate processes: subsequent agreement and subsequent practice as an element of treaty interpretation, and subsequently developing customary international law as an element of treaty interpretation.

Modifying Article 2(4) through Subsequently Evolving Custom

The use of subsequently evolving custom to interpret article 2(4) is problematic if it goes further than filling gaps pursuant to article 31(3)(c) of the VCLT and ostensibly *modifies* the interpretation of the treaty. Assuming that changes in custom would also informally modify the treaty is a controversial point that even the ILC did not venture into. The ILC 'has alluded to the possibility that the emergence of a new rule of customary international law may modify a treaty, depending on the particular circumstances and the intentions of the parties to the treaty'.[18] However, draft article 68(c) in the 1966 draft VCLT proposing that the operation of a treaty may be modified '[b]y the subsequent emergence of a new rule of customary law relating to matters dealt with in the treaty and binding upon all the parties'[19] gave rise to objections by States,

[16] James A Green, 'Questioning the Peremptory Status of the Prohibition of the Use of Force' (2010) 32 *Michigan Journal of International Law* 215, 241.

[17] International Law Commission, 'Yearbook of the International Law Commission 1996, Vol. 1, Part II: Summary Records of the 18th Session', UN Doc A/CN.4/SER.A/1966 (4 May–19 July 1966) ('1966 Yearbook of the ILC, vol. 1, Part II'), 167, paras. 48–49.

[18] International Law Commission, 'Formation and Evidence of Customary International Law – Elements in the Previous Work of the International Law Commission That Could Be Particularly Relevant to the Topic – Memorandum by the Secretariat' UN Doc A/CN.4/659 (14 March 2013), 34, Observation 27, footnote omitted.

[19] 1966 Yearbook of the ILC, vol. 1, Part II, n. 17, 163.

extensive discussions in the Commission, and was ultimately deleted on the recommendation of the Special Rapporteur, Sir Humphrey Waldock. The basis for the objections related to the complex relationship between custom and treaty law including priority of sources, the problem of inter-temporal law and the objection 'to the idea that a new customary norm should necessarily over-ride a treaty provision regardless of the will of the parties'.[20] Ago noted that the provision conflated two issues, namely, the subsequent practice of the parties in the application of the treaty evidencing their agreement to extend or modify its operation, and a subsequently developing rule of customary international law.[21] In essence, the Special Rapporteur observed that paragraph (c) 'concern[s] the impact on a treaty of acts done outside and not in relation to it'.[22]

In summary, in the event that the customary international law prohibition of the use of force subsequently evolved, this would not automatically change the interpretation of article 2(4) of the UN Charter. In practice, the scope of article 2(4) and the customary prohibition would diverge unless the change in the customary rule was accompanied by subsequent practice *in the application of the treaty* evidencing the agreement of ('all, or nearly all' of)[23] the parties to a new interpretation of article 2(4) in line with the new customary rule, and even then only to the extent that an informal modification of a substantive (as opposed to procedural[24]) rule in the UN Charter is permissible. Informal modification of a treaty is generally problematic, since treaties usually contain formal requirements regarding modification or amendment.[25] Informal modification of the UN Charter is particularly problematic because it circumvents the formal mechanism for amendment set out in the Charter and thus potentially usurps the consent of the treaty parties.[26]

20 The latter was raised by the UK Government; see *ibid.*, vol. 2, 90, para. 12.

21 1966 Yearbook of the ILC, vol. 1, Part II, n. 17, 167, paras. 48–49.

22 *Ibid.*, vol. 2, 91, para. 14.

23 1966 Yearbook of the ILC, vol. 1, Part II, n. 17, 165, para. 17, intervention of Mr Tunkin with respect to draft article 68.

24 For example, the practice of UN Security Council abstention votes under article 27(3) of the UN Charter.

25 Ruys, n. 3, 24–8.

26 For example, Corten writes: 'In the context of a treaty law, an evolution of the rule prohibiting the use of force would require ratification by at least two thirds of the States parties, including all permanent members of the Security Council, pursuant to articles 108 and 109 of the UN Charter. By definition this onerous procedure is not applicable in the realm of custom.' Corten, n. 14, 34–5.

EVOLUTIVE INTERPRETATION OF ARTICLE 2(4)

Of course, the interpretation of article 2(4) may still evolve over time through subsequent practice, within the limits posed by the text and the peremptory status of the prohibition. The terms of a treaty may be interpreted either in accordance with the circumstances prevailing at the time of its conclusion (contemporaneous interpretation) or in accordance with circumstances prevailing at the time of its application (evolutive interpretation).[27] Whether the interpretation of terms in a treaty changes over time depends on 'whether or not the presumed intention of the parties upon the conclusion of the treaty was to give a term used a meaning which is capable of evolving over time'.[28] Indications of the parties' intention at the time of concluding the treaty that the interpretation of terms change over time include the language used in the treaty. For example, '(a) Use of a term in the treaty which is "not static but evolutionary". ... (b) The description of obligations in very general terms, thus operating a kind of *renvoi* to the State of the law at the time of its application.'[29] In other words, the use of a term 'whose meaning is inherently more context-dependent'[30] supports a conclusion that an evolutive interpretation was intended by the treaty parties at the time of its conclusion. The use of 'generic' terms or 'the fact that the treaty is designed to be "of continuing duration"',[31] may also indicate an evolutive interpretation was intended.[32] The subsequent agreements and practice of UN Member States under articles 31 and 32 of the VCLT also assist with determining the presumed intention of the treaty parties upon the conclusion of the treaty with respect to evolutive interpretation.[33]

An evolutive interpretation of the UN Charter is justified by the drafters' intention. The UN Charter was designed to be of continuing duration and to govern changing international circumstances. 'The practical quality of the

[27] Georg Nolte, 'First Report on Subsequent Agreements and Subsequent Practice in Relation to Treaty Interpretation' UN Doc A/CN.4/660 (19 March 2013) ('Nolte First Report'), 23, para. 54.

[28] International Law Commission, 'Draft Conclusions on Subsequent Agreements and Subsequent Practice in Relation to the Interpretation of Treaties', Annexed to UN GA Resolution 73/202, A/RES/73/202 (3 January 2019), draft conclusion 8.

[29] Nolte First Report, n. 27, 23–4, para. 56, citing Final report of Chair of Study Group on fragmentation (Martii Koskenniemi).

[30] *Ibid.*, 26, para. 61.

[31] *Ibid.*, footnote omitted.

[32] *Ibid.*

[33] International Law Commission, 'Draft Conclusions on Subsequent Agreements and Subsequent Practice in Relation to the Interpretation of Treaties', n. 28, draft conclusion 8.

UN Charter as the constitution of the UN and the international community at large provides additional support for considering the Charter to be a "living instrument" which must be "capable of growth and development over time to meet new social, political and historical realities often unimagined by its framers."'[34] Absent evidence to the contrary, this provides grounds to conclude that the term 'use of force' was intended to be subjected to evolutive interpretation in order to regulate changing circumstances and new uses of force which were not anticipated in 1945. This conclusion is supported by the approach of the ICJ in the *Nicaragua* case, which 'apparently regarded the Charter provisions as dynamic rather than fixed, and thus as capable of change over time through state practice'.[35] As Thilo Rensmann argues: 'The prevailing view today is that the Charter must be interpreted in a purposive-dynamic rather than an originalist-static manner.'[36] In particular, the term 'use of force' in article 2(4) of the UN Charter is very general and must be context dependent since such usages will change over time with, for example, technological developments. An evolutive interpretation of this provision is also supported by the drafter's intention that the prohibition be all-encompassing. Accordingly, when interpreting the term 'use of force' in article 2(4) of the UN Charter, this work will also examine how the term is currently applied, taking into consideration the current context, not only the original interpretation at the conclusion of the UN Charter in 1945.

Evolutive Interpretation versus Treaty Modification

However, one must be careful to distinguish between the following two concepts. The first is an evolutive interpretation of the terms of a treaty justified by the drafter's intention that its interpretation may change over time, which would allow consideration of, inter alia, subsequent agreements and practice that interpret the terms in a way different to the original interpretation at the time of conclusion of the treaty but still within the scope of potential natural meanings attaching to particular terms. A second and markedly different concept is the use of subsequent practice to *amend or modify* the terms of a treaty beyond the scope intended by the parties to the treaty at the time of its conclusion. The difference is that an evolutive interpretation, including one

34 Thilo Rensmann, 'Reform' in Bruno Simma et al (eds), *The Charter of the United Nations: A Commentary* (Oxford University Press, 3rd ed, 2012), vol. I, 25, 31–2, MN20, footnotes omitted.

35 Christine Gray, *International Law and the Use of Force* (Oxford University Press, 3rd ed, 2008), 9.

36 Rensmann, n. 34, 31–32, MN20, footnote omitted.

arrived at through the effect of subsequent practice in the application of the treaty, is the result of the process of treaty interpretation and clarifies the meaning of the terms of the treaty within the scope intended by the parties at the time of its conclusion. In contrast, an amendment or modification of the terms of a treaty by subsequent practice – outside the VCLT rules on treaty amendment and modification – alters the treaty terms beyond any potential scope for discretion afforded to the parties by the treaty.

The possibility of treaty modification through subsequent practice was not recognised by States at the Vienna Conference and may be considered to have been rejected with the deletion of draft article 38, which had included this possibility. The ILC Committee on Subsequent Agreement and Subsequent Practice in Relation to the Interpretation of Treaties has stated that '[t]he possibility of amending or modifying a treaty by subsequent practice of the parties has not been generally recognized'.[37] In practice, the line between evolutive interpretation and modification may, however, be a fine distinction,[38] and the ICJ has not set out criteria for making such a distinction.[39] Nolte concludes that '[t]he most reasonable approach seems to be that the line between interpretation and modification cannot be determined by abstract criteria but must rather be derived, in the first place, from the treaty itself, the character of the specific treaty provision at hand, and the legal context within which the treaty operates, and the specific circumstances of the case'.[40]

In addition to the limits on treaty modification via subsequent agreement or practice (which remains highly controversial), there are further limitations on the modification of article 2(4) of the UN Charter through subsequent agreement or practice. These arise from the formal amendment procedure set out in the UN Charter itself, and the potential *jus cogens* nature of the norm. The formal amendment procedure for the UN Charter has a very high procedural threshold that is set out in articles 108 and 109(2) and is rarely used.[41] These rules for formal modification supersede rules of formal treaty amendment or *inter se* modification set out in articles 40 and 41 of the

[37] International Law Commission, 'Draft Conclusions on Subsequent Agreements and Subsequent Practice in Relation to the Interpretation of Treaties', n. 28, conclusion 7(3).

[38] Georg Nolte, 'Second Report on Subsequent Agreements and Subsequent Practice in Relation to the Interpretation of Treaties' UN Doc A/CN.4/671 (International Law Commission, 26 March 2014) ('Nolte Second Report'), 51, para. 116 with extensive further references at footnote 245. For discussion, see 50 ff.

[39] *Ibid.*, 68, para. 165.

[40] *Ibid.*

[41] Rensmann, n. 34, 30, MN14.

VCLT.[42] It is controversial whether the UN Charter may be amended by means other than the formal procedure set out in articles 108 and 109, such as through subsequent practice.[43] Modification of the UN Charter through a subsequent agreement outside of the procedure set out in the UN Charter is problematic due to article 103 of the Charter, which provides that '[i]n the event of a conflict between the obligations of the Members of the United Nations under the present Charter and their obligations under any other international agreement, their obligations under the present Charter shall prevail'.[44]

However, maintaining a strict constitutional view that permits only formal amendments to the UN Charter risks delegitimising the United Nations since 'the UN operates on the basis of a number of informally accepted rules' differing from the original framework.[45] 'In consequence the prevailing view assumes that under exceptional circumstances the member States possess the power to override the procedural restraints set forth in Arts 108 and 109.'[46] For example, 'the replacement of the former Soviet Union and the Republic of China (Taiwan) by the Russian Federation and the People's Republic of China without amendment to Art. 23 (1) of the Charter. Counting abstentions as well as affirmative votes as concurring votes under Art. 27 (3) may also be seen as an informal modification'.[47] But these examples relate to the procedural rules of the UN itself, and not to fundamental rules of the international legal order established by the UN Charter, such as the prohibition of the use of force in article 2(4).

[42] Georg Witschel, 'Article 108' in Bruno Simma et al (eds), *The Charter of the United Nations: A Commentary* (Oxford University Press, 3rd ed, 2012), vol. I, 2199, 2204, MN 8.

[43] Rensmann, n. 34, 32, MN24.

[44] See Stuard Ford, 'Legal Processes of Change: Article 2(4) and the Vienna Convention on the Law of Treaties' (1999) 4(1) *Journal of Conflict and Security Law* 75, 85.

[45] Rensmann, n. 34, 33, MN25–26.

[46] *Ibid.*, 33, MN27–28, footnote omitted.

[47] Witschel, n. 42, 661, MN28:

> In this respect see the interesting remarks by the representative of the Secretary-General of the UN, Mr Stavropoulos, 'The constant practice of the Security Council of not treating the voluntary abstention of a permanent member of the Security Council as a vote against a substantive draft resolution before the Council is customary law. . . . Even if the development relating to voluntary abstentions is looked upon as an interpretation of the Charter by subsequent practice, the result cannot be different and the practice must be recognized as being authoritative'.
>
> (Oral Statement of Mr Stavropoulos, Legal Consequences for States of the Continued Presence of South Africa in Namibia (South West Africa) notwithstanding Security Council Resolution 276 (1970), ICJ, Pleadings, Oral Arguments, Documents, II, 39)

In conclusion, using subsequent practice to interpret the UN Charter in a way that amounts to informal modification of its terms remains controversial; rather, '[i]t is presumed that the parties to a treaty, by an agreement subsequently arrived at or a practice in the application of the treaty, intend to interpret the treaty, not to amend or to modify it'.[48] Finally, if the prohibition of the use of force in article 2(4) is a norm of *jus cogens*, this sets further limits on changes to the rule through subsequent practice, subsequent treaties or the subsequent development of customary international law. This is discussed further below.

JUS COGENS AND THE PROHIBITION OF THE USE OF FORCE

Jus cogens norms are peremptory norms of international law, defined in the VCLT as 'a norm accepted and recognized by the international community of States as a whole as a norm from which no derogation is permitted and which can be modified only by a subsequent norm of general international law having the same character'.[49] Although the existence of *jus cogens* norms is now generally accepted,[50] the substantive content and source of *jus cogens* norms remain subject to debate.[51] The distinguishing feature of *jus cogens* norms is their hierarchical superiority (as they override inconsistent customary international law and treaty), that they are not subject to derogation and that States cannot opt out as a persistent objector. This is sometimes justified on the basis of the moral force of the value that the norm protects.[52] Others such as Hugh Thirlway[53] emphasise the non-derogable nature of the norm as a means of identifying norms of *jus cogens* through State practice.

48 International Law Commission, 'Draft Conclusions on Subsequent Agreements and Subsequent Practice in Relation to the Interpretation of Treaties', n. 28, conclusion 7(3). See Nolte Second Report, n. 38, 51–2 for an outline of the controversial debate to which this provision gave rise.

49 VCLT, n. 2, art. 53. The Special Rapporteur of the ILC Committee on the Identification of Customary International Law, Sir Michael Wood, noted that: 'The definition in the Vienna Convention is of general application': Wood First Report, n. 1, footnote 43, referring to para. (5) of the commentary to article 26 of the 'Articles on State Responsibility', Yearbook of the International Law Commission (2001), vol. II, p. 85.

50 Wood First Report, *ibid.*, para. 25 with further references.

51 *Ibid.*, para. 25 with further extensive footnotes.

52 For example, Alexander Orakhelashvili, *Peremptory Norms in International Law* (Oxford University Press, 2006), 50.

53 Thirlway, n. 10, 154 ff.

Is the Prohibition of the Use of Force Jus Cogens?

The prohibition of the use of force is considered by many to be *jus cogens*,[54] although there is no ICJ ruling directly on this point.[55] The ILC stated in its commentary on the Draft Articles on the Law of Treaties that 'the law of the Charter concerning the prohibition of the use of force' is 'a conspicuous example' of a peremptory norm.[56] The ICJ in the *Nicaragua* case referred to the ILC's statement,[57] which some argue 'may indicate an inclination itself to move in that direction, but it does not constitute a determination to that effect'.[58] Various ICJ judges in their separate and dissenting opinions have declared that the prohibition of the use of force is a peremptory norm.[59] In his fourth report,[60] the ILC Special Rapporteur on the topic of peremptory norms of general international law (*jus cogens*), Dire Tladi, included the prohibition of aggression[61] in an illustrative list of jus cogens norms. Tladi canvassed relevant practice in support of the ILC's recognition of the prohibition of aggression as a peremptory norm, including the 1974 GA Definition of Aggression.[62] The ILC Drafting Committee subsequently adopted a draft

54 Article 2(4) is 'usually acknowledged' as *jus cogens*: Albrecht Randelzhofer and Oliver Dörr, 'Article 2(4)' in Bruno Simma et al (eds), *The Charter of the United Nations: A Commentary* (Oxford University Press, 3rd ed, 2012), 200, 231–2, MN67–8. See footnote 182 for list of further references in support.

55 Claus Kreß, 'The International Court of Justice and the Non-Use of Force' in Marc Weller (ed), *The Oxford Handbook of the Use of Force in International Law* (Oxford University Press, 2015), 561, 571.

56 International Law Commission, 'Yearbook of the International Law Commission 1966, Vol. II', n. 12, 247, commentary on article 50, para. 1.

57 *Case concerning Military and Paramilitary activities in and against Nicaragua (Nicaragua v United States of America), Merits, Judgment* (1986) ICJ Reports 14 ('*Nicaragua* case'), para. 190.

58 Kreß, n. 55, 571.

59 For example, *Nicaragua* case, n. 57, Separate Opinion of President Nagendra Singh, 153, Separate Opinion of Judge Sette-Camara, 189; *Oil Platforms (Islamic Republic of Iran v United States of America), Judgment* (2003) ICJ Reports 161 ('*Oil Platforms* case'), Dissenting Opinion of Judge Elarby, para. 1.1, Dissenting Opinion of Judge Al-Khasawneh, para. 9, Separate Opinion of Judge Simma, para. 6; *Legal Consequences of the Construction of a Wall in the Occupied Palestinian Territory (Advisory Opinion)* (2004) ICJ Reports 136, Separate Opinion of Judge Elarby, para. 3.1.

60 International Law Commission, 'Fourth Report on Peremptory Norms of General International Law (jus cogens) by Dire Tladi, Special Rapporteur' UN Doc A/CN.4/727 (31 January 2019).

61 'As a terminological matter, the ... report ... refer[s] to the prohibition of aggression in lieu of the possible alternatives, i.e., the prohibition of the use of force, prohibition of aggressive force and the law of the Charter on the prohibition of force' (*ibid.*, para. 62).

62 *Ibid.*, paras. 62–68.

conclusion setting out an illustrative list of 'the most widely recognised examples of peremptory norms of general international law', which lists as the first example 'the prohibition of aggression or aggressive force'.[63] Scholars arguing in favour of the prohibition of the use of force as a peremptory norm run the gamut between the position that the entire *jus contra bellum* is *jus cogens*;[64] that all of article 2(4) is *jus cogens*;[65] that only the prohibition of the use of force (as opposed to threats of force) in article 2(4) is *jus cogens*;[66] to those who take the view that only a narrow core of the prohibition (i.e. aggression) is *jus cogens*.[67]

James Green has criticised the tendency for uncritical conclusions that the prohibition of the use of force is *jus cogens* and pointed out key issues with characterising the prohibition of the use of force as a peremptory norm.[68] There are two main bases for his critique. The first issue concerns the flexibility and uncertain nature of the scope and content of the *jus contra bellum*. Green notes that the content and scope of a peremptory norm on the use of force is very difficult to determine and that, as set out earlier in the chapter, a wide range of possibilities have been put forward by scholars.[69] This is due to the nature of the prohibition of the use of force and its scope: article 2 (4) sets out two prohibitions (on the threat and use of force) and is subject to two exceptions set out in the UN Charter (article 51 and Chapter VII Security Council authorisation) as well as the 'exception' of valid consent. Not all of the concepts are treated in the same way in the legal discourse and practice of States – for example, the difference in treatment of threats of force and uses of force has led some scholars to argue that the prohibition of the threat of force is not even a customary norm, let alone a peremptory one.[70] In addition, each

[63] International Law Commission, 'Draft Conclusions on Identification and Legal Consequences of Peremptory Norms of General International Law (Jus Cogens)', Yearbook of the International Law Commission (2022), vol. II, Part Two, conclusion 23.

[64] '[I]f the very prohibition of the use of force is peremptory, then every principle specifying the limits on the entitlement of States to use force is also peremptory': Orakhelashvili, n. 52, 50.

[65] Nikolas Stürchler, *The Threat of Force in International Law* (Cambridge University Press, Paperback ed, 2009), 91: the no-threat rule enjoys peremptory status like the rest of article 2(4); Ruys, n. 3, 27, footnote omitted: 'it appears plausible that both Article 2(4) and Article 51 form part of *ius cogens*.'

[66] Corten, n. 14, 200–12.

[67] For example, Lauri Hannikainen, *Peremptory Norms* (Jus Cogens) *in International Law* (Lakimiesliiton Kustannus, 1988), 354–5.

[68] Green, n. 16.

[69] *Ibid.*, 226.

[70] Romana Sadurska, 'Threats of Force' (1988) 82(2) *American Journal of International Law* 239, 249, argues that 'it seems unnecessary for all practical purposes and theoretically dubious to characterize the prohibition of the threat of force as a rule of customary international law';

of these concepts is in turn subject to areas of uncertainty and is informed by or has its origin in different sources of international law. For example, there is continuing uncertainty over the content of the customary international law requirements of necessity and proportionality of self-defence measures,[71] and contested areas of the *jus contra bellum* such as whether there is the right to anticipatory self-defence.[72] This does not necessarily prevent the prohibition of the use of force from having peremptory status but requires either that the norm be framed in a broad way to include either the entire *jus contra bellum*[73] or exceptions to the prohibition of the use of force, or that the *jus cogens* norm be construed restrictively to confine it to the most certain areas (generally, the core of 'aggression').[74] Green argues that 'the inherent uncertainty and flexibility of the prohibition would not seem to be compatible with the conception of peremptory norms as set out in the Vienna Convention on the Law of Treaties'.[75]

The second issue is 'whether there is enough evidence to establish that the prohibition of the use of force is peremptory in nature'.[76] Green argues for a positivist approach to the identification of *jus cogens* norms by examining State practice.[77] This accords with the ILC's indication that 'peremptory norms are formed as a result of a process of widespread acceptance and recognition of such norms *as peremptory* by the international community as a whole'.[78] Green canvasses a range of such practice that does not necessarily bear out the peremptory status of the prohibition of the use of force, observing that 'in notable instances where states have had the opportunity to explicitly affirm the peremptory status of the prohibition, and might reasonably have been expected to do so, there has been a trend toward silence on the issue'.[79] Although most States stayed silent on this point during relevant debates in treaty negotiations, in the Sixth Committee of the General Assembly and the

Green, n. 16, 230. Cf Dissenting Opinion of Judge Weeramantry in *Nuclear Weapons* Advisory Opinion, n. 6, 525, who quotes numerous resolutions and international law documents confirming that threats of force are unlawful under international law.

71 Green, n. 16, 235.

72 *Ibid.*, 236.

73 *Ibid.*, 231.

74 *Ibid.*, 235.

75 *Ibid.*, 226.

76 *Ibid.*, 218.

77 Thirlway sets out an even more stringent test, noting that 'only a court decision could authoritatively invalidate an agreement between States as contrary to *jus cogens*, and thus demonstrate that the category of *jus cogens* exists' (n. 10, 154, footnote omitted).

78 International Law Commission, 'Formation and Evidence of Customary International Law', n. 18, 30, observation 23, emphasis added, footnote omitted.

79 Green, n. 16, 246.

UN Security Council, very rarely has any State actually rejected the *jus cogens* status of the prohibition of the use of force, with nearly all explicit statements on this issue arguing in favour of the peremptory status of the prohibition. 'As such, one may point to a cumulative effect of acceptance across these examples'[80] and the argument could be made that the majority of States have not explicitly affirmed the *jus cogens* nature of the prohibition since it is 'self-evident' or for political reasons.[81] However, Green questions 'whether silence is enough to bestow supernorm status on a rule'.[82]

In conclusion, there is no consensus as to whether and to what extent the prohibition of the use of force is *jus cogens*. The majority position appears to be that the prohibition (or at least a small core of it) is a peremptory norm, however, this position is also subject to powerful critiques. Ultimately, as Green notes, '[t]he only way to reach a firm conclusion on this question is through an extensive and systematic survey of state practice',[83] which is beyond the scope of the present work.

Consequences of Jus Cogens *Nature of the Prohibition*

If the prohibition of the use of force is *jus cogens*, the legal consequences for violation are more stringent. In addition to the consequences of a threat to the peace, breach of the peace or act of aggression set out in Chapter VII of the UN Charter, under customary international law, a prohibited use of force gives rise to international State responsibility and the obligation to cease the unlawful act,[84] make reparation[85] and the right of the victim State to take non-forcible countermeasures.[86] If a use of force in violation of article 2(4) is considered to be a peremptory norm, there are additional consequences of a serious breach of the prohibition, namely, that other States shall co-operate using lawful means to bring the violation to an end, shall not recognise the situation as lawful and shall not render aid or assistance in maintaining the situation.[87] If the entire prohibition of the use of force is *jus cogens*, then even

80 *Ibid.*, 253, footnote omitted.
81 *Ibid.*, 254.
82 *Ibid.*, 255.
83 *Ibid.*, 256.
84 ILC, 'Draft Articles on Responsibility of State for Internationally Wrongful Acts, with Commentaries, in Report of the International Law Commission on the Work of Its Fifty-Third Session' UN Doc A/56/10 (2001), art. 30.
85 *Ibid.*, art. 31.
86 *Ibid.*, art. 22.
87 *Ibid.*, art. 41.

uses of force at the lower boundary of the prohibition in terms of intensity or effects could potentially be a serious breach of a peremptory norm if it 'involves a gross or systematic failure by the responsible State to fulfil the obligation',[88] giving rise to these corresponding consequences.

Furthermore, if the rule in article 2(4) of the UN Charter is *jus cogens*, States cannot legally conclude treaties that are the result of a prohibited threat or use of force or enter into legally binding treaties that conflict with the rule. Under article 52 of the VCLT, '[a] treaty is void if its conclusion has been procured by the threat or use of force in violation of the principles of international law embodied in the Charter of the United Nations'. The ICJ held that this reflects customary international law in the *Fisheries Jurisdiction (UK v Iceland)* case.[89] Regarding the second point, article 53 of the VCLT provides that if at the time of the conclusion of a treaty, it conflicts with a *jus cogens* norm, then the treaty is void *ab initio*. One practical example of this is a treaty purporting to provide 'prospective consent to authorize the use of force by one state against another, irrespective or against its will at the moment when force is being used'. If the prohibition of the use of force is *jus cogens*, then this 'constitutes a derogation from the prohibition ... Such consent embodied in a treaty or in a unilateral act would be void for its conflict with *jus cogens* on the basis of Article 53 VCLT and general international law.'[90] This could conceivably encompass standing authorisations under regional collective security agreements, such as article 4(h) of the Constitutive Act of the African Union,[91] which recognises 'the right of the Union to intervene in a Member State pursuant to a decision of the Assembly in respect of grave circumstances, namely: war crimes, genocide and crimes against humanity'.[92]

The International Law Commission noted 'a certain overlap in the application of the *jus cogens* provisions of ... the draft articles and Article 103 of the Charter because certain provisions of the Charter, notably those of Article 2,

[88] *Ibid.*, art. 40(2).

[89] *Fisheries Jurisdiction (UK v Iceland), Jurisdiction* (1973) ICJ Reports 3, para. 14.

[90] Alexander Orakhelashvili, 'Changing *Jus Cogens* through State Practice? The Case of the Prohibition of the Use of Force and Its Exceptions' in Marc Weller (ed), *The Oxford Handbook of the Use of Force in International Law* (Oxford University Press, 2015), 157, 167, citations omitted.

[91] Organisation of African Unity (adopted 1 July 2000, entered into force 26 May 2001). On article 4(h) of the Constitutive Act of the African Union and article 2(4) of the UN Charter, see Erika de Wet, 'Military Assistance Based on Ex-Ante Consent: A Violation of Article 2 (4) of the UN Charter?' (2020) 93(3–4) *Die Friedens-Warte* 413–29.

[92] On 11 July 2003, a Protocol on the Amendments to the Constitutive Act of the African Union was adopted, which amended article 4(h) to include 'a serious threat to legitimate order'; however, the Protocol has not entered into force.

paragraph 4, are of a *jus cogens* character'.[93] Due to the operation of article 103 of the Charter, the obligations in article 2(4) would prevail over the obligations of UN Member States under any other international agreement in the event of a conflict between the obligations. As noted by the ILC,[94] the difference is that if article 2(4) is *jus cogens*, then a conflicting treaty will be completely void, not merely that the obligation under the UN Charter would prevail over the conflicting obligation. In any case, if the prohibition of the use of force is in fact *jus cogens*, then as Thirlway notes,[95] it is unlikely that States would enter into a treaty that conflicts with this obligation and then later seek to denounce it as void on this basis.

For the purpose of identifying the meaning of a prohibited 'use of force' under international law, the *jus cogens* nature of the norm is relevant to the standard of modification, to which we will now turn.

Modification Standard of the Prohibition of the Use of Force if It Is Jus Cogens

If the prohibition of the use of force is a peremptory norm of international law, then there will be a higher standard applicable for determining whether subsequent State practice (for treaty interpretation) or State practice and *opinio juris* (for customary international law) has modified the scope or content of the norm. This is because a peremptory norm 'can be modified only by a subsequent norm of general international law having the same character'.[96] Notably, the modification standard (i.e. *jus cogens* status of the norm) is only relevant to attempts to make the rule less restrictive, either through interpreting the rule in a way that results in a narrower scope or through new derogations or exceptions to the rule. Making the rule narrower would be inconsistent with the original (peremptory) rule, which means that

93 International Law Commission, 'Yearbook of the International Law Commission 1966, Vol. II', n. 12, Commentary of Special Rapporteur Waldock on the draft convention on the law of treaties, regarding draft article 37: treaties conflicting with a peremptory norm of general international law (*jus cogens*), 24.

94 *Ibid.*

95 Thirlway, n. 10, 154.

96 VCLT, n. 2, art. 53. The ILC has observed that 'at the present time, a modification of a rule of jus cogens would most probably be effected through a general multilateral treaty': International Law Commission, 'Formation and Evidence of Customary International Law', n. 18, 31, observation 24, footnote omitted.

the new narrow interpretation would also have to be a *jus cogens* rule to override the original broader interpretation.[97]

Conversely, making the rule broader does not contravene the original *jus cogens* norm; the 'new' rule would preserve the original *jus cogens* 'core' of the norm and extend it under either the treaty (through an evolutive interpretation of article 2(4)) or custom (through evolving custom). In order for the part of the rule that extends beyond the original scope to also comprise *jus cogens*, it would have to separately meet the requirements for the development of a *jus cogens* norm; that is, it must also be 'a norm accepted and recognized by the international community of States as a whole as a norm from which no derogation is permitted and which can be modified only by a subsequent norm of general international law having the same character'.[98] Of course, it is not necessary for an extended scope of the prohibition of the use of force to be *jus cogens*; it is entirely possible for only the original core to be *jus cogens* and for the 'new' part to be an ordinary treaty or customary rule. If the evolved (expanded) interpretation of the prohibition of the use of force did comprise *jus cogens*, then 'any existing treaty which is in conflict with that norm becomes void and terminates'.[99]

CONCLUSION: WHICH SOURCE TO INTERPRET OR APPLY?

Approaches based on analysing State practice and *opinio juris* in order to determine whether and how the prohibition of the use of force in article 2(4) of the UN Charter has evolved or been modified are flawed. Furthermore, since the two rules are identical in content, States do not differentiate between the two in their application of the prohibition and, most importantly, *the rule in article 2(4) is itself the origin of the customary rule*. It is not appropriate to use the customary prohibition to fill gaps in the interpretation of or to modify article 2(4) (unless the customary norm evolves and is used as an element of interpretation of article 2(4)). The preferable approach then to interpret the meaning of a prohibited 'use of force' under international law is to focus on interpreting the treaty.

97 Cf Corten, n. 14, 210–11, who argues that under article 53 of the VCLT, the only relevant practice is subsequent treaties departing from the peremptory rule, since subsequent State practice that claims an exception or justification 'can influence only the interpretation of the rule, not its status as *jus cogens*'. Corten points out that there is no treaty seeking to derogate from article 2(4), and there are many treaties with saving clauses of the rights and responsibilities under the UN Charter.

98 VCLT, n. 2, art. 53.

99 *Ibid.*, art. 64.

There are several implications of choosing to focus on treaty interpretation to discern the meaning and content of a prohibited 'use of force' between States. There is no hierarchy between these different sources of law,[100] and even if the content of the rule under each source of law is currently identical, there are important differences in the application and interpretation of the two different sources of law:

- *Relevance of State practice*: The relevance of State practice differs according to the method being applied. State practice may be relevant firstly to identification of customary international law (when accompanied by an *opinio juris*); secondly, as subsequent practice of the parties in the application of the treaty under article 31 of the VCLT, which establishes their agreement regarding its interpretation; and, thirdly, as other subsequent practice in the application of the treaty as a supplementary means of interpretation under article 32 of the VCLT.
- *Relevant State practice*: Georg Nolte notes that '[i]t is . . . not always easy to distinguish subsequent agreements and subsequent practice from subsequent "other relevant rules of international law applicable in the relations between the parties" (article 31 (3) (c)). It appears that the most important distinguishing factor is whether an agreement is made "regarding the interpretation" of a treaty.'[101] Accordingly, the main difference in method is to identify whether the State practice is in the application of article 2(4) of the UN Charter and whether such practice (in combination with other instances of State practice) establishes the agreement of the treaty parties regarding its interpretation.
- *Opinio juris*: Unlike the identification of the scope of the customary prohibition of the use of force, examining the interpretation of article 2 (4) through subsequent practice does not require an analysis of whether acts or omissions are accompanied by an *opinio juris*, but only whether it is in the application of the UN Charter and if it establishes agreement of UN Member States regarding its interpretation.
- *Required density of practice*: The quantitative standard is probably higher for identifying whether subsequent practice in the application of the treaty evidences agreement of the parties regarding its interpretation, as

[100] Thirlway, n. 10, 136.

[101] Nolte First Report, n. 27, para. 115; cf Wood First Report, n. 1, para. 17, which states that 'the dividing lines' between the areas of identification of customary international law and subsequent agreements and subsequent practice in relation to the interpretation of treaties 'are reasonably clear'.

this will likely require unanimity or near-unanimous agreement of all treaty parties.[102]

Focusing on treaty interpretation to find the meaning of a prohibited 'use of force' has the advantage of avoiding the problems associated with trying to identify an evolution in the customary rule that have been noted by other scholars, such as 'profound divergences' over method,[103] and legal debates regarding the appropriate equilibrium 'not only between "words" and "deeds" but also between "abstract" and "concrete" statements; between the various aspects of density of State practice (uniformity, extensiveness and duration); between the (relatively more influential) practice of powerful States and that of other members of the international community; or between the practice of the Security Council and that of the General Assembly'.[104] A consequence of this approach is that it does not give greater weight to the practice of more militarily powerful States. However, the practice of those more powerful States is more likely to play an influential role as a form of 'other subsequent practice',[105] since those States tend to be more active in the actual use of force and exchange of claims about the use of force, and therefore generate more relevant practice which could play a subsidiary role in interpretation (though one still needs to consider whether such practice indicates how those parties interpret the treaty). Finally, taking the UN Charter provisions as the starting point imposes certain textual constraints on the interpreter[106] and restricts the range of interpretive possibilities to what is offered by the text.

As Andrea Bianchi notes:

> [T]here are good reasons for considering the provisions of the Charter as the starting point of the inquiry on the international legal regulation of the use of force. The first obvious reason is that there is widespread social consensus on this proposition. In most of the debates before the Security Council, in which

[102] 1966 Yearbook of the ILC, vol. 1, Part II, n. 17, 165, para. 17, intervention of Mr Tunkin with respect to draft article 68.

[103] For example, Corten notes:

> On one side of those debates in the extensive approach; it consists in interpreting the rule in the most flexible manner possible. ... On the other side is what can be categorised as the restrictive approach; it advocates a much stricter interpretation of the prohibition so making it much less likely that new exceptions will be viewed as acceptable. Beyond the validity of the basic arguments advanced by both sides, a review of scholarship reveals that the debate is also, and perhaps above all, about method. The most profound divergences arise over the status and interpretation of the customary prohibition on the use of force. (n. 14, 5, footnotes omitted)

[104] Ruys, n. 3, 51.

[105] VCLT, n. 2, art. 32.

[106] Andrea Bianchi, 'The International Regulation of the Use of Force: The Politics of Interpretive Method' (2009) 22(4) *Leiden Journal of International Law* 651, 658.

> issues of the use of force are discussed, reference is primarily made to the law of the Charter. Also in other fora the 'official discourse' on the use of force relies heavily on the central character of the Charter provisions.[107]

This analysis will therefore start with the UN Charter and focus on the subsequent agreement of the parties as well as other practice in the application of the Charter as a supplementary means of interpretation, rather than seeking to identify State practice and *opinio juris* for the purpose of deriving the content of the rule under customary international law.

[107] *Ibid.*, 659 ff.

PART II

Elements of Prohibited Force

INTRODUCTION

Having unentangled the relationship between the UN Charter and the customary prohibition of the use of force in Part I and thus determined that the most suitable approach to identifying the meaning of prohibited force is to focus on treaty interpretation, Part II will carry out a textual analysis of article 2 (4) of the UN Charter to identify the elements of prohibited force.

Some argue that due to the special nature of the UN Charter, different rules should apply to its interpretation than to other treaties.[1] However, whatever its unique character within the international legal system, the UN Charter is a multilateral treaty, 'and as such subject to the general law of treaties'.[2] Article 5 of the Vienna Convention on the Law of Treaties[3] (VCLT) confirms that '[t]he present Convention applies to any treaty which is the constituent instrument of an international organization ... without prejudice to any relevant rules of the organization'.[4] The approach set out in article 5 of the

1 See, for example, Stefan Kadelbach, 'Interpretation of the Charter' in Bruno Simma et al (eds), *The Charter of the United Nations: A Commentary* (Oxford University Press, 3rd ed, 2012), vol. I, 7, 73–4, who identifies four approaches to interpreting the UN Charter: classical positivism, international constitutionalism, critical approach challenging the first two approaches, and a pragmatic approach combining aspects of positivism with constitutionalism and critical approach.

2 Georg Witschel, 'Article 108' in Bruno Simma et al (eds), *The Charter of the United Nations: A Commentary* (Oxford University Press, 3rd ed, 2012), vol. I, 2199, 2204, MN8, footnote omitted.

3 *Vienna Convention on the Law of Treaties* 1969 (adopted 22 May 1969, entered into force 27 January 1980), 1155 UNTS 331 ('VCLT').

4 Article 5 of the VCLT is considered to reflect customary international law, although the evidence to support this is limited and the ICJ has not yet pronounced itself on this question. However, 'it has been generally recognized that the rules of the Vienna Convention regarding treaty interpretation are applicable to constituent instruments of international organizations, but always "without prejudice to any relevant rules of the organization" ... If it is understood in this broad and flexible sense it is clear that article 5 does reflect customary international law.'

VCLT was confirmed by the International Court of Justice (ICJ) in the *Nuclear Weapons Advisory Opinion*, in which it held that: 'From a formal standpoint, the constituent instruments of international organizations are multilateral treaties, to which the well-established rules of treaty interpretation apply.'[5] The ICJ has held more specifically with respect to the UN Charter that '[o]n the previous occasions when the Court has had to interpret the Charter of the United Nations, it has followed the principles and rules applicable in general to the interpretation of treaties, since it has recognized that the Charter is a multilateral treaty, albeit a treaty having certain special characteristics'.[6]

The starting point for interpreting article 2(4) of the UN Charter is therefore to apply the process set out in the VCLT. The general rule of interpretation and the rule on supplementary means of interpretation are set out in articles 31 and 32 of the VCLT, which both apply as rules of customary international law.[7] Article 31(1) of the VCLT sets out the general rule of interpretation as follows: 'A treaty shall be interpreted in good faith in accordance with the ordinary meaning to be given to the terms of the treaty in their context and in the light of its object and purpose.' According to article 31(3) of the VCLT:

> There shall be taken into account, together with the context:
> (*a*) any subsequent agreement between the parties regarding the interpretation of the treaty or the application of its provisions;
> (*b*) any subsequent practice in the application of the treaty which establishes the agreement of the parties regarding its interpretation;
> (*c*) any relevant rules of international law applicable in the relations between the parties.

Georg Nolte, 'Third Report on Subsequent Agreements and Subsequent Practice in Relation to the Interpretation of Treaties' UN Doc A/CN.4/683 (International Law Commission, 7 April 2015) ('Nolte Third Report'), 32–3, paras. 83–85.

5 *Legality of the Threat or Use of Nuclear Weapons, Advisory Opinion* (1996) ICJ Reports 226, para. 19.

6 *Certain Expenses of the United Nations (Article 17, paragraph 2 of the Charter), Advisory Opinion* [1962] ICJ Reports 151, 157; see also Nolte Third Report, n. 4, 9.

7 International Law Commission, 'Subsequent Agreements and Subsequent Practice in Relation to the Interpretation of Treaties Text of Draft Conclusions 1–5 Provisionally Adopted by the Drafting Committee at the Sixty-Fifth Session of the International Law Commission' UN Doc A/CN.4/L.813 (May 24, 2013) ('ILC'); Georg Nolte, 'First Report on Subsequent Agreements and Subsequent Practice in Relation to Treaty Interpretation' (International Law Commission, 19 March 2013), 6, para. 8, footnotes omitted.

This work will thus apply the following principles to the interpretation of a prohibited 'use of force' under article 2(4) of the UN Charter:

- focus on a textual interpretation of article 2(4) by looking at the 'ordinary meaning to be given to the terms of the treaty in their context and in the light of its object and purpose';[8]
- take into account 'subsequent agreements between the parties regarding the interpretation of the treaty or the application of its provisions' and 'subsequent practice in the application of the treaty which establishes the agreement of the parties regarding its interpretation', together with 'any relevant rules of international law applicable in the relations between the parties';[9]
- where appropriate, consider preparatory work of the UN Charter and 'other subsequent practice' as a supplementary means of interpretation;[10] and
- examine how the term 'use of force' is currently interpreted and applied by States.

Part II will apply these principles to a textual analysis of article 2(4), including subsequent agreements of States, to identify the elements of prohibited force.

8 VCLT, n. 3, art. 31(1).

9 *Ibid.*, art. 31(3). A 'subsequent agreement' is 'an agreement between the parties, reached after the conclusion of a treaty, regarding the interpretation of the treaty or the application of its provisions' (ILC (2013), n. 7, draft conclusion 4, para. 1). 'Subsequent practice' is 'conduct in the application of a treaty, after its conclusion, which establishes the agreement of the parties regarding the interpretation of the treaty' (draft conclusion 4, para. 2.). Such conduct includes tacit consent and pronouncements such as declarations and other official statements. Decisions by a court or tribunal on the interpretation of a treaty (such as the ICJ interpreting the UN Charter) do not count as 'subsequent practice' for the purpose of treaty interpretation and instead 'constitute special means for the interpretation of the treaty in subsequent cases, as indicated, in particular, by article 38 (1) (d) of the Statute of the International Court of Justice': Nolte Third Report, n. 4, 7, para. 17.

10 VCLT, n. 3, art. 32.

4

Contextual Elements of a Prohibited 'Use of Force'

International Relations

INTRODUCTION

The text of article 2(4) reads as follows:

> The Organization and its Members, in pursuit of the Purposes stated in Article 1, shall act in accordance with the following Principles.
>
> (4) All Members shall refrain in their international relations from the threat or use of force against the territorial integrity or political independence of any state, or in any other manner inconsistent with the Purposes of the United Nations.

This chapter will carry out a textual analysis of the terms of article 2(4) of the UN Charter other than 'threat or use of force',[1] in order to delineate the contextual elements of prohibited force. These terms – 'all Members', 'international relations' and 'against the territorial integrity or political independence of any state, or in any other manner inconsistent with the Purposes of the United Nations' – are fundamental, contextual elements that must be present in order for a 'use of force' to fall within the scope of article 2(4). This chapter will briefly examine each of these terms in turn to understand how they delineate the scope and context of a prohibited 'use of force'.

'ALL MEMBERS'

States Only

In the first place, the prohibition in article 2(4) binds only States, as confirmed by State practice and case law.[2] With respect to the parallel customary rule, it

[1] 'Threat' of force is discussed in Chapter 6 with respect to intention.

[2] Claus Kreß, 'The State Conduct Element' in Claus Kreß and Stefan Barriga (eds), *The Crime of Aggression: A Commentary* (Cambridge University Press, 2017), 412, with further references;

is an interesting question whether the customary prohibition also applies only to States or if it also binds non-State actors, international organisations or individuals.[3]

Member States Only

As a treaty, the provisions of the UN Charter are clearly binding on its parties, that is, the Member States of the United Nations. Non-Member States are bound by the prohibition only indirectly through the UN Charter (since they could be subject to enforcement action/sanctions for failing to comply with the relevant principles),[4] but the source of their legal obligation is customary international law.

Use of Force by Non-State Armed Groups

In certain circumstances, State support or involvement in forcible acts of other States, or in forcible acts of non-State actors against another State will violate the prohibition of the use of force.[5] However, this is relevant not to who are the addressees of the prohibition (States) but to what acts or level of support will result in attribution to a State or amount to an indirect 'use of force' in violation of article 2(4). With respect to attribution, the general principles of State responsibility apply, as set out in articles 4 to 11 of the International Law Commission (ILC) Articles on State Responsibility. In particular, article 8 of the ILC Articles on State Responsibility provides that:

> The conduct of a person or group of persons shall be considered an act of a State under international law if the person or group of persons is in fact acting on the instructions of, or under the direction or control of, that State in carrying out the conduct.

The International Court of Justice (ICJ) had applied a similar standard of attribution in the *Nicaragua* case, in which it held that:

cf Tarcisio Gazzini, *The Changing Rules on the Use of Force in International Law* (Manchester University Press, 2005), 188, who notes that '[i]t has been suggested, in particular, that Art. 2(4) of the Charter should be read as imposing the prohibition on threat or use of force not only on States but also on individuals' (citing A-M Slaughter and W Burke-White, 'An International Constitutional Moment' (2002) 43 *Harvard International Law Journal* 1, 2), although he does not adopt a position on this issue.

3 See discussion in Chapter 3.

4 See Chapter 2 for a discussion of article 2(6).

5 See Chapter 6.

> For this conduct to give rise to legal responsibility of the United States, it would in principle have to be proved that that State had *effective control* of the military or paramilitary operations in the course of which the alleged violations were committed.[6]

Although the International Criminal Tribunal for the former Yugoslavia in the *Tadic* case applied a different test for attribution of 'overall control',[7] this has been criticised by both the ILC[8] and the ICJ, which declined to adopt this standard.[9] Other forms of support that do not meet the standard for attribution of the conduct of the non-State armed group to a State may nevertheless constitute an indirect 'use of force' by a State under article 2(4) of the UN Charter. Indirect force is discussed further in Chapter 5.

'SHALL REFRAIN ... FROM'

This is obligatory language that reflects the binding legal obligation set out in article 2(4).

'IN THEIR INTERNATIONAL RELATIONS'

The confinement of the prohibition of the threat or use of force by States to those 'in their international relations' 'continues the tradition of article I of the Kellogg-Briand Pact, which confines the scope of application of the prohibition of the recourse to war as an instrument of national policy to the realm of the "solution of international controversies"'.[10] This section will discuss the meaning of the term 'international relations' and whether it requires that the object of a prohibited use of force be another State, as well as looking at the types of acts that fall within and outside the scope of this term.

6 *Merits, Judgment* (1986) ICJ Reports 14, para. 115, emphasis added. The ICJ later applied the test in article 8 of the ILC Draft Articles on State Responsibility in the *Armed Activities on the Territory of the Congo (Democratic Republic of the Congo v Uganda)* (2005) ICJ Reports 168, para. 160.

7 *Prosecutor v Duško Tadic*, ICTY Appeals Chamber Judgment of 15 July 1999, IT-94-1-A, para. 120 ff.

8 ILC, 'Draft Articles on Responsibility of States for Internationally Wrongful Acts, with Commentaries, in Report of the International Law Commission on the Work of Its Fifty-Third Session' UN Doc A/56/10 (2001), commentary to art. 8 at para. 5.

9 *Case concerning Application of the Convention on the Prevention and Punishment of the Crime of Genocide (Bosnia and Herzegovina v Serbia and Montenegro), Judgment* (2007) ICJ Reports 43, para. 403.

10 Kreß, n. 2, 432, footnote 93, citing K Sellars, *Crimes against Peace and International Law* (Cambridge University Press, 2013), 25.

Another State?

The wording of article 2(4), in particular the terms 'international relations' and 'in any other manner', does not explicitly require the damage to be to another State.[11] The reference to 'international relations' implies that a prohibited use of force must affect the *relations* between the State using force and another State. This leaves open the possibility that the actual damage is not to a State but affects inter-State relations. With respect to the phrase, 'in any other manner', the second half of article 2(4) was introduced to prevent loopholes in interpretation (see discussion of this term later in the chapter). Thus, interpreting the term 'international relations' to prohibit another type of use of force (in addition to uses of force against the territorial integrity or political independence *of a State*) would comply with this intended purpose of making the prohibition more expansive. Furthermore, a natural reading of the second part of article 2(4) is to read the listed elements conjunctively (i.e. as alternatives). This would result in the following categories of prohibited conduct: firstly, uses of force in the international relations of Members against the territorial integrity or political independence of any State, and secondly, uses of force in the international relations of Members in any other manner inconsistent with the Purposes of the United Nations.[12]

This interpretation would potentially encompass a use of force that is in 'international relations' outside the context of State damage, such as damage to *terra nullius*. Claus Kreß notes that '[i]t is an unsettled question whether the use of force by a state ... on terra nullius occurs in international relations and thus within the meaning of article 2(4) of the UN Charter'.[13] Since there are hardly any areas of *terra nullius* (rare examples include Bir Tawil between Egypt and Sudan, an area that neither claims, and parts of Antarctica), this

[11] Kreß, n. 2, 434–5: 'the text of article 2(4) does not unambiguously require a use of force against another state. As a matter of textual interpretation, the words "international relations" can be construed so as to cover any use of force by a state outside its territory.'

[12] Kelsen supports this interpretation (Hans Kelsen, *The Law of the United Nations: A Critical Analysis of Its Fundamental Problems* (Stevens, 1950), 726–7):

> The phrase 'or in any other manner inconsistent with the Purposes of the United Nations' is an addition to the words 'against the territorial integrity, etc.' The meaning is: the Members shall refrain from the threat or use of force not only against the territorial integrity and political independence of any state; they shall refrain from the threat or use of force also in any other manner inconsistent with the Purposes of the United Nations, that is to say: with the provisions of Article I of the Charter.

Kreß (n. 2, 432–5) has also argued that the term 'in any other manner' leaves open the possibility that the use of force does not have to be directed against another State.

[13] Kreß, n. 2, 434, footnote omitted.

issue is unlikely to be raised in practice. However, both on Earth (with respect to the high seas)[14] and in outer space (with respect to celestial bodies),[15] there are vast areas which do not form part of the territory of any State and are not subject to claims of sovereignty, so it is conceivable that a 'use of force' could be directed against these environments (for instance, as part of a malicious attack, or in the process of exploiting natural resources located in these environments), thus raising the question of whether such an act occurs in 'international relations' even though no State suffers direct damage.

Object and Purpose

The object and purpose of the UN Charter and in particular article 2(4) are also relevant to determining whether the range of interpretive possibilities of the term 'international relations' includes damage to objects without a nexus to another State.[16] Subsequent agreements with respect to article 2(4) of the UN Charter demonstrate the agreement of Member States that the primary purposes of that provision are international peace and security and the sovereign equality of States.[17] The Friendly Relations Declaration emphasises international peace and security as among the fundamental purposes of the UN Charter[18] and sets out related principles that are 'interrelated with'[19] the prohibition of the use of force, including the obligation to settle international disputes by peaceful means[20] and the principle of sovereign equality of States.[21] Resolution 42/22 (1987) also notes that the principle of peaceful settlement of disputes 'is inseparable from the principle of refraining from the

[14] *United Nations Convention on the Law of the Sea*, 1994 UNTS 397 (concluded 10 December 1982, entered into force 16 November 1994), article 89 provides that '[n]o State may validly purport to subject any part of the high seas to its sovereignty'.

[15] With respect to celestial bodies, the Outer Space Treaty provides that '[o]uter space, including the Moon and other celestial bodies, is not subject to national appropriation by claim of sovereignty, by means of use or occupation, or by any other means'. *Treaty on Principles Governing the Activities of States in the Exploration and Use of Outer Space, including the Moon and Other Celestial Bodies* (adopted 27 January 1967, entered into force 10 October 1967), 610 UNTS 205, art. II.

[16] *Vienna Convention on the Law of Treaties* 1969 (adopted 22 May 1969, entered into force 27 January 1980), 1155 UNTS 331 ('VCLT'), art. 1.

[17] For a discussion of subsequent agreements regarding article 2(4) of the UN Charter, see Chapter 5.

[18] UN General Assembly, *Resolution 2625: Declaration on Principles of International Law concerning Friendly Relations and Cooperation among States in Accordance with the Charter of the United Nations*, UN Doc A/Res/2625(XXV) (24 October 1970) ('Friendly Relations Declaration'), first preambular para.

[19] *Ibid.*, para. 2.

[20] *Ibid.*, principle 2.

[21] *Ibid.*, principle 5.

threat or use of force in their international relations'.[22] Resolution 42/22 explicitly reaffirms the purpose of article 2(4) is the 'establishment of lasting peace and security for all States'.[23] In the 2005 World Summit Outcome Document (adopted by consensus), the UN General Assembly emphasised the purposes of the UN Charter as international peace and security and sovereign equality of States. In that document, the UN General Assembly 'reaffirm[ed] that the purposes and principles guiding the United Nations are, inter alia, to maintain international peace and security, to develop friendly relations among nations based on respect for the principles of equal rights and self-determination of peoples and to take other appropriate measures to strengthen universal peace'.[24] These two primary values protected by article 2(4) – international peace and security and the sovereign equality of States – give rise to arguments for and against including uses of force that are not against a State, depending on which purpose is emphasised, as discussed below.

STATE SOVEREIGNTY Article 2(4) of the UN Charter protects sovereign equality by prohibiting the use of force to settle international disputes. The term 'of any state' suggests that the protected object of article 2(4) is States, and in particular their 'territorial integrity' and 'political independence'. This is also supported by the Friendly Relations Declaration, which holds that the principle of sovereign equality of States includes the inviolability of the territorial integrity and political independence of the State.[25] (The protected interest of State sovereignty in article 2(4) read together with articles 2(3) and 2(7) also supports an interpretation of a 'use of force' as requiring a coercive intent – this is discussed further in Chapter 6.) The protected object of State sovereignty tends to exclude the use of force against objects with no sufficient nexus to another State from the scope of article 2(4).

INTERNATIONAL PEACE AND SECURITY However, the second and arguably main purpose of article 2(4), the maintenance of international peace and security, may concern damage to non-State objects (objects with no sufficient

[22] UN General Assembly, *Resolution 42/22: Declaration on the Enhancement of the Effectiveness of the Principle of Refraining from the Threat or Use of Force in International Relations*, UN Doc A/Res/42/22 (18 November 1987), para. 16.

[23] *Ibid.*, preambular para. 21.

[24] UN General Assembly, 2005 *World Summit Outcome*, UN Doc A/RES/60/1 (24 October 2005), para. 77.

[25] Friendly Relations Declaration, n. 18, principle 1(d). Another possibility is to construe the protected value of State sovereignty to include the right of a State's people and the protection of their common life: see Kreß, n. 2, 418 ff.

nexus to another State) under certain circumstances. This possibility is supported firstly by the Purposes of the United Nations, and secondly by reading article 2(4) in the context of the collective security framework provided for in the Charter.[26] The Purposes are referred to in the *chapeau* of article 2, which provides: 'The Organization and its Members, in pursuit of the Purposes stated in Article 1, shall act in accordance with the following Principles' (one of which is of course the principle of the prohibition of the use of force in article 2(4)). The first of the Purposes set out in article 1 in paragraph 1 is

> To maintain international peace and security, and to that end: to take effective collective measures for the prevention and removal of threats to the peace, and for the suppression of acts of aggression or other breaches of the peace, and to bring about by peaceful means, and in conformity with the principles of justice and international law, adjustment or settlement of international disputes or situations which might lead to a breach of the peace.

The Preamble of the UN Charter (which according to article 31(2) of the VCLT comprises part of the context for the purpose of treaty interpretation) further supports this as the primary value of article 2(4). The Preamble states in its opening lines, '[w]e the peoples of the United Nations determined to save succeeding generations from the scourge of war'. In the first meeting of Commission 1 (responsible for drafting the general provisions of the UN Charter including the preamble, Purposes and Principles) at the San Francisco Conference, the President of the Commission, Mr Rolin of Belgium, stated with respect to the 'first object' of the maintenance of peace: 'We are not state worshippers, and when we speak of the prevention of war we have, of course, in mind only what sufferings war is causing to humanity'.[27] In its Advisory Opinion on *Certain Expenses*, the ICJ held that '[t]he primary place ascribed to international peace and security is natural, since the fulfilment of the other purposes will be dependent upon the attainment of that basic condition'.[28]

The primary purpose of article 2(4) as the maintenance of international peace and security is also supported by the context of the collective security framework provided for in the Charter.[29] The UN Charter sets out two

[26] Kelsen, n. 12, 13.

[27] UNCIO, 'First Session of Commission I, June 14, 1945', vol. VI, Doc 1006 I/6 (15 June 1945), 12.

[28] *Certain Expenses of the United Nations (Article 17, paragraph 2 of the Charter), Advisory Opinion* (1962) ICJ Reports 151, 168.

[29] For a historical account of the Dumbarton Oaks conference (where the four Great Powers met to lay out the framework for the future UN, prior to the San Francisco conference), see Robert C Hilderbrand, *Dumbarton Oaks: The Origins of the United Nations and the Search for Postwar Security* (University of North Carolina Press, 1990) explaining the factors that lead to

exceptions to the prohibition of the use of force, namely, self-defence in response to an armed attack under article 51 and the authorisation of force by the UN Security Council acting under Chapter VII. These provisions (article 2(4), article 51 and Chapter VII) together comprise the collective security system of the United Nations; under international law in the post-Charter era, States do not have a right to unilaterally use force but must settle their international disputes by peaceful means. This system is supplemented by the customary international law duty of non-intervention (in recognition of the sovereign equality of States). The context of article 2(4) and its relationship with other Charter provisions illuminates the interpretation of article 2(4) by emphasising its primary aim of maintaining international peace and security. In this light, the purpose of maintaining international peace and security points towards the inclusion of forcible acts against non-State objects within the scope of the prohibition, when those acts affect the international relations between States and therefore endanger international peace and security.

In sum, the text of article 2(4) does not unambiguously require that a State be the object or target of a 'use of force', and the primary value protected by article 2(4) of international peace and security supports a broad interpretation. During the drafting of the 1970 Friendly Relations Declaration, '[t]hose who discussed the point generally agreed that the term had the effect of limiting the prohibition in Article 2, paragraph 4, to disputes between States'.[30] However, this does not constitute a 'subsequent agreement' within the meaning of article 31(3) of the VCLT, and such an interpretation remains to be either confirmed or rejected through the subsequent agreement and subsequent practice of States. So far this author is not aware of any State practice seeking to extend the interpretation of article 2(4) beyond damage to States. While a broader interpretation remains textually open, since article 2(4) also protects States' sovereignty and territorial integrity, it is likely that another State must be the object/target in order for a 'use of force' to be in 'international relations' and fall within the scope of article 2(4).

Required Nexus

This then raises the question of the required nexus between the object/target of a use of force and another State, particularly with respect to forcible acts against non-State objects such as nationals of a State, individuals present

the Great Powers establishing the UN with a watered-down power and authority, and what the objectives and motives of the drafters were.

30 First Report of the Special Committee on Principles of International Law concerning Friendly Relations and Co-operation among States, UN Doc A/5746 (16 November 1964), para. 36.

within the territory of a State or private property such as private and merchant vessels or aircraft registered to a State. In some cases, attacks on individuals due to their nationality have been regarded as armed attacks (and therefore uses of force under article 2(4)) against the State of nationality, such as the Entebbe incident, where all hostages were released apart from those of Israeli nationality.[31] In certain circumstances, article 2(4) applies to uses of force by a State against private vessels and aircraft registered to another State. This results from article 3(g) of the Annex to 1974 General Assembly Resolution 3314, which lists as an act of aggression an 'attack by the armed forces of a State on the ... marine and air fleets of another State'. The issue of required nexus to another State is of particular relevance to emerging forms of practice in disputed maritime zones such as in the South China Sea, firstly, with respect to '[t]he use of Coast Guard and other maritime law enforcement agency vessels and officials, and indeed merchant vessels and fishing vessels under obvious governmental orders, to enforce presence and to employ force in disputed maritime areas' and, secondly, to 'the use of private citizens – especially fishermen – to assert claims, act as state proxies in confrontation situations, or to provoke harassment which is then used to justify escalated intervention by more formal state forces such as Coast Guard vessels'.[32] For non-State objects/targets that do not have a close association with a State, more will be required to bring the act within 'international relations' and into the scope of article 2(4), such as the presence of other factors including the gravity of the (potential) effects, a coercive or hostile intent against a State or a pre-existing dispute between States.

Political Context

If there is a pre-existing dispute between the States concerned, such as contested territory, this may bring the use of force within the realm of 'international relations' and thus within the scope of the *jus contra bellum*.[33] The political context may be relevant to whether the act itself constitutes a 'use of force', since it may increase the gravity of the act and indicate a hostile

[31] See Claus Kreß and Benjamin K Nußberger, 'The Entebbe Raid – 1976' in Tom Ruys and Olivier Corten (eds), *The Use of Force in International Law: A Case-Based Approach* (Oxford University Press, 2018), 220.

[32] Rob McLaughlin, 'Some Contributions from Asia to the Development of LOAC', Speech Delivered at International Law Association Meeting, South Africa (2016) (on file with author).

[33] Tom Ruys, 'The Meaning of "Force" and the Boundaries of the *Jus Ad Bellum*: Are "Minimal" Uses of Force Excluded from UN Charter Article 2 (4)?' (2014) 108(2) *American Journal of International Law* 159, 206.

or coercive intention. A pre-existing dispute between States or otherwise hostile relations could thus explain why friendly States do not view certain acts as an unlawful 'use of force', which, if committed by an unfriendly State, would be so regarded. The State experiencing the forcible act (the 'victim' State) will interpret the *intention* or motivation of the forcible act and the perceived threat to its security (*gravity*) taking into account this political context; thus, the interpretation of the situation is influenced by this context, meaning that the State could in fact be applying the same criteria for a 'use of force' but to differently viewed 'facts'. For example, when on 1 March 2007, 170 Swiss Army infantry troops armed with rifles lost their bearings and crossed the border into Liechtenstein, the incursion did not provoke any official protest.[34] It is easy to imagine that the response and legal characterisation of such an incursion would be vastly different if it occurred between States with heightened tensions or pre-existing disputes, such as India/Pakistan or Democratic People's Republic of Korea/South Korea. The relationship between intention, gravity and international relations is explored further in Chapter 8. A 'use of force' in the context of an existing international dispute may also relate to whether the act is 'in any other manner inconsistent with the Purposes of the United Nations' (the second part of article 2(4), discussed later), since such a use of force is inconsistent with the Purpose to maintain international peace and security through the peaceful settlement of international disputes (article 1(1), UN Charter).

The remainder of this section will look at particular categories of acts falling within and outside the scope of the term 'international relations'.

Extra-Territorial Sovereign Manifestations of a State

The classic paradigm is a use of force by a State on the territory of another State,[35] but 'international relations' also covers a use of force against an extraterritorial sovereign manifestation of a State including on the high seas or on the territory of the State using force, such as armed forces or embassies.[36]

Disputed Territory and Armistice Lines

In the case of disputed territory that is claimed by more than one State, the prohibition of the use of force acts in favour of the State in de facto control of

34 Peter Stamm, 'Switzerland Invades Liechtenstein', *The New York Times* (13 March 2007), sec. Opinion. www.nytimes.com/2007/03/13/opinion/13iht-edstamm.4893796.html.

35 Kreß, n. 2, 432.

36 *Ibid.*, 433.

the territory even against the State holding the sovereign title.[37] This is an example of a use of force against another State that does not violate its territorial integrity. Kreß suggests that what is being protected by the prohibition in such a case is 'the peaceful common life on the disputed territory and the maintenance of international peace and security'.[38] However, this interpretation is without prejudice to the right of a victim State to act in self-defence against a State that has established military occupation over its territory as a result of an armed attack under article 51;[39] a State may not use force against a State in de facto control of its territory unless it is in self-defence or with UN Security Council authorisation.[40] A 'use of force' is also in 'international relations' and falls within the scope of article 2(4) if it '"violate[s] international lines of demarcation, such as armistice lines, established by or pursuant to an international agreement to which it is a party or which it is otherwise bound to respect", provided that these lines run between two states'. Kreß argues that in the case of disputed territory and armistice lines, 'international law subordinates the protection of territorial sovereignty to the protection of a peaceful common life on a certain piece of territory and the maintenance of international peace and security'.[41] With respect to entities whose statehood is disputed (e.g. North and South Vietnam during the Vietnam War; North and South Korea during the Korean War; Taiwan; Kosovo; Abkhazia; South Ossetia), the situation is more complicated. The *jus contra bellum* does not require all States to recognise the statehood of the entity in question, and it is an open question if article 2 (4) covers a use of force violating an 'international demarcation line delimiting the territory of a non-State political entity'.[42]

Use of Force by a State within Its Own Territory

An interesting question is raised as to whether and when a use of force by a State within its own territory is in 'international relations' and falls within the

37 *Ibid.*, citing art. 2(3); Olivier Corten, *The Law against War: The Prohibition on the Use of Force in Contemporary International Law* (Hart Publishing, 2010), 149–50.

38 Kreß, n. 2, 432.

39 *Ibid.*, 433. For a discussion of this question, see Tom Ruys and Felipe Rodríguez Silvestre, 'Illegal: The Recourse to Force to Recover Occupied Territory and the Second Nagorno-Karabakh War' (2021) 32(4) *European Journal of International Law* 1287; Dapo Akande and Antonios Tzanakopoulos, 'Legal: Use of Force in Self-Defence to Recover Occupied Territory' (2021) 32(4) *European Journal of International Law* 1299.

40 Corten, n. 37, 149–50; Tomohiro Mikanagi, 'Establishing a Military Presence in a Disputed Territory: Interpretation of Article 2(3) and (4) of the UN Charter' (2018) 67(4) *International & Comparative Law Quarterly* 1021.

41 Kreß, n. 2, 433.

42 Corten, n. 37, 152.

scope of article 2(4). Differing views were expressed on the inclusion of the use of force within a State within the scope of the prohibition during the drafting of the 1970 Friendly Relations Declaration. In the 1966 meeting of the Special Committee on Principles of International Law concerning Friendly Relations and Co-operation among States ('Special Committee'), one representative suggested the Special Committee include a statement that 'the prohibition on the threat or use of force did not in any way affect the use of force within a State'.[43] In the 1970 meeting of the Special Committee,

> [t]he Italian delegation reiterated, with respect to the prohibition of the threat or use of force, its firm opinion that that prohibition was, according to the Charter, a general prohibition which must be complied with under any circumstances other than the exceptions contemplated in the Charter ... including, inter alia, the high seas, outer space and, as his delegation had stressed at the Committee's eighty-ninth meeting in 1968 ... even the very territory of the States to which the prohibition was addressed.[44]

However, this point was not further discussed and does not appear in the text of the Friendly Relations Declaration.

The use of force within a State's own territory can be further broken down into several types of incidents, namely, a use of force by a State in its own territory: (a) against its own population, (b) against territorial incursion by the armed forces of another State, and (c) against foreign private actors such as individuals, merchant vessels or civilian aircraft. These are briefly dealt with in turn in the following sections.

A. Use of Force within a State's Own Territory against Its Own Population

The *Nuclear Weapons Advisory Opinion* can be interpreted as excluding uses of force by a State 'within its own boundaries' from the scope of the prohibition in article 2(4) since the Court decided not to deal with this issue.[45] However, the contrary interpretation is also possible, since the ICJ stated that '[t]he terms of the question put to the Court by the General Assembly in resolution 49175 K ("Is the threat or use of nuclear weapons in any circumstance permitted under international law?") could in principle also cover a

43 Second Report of the 1966 Special Committee on Principles of International Law concerning Friendly Relations and Co-operation among States, UN Doc A/6230 (27 June 1966), para. 54.

44 Sixth Report of the Special Committee on Principles of International Law concerning Friendly Relations and Co-operation among States, UN Doc A/8018 (31 March to 1 May 1970), para. 136.

45 *Legality of the Threat or Use of Nuclear Weapons, Advisory Opinion* (1996) ICJ Reports 226, para. 50.

threat or use of nuclear weapons by a State within its own boundaries', and decided that it was not called upon to deal with an internal use of nuclear weapons because no State addressing the Court raised this issue.[46] Kreß notes that 'it would probably overstate the significance' of the Court's statement to conclude that the Court would totally exclude all uses of force by a State within its territory from the prohibition,[47] but he does note that it is uncontroversial that a use of force by a State *against its own population* within its territory would not fall within the scope of the prohibition,[48] although this may well violate other norms of international law including international human rights and humanitarian law.

B. Legal Basis for Forceful Response by a State to Small-Scale Territorial Incursions by Armed Forces of Another State

It is controversial whether a use of force by a State within its own territory against small-scale intruding police or military units of another State (including ships and aircraft) falls within the scope of the prohibition of the use of force in article 2(4). The crux of the debate is the legal basis for a forcible response by a State to low-scale incursions within its own territory, with some arguing that the legal basis is law enforcement based on the exercise of sovereign jurisdiction,[49] and others arguing that the legal basis is the *jus contra bellum* as it engages international relations (and that it is therefore restricted with respect to territorial incursion falling short of armed attack).[50]

Ian Brownlie argued that forcible response to aerial trespass (but not maritime trespass)[51] is a justified exception to the prohibition of the use of force, separate from self-defence. He sets out some specific requirements that must be met for the exception to apply:

> In general the practice seems to be that there is no right to shoot down trespassers unless they refuse or appear to refuse to land. However, if the penetration is by unidentified fast aircraft which persist in a deliberate and deep penetration of airspace, it may be that, in view of the destructive power of even a single nuclear weapon carried by an aircraft, the territorial sovereign

46 *Ibid.*

47 Kreß, n. 2, 432.

48 *Ibid.*

49 For example, Albrecht Randelzhofer and Oliver Dörr, 'Article 2(4)' in Bruno Simma et al (eds), *The Charter of the United Nations: A Commentary* (Oxford University Press, 3rd ed, 2012), 200, 215, MN34, with footnote listing concurring scholars.

50 For example, Ruys, n. 33.

51 Ian Brownlie, *International Law and the Use of Force by States* (Clarendon, 1963), 374, emphasis added.

> is justified in taking without any warning violent and immediate preventive measures.[52]

He argued that '[t]his is a rare instance in which a use of force may be justified although no actual attack has occurred'.[53]

Judge Stephen Schwebel in his dissenting opinion in the *Nicaragua* case argued that 'contemporary international law recognizes that a third State is entitled to exert measures of force against the aggressor on its own territory and against its own armed forces and military resources'.[54] Judge Schwebel quotes the Thirteen Powers draft definition of aggression,[55] which specified that

> [w]hen a State is a victim in its own territory of subversive and/or terrorist acts by irregular, volunteer or armed bands organized or supported by another State, it may take all reasonable and adequate steps to safeguard its existence and its institutions, without having recourse to the right of individual or collective self-defence against the other State under Article 51 of the Charter.

Olivier Corten and Mary Ellen O'Connell also argue that the basis for forcible response to territorial incursions falling short of armed attack is law enforcement. Corten argues that 'the State has sovereign rights over its territory, authorising it to deploy military forces there without having to appeal to any rule creating an exception whatsoever, whether self-defence or not'.[56]

Tom Ruys disagrees that minimal uses of force within a State's own territory are justified by law enforcement rights under other legal regimes for land/sea/air, because none of the other legal frameworks cited 'provide[] a legal basis for forcible action against unlawful territorial incursions by military or police forces of another state'.[57] He makes the argument that forcible response to small-scale incursions falls within the scope of article 2(4) of the UN Charter but frames the argument in terms of the gravity threshold for a 'use of force', rather than in terms of 'international relations'. He notes that there are theoretical reasons against the idea that there is a gravity threshold for article 2(4), including that armed confrontations between police/military of two States involve 'international relations', and the law enforcement paradigm is

52 *Ibid.*, 373–4, footnotes omitted.
53 *Ibid.*, 374.
54 *Case concerning Military and Paramilitary activities in and against Nicaragua (Nicaragua v United States of America), Merits, Judgment* (1986) ICJ Reports 14, Dissenting Opinion of Judge Schwebel 176.
55 *Ibid.*, para. 163.
56 *Ibid.*, 405.
57 Ruys, n. 33, 181.

hierarchical and therefore not suited to equal sovereigns.[58] According to Ruys, the way States treat these confrontations in their legal discourse shows that even when they use force within their own territory in response to an unlawful incursion, this falls within the *jus contra bellum*, and therefore, no *de minimis* gravity threshold exists.[59]

The wording of the text of article 2(4) leaves the interpretation of 'international relations' in this respect uncertain. As can be seen from the previous discussion, a use of force by a State in response to small-scale territorial, maritime or aerial incursion raises several intertwined issues, such as the gap between 'use of force' and an 'armed attack' giving rise to a right of self-defence, the relationship of the *jus contra bellum* and other applicable legal frameworks such as law of the sea and law enforcement, whether there is a gravity threshold for a 'use of force' under article 2(4) and if a hostile or coercive intention is required to enliven article 2(4). But the main legal issue with respect to whether such incidents fall within the scope of the prohibition of the use of force under article 2(4) is the 'international relations' element. As Christian Henderson notes, it is not a matter of 'quantifying the use of force' in terms of its gravity but rather determining whether 'international relations' are engaged, at which point the prohibition of the use of force becomes applicable.[60] The relationship between 'international relations', gravity and intention is discussed further in Chapter 8.

C. Law Enforcement against Foreign Private Actors within or outside Own Territory

There is greater agreement among scholars that law enforcement by a State against foreign private actors within its territory does not usually fall within the scope of article 2(4) as it is not in 'international relations'.[61] Ruys draws a

[58] *Ibid.*, 180.

[59] *Ibid.*, 170ff; See also Yoram Dinstein, *War, Aggression and Self-Defence* (Cambridge University Press, 5th ed, 2011), 213, footnote 130 on the basis for forcible response by the territorial State against small-scale incursion:

> It has been suggested that the problem may be solved by excluding from the 'proscribed categories of article 2(4)' of the Charter the enforcement by a State of its territorial rights against an illegal incursion (Schachter, *supra* note 517, at 1626). But, in the present writer's opinion, the span of the prohibition of the use of inter-State force, as articulated in Article 2(4), is subject to no exception other than self-defence and collective security (see supra 244). When one State uses force unilaterally against another, even within its own territory, this must be based on the exercise of self-defence against an armed attack.

[60] Christian Henderson, *The Use of Force and International Law* (Cambridge University Press, 2018), 68.

[61] Kreß, n. 2, 434.

distinction between the previous example discussed (use of force by a State within its own territory in response to incursions by armed forces of another State) and law enforcement against foreign individuals, merchant vessels and civilian aircraft. He argues this is different to the previous categories because there is a clear legal basis in other legal frameworks such as law of the sea, air law and the UN Basic Principles on the Use of Force and Firearms by Law Enforcement Officials.[62] Since States must be able to take enforcement measures within their jurisdiction, it does not engage international relations.[63] States generally do not invoke use of force language for measures taken under those regimes, even if they go beyond what is lawful.[64] However, such acts could be a prohibited 'use of force' if it 'directly arises from a dispute between sovereign states'[65] since law enforcement is hierarchical so it cannot apply between sovereign States and thus international relations are engaged.[66]

However, as discussed in further detail in the case study on excessive or unlawful maritime law enforcement and 'use of force' in Chapter 8, the issue is not so straightforward. There is mixed State practice regarding these types of incidents. Whether purported law enforcement against foreign private actors is characterised by States as an unlawful 'use of force' in 'international relations' under article 2(4) depends on a number of factors, including the gravity of the physical means or effects, intention, nexus of the object of the use of force and another State and if there is a political dispute between the States concerned. Such incidents highlight the complex relationship between these different elements of a prohibited 'use of force'. This is explored further in Chapter 8.

Conclusion

In sum, it is generally agreed that the following uses of force by a State are usually in its 'international relations' and therefore fall within the scope of article 2(4):

- Use of force on the territory of another State or against its extraterritorial sovereign manifestations.
- Use of force to reclaim disputed territory not within de facto control.
- Use of force in violation of international demarcation lines.
- Use of force directly arising from a political dispute between States.

62 Ruys, n. 33, 201 ff.
63 *Ibid.*, 202.
64 *Ibid.*, 203.
65 *Ibid.*, 209.
66 *Ibid.*, n. 33, 201.

It is also generally accepted that the following uses of force by a State are not in its 'international relations' and therefore usually fall outside the scope of article 2(4):

- Use of force by a State within its own territory against its own population.
- Use of force by a State in the exercise of its law enforcement jurisdiction against private foreign actors absent other factors (such as an existing international dispute, excessive force, coercive intent, or lack of sufficient connection to law enforcement jurisdiction).
- Use of force by a State against objects with no close association with another State. For non-State objects/targets that do not have a close association with a State, more will be required to bring the act within the scope of article 2(4), such as the presence of other factors including the gravity of the (potential) effects, a pre-existing dispute between States or a coercive intent against a State. The interplay of the various elements of a 'use of force' is discussed in more detail in Chapter 8.

It is controversial whether or under what circumstances the following uses of force by a State are in its 'international relations' and therefore fall within the scope of article 2(4):

- Use of force against entities falling short of Statehood.
- Use of force with no nexus to another State but against an international organisation or on *terra nullius*.
- Use of force within a State's own territory against small-scale incursions by armed forces of another State.
- Use of force by a State in the exercise of its law enforcement jurisdiction against private foreign actors in the presence of additional factors. This is discussed further in Chapter 6.

'AGAINST THE TERRITORIAL INTEGRITY OR POLITICAL INDEPENDENCE OF ANY STATE OR IN ANY OTHER MANNER INCONSISTENT WITH THE PURPOSES OF THE UNITED NATIONS'

Against the Territorial Integrity...

Despite the arguments by some scholars that these terms permit uses of force for a benign purpose,[67] the second part of article 2(4) was introduced to

[67] Kreß, n. 2, 431: 'For an early exposition of this view, see Stone, supra note 6, at 95–96; for a prominent later version, see W. M. Reisman, "Coercion and Self-Determination: Construing Charter Article 2(4)", *American Journal of International Law*, 78 (1984), 642–45.'

ensure the prohibition was all-encompassing. This is made clear in the *travaux préparatoires*.[68] For instance, at the San Francisco Conference, '[t]he Delegate of the United States made it clear that the intention of the authors of the original text was to state in the broadest terms an absolute all-inclusive prohibition; the phrase "or in any other manner" was designed to insure that there should be no loopholes'.[69] This view was later confirmed during the drafting of the 1970 Friendly Relations Declaration. In the 1964 meeting of the Friendly Relations Special Committee, representatives who commented on the term 'against the territorial integrity or political independence of any State' said that this term

> did not limit or circumscribe the prohibition on the threat or use of force contained in the same Article. It had been inserted at the United Nations Conference on International Organization, San Francisco, in order to guarantee the territorial integrity and political independence of small and weak States, and was not intended to mean that one State could use force against another on the pretext that it had no designs on the latter's territorial integrity or political independence but sought to maintain the established constitutional order or to protect a minority, or on any other pretext.[70]

Furthermore, the notion of a permissible use of force for a benign purpose is not supported by State practice, was implicitly rejected by the ICJ[71] and is

[68] Under article 32 of the VCLT,

> [r]ecourse may be had to supplementary means of interpretation, including the preparatory work of the treaty and the circumstances of its conclusion, in order to confirm the meaning resulting from the application of article 31, or to determine the meaning when the interpretation according to article 31:
>
> (*a*) leaves the meaning ambiguous or obscure; or
> (*b*) leads to a result which is manifestly absurd or unreasonable.

[69] Vol. VI, 335. See also Brownlie, n. 51, 267, who draws the same conclusion that the *travaux préparatoires* support a broad reading of this provision: 'The conclusion warranted by the *travaux préparatoires* is that the phrase under discussion was not intended to be restrictive but, on the contrary, to give more specific guarantees to small states and that it cannot be interpreted as having a qualifying effect' (Footnote omitted).

[70] First Report, n. 30, Doc A/5746, para. 37.

[71] In the *Corfu Channel* case, in response to the UK's justification of its minesweeping operation in Albanian territorial waters, the ICJ held that: 'The Court can only regard the alleged right of intervention as the manifestation of a policy of force, such as has, in the past, given rise to the most serious abuses and such as cannot, whatever be the present defects in international organization, find a place in international law' (*Corfu Channel Case (UK v Albania), Merits, Judgment* (1949) ICJ Reports 4, 35). For a legal analysis of this finding arguing that the Court thereby implicitly rejected the argument that a use of force for a benign purpose falls outside the scope of article 2(4), see Claus Kreß, 'The International Court of Justice and the Non-Use

overwhelmingly rejected by scholars.[72] Therefore, an otherwise prohibited use of force cannot be legally justified by arguing that it has a limited purpose.

Consent

This wording of article 2(4) does carve out an exclusion from the prohibition in the case of consent, which is not a circumstance precluding wrongfulness but forms an intrinsic part of the primary rule itself.[73] According to the International Law Commission:

> the consent of the State must be *valid in international law, clearly established, really expressed (which precludes merely presumed consent), internationally attributable to the State and anterior to the commission of the act to which it refers.*[74]

of Force' in Marc Weller (ed), *The Oxford Handbook of the Use of Force in International Law* (Oxford University Press, 2015), 561, 573–4.

[72] Kreß, n. 2, 431. See Kreß for an overview of the different positions on these issues with extensive references. Note that Kreß's analysis is referring to the slightly different formulation that was used in the definition of the crime of aggression in article 8 *bis*(2) of the Rome Statute, which itself is taken from the language used in article 1 of the 1974 Definition of Aggression. That formulation is 'against the sovereignty, territorial integrity or political independence of another State, or in any other manner inconsistent with the Charter of the United Nations'. It mentions 'sovereignty' and is slightly broader by including uses of force 'in any other manner inconsistent with the *Charter* of the United Nations' (emphasis added) rather than only the Purposes of the United Nations.

[73] James Crawford, Second Report on State Responsibility, UN Doc A/CN.4/498/Add.2 (30 April 1999), 12–13, para. 240(b). See also ILA Committee on the Use of Force, 'Final Report on Aggression and the Use of Force' (2018), 18–20. Cf Federica I Paddeu, 'Military Assistance on Request and General Reasons against Force: Consent as a Defence to the Prohibition of the Use of Force' (2020) 7(2) *Journal on the Use of Force and International Law* 227, arguing that consent should be reconstrued as a defence and not part of the primary rule.

[74] (1979) Yearbook of the International Law Commission, vol. 2, Part II, 112. See further Corten, n. 37, 250 ff, who looks at the conditions for lawful military intervention by consent. A matter of some controversy is whether a State may lawfully militarily intervene in an internal conflict within another State at the invitation of the government of that State. This controversy raises two potential issues: the identity of the legitimate government, and whether it is permitted to intervene in such a conflict even with the consent of the central authorities. On these points, see Corten, n. 37, 276–7, 280–1, 284, 287. The purpose of a government's invitation to another State to military intervene on its territory has been argued to be potentially relevant with respect to two contexts: firstly, an internal conflict engaging the right to self-determination, and, secondly, a government which is massively violating the human rights of its own population. For further exposition of these issues, see Kreß, n. 2, 429–31. For a comprehensive general assessment of this topic, see Erika de Wet, *Military Assistance on Request and the Use of Force* (Oxford University Press, 2020).

CONCLUSION

The factors discussed in this chapter delineate the scope and context of the prohibition of the use of force in article 2(4). In other words, they are fundamental contextual elements which must be present in order for a 'use of force' to fall within the scope of article 2(4) and be unlawful under that provision. Accordingly, a 'use of force' must take place within the context of the following fundamental requirements to fall within the scope of article 2(4):

- Two or more States: The use of force must be by a State. It is likely that the object/target of the 'use of force' must have a sufficient nexus to another State for the 'use of force' to be in 'international relations' and fall within the scope of article 2(4).
- In international relations.
- 'Against the territorial integrity or political independence of any state or in any other manner inconsistent with the Purposes of the United Nations'.

From the above analysis of these terms, the following can be concluded regarding acts that fall within and outside the scope of article 2(4):

Uses of force falling outside the scope of article 2(4):

- Use of force by non-UN Member States (although they are bound by the identical customary international law prohibition of the use of force; see Part I).
- Uses of force that are not committed by a State (including indirectly – see discussion of indirect force in Chapter 5) and are not attributable to a State.
- Uses of force not in international relations. It is generally accepted that the following uses of force by a State are not in its 'international relations' and therefore usually fall outside the scope of article 2(4):
  1. Use of force by a State within its own territory against its own population.
  2. Use of force by a State in the exercise of its law enforcement jurisdiction against private foreign actors absent other factors (such as an existing international dispute, excessive force, coercive intent or lack of sufficient connection to law enforcement jurisdiction).
- Use of force falling within an exception to the prohibition recognised in the UN Charter, namely, forcible acts in lawful self-defence or validly authorised by the UN Security Council.
- Use of force that is validly consented to.

Uses of force falling within the scope of article 2(4):

- Use of force on the territory of another State or against its extraterritorial sovereign manifestations.
- Use of force to reclaim disputed territory not within de facto control.
- Use of force in violation of international demarcation lines.
- Use of force directly arising from a political dispute between States.
- Use of force for a benign purpose, provided the other requirements of article 2(4) are met. The limited purpose of the use of force does not exclude it from the scope of this provision.

Uses of force for which it is unclear if they fall within scope of article 2(4):

It is controversial whether or under what circumstances the following uses of force by a State are in its 'international relations' and therefore fall within the scope of article 2(4):

- Use of force against entities falling short of Statehood.
- Use of force with no nexus to another State, such as against an international organisation or on *terra nullius*.
- Use of force by a State within its own territory against small-scale incursions by armed forces of another State.
- Use of force by a State in the exercise of its law enforcement jurisdiction against private foreign actors in the presence of other factors (such as an existing international dispute, excessive force, coercive intent or lack of sufficient connection to law enforcement jurisdiction).

5

Elements of 'Use of Force'

Means

INTRODUCTION

Having interpreted the meaning of the contextual elements of article 2(4) of the UN Charter, the following two chapters will apply a process of textual interpretation to the term 'use of force' in that article. Chapter 5 will firstly set out subsequent agreements regarding article 2(4), and then examine whether 'use of force' means physical/armed force only, and if a particular type of means is required. Chapter 6 will look at the required effects of an unlawful 'use of force', and if gravity and intent are required elements of a 'use of force' under article 2(4).

SUBSEQUENT AGREEMENTS REGARDING ARTICLE 2(4)

Subsequent agreements on the interpretation of the prohibition of the use of force in article 2(4) of the UN Charter include 1970 UN General Assembly (GA) Resolution 2625 (XXV), the Declaration on Principles of International Law concerning Friendly Relations and Co-operation among States in accordance with the Charter of the United Nations ('Friendly Relations Declaration'); the General Assembly's 1974 Definition of Aggression,[1] 1987 General Assembly Resolution 42/22 and the 2005 World Summit Outcome Document. These subsequent agreements may contribute to clarifying the meaning of the treaty[2] and its object and purpose.[3] This may be done by:

[1] UN General Assembly, *Resolution 3314: Definition of Aggression*, UN Doc A/Res/29/3314 (14 December 1974) ('1974 Definition of Aggression').

[2] International Law Commission, 'Draft Conclusions on Subsequent Agreements and Subsequent Practice in Relation to the Interpretation of Treaties', annexed to UN GA Resolution 73/202 (A/RES/73/202, 3 January 2019), conclusion 7(1).

[3] Georg Nolte, 'Second Report on Subsequent Agreements and Subsequent Practice in Relation to the Interpretation of Treaties' UN Doc A/CN.4/671 (International Law Commission, 26 March 2014) ('Nolte Second Report'), 14, para. 27.

- determining whether a special meaning was intended by the treaty parties, and if so, what it is;[4]
- after determining the 'ordinary meaning' of the terms of a treaty, subsequent agreements and subsequent practice may be consulted to determine 'whether such conduct confirms or modifies the preliminary result arrived at by the initial textual interpretation or by other means of interpretation';[5] and
- contributing, 'in their interaction with other means of interpretation, to the clarification of the meaning of a treaty. This may result in narrowing, widening, or otherwise determining the range of possible interpretations, including any scope for the exercise of discretion which the treaty accords to the parties.'[6]

There is debate over whether an international organisation's 'own practice' (such as UN General Assembly and UN Security Council resolutions) should be characterised as a form of subsequent agreement and practice under article 31(3) of the Vienna Convention on the Law of Treaties (VCLT).[7] However, the International Court of Justice (ICJ) has recognised three types of practice that may bear on the interpretation of a constituent instrument of an international organisation (such as the UN Charter):

> (a) the subsequent practice of the parties to constituent instruments of international organizations under articles 31 (3) (b) and 32 of the Vienna Convention; (b) the practice of organs of an international organization; (c) a combination of practice of organs of the international organization of subsequent practice of the parties.[8]

The practice of organs of the international organisation may have a different weight with respect to interpretation than the practice of the parties to the constituent instrument themselves.[9] With respect to (b) the jurisprudence of the ICJ shows that practice of organs of the United Nations such as the General Assembly and the Security Council in the application of the Charter may be relevant as a form of other subsequent practice under article 32 of the VCLT (i.e. as a supplementary means of interpretation),

4 *Ibid.*, 12, para. 21.
5 *Ibid.*, citation omitted.
6 International Law Commission, n. 2, conclusion 7(1).
7 See Georg Nolte, 'Third Report on Subsequent Agreements and Subsequent Practice in Relation to the Interpretation of Treaties' UN Doc A/CN.4/683 (International Law Commission, 7 April 2015) ('Nolte Third Report'), 26–8, paras. 69–73.
8 *Ibid.*, 12, paras. 31 and 32.
9 *Ibid.*, 29–30, paras. 76–78.

independently of the practice or acceptance of all parties to the UN Charter.[10] Such resolutions will carry more weight when they deal with an area for which the burden of obligation falls on those bodies, such as the Security Council determining what is an act of aggression under article 39 of the Charter. But since that is a political rather than a legal determination, it does not have a direct bearing on the interpretation of the term 'use of force' in article 2(4) of the UN Charter.

An example of the practice referred to in (c) is the practice of the UN Security Council and UN General Assembly in the application of the UN Charter that is generally accepted by UN Member States. For example, when a UN Security Council resolution is passed without dissenting votes and is accompanied by the general acceptance of UN Member States, then this may be considered as potentially relevant subsequent conduct confirmed by the practice of the parties demonstrating their agreement regarding the interpretation of the UN Charter under article 31(3)(b) of the VCLT. Nolte observes that the ICJ applied this approach in its *Namibia* Advisory Opinion, where the Court interpreted the term 'concurring votes' in article 27(3) of the UN Charter as including voluntary abstentions 'primarily by relying on the practice of the organ concerned in combination with the fact that it was then "generally accepted" by member States'.[11] Nolte notes that '"[g]eneral acceptance" requires "at a minimum" acquiescence'.[12] If the UN General Assembly or UN Security Council pass a resolution with dissenting votes, this may constitute other subsequent practice as a supplementary means of interpretation under article 32 of the VCLT but not as practice establishing the agreement of the parties regarding the interpretation of the UN Charter under article 31(3) of the VCLT.[13]

[10] *Ibid.*, 16–19, paras. 43–51; see especially *Certain Expenses of the United Nations (Article 17, paragraph 2 of the Charter), Advisory Opinion* (1962) ICJ Reports 151,168:

> Proposals made during the drafting of the Charter to place the ultimate authority to interpret the Charter in the International Court of Justice were not accepted; the opinion which the Court is in course of rendering is an advisory opinion. As anticipated in 1945, therefore, each organ must, in the first place at least, determine its own jurisdiction. If the Security Council, for example, adopts a resolution purportedly for the maintenance of international peace and security and if, in accordance with a mandate or authorization in such resolution, the Secretary-General incurs financial obligations, these amounts must be presumed to constitute 'expenses of the Organization'.

[11] Nolte Third Report, n. 7, 19, para. 52.

[12] *Ibid.*, 30, para. 80, footnote omitted.

[13] *Ibid.*, 30, para. 79.

The decisions of plenary bodies, such as resolutions of the UN General Assembly, may be characterised in certain circumstances as a form of subsequent *agreement* regarding the interpretation of the constituent instrument.[14] Thus, when a UN General Assembly resolution is passed without dissent (e.g. by acclamation), then this may be considered in certain circumstances as a form of subsequent agreement regarding the interpretation of the UN Charter. The ICJ has considered UN General Assembly resolutions when interpreting provisions of the UN Charter but has made clear that mere adoption is not sufficient and has taken into account the attitudes of States towards such resolutions.[15] Since subsequent agreement between the parties is a means of authentic interpretation of the treaty under article 31(3)(a) of the VCLT because it demonstrates the shared understanding of the parties regarding the interpretation of a treaty, UN General Assembly resolutions may be valued as evidence of such a shared understanding when they are passed without objection (i.e. unanimously or by consensus). This is the case with each of the resolutions discussed below.

1970 Friendly Relations Declaration

The most important and comprehensive subsequent agreement of UN Member States on the interpretation of article 2(4) of the UN Charter is the Friendly Relations Declaration, which was adopted on 24 October 1970 by consensus by the UN General Assembly on the twenty-fifth anniversary of the United Nations. Principle 1 of the Declaration proclaims:

> The principle that States shall refrain in their international relations from the threat or use of force against the territorial integrity or political independence of any State, or in any other manner inconsistent with the purposes of the United Nations.

In the elaboration of this principle, UN Member States took a clear position on the interpretation of article 2(4) with respect to its scope of application to include the following: international boundaries, international lines of demarcation such as armistice lines;[16] forcible acts of

[14] *Ibid.*, 24–6, para. 67, with extensive further references.
[15] *Ibid.*
[16] 'Every State has the duty to refrain from the threat or use of force to violate the existing international boundaries of another State or as a means of solving international disputes, including territorial disputes and problems concerning frontiers of States.' Principle 1, para. 4; 'Every State likewise has the duty to refrain from the threat or use of force to violate international lines of demarcation, such as armistice lines, established by or pursuant to an

reprisal;[17] using force to deprive peoples of the right to self-determination;[18] certain forms of interference in civil strife or terrorist acts in another State[19] and military occupation or territorial acquisition resulting from the threat or use of force.[20] (Paragraph 8 of Principle 1 of the Friendly Relations Declaration refers to 'organizing or encouraging the organization of irregular forces or armed bands, including mercenaries, for incursion into the territory of another State', however unlike other paragraphs listed under Principle 1, it does not link the legality of this action to a threat or use of force.[21] Indirect force is discussed in more detail later.) In addition to comprising subsequent agreement of UN Member States on the interpretation of article 2(4), the ICJ relied on the Friendly Relations Declaration in the *Nicaragua* case as an indication of States' *opinio juris* on the existence and content of the customary prohibition of the use of force[22] due to its references to 'all States',[23] 'principle',[24] 'States', 'every State',[25] 'a violation of international law and the Charter'[26] and the statement that '[t]he principles of the Charter

international agreement to which it is a party or which it is otherwise bound to respect. Nothing in the foregoing shall be construed as prejudicing the positions of the parties concerned with regard to the status and effects of such lines under their special régimes or as affecting their temporary character.' Principle 1, para. 5.

17 'States have a duty to refrain from acts of reprisal involving the use of force.' Principle 1, para. 6.

18 'Every State has the duty to refrain from any forcible action which deprives peoples referred to in the elaboration of the principle of equal rights and self-determination of their right to self-determination and freedom and independence.' Principle 1, para. 7.

19 'Every State has the duty to refrain from organizing, instigating, assisting or participating in acts of civil strife or terrorist acts in another State or acquiescing in organized activities within its territory directed towards the commission of such acts, when the acts referred to in the present paragraph involve a threat or use of force.' Principle 1, para. 9.

20 'The territory of a State shall not be the object of military occupation resulting from the use of force in contravention of the provisions of the Charter. The territory of a State shall not be the object of acquisition by another State resulting from the threat or use of force. No territorial acquisition resulting from the threat or use of force shall be recognized as legal.' Principle 1, para. 10.

21 In the case *Certain Activities Carried Out by Nicaragua in the Border Area (Costa Rica v. Nicaragua) and Construction of a Road in Costa Rica along the San Juan River (Nicaragua v. Costa Rica)*, Vice-President Yusuf considered this paragraph in the context of a violation of territorial integrity rather than a use of force: Judgment of 16 December 2015, 2015 ICJ Reports, 665, Declaration of Vice-President Yusuf, 743, para. 8.

22 *Case concerning Military and Paramilitary Activities in and against Nicaragua (Nicaragua v United States of America), Merits, Judgment* (1986) ICJ Reports 14, para. 191.

23 *Ibid.*, 10th preambular paragraph.

24 *Ibid.*, Principle 1.

25 *Ibid.*

26 *Ibid.*, Principle 1, para. 1.

which are embodied in this Declaration constitute basic principles of international law'.[27]

1974 Definition of Aggression

1974 GA Resolution 3314 annexing the Definition of Aggression was adopted by acclamation (consensus) and was the first time that the international community agreed on a definition of aggression.[28] Despite the significance of the 1974 Definition of Aggression, one should be careful about characterising the 1974 Definition as a 'subsequent agreement' regarding the interpretation of article 2(4), since it is actually defining aggression as a guideline for the UN Security Council's political determination. Thomas Bruha argues that because of the politically negotiated nature of the 1974 Definition and its constructive ambiguity, the Definition must be read as a whole and in its context. One cannot extract elements of the 'definition' without taking this into account (as Bruha argues the ICJ did in the *Nicaragua* case). But given the wording in the Definition itself, which refers to uses of force, and the relationship between use of force and aggression – the annex to 1974 GA Resolution 3314 itself notes that 'aggression is the most serious and dangerous form of the illegal use of force'[29] – it is sound to infer a shared agreement or understanding that those acts listed in the Definition constitute 'use of force' under article 2(4)).

1987 GA *Resolution 42/22*

1987 GA Resolution 42/22 (adopted by consensus) was a Declaration on the Enhancement of the Effectiveness of the Principle of Refraining from the Threat or Use of Force in International Relations. This resolution reflects provisions of the 1970 Friendly Relations Declaration regarding

[27] *Ibid.*, para. 3 of Declaration.

[28] See Thomas Bruha, 'The General Assembly's Definition of the Act of Aggression' in Claus Kreß and Stefan Barriga (eds), *The Crime of Aggression: A Commentary* (Cambridge University Press, 2017), 142 for an in-depth analysis of the 1974 Definition of Aggression, including the negotiations leading up to it. Bruha notes the purpose of the 1974 Definition, which began with three groups: non-aligned, pushing for an extensive, legal definition to protect their interests as newly independent States; Western, seeking to make the definition a discretionary guideline for the UN Security Council's political determination of aggression; and the Soviet Union, which was in between the two.

[29] 1974 Definition of Aggression, n. 1, Fifth preambular para.

non-intervention.[30] Like the Friendly Relations Declaration, Resolution 42/22 confirms States' view that the prohibition of the threat or use of force is universal and binding, referring to the prohibition as a 'principle',[31] holding that '[e]very State' has the duty to comply with the prohibition[32] and explicitly stating that '[t]he principle of refraining from the threat or use of force in international relations is universal in character and is binding, regardless of each State's political, economic, social or cultural system or relations of alliance'.[33]

2005 World Summit Outcome Document

The 2005 World Summit at the United Nations Headquarters in New York was attended by over 170 Heads of State and Government. This summit produced and adopted by consensus the 2005 World Summit Outcome Document, which is historically and symbolically important as a united stand by UN Member States to reaffirm their commitment to the UN Charter and its purposes and principles in the face of modern challenges to the international order and human security. The principal importance of the 2005 World Summit Outcome Document for our purposes is that in it, the Member States of the UN 'reaffirm that the relevant provisions of the Charter are sufficient to address the full range of threats to international peace and security'.[34] This affirms States' view of the continued relevance of the collective security framework of the UN Charter. The Outcome Document abridges the wording of article 2(4) in a way that makes it broader, by leaving out

30 'Reaffirming the duty of States to refrain in their international relations from military, political, economic or any other form of coercion aimed against the political independence or territorial integrity of any State'(*ibid.*, preambular para. 18); para. (6) 'States shall fulfil their obligations under international law to refrain from organizing, instigating, or assisting or participating in paramilitary, terrorist or subversive acts, including acts of mercenaries, in other States, or acquiescing in organized activities within their territory directed towards the commission of such acts.'; para. (7) 'States have the duty to abstain from armed intervention and all other forms of interference or attempted threats against the personality of the State or against its political, economic and cultural elements.'; para. (8) 'No State may use or encourage the use of economic, political or any other type of measures to coerce another State in order to obtain from it the subordination of the exercise of its sovereign rights and to secure from it advantages of any kind.'

31 UN General Assembly, *Resolution 42/22: Declaration on the Enhancement of the Effectiveness of the Principle of Refraining from the Threat or Use of Force in International Relations*, UN Doc A/Res/42/22 (18 November 1987), annex, preambular paras. 1 and 1(2).

32 *Ibid.*, annex, para. 1(1).

33 *Ibid.*, annex, para. 1(2).

34 UN General Assembly, 2005 World Summit Outcome, UN Doc A/RES/60/1 (24 October 2005), para. 79.

reference to 'against the territorial integrity or political independence of any State'[35] and replacing reference to 'against the Purposes' of the Charter with the threat or use of force 'inconsistent with the Charter'.[36] The document states[37] '[w]e rededicate ourselves to ... refrain in our international relations from the threat or use of force in any manner inconsistent with *the purposes and principles of the United Nations*'. Although the earlier parts of the sentence which mention upholding the sovereign equality of States and respecting their territorial integrity and political independence could probably be said to implicitly cover the other parts of article 2(4), it is not clear what, if anything, this shows about the way that States interpret article 2(4).

Listed 'Uses of Force' in Subsequent Agreements

The aforementioned UN General Assembly resolutions passed by acclamation (consensus) show that UN Member States have taken a position regarding the interpretation of article 2(4) of the UN Charter with respect to its primary purposes and certain acts which fall within its scope. In particular, the 1970 Friendly Relations Declaration and the 1974 GA Definition of Aggression clearly demonstrate UN Member States' subsequent agreement that the prohibition of the use of force in article 2(4) includes the following specific acts listed in those documents:

- The 'use of force to violate the existing international boundaries of another State or as a means of solving international disputes, including territorial disputes and problems concerning frontiers of States';[38]
- The 'use of force to violate international lines of demarcation, such as armistice lines, established by or pursuant to an international agreement to which it is a party or which it is otherwise bound to respect';[39]
- Forcible acts of reprisal;[40]
- '[A]ny forcible action which deprives peoples referred to in the elaboration of the principle of equal rights and self-determination of their right to self-determination and freedom and independence';[41]

35 *Ibid.*, paras. 5 and 77.
36 *Ibid.*, para. 77.
37 *Ibid.*, para. 5, emphasis added.
38 Friendly Relations Declaration, Principle 1, para. 4.
39 *Ibid.*, Principle 1, para. 5.
40 *Ibid.*, Principle 1, para. 6.
41 *Ibid.*, Principle 1, para. 7.

- '[M]ilitary occupation resulting from the use of force in contravention of the provisions of the Charter';[42]
- Acquisition of the territory of a State resulting from the threat or use of force;[43]
- 'The invasion or attack by the armed forces of a State of the territory of another State, or any military occupation, however temporary, resulting from such invasion or attack, or any annexation by the use of force of the territory of another State or part thereof';[44]
- 'Bombardment by the armed forces of a State against the territory of another State or the use of any weapons by a State against the territory of another State';[45]
- 'The blockade of the ports or coasts of a State by the armed forces of another State';[46]
- 'An attack by the armed forces of a State on the land, sea or air forces, or marine and air fleets of another State';[47]
- 'The use of armed forces of one State which are within the territory of another State with the agreement of the receiving State, in contravention of the conditions provided for in the agreement or any extension of their presence in such territory beyond the termination of the agreement'.[48]
- The following forms of indirect uses of force are also prohibited:
  - 'The sending by or on behalf of a State of armed bands, groups, irregulars or mercenaries, which carry out acts of armed force against another State of such gravity as to amount to the acts listed above, or its substantial involvement therein.[49]
  - 'The action of a State in allowing its territory, which it has placed at the disposal of another State, to be used by that other State for perpetrating an act of aggression against a third State'.[50]

The 1974 Definition of Aggression shows that UN Member States interpret the concept of 'armed force' quite broadly. However, these subsequent agreements of UN Member States leave unclear whether article 2(4) prohibits 'armed' force only, and what the elements of a prohibited 'use of force' are.

[42] *Ibid.*, Principle 1, para. 10.
[43] *Ibid.*
[44] 1974 Definition of Aggression, n. 1, art. 3(a).
[45] *Ibid.*, art. 3(b).
[46] *Ibid.*, art. 3(c).
[47] *Ibid.*, art. 3(d).
[48] *Ibid.*, art. 3(e).
[49] *Ibid.*, art. 3(g).
[50] *Ibid.*, art. 3(f).

As there are no statements in the *travaux préparatoires* that a special meaning of the term 'use of force' was intended by the parties under article 31(4) of the VCLT, Chapters 5 and 6 will now examine the ordinary meaning of this term.

ORDINARY MEANING

According to article 111 of the UN Charter, the Chinese,[51] French,[52] Russian,[53] English[54] and Spanish[55] texts are equally authentic. However, all of these language versions employ the same terms for 'use of force' and do not appear to add any further connotations to this term which could assist with shedding light on its interpretation.[56]

According to the Oxford English Dictionary (OED), the noun 'use' means '[t]he act of putting something to work, or employing or applying a thing, for any (esp. a beneficial or productive) purpose; the fact, state, or condition of being put to work, employed, or applied in this way; utilization or appropriation, esp. in order to achieve an end or pursue one's purpose'.[57]

51 各会员国在其国际关系上不得使用威胁或武力，或以与联合国宗旨不符之任何其他方法，侵害任何会员国或国家之领土完整或政治独立。The Chinese text emphasises 'states' ('all member states' and 'any member states or states') and re-orders the two final subclauses, but these differences do not appear to change the meaning of the text. (I thank Yuwen Fan for her translation of the Chinese text into English and her observations.)

52 Les Membres de l'Organisation s'abstiennent, dans leurs relations internationales, de recourir à la menace ou à l'emploi de la force, soit contre l'intégrité territoriale ou l'indépendance politique de tout État, soit de toute autre manière incompatible avec les buts des Nations Unies.

53 Все Члены Организации Объединенных Наций воздерживаются в их международных отношениях от угрозы силой или ее применения как против территориальной неприкосновенности или политической независимости любого государства, так и каким-либо другим образом, несовместимым с Целями Объединенных Наций.

54 All Members shall refrain in their international relations from the threat or use of force against the territorial integrity or political independence of any state, or in any other manner inconsistent with the Purposes of the United Nations.

55 Los Miembros de la Organización, en sus relaciones internacionales, se abstendrán de recurrir a la amenaza o al uso de la fuerza contra la integridad territorial o la independencia política de cualquier Estado, o en cualquier otra forma incompatible con los Propósitos de las Naciones Unidas.

56 The Russian language version of article 2(4) does appear to slightly differ from the others with respect to the term 'against the territorial integrity': против территориальной неприкосновенности. Неприкосновенность. Here, the translation for 'integrity' would mean 'inviolability'. This carries a different connotation, as the term 'territorial integrity' indicates unity or wholeness of the territory rather than only 'inviolability' of State borders. (I am indebted to Nino Burdiladze for her translation of the Russian text and these observations.)

57 'Use, N', *OED Online* (Oxford University Press, December 2018), www.oed.com/view/Entry/220635.

The following definition of 'force' in the OED most closely corresponds to the way this term is employed in article 2(4):

> '5. a. Physical strength or power exerted upon an object; *esp.* the use of physical strength to constrain the action of persons; violence or physical coercion'.
>
> 'b. *esp.* in phr. ***by force*** = by employing violence, by violent means, also †under compulsion. †Formerly also ***through, with, of force***'
>
> 'c. *spec.* in *Law*: Unlawful violence offered to persons or things'.[58]

This naturally leads to the question of whether the term 'force' in article 2(4) is confined to this 'ordinary meaning' of physical/violent means only and whether it requires certain types of physical effects.

MEANS

This section will discuss whether 'force' in article 2(4) of the UN Charter is restricted to particular means, namely, if 'force' means physical/armed force only, if a weapon must be employed, what is considered a 'weapon' and if a release of kinetic energy is required for an act to qualify as a prohibited 'use of force'.

Physical/Armed Force Only?

The role of article 2(4) in the UN collective security system and its primary objective of the maintenance of international peace and security supports interpreting the term 'use of force' as confined to armed/physical force only. This is because forms of non-physical coercion do not directly concern international peace and security but relate more to sovereign equality and the non-intervention principle. Some scholars such as Nikolas Stürchler have argued that the latter (i.e. freedom of choice for States) is not the primary concern of article 2(4). This understanding of article 2(4) excludes non-forcible forms of intervention from the scope of the prohibition of the use of force. This interpretation is further borne out by the following factors: firstly, the choice of the drafters to employ the term 'use of force' to overcome the problems associated with the term 'war'; secondly, references to 'force' elsewhere in the UN Charter refer to 'armed force'; and thirdly, that economic

[58] 'Force, n.1', *OED Online* (Oxford University Press, December 2018), www.oed.com/view/Entry/72847#eid4006249.

coercion was explicitly rejected by the drafters as a form of 'force' falling under article 2(4).

Regarding the choice of term 'use of force', as discussed earlier, the historical context of article 2(4) was intended to address the problems of the Covenant of the League of Nations and the Kellogg–Briand Pact, which used the restrictive notion of 'war'.[59] References to 'armed force' in the UN Charter further support this interpretation of force (referred to later). In particular, preambular paragraph 7 of the Charter refers to armed force, stating one of the goals of the Charter is 'to ensure, by the acceptance of principles and the institution of methods, that armed force shall not be used, save in the common interest'. With respect to other forms of non-forcible coercion such as economic coercion, the proposal of the Brazilian delegate to the San Francisco conference to include 'the threat or use of economic measures' under article 2(4) was rejected by the drafting committee.[60] The counter-argument, that the explicit reference to 'armed force' in other parts of the UN Charter might indicate that the absence of the qualifier 'armed' in article 2(4) shows that the drafters did not intend to restrict the term 'force' in this way, is less plausible if the latter provision is read in its historical context and in the light of the exclusion of economic coercion. It is then far more persuasive to hold that 'force' in article 2(4) only refers to *armed* force.

The question of whether article 2(4) extends to other forms of coercion was re-opened and subject to extensive debates in the drafting of the Friendly Relations Declaration, but there was ultimately no subsequent agreement overturning the drafter's clear intent on this point. In each session of the

59 See Part I discussion of how the customary international law rule arose. See also Rüdiger Wolfrum, 'Preamble' in Bruno Simma et al (eds), *The Charter of the United Nations: A Commentary* (Oxford University Press, 3rd ed, 2012), vol. I, 45. See Olivier Corten, *The Law against War: The Prohibition on the Use of Force in Contemporary International Law* (Hart Publishing, 2010), 52, footnote 13 for a list of statements by States in the debates in the UN General Assembly preceding votes on major resolutions on the boundaries of the prohibition, reaffirming that article 2(4) prohibits all measures 'short of war'.

60 UNCIO, vol. VI, UN Doc 784/I/1/27 (5 June 1945), 335. But note, UNCIO, vol. VI p400, UN Doc 885/I/1/34 (9 June 1945), Report of the Rapporteur of Committee 1 to Commission I, regarding article 2(4):

> The Committee likes it to be stated in view of the Norwegian amendment to the same paragraph that the unilateral use of force or similar coercive measures is not authorized or admitted. The use of arms in legitimate self-defense remains admitted and unimpaired. The use of force, therefore, remains legitimate only to back up the decisions of the Organization at the start of a controversy or during its solution in the way that the Organization itself ordains. The intention of the Norwegian amendment is thus covered by the present text.

Special Committee,[61] delegates debated this issue and could not reach agreement about the definition of 'force' in article 2(4) and, in particular, whether it included armed force only or also other forms of pressure threatening the territorial integrity or political independence of a State, such as economic coercion. Many (mostly newly independent and developing) States were in favour of a broad interpretation of 'force' to include not only armed force but also economic, political and other forms of pressure or coercion.[62] Several proposals included provisions to the effect that the term 'force' should be interpreted broadly to cover not only armed force but also economic, political and other forces of pressure,[63] particularly those which 'had the effect of undermining the territorial integrity or political independence of a State'.[64] Some States in favour of a broad interpretation of the term 'force' beyond armed force were nevertheless cautious about including other forms of

61 In particular, the 1967 session of the Special Committee extensively discussed 'economic, political and other forms of pressure or coercion': Third Report of the Special Committee on Principles of International Law concerning Friendly Relations and Co-operation among States, UN Doc A/6799 (26 September 1967) ('Third Report'), see para. 51 ff for summary of debate.

62 See First Report of the Special Committee on Principles of International Law concerning Friendly Relations and Co-operation among States, UN Doc A/5746 (16 November 1964) ('First Report'), annex B, p99 section D: India (SR.3, pp. 7, 8, SR.17, p4), Czechoslovakia (SR.4, p6, SR.8, pp.4–6), Yugoslavia (SR.4, p.9, SR.9, pp.20–21, SR.17, pp.5–9) Nigeria, (SR.4, p.10, SR.7, p.23), Union of Soviet Socialist Republics (SR.5, p.8, SR.14, pp.10–11), Ghana (SR.5, p.17, SR.10, p.14), Romania (SR.7, p.17, SR.16, pp.4–5), United Arab Republic (SR.8, p.9), Poland (SR.9, p.8), Madagascar (SR.9, p.17), and Burma (SR.9, pp.18–19). Fifth Report of the Special Committee on Principles of International Law concerning Friendly Relations and Co-operation among States, UN Doc A/7619 (October 1969) ('Fifth Report'), para. 124 (Nigeria); Sixth Report of the Special Committee on Principles of International Law concerning Friendly Relations and Co-operation among States, UN Doc A/8018 (31 March to 1 May 1970) ('Sixth Report'), para. 114 (Venezuela), 120 (Romania), para. 182 (Nigeria), para. 194 (Czechoslovakia).

63 For example, in the Second Report of the 1966 Special Committee on Principles of International Law concerning Friendly Relations and Co-operation among States, UN Doc A/6230 (27 June 1966) ('Second Report') at para. 64, it was noted that Chile's proposal included provisions 'to the effect that the principle under consideration should be formulated in the light of the practice of States and of the United Nations during the past twenty years and that the term "force" should be broadly understood to cover not only armed force, but also all forms of political, economic or other pressure.'; Third Report, n. 61, UN Doc A/6799, para. 51: 'paragraph 5 of the 1966 proposal of Czechoslovakia and paragraph 2 (b) of the proposal of Algeria, Cameroon, Ghana, India, Kenya, Madagascar, Nigeria, Syria, the United Arab Republic and Yugoslavia … contained provisions to the effect that economic, political and other forms of pressure against the territorial integrity or political independence of any State were prohibited uses of force'.

64 Fourth Report of the Special Committee on Principles of International Law concerning Friendly Relations and Co-operation Among States, UN Doc A/7326 (1968) ('Fourth Report'), para. 50.

coercion within the concept 'in order to avoid enlarging the scope of self-defence'.[65]

Textual arguments in favour of a broad interpretation of 'force' included the terms 'in any other manner' in article 2(4) of the UN Charter,[66] and the fact that since other provisions of the UN Charter refer to 'armed force' (the Preamble and articles 41, 42, 43, 44 and 46) it is to be presumed that the drafters of the Charter did not intend to limit the term 'force' in article 2(4) in this way.[67] The newly independent States emerging after the process of decolonisation noted that they had not had a chance to shape the interpretation of article 2(4) during the San Francisco Conference and argued that 'economic and political forms of pressure were sometimes even more dangerous than armed force, particularly for developing countries'.[68] 'Many representatives emphasized the need to interpret the term "force" in the light of developments subsequent to the drafting of the Charter.'[69] Reference was made to the fact that various international declarations, resolutions and treaties had included a broad understanding of 'force' and recognised the duty of States to refrain from undue pressure, including economic or other forms of pressure, such as the Bandung, Belgrade and Cairo Declarations, UN General Assembly Resolutions 2131 (xx) and 2160 (xxi), the Charter of the Organization of African Unity and article 51 VCLT and the Declaration on the Prohibition of Military, Political or Economic Coercion adopted by the Vienna Conference on the Law of Treaties.[70]

The third report of the Special Committee sums up 'the arguments advanced during the debate in favour of a broad interpretation of the term "force" in formulating the principle of the prohibition of the threat or use of force':

> (a) a considerable number of delegations, both in the Special Committee and in the General Assembly, had expressed themselves in favour of a broad interpretation of the term 'force'; (b) that interpretation was supported by a large sector of opinion and by many writers; (c) that interpretation was recognized in recent international documents such as the Programme for Peace and International Co-operation adopted by the Second Conference of Heads of State or Government of Non-Aligned Countries held at Cairo in

[65] For example, First Report, n. 62, annex B, 99, section D 'Mexico (SR.9, pp.14–15)'; Fourth Report, *ibid.*, para. 127 (Chile); Second Report, n. 63, para. 70.

[66] Fifth Report, n. 62, para. 90.

[67] Second Report, n. 63, para. 66.

[68] Fourth Report, n. 64, para. 52.

[69] Second Report, n. 63, para. 71.

[70] *Ibid.*, para. 73; Fifth Report, n. 62, paras. 52 and 91.

> 1964; (d) it was necessary to take into account the purposes aimed at in drafting the principle, so that the wording adopted could be made appropriate and useful by taking into account the practices and possibilities of international relations as they existed in reality; (e) it would not be realistic to limit the formulation of the principle to an examination of the provisions of the Charter, in an effort to make a distinction between *lex lata* and *lex ferenda*; (f) economic and political forms of pressure were sometimes as dangerous as armed force, particularly for developing countries, new States and peoples under colonial domination, and could accomplish the same illicit results; they constituted a violation of international law and a threat to the maintenance of international peace and co-operation; (g) the existence of international relations based on the free consent of independent sovereign States necessarily implied prohibition both of armed force and of other forms of pressure and coercion; (h) the authors of the Charter, in drafting Article 2, paragraph 4, had used the generic term 'force' without any qualification, and consequently a broad interpretation of that term was perfectly compatible with the text of that provision; (i) there was nothing in the *travaux préparatoires* of the San Francisco Conference to preclude a broad interpretation of 'force' in Article 2, paragraph 4, of the Charter; (j) the very fact that the San Francisco Conference had rejected a Brazilian amendment that a reference to economic forms of pressure be added was proof that such a reference was not considered necessary in view of the broad meaning of the term 'force' in Article 2, paragraph 4, of the Charter; (k) the notion and conditions of self-defence had not yet been clearly defined, and hence no argument for the exclusion of the various forms of pressure could be based on that notion.[71]

On the other hand, many States strongly maintained that 'force' within the meaning of article 2(4) was confined to armed force.[72] Delegates of these States opposed the inclusion of economic, political and other forms of

[71] Third Report, n. 61, para. 55.

[72] See for example, First Report, n. 62, annex B, 99, section D: Argentina (S.R., p. 11), United States of America (SR.3, p. 12, SR.15, pp. 17–18), United Kingdom (SR.5, pp. 12–13, SR.16, p. 12), France (SR.6, pp. 5–6), Italy (SR.7, p. 6), Netherlands (SR.7, p. 8), Lebanon (SR.7, p. 14), Australia (SR.10, p. 7, SR.17, p. 12), Sweden (SR.10, p. 10), Guatemala (SR.14, p. 7) and Venezuela (SR.16, p. 16). Fourth Report, n. 64: para. 114 (USA, stressing that 'the term "force" in Article 2, paragraph 4, of the Charter related exclusively to armed or military force and did not cover non-military acts, even of a coercive character'.); para. 117 (Canada – 'use of force' with respect to acts of reprisal means exclusively 'armed force'); para. 119 (UK); para. 131 (Australia). Fifth Report, n. 62, para. 128 (Italy); Sixth Report, n. 62, para. 106 (Argentina), para. 227 (The United Kingdom of Great Britain and Northern Ireland), para. 256 (USA).

coercion within the scope of article 2(4). The third report of the Special Committee sums up their arguments as follows:

> In their turn, those representatives who considered that the term 'force' in Article 2, paragraph 4, of the Charter meant only armed force put forward the following arguments: (a) the intention of the authors of the Charter was clearly to limit the term 'force' to armed force; (b) the *travaux préparatoires* of the Charter argued against those who held that, because the term 'force' in Article 2, paragraph 4, was not qualified by the adjective 'armed', that term should be given a broad interpretation which covered other forms of pressure; (c) the San Francisco Conference rejected a Brazilian amendment designed to broaden the prohibition laid down in Article 2, paragraph 4, by adding the words 'and the threat or use of economic measures'; (d) the very fact that Brazil had found it necessary to submit its amendment was proof, and the rejection of that amendment conclusive proof of the meaning which should be given to the word 'force' in Article 2, paragraph 4, of the Charter; (e) in Article 44 of the Charter the term 'force' was also used without any qualification, and there was no doubt that it referred exclusively to armed force; (f) if Article 2, paragraph 4, was analysed in the context of the other provisions of the Charter, the legal conclusion reached was that the term 'force' used in that paragraph could be interpreted only to mean armed force; (g) a broad interpretation of the term 'force' in Article 2, paragraph 4, of the Charter would completely alter the existing relationship between that Article and the provisions of Chapter VII of the Charter; (h) a broad interpretation of the term 'force' in Article 2, paragraph 4 would also imply a broader interpretation of the inherent right of individual or collective self-defence provided for in Article 51 of the Charter, although it was obvious that the protection established in that Article was intended to operate solely in the case of the threat or illegitimate use of force and until such time as the Security Council had taken the necessary steps to maintain international peace and security; (i) a broad interpretation of the term 'force' would undermine the integrity of the Charter as a legal instrument – an outcome which could not be accepted on the pretext of progressive development; (j) any attempt to amend the Charter must be made in accordance with the procedure laid down in Article 108; (h) most writers supported a limitative interpretation of the term 'force' in Article 2, paragraph 4, of the Charter.[73]

It was also argued that 'apart from basic legal objections to the inclusion of economic and political pressures in the definition of force, there was no legally satisfactory definition of economic and political pressures'.[74]

[73] Third Report, n. 61, para. 56. For further elaboration of arguments, see also Second Report, n. 63, paras. 67–69; Fourth Report, n. 64, para. 51; Fifth Report, n. 62, para. 92.

[74] Second Report, n. 63, para. 75.

The Friendly Relations Declaration left open the issues of whether a prohibited use of force must be 'armed', and whether coercion falls within the scope of the prohibition. Although the Declaration was adopted by acclamation (consensus), seventy-nine delegations made statements on the formulation of the draft declaration at the time of its adoption,[75] and the Rapporteur of the Sixth Committee, Mr Owada, noted that 'the text of the declaration should be read in conjunction with the statements made for the record which are included in the relevant part of the summary records of the Sixth Committee, contained in documents A/C.6/SR.1178 to 1184'.[76] The delegate for the UK, Sir Vincent Evants, drew

> attention to the statements summarized in paragraphs 90 to 273 of the Special Committee's report [A/8018] and in the summary records of the 1178th to 1184th meetings of the Sixth Committee. Individual delegations have made it clear that the acceptance of the declaration by their Governments is subject to the views and positions there expressed and the declaration must consequently be read in conjunction with [those] records.[77]

In particular, the delegate for Nigeria, Mr Shittabey, on behalf of the African Group of States expressed regret over 'the Committee's failure to accept the legitimate notion that the expression "force" as employed in the principle of the non-use of force denotes economic and political pressures as well as every kind of armed force'.[78]

In the text of the adopted Declaration, the prohibition of coercion is mentioned twice, firstly in the ninth preambular paragraph which '*[r]ecall[s]* the duty of States to refrain in their international relations from military, political, economic or any other form of coercion aimed against the political independence or territorial integrity of any State' (emphasis added). The prohibition of coercion is also included with respect to the principle of the duty of non-intervention.[79] However, the Special Committee reached no ultimate agreement on the issue of whether the prohibition of the use of force

[75] UN General Assembly, *Verbatim Record of Plenary Meeting No. 1860*, UN Doc A/PV.1860 (6 October 1970), para. 24. Thomas Bruha (n. 28, at 142, 151) observes that these interpretive declarations were 'a kind of substitute for votes'.

[76] UN General Assembly, *Verbatim Record Plenary Meeting No. 1860*, Ibid., para. 25.

[77] *Ibid.*, para. 83.

[78] *Ibid.*, para. 60.

[79] Para. 2: 'No State may use or encourage the use of economic political or any other type of measures to coerce another State in order to obtain from it the subordination of the exercise of its sovereign rights and to secure from it advantages of any kind.'

includes the prohibition of other forms of coercion.[80] Some delegations expressed their understanding that '[t]he forms of coercion referred to in [preambular paragraph 9] were examples of unlawful forms of the threat or use of force, which was prohibited under the Charter',[81] and others criticised the fact that 'the principle concerning the prohibition of political, economic and other forms of coercion' was 'covered only in the preamble and not in the operative part' and considered that it should have been placed in the principle concerning the non-use of force or in the general part of the declaration.[82]

Ultimately the lack of agreement regarding the definition of 'force' with respect to the principle of the non-use of force in the 1970 Friendly Relations Declaration was left unresolved. Accordingly, the 1970 Friendly Relations Declaration does not constitute a subsequent agreement regarding whether or not 'force' in article 2(4) refers to physical/armed force only.

Another potential subsequent agreement regarding whether 'force' in article 2(4) refers to armed/physical force only is the 1974 Definition of Aggression. Article 1 of the 1974 Definition provides that:

> Aggression is the use of armed force by a State against the sovereignty, territorial integrity or political independence of another State, or in any other manner inconsistent with the Charter of the United Nations, as set out in this Definition.[83]

The introduction of the qualifier 'armed' before 'force' is the most significant difference to the text of article 2(4).[84] On first glance, the use of the term

80 First Report, n. 62, para. 42: 'the Special Committee was unable to arrive at a consensus on a comprehensive definition of "force" in view, *inter alia*, of a disagreement as to whether the term embraced political, economic and other forms of pressure'.

81 For example, Sixth Report, n. 62, para. 120, Romania.

82 *Ibid.*, para. 194, Czechoslovakia.

83 The Explanatory note:

> in this Definition the term 'State':
> (A) is used without prejudice to questions of recognition or to whether a State is a member of the United Nations;
> (B) includes the concept of a 'group of States' where appropriate.

84 Bruha, n. 28, 159 sets out the differences between article 1 of the 1974 Definition and article 2 (4) of the UN Charter (footnote omitted):

> The other deviations from article 2(4) of the UN Charter concern the following: explicit mention of the use of 'armed' force; the added reference to 'sovereignty'; the replacement of 'any' state by 'another' state; the clause 'inconsistent with the Charter' instead of 'inconsistent with the purposes of the United Nations'; and the final clause 'as set out in this definition'. Whereas the last two variations are to be seen as additional escape clauses to defend one's own military actions against the accusation of aggression, the others are less significant or of more historical importance: (i) the adjective 'armed'

'armed' tends to bolster the view that article 2(4) of the UN Charter is directed at armed force only, since that article forms part of the collective security framework of the UN (which is also the context of the Definition of Aggression, for the purposes of providing guidance to the UN Security Council in making a determination under article 39 of the Charter). As discussed, the debates leading up to the Friendly Relations Declaration did not resolve the disagreements between States about whether article 2(4) was confined to armed force only, so the use of the qualifier 'armed' in article 1 of the Definition of Aggression could be viewed as a progressive development of international law through the subsequent agreement of the parties regarding the interpretation of article 2(4). Bruha argues that the use of this adjective 'ended the discussion on "economic" or "ideological" aggression, which had lost much of its significance in the atmosphere of détente looming at that time'.[85] However, since article 1 is defining *aggression*, the most serious form of illegal use of force, it does not follow that all illegal uses of force involve *armed* force. Hence, article 1 of the Definition of Aggression does not unequivocally indicate agreement of the UN Member States regarding the interpretation of article 2(4) as referring to armed force only.[86]

In absence of a subsequent agreement regarding the interpretation of 'force' in article 2(4), according to article 32 of the VCLT:

> Recourse may be had to supplementary means of interpretation, including the preparatory work of the treaty and the circumstances of its conclusion, in order to confirm the meaning resulting from the application of article 31, or to determine the meaning when the interpretation according to article 31:
>
> (*a*) leaves the meaning ambiguous or obscure.

Accordingly, given the ambiguity of the text of article 2(4) regarding the meaning of 'force' and in the absence of a subsequent agreement regarding its interpretation, one should revert to the clear drafter's intent expressed in San Francisco by the rejection of the Brazilian proposal to include economic coercion, that 'force' does not extend to other forms of non-armed/non-

before force ended the discussion on 'economic' or 'ideological' aggression, which had lost much of its significance in the atmosphere of détente looming at that time; (ii) the inclusion of the word 'sovereignty' met the respective 'sensibility' of the newly established states of the South, and was considered harmless by the other groups; (iii) likewise, the replacement of 'any' by 'another' state, as already contained in the Soviet and non-aligned countries drafts, was also considered to have no practical impact.

85 *Ibid.*, 159.

86 For a discussion of whether economic coercion is otherwise unlawful under international law, see Antonios Tzanakopoulos, 'The Right to Be Free from Economic Coercion' (2015) 4 *Cambridge Journal of International and Comparative Law* 616.

physical coercion. Despite some earlier scholarly views,[87] the position that 'force' in article 2(4) includes only armed/physical force and excludes other forms of non-armed coercion is today overwhelmingly supported by scholars.[88]

Weapons

The ICJ has confirmed that article 2(4) does 'not refer to specific weapons'; articles 2(4), 51 and 42 of the UN Charter 'apply to any use of force regardless

[87] For example, in the negotiations of the Friendly Relations Special Committee during the discussion on the meaning of 'force' in article 2(4), it was noted that Kelsen 'supported the view that the use of force under Article 2, paragraph 4, of the Charter included both use of arms *and violations of international law which involved an exercise of power in the territorial domain of other States without the use of arms.*' Second Report, n. 63, para. 66, citing Hans Kelsen, *The Law of the United Nations: A Critical Analysis of Its Fundamental Problems* (Stevens, 1950), emphasis added by author. However, Ian Brownlie (*International Law and the Use of Force by States* (Clarendon, 1963)) argued in response to Kelsen that:

> It is true that the travaux préparatoires do not indicate that the phrase applied only to armed force but there is no evidence either in the discussions at San Francisco or in state or United Nations practice that it bears the meaning suggested by Kelsen. Indeed, in view of the predominant view of aggression and the use of force in the previous twenty years it is very doubtful if it was intended to have such a meaning.
>
> (361 ff, citation omitted)

But interestingly, Brownlie argued that although 'it is very doubtful if [article 2(4)] applies to economic measures of a coercive nature', 'it is correct to assume that paragraph 4 applies to force other than armed force' (footnotes omitted).

[88] For example, Robert Kolb, *Ius contra bellum: Le droit international relatif au maintien de la paix: précis* (Helbing & Lichtenhahn, 2e éd, 2009), 246; Tom Ruys, 'The Meaning of "Force" and the Boundaries of the *Jus Ad Bellum*: Are "Minimal" Uses of Force Excluded from UN Charter Article 2 (4)?' (2014) 108(2) *American Journal of International Law* 159, 163; Albrecht Randelzhofer and Oliver Dörr, 'Article 2(4)' in Bruno Simma et al (eds), *The Charter of the United Nations: A Commentary* (Oxford University Press, 3rd ed, 2012), 200, 208, MN16; Claus Kreß, 'The State Conduct Element' in Claus Kreß and Stefan Barriga (eds), *The Crime of Aggression: A Commentary* (Cambridge University Press, 2017), 412; Mary Ellen O'Connell, 'The Prohibition of the Use of Force' in Nigel D White and Christian Henderson (eds), *Research Handbook on International Conflict and Security Law:* Jus ad Bellum, Jus in Bello *and* Jus post Bellum (Elgar, 2013), 89, 101; Christian Henderson, *The Use of Force and International Law* (Cambridge University Press, 1 ed., 2018), 55: the *travaux préparatoires* of the UN Charter, subsequent resolutions and subsequent State practice 'would seem to confirm that the prohibition is targeted towards armed force, to the exclusion of the other types of force.' Of recent scholars who have analysed the concept of 'force' in article 2(4), Corten refrains from stating an opinion about whether the concept of 'force' extends further than armed force, deliberately leaving the question open. Instead, he focuses on whether there is a threshold for conduct to qualify as a 'use of force' as opposed to a 'simple police measure', arguing in the affirmative.

of the weapons employed'.[89] The ICJ's view has been affirmed by States in the comment to article 3(b) of the 1974 Definition of Aggression. Article 3(b) 1974 Definition of Aggression lists as an act of aggression: 'Bombardment by the armed forces of a State against the territory of another State or *the use of any weapons* by a State against the territory of another State' (emphasis added). The comment annotated to article 3(b) refers to paragraph 20 of the 1974 GA Special Committee report, which states: 'the Special Committee agreed that the expression "any weapons" is used without making a distinction between conventional weapons, weapons of mass destruction and any other kind of weapon.' This makes clear States' agreement that at least with respect to aggression (and there is no apparent reason it should not extend to all illegal uses of force), the type of weapon used does not affect the lawfulness of the use of force under the *jus contra bellum*. Although explicitly referring to use of weapons, this term is broadly understood in the annotated comment of the Special Committee. It could also further be argued that as article 3(b) of the 1974 Definition refers to the most serious uses of force (i.e. aggression), it is not necessary that all uses of force (those below the threshold of an act of aggression) should require the employment of a weapon. In any event, the ICJ's well-known statement does not explicitly state that a weapon must be employed for an act to fall under article 2(4) of the UN Charter, merely that no specific weapon is referred to by article 2(4) and that article 2(4) applies 'to any use of force regardless of the weapons employed'. Although this does imply that some kind of weapon should be employed, it is not explicitly stated. Apparently, then, the type of weapon is not relevant to whether an act falls under the scope of article 2(4). But this still leaves the question: is the use of a weapon required at all for an act to fall under the prohibition of the use of force in article 2(4), and if so, what is a 'weapon'?

Is Use of a 'Weapon' Required by Article 2(4)?

The question of whether a 'weapon' is required by article 2(4) and the definition of 'weapon' is particularly relevant to new forms of technology that may be used to commit acts of violence or create a military effect, such as cyber operations (e.g. to attack satellite systems by spoofing telemetry data),[90]

[89] *Legality of the Threat or Use of Nuclear Weapons, Advisory Opinion* (1996) ICJ Reports 226 ('*Nuclear Weapons*'), para. 39.

[90] Kazuto Suzuki, 'A Japanese Perspective on Space Deterrence and the Role of the U.S.-Japan Alliance and Deterrence in Outer Space' in Scott W Harold et al (eds), *The U.S.-Japan Alliance and Deterring Gray Zone Coercion in the Maritime, Cyber, and Space Domains* (RAND Corporation, 2017), 91–7: 'Spoofing is a technique to provide false information about a satellite's location, position, and health (in this case, its mechanical condition). It can be

the use of radio frequencies (for jamming and disrupting space systems including satellite signals – discussed further below), or an electromagnetic pulse to damage electrical power and control systems, which could lead to the meltdown of a nuclear reactor.[91] Could these means be considered 'weapons', and is the use of a weapon required by article 2(4)? Of course, textually, in article 2(4) there is no mention of weapons. Any requirement for a 'use of force' to be effected by a 'weapon' must therefore derive from the interpretation of the term 'use of force' in that provision. As seen earlier, the ordinary meaning of the term also does not require the use of weapons but merely 'physical strength or power exerted upon an object; *esp.* the use of physical strength to constrain the action of persons; violence or physical coercion' and 'violent means'.[92]

What Is a 'Weapon'?

The answer to whether a 'use of force' requires the use of a weapon is made clearer when one considers what a 'weapon' is. Some objects (conventional weapons, weapons of mass destruction) are clearly understood to be weapons because they are created, designed and employed to achieve physical damage. But almost anything can achieve physical damage depending on how it is used – so it is either its employed function (which could entail an element of hostile intent) and/or its effect (the harm or damage caused) that determines its character as a 'weapon'. As Christian Henderson notes, '[t]he design of an object as a weapon does not appear to be the determining factor as to whether an action constitutes "force"; rather a weapon is instead "a thing designed *or used* for inflicting bodily harm or physical damage"'.[93] Take the example of an unarmed ballistic missile, such as the Hwasong-12 ballistic missiles that it is believed North Korea launched on 28 August and 15 September 2017 over Hokkaido, Japan.[94] These appear to be single-stage intermediate-range ballistic missile designed to deliver a payload of a single (conventional or nuclear)

done by either hacking satellite frequencies or providing false signals to ground station networks', which 'can direct the satellite onto a collision course with another satellite'.

91 This possibility was mentioned by the ICJ in its *Nuclear Weapons* Advisory Opinion, n. 89, para. 35, though in the context of the electromagnetic pulse generated by nuclear weapons.

92 'Force, n.1', *OED Online*, n. 58.

93 Henderson, n. 88, 56, citing the OED with emphasis added and *Black's Law Dictionary* for the definition of 'weapon'. He also notes the Stuxnet attack and that 'a computer may be used as a weapon for inflicting physical damage.' 57, citation omitted.

94 Arms Control Association, 'Chronology of US-North Korean Nuclear and Missile Diplomacy' (2018), www.armscontrol.org/factsheets/dprkchron.

warhead.[95] An intermediate or long-range ballistic missile is a large, high-speed rocket-fuel propelled projectile and so, even unarmed, could be employed as a 'weapon'. On the other hand, the unarmed missiles themselves are weapon *delivery systems* that do not actually carry weapons. In other words, an unarmed missile does not belong to the category of conventional weapon, but it has features that allow it to be employed in a way that will achieve the same effect as conventional weapons if it strikes a target (namely, the kinetic energy of the missile will be transferred to the object that it strikes; the friction will ignite the rocket fuel and the missile will explode). Therefore, to be employed as a weapon, an unarmed ballistic missile must have a physical effect, which it would only have by actually striking a target (as opposed to its usual function and effect of describing a ballistic trajectory and landing in water).[96] Therefore, it is not helpful to speak of 'weapons', since in the discussion of what is a 'weapon' and whether use of a 'weapon' is required, 'weapons' is really a signifier standing for other potential requirements for an act to constitute a prohibited use of force under article 2(4), namely, kinetic/physical means, kinetic/physical effects, object of harm, directness of harm and possibly, hostile intent and gravity. These elements will now be considered.

Kinetic/Physical Means

'Kinetic' is defined as '[p]roducing or causing motion'.[97] Although the scholarly literature often refers to 'kinetic force', it is more accurate to speak of *kinetic energy* and the transfer or release of kinetic energy to other objects. In conventional weapons, the transfer of kinetic energy occurs when, for example, a bullet that is discharged from a firearm strikes an object and transfers its kinetic energy to that object in the form of kinetic energy and heat, causing physical damage. Since the prohibition of the use of force in article 2(4) undoubtedly covers the use of chemical, biological and nuclear

95 38 North, 'A Quick Technical Analysis of the Hwasong-12' (19 May 2017), www.38north.org/2017/05/hwasong051917/.

96 In the absence of any physical effect, the missile passing through airspace would not violate article 2(4) because there is no use of armed/physical force. It is more likely that an unarmed ballistic missile passing through another State's airspace would be denounced as a violation of UN Security Council resolutions (in the case of North Korea), a violation of sovereignty and possibly responded to as an imminent armed attack (i.e. shot down). If the missile does not land or hit any target within the State it is overflying, then in the absence of physical effect arguably it would not be a violation of the prohibition of the use of force in article 2(4).

97 'Kinetic, Adj. and N', *OED Online* (Oxford University Press, December 2018), www.oed.com/view/Entry/103498.

weapons,[98] a kinetic release of energy is clearly not always required for an act to fall within the scope of the prohibition. Other examples that may fall under the category of forcible acts through employing means other than the release of kinetic energy may include cyber operations;[99] certain types of interference with space systems such as 'deliberate interference and "soft kill" techniques against satellites, such as laser dazzling and radio frequency jamming'[100] or spoofing;[101] non-conventional weapons such as chemical, biological or nuclear weapons;[102] use of the environment as a weapon[103] such as diverting a river or spreading fire across a border; and other measures such as contaminating a water source, releasing harmful substances into the air and expulsion of populations.[104]

98 Brownlie considers whether 'weapons which do not involve any explosive effect with shock waves and heat involves a use of force [such as] bacteriological, biological, and chemical devices such as poison gas and "nerve gases".' These could be regarded as a use of force on two grounds, firstly that they are 'commonly referred to as "weapons"', and, secondly, 'the fact that these weapons are employed for the destruction of life and property, and are often described as "weapons of mass destruction".' Brownlie, n. 87, 362.

99 For an overview, see Marco Roscini, *Cyber Operations and the Use of Force in International Law* (Oxford University Press, 2014).

100 Dean Cheng, 'Space Deterrence, the U.S.-Japan Alliance, and Asian Security: A U.S. Perspective', in Harold et al, n. 90, 74, 78.

101 Suzuki, n. 90, 97.

102 On the characteristics and effects of nuclear weapons, see *Nuclear Weapons* Advisory Opinion, n. 89, para. 35:

> The Court has noted the definitions of nuclear weapons contained in various treaties and accords. It also notes that nuclear weapons are explosive devices whose energy results from the fusion or fission of the atom. By its very nature, that process, in nuclear weapons as they exist today, releases not only immense quantities of heat and energy, but also powerful and prolonged radiation. According to the material before the Court, the first two causes of damage are vastly more powerful than the damage caused by other weapons, while the phenomenon of radiation is said to be peculiar to nuclear weapons. These characteristics render the nuclear weapon potentially catastrophic. The destructive power of nuclear weapons cannot be contained in either space or time. They have the potential to destroy all civilization and the entire ecosystem of the planet. The radiation released by a nuclear explosion would affect health, agriculture, natural resources and demography over a very wide area. Further, the use of nuclear weapons would be a serious danger to future generations. Ionizing radiation has the potential to damage the future environment, food and marine ecosystem, and to cause genetic defects and illness in future generations.

See also the Dissenting Opinion of Judge Weeramantry, 468.

103 On ecological aggression, see Dissenting Opinion of Judge Weeramantry in *Nuclear Weapons* Advisory Opinion, *ibid.*, 503.

104 Brownlie, n. 87, 362–3, footnotes omitted: 'More difficult to regard as a use of force are deliberate and forcible expulsion of population over a frontier, release of large quantities of water down a valley, and the spreading of fire through a built up area or woodland across a

Not all of these examples are necessarily 'uses of force' within the meaning of article 2(4); this is merely to illustrate the different means through which it is possible to create physical effects without the kinetic release of energy typically associated with a conventional weapon. One factor that may contribute to the characterisation of some of these non-'kinetic' means as a 'use of force' is indeed their *effect*. In sum, physical means are not essential for an act to be characterised as a 'use of force' within the meaning of article 2(4) but rather a certain physical effect. Henderson argues that 'a consideration of the *effects* of the action takes on a greater importance the further one moves away from what we might consider to be conventional weapons'.[105] This approach also coincides with the Tallinn Manual's commentary on the definition of the use of force with respect to cyber operations, which sets out indicative factors for whether a cyber operation is a 'use of force', focusing on its effects rather than its means.[106]

Indirect Use of Force

In addition, with respect to means, the 1970 Friendly Relations Declaration and the 1974 GA Definition of Aggression clearly demonstrate UN Member States' subsequent agreement that the prohibition of the use of force in article 2(4) includes the following forms of indirect uses of force: 'The action of a State in allowing its territory, which it has placed at the disposal of another State, to be used by that other State for perpetrating an act of aggression against a third State';[107] 'The sending by or on behalf of a State of armed bands, groups, irregulars or mercenaries, which carry out acts of armed force against another State of such gravity as to amount to the acts listed above, or its substantial involvement therein';[108] and 'organizing or encouraging the organization of irregular armed forces or armed bands, including mercenaries, for incursion into the territory of another State'.[109] These refer to indirectness of means, rather than of effects, and are discussed further in Chapter 7 (anomalous examples of 'use of force').

frontier.' See also UN Security Council Debates, *1606th Meeting* (4 December 1971), para. 161 in which India claimed that mass expulsions (India/Bangladesh) were a use of force.

105 Henderson, n. 88, 59, for example, cyber attacks and the arguments of some scholars that the physical effects are what count.

106 Michael N Schmitt (ed), *Tallinn Manual 2.0 on the International Law Applicable to Cyber Operations* (Cambridge University Press, 2017), Commentary to rule 69, para. 9.

107 1974 Definition of Aggression, n. 1, art. 3(f)).

108 *Ibid.*, art. 3(g).

109 Friendly Relations Declaration, para. 8 of principle 1 (duty to refrain from the threat or use of force).

CONCLUSION

The above textual analysis of article 2(4) of the UN Charter supports the following conclusions regarding the interpretation of the term 'use of force' with respect to its required means:

- ***Means:***
  - *Type of force*: Article 2(4) refers to physical force and not to non-physical forms of coercion.
  - *Type of weapon*: It is not necessary that a 'weapon' be used; what counts are the (physical) effects.
  - *Kinetic energy*: It is not required that kinetic energy be released.
  - *Physical means*: This is not essential, as what counts are the physical effects.

Chapter 6 will explore the required physical effects of a 'use of force', as well as whether a particular intention is required.

6

Elements of 'Use of Force'

Effects, Gravity and Intention

INTRODUCTION

This chapter will continue the analysis of the meaning of a 'use of force' in article 2(4) of the UN Charter with respect to its required effects, whether there is a gravity threshold for an unlawful use of force, and if a particular intent is required to bring a forcible act within the scope of this provision.

EFFECTS

Building on the previous chapter's conclusions that 'force' in article 2(4) includes physical force (and not non-physical forms of coercion) but that physical means are not necessarily required, this section will show that it is the *effects* of a 'use of force' that are likely to be decisive in its characterisation as such[1] and will analyse the type of effects that are relevant. The following section will evaluate the required nature of the effects of a 'use of force' under article 2 (4) by discussing if the relevant harm is confined to harm to persons and property only, the required level of directness between the act and its harmful effect, whether the effect should be permanent or if temporary effects suffice and if the effect should actually ensue or if merely potential effects count.

Physical Harm to Persons or Objects

Although it is clear that a forcible act that directly results in physical harm to persons or property (and that meets the other requirements of article 2(4)) will

[1] For a different (policy- rather than legal-based) argument that the consequences (i.e. effects) of a 'use of force' are what count, see Michael N Schmitt, 'Computer Network Attack and the Use of Force in International Law: Thoughts on a Normative Framework (1999) 37 *Columbia Journal of Transnational Law* 1998–9, 900–23.

be characterised as a 'use of force' under article 2(4),[2] there is nothing explicit in the text of article 2(4) itself that restricts its scope to physical harm or harm to certain objects. A physical effect may not always be required for an act to constitute a prohibited 'use of force'.[3] However, *non*-physical effects alone (such as psychological, economic or more abstract forms of harm) are not likely to be legally relevant to the determination of whether an act is a 'use of force'. During the 1964 meeting of the Friendly Relations Special Committee, '[i]t was … pointed out that force could not be exercised in the abstract; when used, it was directed against an international legal entity, including its political organization, population and territory'.[4] More abstract forms of harm, such as breaking a diplomatic bag[5] or an unauthorised visit by a Head of State such as the visit by Turkish prime minister Ahmet Davutoglu to visit an Ottoman tomb within the Syrian border on 10 May 2015, which the Syrian government called 'a clear aggression',[6] are unlikely to be widely considered by States as a 'use of force' and will fall instead under other legal principles such as the principle of non-intervention.

Christian Henderson states, '[i]t may also be that humans are neither killed or injured, nor property damaged or destroyed, when the prohibition is engaged'.[7] This is due to the emphasis in article 2(4) on territorial integrity and political independence, which does not require harm to persons or property. This is a similar argument to that in Chapter 4 regarding the interpretation of 'international relations' and whether uses of force against objects with no nexus to another State fall within the scope of the prohibition. The object or target of the 'use of force' can therefore be relevant to both elements: whether the act is in 'international relations' and whether it is in fact

[2] Michael N Schmitt (ed), *Tallinn Manual 2.0 on the International Law Applicable to Cyber Operations* (Cambridge University Press, 2017), commentary to rule 69, para. 8: '[a]cts that injure or kill persons or physically damage or destroy objects are uses of force'.

[3] There are some notable exceptions to the requirement for direct physical effects, such as an unresisted invasion, and potentially, certain forms of non-kinetic and indirect uses of force such as interfering with satellites and jamming or disrupting radio or television signals. These exceptions and their implications for the interpretation of a 'use of force' under article 2(4) are discussed in more detail in Part III.

[4] First Report of the Special Committee on Principles of International Law concerning Friendly Relations and Co-operation among States, UN Doc A/5746 (16 November 1964), para. 37.

[5] Yoram Dinstein, *War, Aggression and Self-Defence* (Cambridge University Press, 5th ed, 2011), 208.

[6] Reuters, 'Turkish Prime Minister's Visit to Tomb in Syria Likely to Anger Damascus' *The Guardian* (11 May 2015), www.theguardian.com/world/2015/may/11/turkish-prime-ministers-visit-to-tomb-in-syria-likely-to-anger-damascus.

[7] Christian Henderson, *The Use of Force and International Law* (Cambridge University Press, 1st ed, 2018), 58–9.

a 'use of force'. A forcible act that targets or causes damage to something other than a person or an object is likely to fall outside the scope of the prohibition on both counts.

Directness

The physical effect of a 'use of force' must be 'sufficiently direct'.[8] The commentary to rule 69 in the Tallinn Manual 2.0 (which defines a 'use of force' with respect to cyber operations) suggests that the criterion of directness relates to States' perception of the military nature of the act, since '[i]n armed actions ... cause and effect are closely related'.[9] Directness here refers not to the time elapsed between the use of force and its effect (since in the case of nuclear weapons[10] or cyber operations[11] for example, some of the most damaging effects may be delayed) but rather to proximity, that is, the lack of intermediate steps between the action and its result. This means that the use of force should be the proximate cause of harm. This would exclude non-physical 'force' such as cyber operations adversely affecting financial markets or the electricity grid. The potential problem with including such acts within the scope of article 2(4) is a lack of sufficient directness of the physical effects, rather than the effects themselves, since clearly interruptions to a power supply of, for instance, a nuclear power plant or a hospital can lead to physical harm to persons and property, or in the case of interruption of power supply or radio signals to a military facility, this could yield a military advantage to the attacking State.

8 Claus Kreß, 'The State Conduct Element' in Claus Kreß and Stefan Barriga (eds), *The Crime of Aggression: A Commentary* (Cambridge University Press, 2017), 412, 425.

9 *Tallinn Manual* 2.0, n. 2, para. 9.

10 Judge Weeramantry notes in his dissenting opinion in the *Legality of the Threat or Use of Nuclear Weapons* Advisory Opinion (1996) ICJ Reports 226, 469 (citation omitted) that:

> Unlike other weapons, whose direct impact is the most devastating part of the damage they cause, nuclear weapons can cause far greater damage by their delayed after-effects than by their direct effects. The detailed technical study, *Environmental Consequences of Nuclear War*, while referring to some uncertainties regarding the indirect effects of nuclear war, states: 'What can be said with assurance, however, is that the Earth's human population has a much greater vulnerability to the indirect effects of nuclear war, especially mediated through impacts on food productivity and food availability, than to the direct effects of nuclear war itself'.

11 A main characteristic of cyber operations is 'that they often produce the intended prejudicial effects indirectly as the consequence of the alteration, deletion, or corruption of data or software or the loss of functionality of infrastructure.' Marco Roscini, *Cyber Operations and the Use of Force in International Law* (Oxford University Press, 2014), 49, citing Harrison Dinniss.

Permanent and Temporary Effects

The text of article 2(4) does not reveal whether the effects of an act must be permanent for it to be characterised as a 'use of force'. The Tallinn Manual 2.0 does not explicitly list permanence of effects as a criterion for characterising a cyber operation as a 'use of force', but the application of its listed criteria (severity, immediacy, directness, invasiveness, measurability of effects, military character, State involvement and presumptive legality) would implicitly include certain cyber operations with only temporary effects, for example, if there is a severe and immediate effect of a military character.[12] Acts which do not cause permanent damage but which could potentially be regarded as a 'use of force' include cyber operations such as Denial of Service[13] and non-kinetic, non-cyber operations that interfere with satellites such as dazzling with lasers, electromagnetic interference for orbital jamming, terrestrial jamming, hijacking, spoofing or scanning.[14] For instance, Kazuto Suzuki notes that

> [j]amming space-based or terrestrial receivers of satellite signals by overwhelming them with energy is one way to interfere with space-based communication, GPS signals, and radio frequency sensors. In 2013, for example, North Korea directed a very strong radio frequency signal toward South Korea to disrupt GPS signals. This mass-scale jamming caused huge confusion for air traffic and other vital socioeconomic infrastructures.[15]

It is not clear if these acts which cause temporary physical effects would be considered uses of force by States. For instance, in response to further GPS disruption by the DPRK in 2016, South Korea wrote to the UN Security Council that '[t]he GPS jamming by DPRK is an act of provocation that poses a threat to the security of the Republic of Korea'[16] but did not invoke the

[12] *Tallinn Manual* 2.0, n. 2, commentary to rule 69, para. 9.

[13] 'The non-availability of computer system resources to their users. A denial of service can result from a "cyber operation" ...' *ibid*., 564.

[14] Space Security Index, *Electromagnetic Interference with Space Systems* (November 2020), https://spacesecurityindex.org/2020/11/electromagnetic-interference-with-space-systems/.

[15] Kazuto Suzuki, 'A Japanese Perspective on Space Deterrence and the Role of the U.S.-Japan Alliance and Deterrence in Outer Space', in Scott W Harold et al (eds), *The U.S.-Japan Alliance and Deterring Gray Zone Coercion in the Maritime, Cyber, and Space Domains* (RAND Corporation, 2017), 91, 97.

[16] *Letter dated 5 April 2016 from the Permanent Representative of the Republic of Korea to the United Nations addressed to the President of the Security Council* (5 April 2016) UN Doc S/2016/315, para. 2.

language of article 2(4) of the UN Charter or the right of self-defence under article 51. Uses of force which have only temporary effects are not excluded from a textual interpretation of article 2(4), but it remains to be seen whether subsequent practice of States will demonstrate their agreement regarding such an interpretation. Significant problems of attribution for these types of non-kinetic operations may complicate State's response and legal characterisation of these acts.

It is interesting to consider whether acts with temporary effects would require a higher gravity threshold (or some other factor) to qualify as a prohibited use of force; in the aforementioned examples of cyber attacks and interference with satellites, it is the gravity (e.g. military nature) of the effects or of the potential effects (e.g. in the case of GPS disruption, potential aviation disasters) that is important rather than the actual direct (temporary) damage/disruption of function. With increasing reliance by States on satellite technology (for instance, the reliance of the United States on satellite technology with respect to its military presence and potential military operations in geographically distant theatres such as the South China Sea[17]), it is entirely plausible that even acts with only a temporary effect of disabling or interfering with space systems may in future be treated by States as violating the prohibition of the use of force. Uses of force in outer space are further analysed and discussed in Chapter 8.

Actual or Potential Effects

The wording of article 2(4) of the UN Charter with respect to the threat or use of force is distinguished from article 51 regarding temporality. The phrase 'if an armed attack occurs' has been the subject of much controversy and debate as to whether it limits the right of self-defence to after an armed attack 'occurs'.[18] However, article 2(4) does not mention effects or temporality at all (which is sensible, given that unlike article 51, it does not define conditions for the exercise of a right) but only refers to the terms 'threat' and 'use' of force. It is therefore textually ambiguous whether any physical effect (i.e. harm) must actually ensue for such acts to fall within the scope of the prohibition of the

[17] Dean Cheng, 'Space Deterrence, the U.S.-Japan Alliance, and Asian Security: A U.S. Perspective' in Harold et al, n. 15, 74, 75.

[18] The International Law Association Committee on the Use of Force's 'Final Report on Aggression and the Use of Force' (2018) ('2018 Report') notes that '[t]he ensuing debate over the legality of anticipatory self-defence has been one of the most hotly contested issues surrounding the right to self-defence under international law' (18 with further references).

use of force, or if it is sufficient if there is a potential for physical effects/harm to result.

State practice is mixed and insufficient to draw a definite conclusion regarding whether potential harmful effects would suffice to constitute a prohibited 'use of force' under article 2(4). There are some notable examples of merely potential effects being treated as a 'use of force' and even an 'armed attack', such as the attempted assassination of former US President George Bush in Kuwait in 1993 (discussed in Chapter 8).[19] But of recent alleged State-sponsored assassinations and attempted assassinations involving the use of radioactive (Litvinenko) or chemical weapons (Skripal – analysed in greater detail in Chapter 8, and the assassination of Kim Jong-nam allegedly by North Korean agents in Malaysia on 13 February 2017 with XV nerve agent), article 2(4) was only invoked in relation to the Skripal incident and by only one State (the UK).[20] It is therefore unclear if potential effects would suffice to meet the requirements of article 2(4).

It may be that acts with merely potential effects would only meet the threshold of a 'use of force' under article 2(4) if they occur in combination with other elements, such as a higher gravity of the potential effects, a clear hostile or coercive intention, or a particularly close connection between another State and the object/target of the act. These considerations may relate to the element of 'international relations', since the targeted (attempted) killing of an individual may rise to the level of an international incident due to the use of a prohibited weapon with serious potential effects for the population of the territorial State (as was the case in the attempted assassination of Sergei Skripal with the prohibited nerve agent Novichok). The notion of a combined threshold of elements for an act to constitute a 'use of force' and the relationship between the elements of a 'use of force' and contextual elements such as 'international relations' is explored in more detail in Part III.

Conclusion

It is clear that forcible acts with direct (i.e. sufficiently proximate) physical effects on persons or objects may constitute a 'use of force' and fall within the scope of the prohibition of the use of force in article 2(4) if the other

[19] Henderson observes in relation to this example that 'mere attempts to use force by one state against another have been construed as armed attacks, and therefore by implication a use of force in breach of the prohibition' (n. 7, 59).

[20] Marc Weller, 'An International Use of Force in Salisbury?', *EJIL: Talk!* (14 March 2018), www.ejiltalk.org/an-international-use-of-force-in-salisbury/.

requirements of that provision are met. It is textually unclear and remains to be seen through the subsequent practice of States if forcible acts with only temporary effects would fall within the scope of the prohibition in article 2(4). It is similarly legally uncertain if forcible acts with potential but unrealised effects would suffice to constitute a prohibited 'use of force' under article 2(4). It is likely that other elements of a 'use of force' will be decisive for determining whether such acts meet the definition of this term. The rest of this chapter will consider if there is a requirement for a particular gravity or intention for a prohibited 'use of force'.

GRAVITY

It is debated among legal scholars whether there is a '*de minimis*' gravity threshold for a prohibited use of force under article 2(4) of the UN Charter. The concept of a gravity threshold for prohibited uses of force under article 2 (4) of the UN Charter is a hotly contested topic in three respects: firstly, whether there is a lower gravity threshold that a forcible act must reach before it will constitute a 'use of force' and fall within the scope of article 2(4); secondly, if there is such a threshold, how high or low it is and how it is to be assessed; and thirdly, the implications of the previous two issues for the 'gap conundrum'.

This conundrum refers to the gap between the gravity threshold of an unlawful 'use of force' under article 2(4) of the UN Charter, and the gravity threshold of an 'armed attack' under article 51, which would permit a use of force in self-defence by the victim State. In the *Nicaragua* case, the International Court of Justice (ICJ) found it 'necessary to distinguish the most grave forms of the use of force (those constituting an armed attack) from other less grave forms'.[21] The problem resulting from this approach was pointed out by Judge Jennings in that case:

> The original scheme of the United Nations Charter, whereby force would be deployed by the United Nations itself, in accordance with the provisions of Chapter VII of the Charter, has never come into effect. Therefore an essential element in the Charter design is totally missing. In this situation it seems dangerous to define unnecessarily strictly the conditions for lawful self-defence, so as to leave a large area where both a forcible response to force is

[21] *Case concerning Military and Paramilitary Activities in and against Nicaragua (Nicaragua v United States of America), Merits, Judgment* (1986) ICJ Reports 14 ('*Nicaragua* case'), para. 191.

> forbidden, and yet the United Nations employment of force, which was intended to fill that gap, is absent.[22]

Clearly then, the gravity threshold for prohibited uses of force is of utmost relevance to the permissibility question, with respect to acts falling below the threshold for an unlawful 'use of force' (and hence permissible under *jus contra bellum*) and with respect to acts above the threshold for a 'use of force' but not amounting to an 'armed attack' (in respect of which States are not permitted to respond using force under the *jus contra bellum*). It is a matter of controversy how high the gravity threshold for an 'armed attack' is.[23] Notwithstanding where the upper limit of the 'gap' between an unlawful 'use of force' under article 2(4) and an 'armed attack' under article 51 falls, the lower limit of the gap – that is, the lower threshold of a 'use of force' – also affects the size of the gap between the two.[24] A very low gravity threshold for an unlawful 'use of force' increases the size of the 'gap' and reduces the range of forcible measures lawfully available to States in their international relations, such as with respect to security measures. Conversely, a relatively high threshold of a prohibited 'use of force' reduces the size of the 'gap' but is also more permissive, since a wider range of forcible measures would be lawfully available to States before the prohibition in article 2(4) is engaged. Therefore, the view that one takes of a *de minimis* threshold for 'use of force' under article 2(4) is likely to be influenced by one's position on the aforementioned matters, including one's position on the appropriate balance between State security and international peace and security, which is liable to be affected by a more permissible regime of potentially escalatory forcible acts. The treatment of these matters in scholarship is analysed next.

Ian Brownlie does not directly discuss the concept of a gravity threshold for article 2(4). He notes that

> from the point of view of assessing responsibility ex post facto, the distinction [between a use of force and 'frontier incidents'] is only relevant in so far as the minor nature of an attack is prima facie evidence of absence of intention to attack, of honest mistake, or simply the limited objectives of an attack. When

[22] Dissenting Opinion of Judge Jennings, *ibid.*, 533–4.

[23] See discussion in ILA Committee on the Use of Force, 2018 Report, n. 18, 6.

[24] As discussed in the Introduction, some States and scholars take the (minority) position that there is no gap between a prohibited 'use of force' under article 2(4) and an 'armed attack' under article 51, which entails clear consequences for justifying the use of force in self-defence.

the justification of self-defence is raised the question becomes one of fact, viz., was the reaction proportionate to the apparent threat.[25]

According to this position, a lower gravity intensity is an indicator of lack of intention, which is relevant either to whether it is actually an 'armed attack' (if intention is a criterion) or to the necessity of using force in self-defence. The relationship between gravity and intention is discussed in Chapter 8.

The more recent discussion by scholars including Olivier Corten,[26] Tom Ruys[27] and Mary Ellen O'Connell[28] frames the question as to whether there is a '*de minimis*' threshold for a use of force under article 2(4). A note on this terminology: in terms of legal doctrine, '*de minimis*' is often short for '*de minimis non curat lex*' – a common law principle available for judges to apply to prevent the strict application of the law to trifles but which does not render the conduct itself lawful.[29] 'The defence of *de minimis* does not mean that the act is justified; it remains unlawful, but on account of its triviality it goes unpunished.'[30] It is an interesting question to consider whether this principle would be applicable in proceedings before the ICJ regarding an article 2(4) violation claim. For violations of the prohibition of the use of force, it is rare that legal claims are brought, and if we limit ourselves to those uses of force that are adjudicated, then we would probably find a much higher gravity threshold for uses of force since States are more likely to bring more grave cases with clearer evidence for adjudication, given the risks, uncertainty and expense of litigation. The term '*de minimis*' can also be used in the sense employed by Corten, Ruys and O'Connell. The Merriam-Webster dictionary defines '*de minimis*' as 'lacking significance or importance: so minor as to merit disregard'.[31] It is in this latter sense that the term is used in the present discussion.

[25] Ian Brownlie, *International Law and the Use of Force by States* (Clarendon, 1963), 365–6, footnote omitted.

[26] Olivier Corten, *The Law against War: The Prohibition on the Use of Force in Contemporary International Law* (Hart Publishing, 2010).

[27] Tom Ruys, 'The Meaning of "Force" and the Boundaries of the *Jus Ad Bellum*: Are "Minimal" Uses of Force Excluded from UN Charter Article 2 (4)?' (2014) 108(2) *American Journal of International Law* 159.

[28] Mary Ellen O'Connell, 'The Prohibition of the Use of Force' in Nigel D White and Christian Henderson (eds), *Research Handbook on International Conflict and Security Law:* Jus ad Bellum, Jus in Bello *and* Jus post Bellum (Elgar, 2013), 89.

[29] Duhaime's Law Dictionary, *De Minimis Non Curat Lex Definition*, www.duhaime.org/LegalDictionary/D/DeMinimisNonCuratLex.aspx.

[30] 2004 Supreme Court of Canada decision of *Canadian Foundation for Youth v Attorney General*, Justice B. Wilson, in dissent.

[31] Merrian-Webster Dictionary, 'De Minimis', www.merriam-webster.com/dictionary/de minimis.

The three scholars mentioned earlier devote considerable attention to the question of a *de minimis* threshold and fundamentally disagree on this point. Corten and O'Connell take the position that the prohibition of the use of force contains a *de minimis* threshold; Ruys posits it does not. Corten argues that 'it can be concluded that there is a threshold below which the use of force in international relations, while it may be contrary to certain rules of international law, cannot violate article 2(4). The conclusion holds not just on land but also at sea and in the air.'[32] On land, he discusses instances of hot pursuit, unlawful arrest and international abductions as police measures falling outside the scope of law enforcement co-operation treaties and not treated as violations of article 2(4).[33] His discussion of police/military measures at sea makes a stronger distinction between police measures (hot pursuit, inspections, prevention of pollution) and the use of inter-State armed force.[34] The discussion of measures in the air relates to illegal trespass and shooting down of aeroplanes as a police measure to guarantee air safety or in self-defence of individual aircraft (not the State).[35] As to where to place the threshold, Corten argues that the factors determining this are where the action took place (if within the State's zone of jurisdiction or not, i.e. can it be considered as an enforcement measure within its jurisdiction?) and the context in which the action occurred (whether there is pre-existing inter-State tension or an international dispute).[36]

According to O'Connell, 'under the best interpretation, Article 2(4) prohibits any use of armed force or armed force equivalent by a state against another state when the force involved is more than de minimis'.[37] She excludes law/maritime enforcement, terrorist attacks by or attributable to States, limited force to rescue hostages, border incursions and serious violations of maritime space including submarines in territorial waters, shooting down planes (e.g. Gulf of Sidra incident) and cyber operations from the scope of article 2(4). '[T]he type of force associated with law enforcement does not come within the Article 2(4) prohibition. Shooting across the bow of a ship, shooting at the legs of a person evading arrest and dropping a bomb on an oil tanker to prevent coastal pollution are all examples of such minimal or de minimis armed force.'[38] She bases this conclusion on the interpretation of ICJ

[32] Corten, n. 26, 55.
[33] *Ibid.*, 53–5.
[34] *Ibid.*, 55–60.
[35] *Ibid.*, 60–7.
[36] *Ibid.*, 73–4.
[37] O'Connell, n. 28, 99.
[38] *Ibid.*, 102, footnote omitted.

judgments (namely, the *Corfu Channel* case, *Nicaragua* case, *Oil Platforms* case, the *Wall* Advisory Opinion and the *DRC v Uganda* case)[39] and examples from State practice, and acknowledges that '[t]here is no express authority on the point'.[40] Examples of State practice that O'Connell provides include the 1981 Gulf of Sidra incident (in which the United States shot down Libyan planes), the 31 March 1999 border incursion by three US soldiers into Serbia, Iranian detention of British sailors in 2007 during the Iraq war, North Korean Navy submarines in Japanese territorial waters, and the 1982 Swedish attempt to bring a submarine to the surface with depth charges and mines. With respect to the latter, she states that '[p]lainly the use of depth charges and mines constitutes armed force, but in this case the use did not violate Article 2(4) because it was a minimal use to detain the submarine'.[41] This example implies that it is not the amount or intensity of force or its (potential) effects that are relevant to determining whether the threshold is met but its purpose.

In contrast to Corten and O'Connell, Ruys argues there is no *de mininis* threshold for a 'use of force' under article 2(4). He disagrees with Corten that minimal uses of force within a State's own territory are justified by law enforcement rights under other legal regimes for land/sea/air, because '[n]one of the conventions cited provides a legal basis for forcible action against unlawful territorial incursions by military or police forces of another state'.[42] He argues that there are theoretical reasons against the idea that there is a gravity threshold for article 2(4): armed confrontations between police/military of two States involve 'international relations', and the law enforcement paradigm is hierarchical and therefore not suited to equal sovereigns.[43] It also cannot be justified by reference to other legal frameworks. According to Ruys, Corten's arguments depend heavily on omission, that is, interpreting a failure by States to protest or raise articles 2(4) or 51 as indicating their *opinio juris* that those provisions do not apply to the incidents in question.

Christian Henderson makes a more nuanced observation about a *de minimis* gravity threshold, noting 'the *de minimis* threshold is normally based upon the distinction between law enforcement actions and uses of force',[44] and that this distinction is more complex than whether a certain gravity threshold is

39 *Ibid.*, 102–4.
40 *Ibid.*, 102.
41 *Ibid.*, 106.
42 Ruys, n. 27, 181.
43 *Ibid.*, 180.
44 Henderson, n. 7, 69.

met.[45] He observes that it is not a matter of 'quantifying the use of force'[46] in terms of its gravity but rather determining whether 'international relations' are engaged, at which point the prohibition of the use of force becomes applicable.[47] Henderson argues that 'the gravity of the use of force against such private actors does not by itself determine the applicability of the prohibition ... Indeed, it is more a qualitative – state or private – as opposed to quantitative – small- or large-scale – distinction, making a clear *de minimis* threshold hard to discern' and that 'when the "international relations" between states are engaged there is little state practice supportive of a *de minimis* threshold in the context of incidences involving armed force.'[48]

This author takes a slightly different view to Henderson. With respect to the prohibition of the use of force, gravity of effects is relevant to two separate elements of article 2(4). Firstly, it is relevant to the contextual element of whether the act occurs in 'international relations'. For example, acts of a higher gravity are more likely to be perceived by States as of a military rather than law enforcement nature and thus as engaging their international relations (discussed in Chapter 8). Also, acts of higher gravity may evince a hostile or coercive intention (discussed in the following section) with respect to another State and thus engage 'international relations' on that basis. The second point of relevance of gravity is to the question of whether the act constitutes a 'use of force' at all. Since, as Ruys convincingly argues, State practice makes clear that when 'international relations' are engaged, 'any actual armed confrontation between two states, even if small-scale or localized, comes within the ambit of the *jus ad bellum*',[49] it does appear that there is no *de minimis* gravity threshold. However, gravity of effects remains a relevant factor in the assessment of whether an act constitutes a 'use of force'. As the preceding discussion of effects noted, gravity may be an especially relevant factor in converting some types of acts into a 'use of force', such as when the act has only temporary effects, or merely potential but unrealised effects. The relationship between these different elements of a 'use of force' and the contextual elements of article 2(4) such as 'international relations' is the subject of Chapter 8 and is explored through case studies of subsequent State practice.

45 *Ibid.*, 68–9, 74.
46 *Ibid.*, 68.
47 *Ibid.*, 74.
48 *Ibid.*.
49 Ruys, n. 27, 209.

A further consideration is that the (perceived) gravity of a use of force is strongly influenced by the domain in which it takes place, namely, land, sea, air or outer space. These domains differ in the following relevant ways: firstly, the type of acts that are possible or frequent in those domains (e.g. interdiction of vessels, satellite interference); secondly, the perceived or actual security threat to the State (i.e. potential effects and security interests at stake); and, thirdly, the legal rights and obligations of States under other applicable legal frameworks (e.g. different maritime spaces under the law of the sea). Within several of these domains, it may be relevant whether the forcible act took place vis-a-vis the States concerned:

- within a State's own territory (land/air/sea – internal waters, territorial waters);
- within territory of another State (land/air/sea);
- within territory governed by a special regime allocating rights and duties between States (Exclusive Economic Zone and contiguous zone, international straits, archipelagic waters, etc);
- within a space beyond the territory of any State (international airspace/ high seas/Antarctica/outer space, the Moon and other celestial bodies);
- on movable objects: ships, submarines, aircraft, spacecraft, satellites and other man-made space objects registered to a State; or
- on extra-territorial manifestations of the State: e.g., embassies and diplomatic premises and warships.

As noted by Judge Alejandro Alvarez in the *Corfu Channel* case:

> Sovereignty confers rights upon States and imposes obligations on them. These rights are not the same and are not exercised in the same way in every sphere of international law. I have in mind the four traditional spheres – terrestrial, maritime, fluvial and lacustrine – to which must be added three new ones – aerial, polar and floating (floating islands). The violation of these rights is not of equal gravity in all these different spheres.[50]

Conclusion

Ultimately, the controversy regarding the gravity threshold of a 'use of force' under article 2(4) is not solved by the text of that provision, which neither specifies nor excludes a gravity threshold for an act to constitute a 'use of force'

[50] *Corfu Channel Case (UK v Albania), Merits, Judgment* (1949) ICJ Reports 4 ('*Corfu Channel* case'), Separate Opinion of Judge Alvarez, 43.

and therefore fall within the scope of the prohibition. Accordingly, the matter is uncertain at the legal of textual interpretation. The issue of whether article 2 (4) has a *de minimis* gravity threshold depends on the subsequent practice of States in their application of this provision. The analysis of subsequent practice by other scholars in relation to this issue, especially by Corten and Ruys, demonstrates that the interpretation of this practice and the conclusion of whether a 'use of force' has a gravity threshold is strongly influenced by the position one takes regarding the legal significance of silence and inaction. This author finds Ruys' analysis of State practice on this matter convincing and agrees that there is no *de minimis* gravity threshold as such for a prohibited 'use of force' under article 2(4). However, this section has argued that gravity is nonetheless a relevant factor to an assessment of whether an act violates article 2(4) on two bases: firstly, as a factor relevant to whether the act occurs in 'international relations' (e.g. as an indicator of intention), and, secondly, as a relevant factor to whether the act constitutes a 'use of force' for acts that may otherwise not meet the threshold of the definition, for instance, because its effects are temporary or only potential. The complex relationship between 'international relations' and of gravity and intention as elements of a 'use of force' is illustrated in further detail in Part III.

INTENTION

Although intention is regarded by some as a requirement for an 'armed attack' under article 51 of the UN Charter,[51] this is disputed, since hostile intent is perhaps better considered in terms of whether a use of force in self-defence is necessary.[52] The picture is even less clear when it comes to a 'use of force' under article 2(4). According to the commentary to the International Law Commission (ILC) Draft Articles on State Responsibility, intention is not a necessary requirement for an act to be internationally wrongful; whether intention is necessary depends on the obligation in question.[53] It is not clear from the text of article 2(4) if a prohibited 'use of force' entails a particular intention. Whether a particular intention is an element of a prohibited 'use of

[51] See Tom Ruys, *'Armed Attack' and Article 51 of the UN Charter* (Cambridge University Press, 2010), 29 for an overview of ICJ case law and State practice in support of this position.

[52] 2018 Report, n. 18, 6–7.

[53] See ILC, 'Draft Articles on Responsibility of State for Internationally Wrongful Acts, with Commentaries, in Report of the International Law Commission on the Work of Its Fifty-Third Session' UN Doc A/56/10 (2001) ('ILC Draft Articles'), commentary to article 2, at paras. 3 and 10. Paragraph 10: 'In the absence of any specific requirement of a mental element in terms of the primary obligation, it is only the act of a State that matters, independently of any intention.'

force' under article 2(4) is illuminated by examining the other prohibition in that provision which is more clearly associated with coercion, namely, the 'threat … of force'. If prohibited threats to use force require a coercive intent and the two prohibitions of threats and use of force are coupled, this would indicate that the latter also requires a coercive intent. This section will firstly examine these questions and then analyse if and what kind of intention may be required for an act to constitute prohibited force, and problems of evidence and proof.

Intention and 'Threat … of Force'

The meaning of prohibited threats of force in article 2(4), similar to its counterpart of prohibited force, has received relatively little treatment in scholarship[54] and jurisprudence.[55] The ICJ's jurisprudence does not make clear whether coercion is required for an unlawful 'threat of force'. The *Corfu Channel* case could be interpreted this way, since in that case the ICJ held that the UK was entitled to make threats if the purpose was to deter Albania from firing on its ships, but it was not entitled to make a demonstration of force 'for the purpose of exercising political pressure' on Albania.[56] However, this case is of little precedential value in determining the meaning of article 2 (4), because it is so ambiguous and has been cited in support of diametrically opposed positions.[57]

The two main scholars who have examined the meaning of threats of force in article 2(4), Nikolas Stürchler[58] and Romana Sadurska, have different views

54 See Romana Sadurska, 'Threats of Force' (1988) 82(2) *American Journal of International Law* 239; Nikolas Stürchler, *The Threat of Force in International Law* (Cambridge University Press, 2009); Corten, n. 26, 92–125; Nicholas Tsagourias, 'The Prohibition of Threats of Force' in Nigel D White and Christian Henderson (eds), *Research Handbook on International Conflict and Security Law:* Jus ad Bellum, Jus in Bello *and* Jus post Bellum (Elgar, 2013), 67.

55 *Corfu Channel* case, n. 50; *Nicaragua* case, n. 21; *Nuclear Weapons* Advisory Opinion, n. 10.

56 *Corfu Channel* case, n. 50, 35; Stürchler, n. 54, 90.

57 See Claus Kreß, 'The International Court of Justice and the Non-Use of Force' in Marc Weller (ed), *The Oxford Handbook of the Use of Force in International Law* (Oxford University Press, 2015), 561, 575 (footnotes with further references omitted):

> While the use of the term 'force' may be taken to suggest that the ICJ *implicitly* qualified Operation Retail as an unlawful use of force, it is also *possible* to interpret the Court's avoidance of any explicit reference to Article 2(4) as implying the view that the threshold for a use of force in its technical legal meaning had not been reached.

58 Stürchler summarises his interpretation of the term as follows:

> In order for there to be a violation of article 2(4), a state must *credibly communicate its readiness to use force in a particular dispute*. … specifically, article 2(4) outlaws (1) explicit promises to resort to force and (2) demonstrations of force, the latter defined as

on whether coercion is a necessary element of prohibited threats. Stürchler argues that coercion is not an essential element of a prohibited 'threat of force'. Despite article 2(7) of the Charter, which guarantees States freedom of choice, the primary purpose of the UN Charter is the prevention of war rather than freedom of choice (i.e. freedom from coercion).[59] He gives the example of a war-mongering State that is no longer trying to ensure compliance with anything – a threat or use of force by that State is thus not coercive (no compliance is sought), but it is still unlawful.[60] But coercion could still be a 'strong indicator'[61] in determining the unlawfulness of threats under article 2 (4), in which case what distinguishes unlawful threats from unlawful intervention is the 'military dimension'.[62] The relevance of coercion as a criterion is in showing 'that the threat of force is not, when properly understood, the mere preparation for the use of force.'[63] Rather, threats can be ends in themselves by ensuring compliance at a much lower cost than an actual use of force. Sadurska agrees that the prohibition of threats of force is aimed at international security rather than the individual liberty of each State from external pressure[64] but takes as her starting point a concept of threat of force as 'a form of coercion because it aims at the deliberate and drastic restriction or suppression by one actor of the choices of another'.[65] Hence, it is uncertain whether coercion constitutes an essential ingredient of a prohibited threat of force, although, at the very least, it may be considered a strong indicator of unlawfulness.

Relationship of 'Threat' to 'Use' of Force

Even if coercion were a necessary element of a prohibited threat of force, it is unclear what consequence this would have for whether coercion is required for a prohibited *use* of force. This depends on the relationship between threats and uses of force under article 2(4) (whether they are coupled or uncoupled), and whether the two prohibitions of 'threat' and 'use' of force are regarded as a continuum or as separate but related prohibitions (and therefore distinct

> any militarised act that reveals hostile intent; and (3) the use of force may also constitute a threat of force if the purpose of a military operation is to signal that more force may be forthcoming.
>
> (n. 54, 273–4)

[59] *Ibid.*, 61.
[60] *Ibid.*.
[61] *Ibid.*.
[62] *Ibid.*, 60.
[63] *Ibid.*, 61.
[64] Sadurska, n. 54, 249–50, footnote omitted.
[65] *Ibid.*, 241.

concepts). Stürchler identifies three possibilities for the direct relationship between 'threat' and 'use' of force in article 2(4).[66] The two (minority) possibilities for the relationship between the prohibition of the threat of force and the use of force both hold that the two prohibitions are uncoupled. These two related though opposed possibilities are predicated on differing models, namely, the spiral and deterrence models of international conflict.[67] The first 'uncoupled' option emphasises that threats can spiral into armed conflict and takes the position that threats are unlawful under any circumstances, even if the force threatened would be lawful, such as the threat to use force in self-defence.[68] The second option holds that threats can serve peace through deterrence and are more justifiable than uses of force since the consequences are lower and threats are more likely than actual uses of force to be proportionate. Therefore, according to this view, as propounded by Sadurska, threats to use force may be lawful even if the force threatened would be unlawful.[69] The basic idea is that the rationale behind prohibiting threats or use of force differs in its application to those two concepts, since uses of force are destabilising to international peace and security, whereas threats of force do not always have destructive effects (lower gravity) and can sometimes help maintain international security (purposes of UN Charter).[70] This asymmetry theory has been critiqued as inconsistent with the UN Charter drafters' intention and with State practice,[71] although Stürchler cogently argues that 'States rely on these themes [of the deterrence and spiral models of conflict] in order to judge the permissibility or otherwise of countervailing threats', especially in the context of protracted conflict.[72] The final (and mainstream) position is that threats are coupled to a use of force so that if the force threatened would be unlawful, the threat is unlawful.[73] ICJ jurisprudence and State practice tend to confirm that threats and use of force are coupled and that the threat of force is justified in self-defence.[74] According to the ICJ in its *Nuclear Weapons* Advisory Opinion, 'the notions of "threat" and "use" of force . . . stand together in the sense that if

66 *Ibid.*, 38–64.
67 Stürchler, n. 54, 45–7.
68 *Ibid.*
69 See Sadurska, n. 54.
70 *Ibid.*, 250.
71 For example, Corten, n. 26, 111ff critiques the asymmetry theory between threats and force put forward by Romana Sadurska by setting out State practice that is inconsistent with this argument.
72 Stürchler, n. 54, 250.
73 Brownlie, n. 25, 36: 'If the promise is to resort to force in conditions in which no justification for the use of force exists, the threat itself is illegal.'
74 Stürchler, n. 54, 91.

the use of force itself in a given case is illegal – for whatever reason – the threat to use such force will likewise be illegal'.[75]

The ICJ's above statement in the *Nuclear Weapons* Advisory Opinion also appears to interpret threats and uses of force as a continuum: concepts that share the same elements but are differentiated merely in form (with threats as a potential but as yet unrealised 'use' of force). Stürchler takes a different view and asserts that threats of force are a separate though related prohibition to the prohibition of the use of force. According to Stürchler, threats do not fit easily into a forcible intervention –> use of force continuum since threats can be broken down along two axes of method (words/actions) and motivation (compellence/deterrence); that is, not all threats are forcible since they may but do not necessarily involve demonstrations of force, and some uses of force are better characterised as threats of further force.[76] Furthermore, threats may but do not necessarily involve coercion and can be ends in themselves and not a prelude to a use of force. Stürchler concludes: 'The dichotomy of threat and use, as suggested by the formulation of article 2(4), is misleading. Although the threat and use of force are conceptually different, that does not mean that they exclude each other in the field.'[77] If one adopts the view of the ICJ that threats and uses of force are coupled and form a continuum, then if 'threat of force' requires coercive intent, the same holds true for 'use of force'. However, different views may be taken on each of these issues with respect to the 'threat of force', and the text of article 2(4) remains open to different interpretations on this point.

Intention and 'Use of Force'

There is a similar lack of consensus among scholars focusing on the meaning of 'use of force' as to whether intention is an element of a prohibited 'use of force'. Ian Brownlie argues that intention is not part of the criteria of prohibited use of force and believes this is a good thing, because to hold otherwise would create unacceptable loopholes in the prohibition.[78] In contrast to Brownlie, Corten argues that '[s]uch an intention appears to be an essential characteristic of the use of force under the Charter'.[79] Henderson also argues that 'it is clear that there must be an intention to use force, or an *animus*

[75] *Nuclear Weapons*, Advisory Opinion, n. 10, para. 47.
[76] Stürchler, n. 54, 262.
[77] *Ibid.*
[78] Brownlie, n. 25, 377.
[79] Corten, n. 26, 76.

belligerandi, in order to breach the prohibition of the threat or use of force'.[80] Ruys notes that 'state practice reveals that, when faced with territorial incursions ostensibly or allegedly lacking hostile intent, territorial states often refrain from invoking the language of Article 2(4) or 51'.[81] However, he notes that this does not necessarily reflect a legal conviction and that State responsibility is 'objective' so does not require intent unless this forms part of the primary rule.[82] For small-scale incursions, Ruys states that 'the key is to determine whether they reflect a hostile intent' to exclude unintentional or harmless acts.[83] With respect to law enforcement within a State's own territory, Ruys argues that manifest hostile intent is sufficient but not necessary for an act to be a 'use of force'.[84]

Adding to the lack of clarity is that the scholarly literature is not consistent in the use of this term. A hostile intention may refer to an intended *action*, intended *effects* or intended *coercion*. The difference is significant, because it may capture or exclude different categories of forcible acts. To speak of a mental state of an abstract entity such as a State is a fiction, since States have neither a physical body nor mind and can only act indirectly through individuals. Therefore, a mental element attaching to a State obligation (in this case, to refrain from the 'use of force' under article 2(4) of the UN Charter) would be satisfied if it is held by a person whose conduct is attributable to the State under the rules set out in the ILC Articles on State Responsibility relating to attribution.[85] This could be either the individual using force (e.g. a soldier) or directing the use of force (a military commander or government official). With respect to what is meant by a hostile intention, at the very least, it requires 'that the State in question is *aware* it is undertaking an action against another State'.[86]

Intended Action

If a hostile intent means intended *action*, this would rule out forcible acts that are accidental, but it would not necessarily rule out mistaken acts. Ruys argues that State practice shows there is a distinction between incursions that are accidental and 'the accidental projection of armed force ... across a border' (e.g. shots or shells fired). 'In the latter scenario ... the territorial state is not

80 Henderson, n. 7, 75.
81 Ruys, n. 27, 189.
82 *Ibid.*, 190–1.
83 *Ibid.*, 172–3.
84 *Ibid.*, 190–1.
85 ILC Draft Articles, n. 53, arts. 4 to 11.
86 Corten, n. 26, 78, emphasis in original.

necessarily precluded from characterizing the act as a use of force'.[87] The text of article 2(4) strongly indicates that an intended action is required, through the italicised words: 'All Members *shall refrain* in their international relations from the threat or use of force against the territorial integrity or political independence of any state, or in any other manner inconsistent with the Purposes of the United Nations.'

Intended Effect

If a hostile intent means an intention to have a certain *effect*, this could rule out mistake, since the action itself is intended but the target, effect or the factual basis may be mistaken. Corten notes that use of force in error was raised in the *travaux préparatoires* of the 1974 GA Definition of Aggression and 'States unanimously excluded the possibility of characterising an act committed by mistake as an aggression'.[88] However, as Corten acknowledges, a problem with this analysis is that although intention may be a requirement for an act of aggression, a use of force may not necessarily amount to aggression. He goes on to argue that 'a review of practice as a whole allows us to affirm that States consider an act, even of a military type, committed by mistake, does not constitute an aggression or even a use of force by one State against another contrary to article 2(4)'.[89] Such practice includes instances of aerial incursion, incursion by South African police into Basutoland (then a British colony) on 26 August 1961, a mistaken attack by UAR on the Federation of South Arabia due to 'pilot's error' on 15 July 1965, and a mistaken firing of five shells by Swiss artillery onto the territory of Liechtenstein during a military exercise on 14 October 1968.[90] In none of these cases did States invoke article 2(4) (although this does not exclude the characterisation of these incidents as internationally wrongful on other legal grounds, such as a violation of sovereignty).

Defining a hostile intent for the purposes of article 2(4) as an intention to produce a particular effect could also rule out deliberate acts with no intention to have a forcible effect within another State. For example, Corten notes that

> [d]uring the discussion before the adoption of General Assembly resolution 3314 (XXIX), Iraq's representative raised the case of a regiment that crosses a State border, knowingly and without authorisation, to go sunbathing on a

[87] Ruys, n. 27, 191.
[88] Corten, n. 26, 79 and footnote 195 with extensive references.
[89] *Ibid.*, 79.
[90] *Ibid.*, 80 with further references.

> beach. No State characterised such a hypothesis as a use of force in the debates in the General Assembly, whether in the Sixth Commission or in the special committee on the definition of aggression.[91]

Corten contrasts this situation with deliberate acts which do not directly target the territorial State but which nevertheless use force, for example, targeted operations such as rescue of nationals abroad and targeted killing. He argues that in respect of targeted operations,

> [i]f the intervening State's objective is not to challenge another State, and if consequently it uses very limited military means, article 2(4) will not be invoked (as in the Rainbow Warrior or 1990 Liberia precedents). If the military action is against another State that supposedly supports 'terrorists' or threatens nationals of the intervening State, the action will involve the rules on the prohibition of the use of force (as in the Mayaguez or Entebbe precedents).[92]

The fundamental point is that:

> For the prohibition of the use of force to be applicable, it is necessary but sufficient for a State to decide to take action that it knows will involve defying another State, whether its central government, its agents, its population, its territory or its infrastructure. … If such an intention is found, article 2(4) will be applicable, regardless of any more general motive for the intervention.[93]

This point relates to a coercive intent and is addressed in the following section.

With respect to intended effects, there is nothing in the text of article 2(4) to indicate or to exclude this as necessary for a prohibited 'use of force'. (There is also a question of whether the notion of hostile intent would require an intended harmful effect or if some other mental State would suffice, such as negligence, recklessness or reasonable foreseeability. But this is going even further beyond the text.) It will therefore depend upon the subsequent practice of States in their application of article 2(4). As set out earlier, there is practice indicating that States do not usually invoke article 2(4) in cases of mistake of fact.

Coercive Intent

Finally, hostile intent may refer to a coercive intent. Corten argues that '[t]he only intention to be considered is that of forcing the will of another State'.[94]

91 *Ibid.*, 84, footnote omitted.
92 *Ibid.*, 91.
93 *Ibid.*, 89–90.
94 *Ibid.*, 76–7.

Corten sees this requirement as so essential that 'when a State takes even limited military measures and admits that such measures are part of a policy conducted against one State, there is no doubt that article 2(4) is applicable'.[95] The position that coercive intent is a requirement for a prohibited use of force finds some support in a textual interpretation of article 2(4), due to the relationship between the prohibition of threats and uses of force (as discussed earlier); the relationship of the non-intervention principle and the principle of the non-use of force; and the object and purpose of the prohibition of the use of force in article 2(4).

The principle of non-intervention is found in customary international law and is a 'corollary of the sovereign equality of States' set out in article 2(1) of the UN Charter.[96] In the *Nicaragua* case, the ICJ defined the content of the principle of non-intervention (as it related to the dispute in question) as follows:

> the principle forbids all States or groups of States to intervene directly or indirectly in internal or external affairs of other States. A prohibited intervention must accordingly be one bearing on matters in which each State is permitted, by the principle of State sovereignty, to decide freely. One of these is the choice of a political, economic, social and cultural system, and the formulation of foreign policy. Intervention is wrongful when it uses methods of coercion in regard to such choices, which must remain free ones.[97]

Henderson argues that intention is necessary for a breach of the prohibition of the use of force in article 2(4) because '[f]orce ... is a particular kind of intervention'.[98] He follows the ICJ's approach in *Nicaragua* and views a 'use of force' as 'a more specific form of intervention' 'involving physical coercion'.[99] This is yet another continuum approach; since intervention requires coercion and a use of force is a form of intervention, a use of force also requires coercion. However, it is not clear from the judgment whether a use of force must always be coercive. Just as an unlawful intervention can be forcible or non-forcible, it is arguable that a prohibited use of force can violate the principle of non-intervention or not. In other words, not all violations of the prohibition of the use of force in article 2(4) will necessarily comprise violations of the principle of non-intervention. For example, a non-combatant evacuation of nationals from a generalised situation of violence or civil unrest

95 *Ibid.*, 78.
96 *Nicaragua* case, n. 21, para. 202.
97 *Ibid.*, para. 205.
98 Henderson, n. 7, 50.
99 *Ibid.*, 52.

abroad is not aimed at coercing a choice 'on matters in which each State is permitted, by the principle of State sovereignty, to decide freely' such as 'the choice of a political, economic, social and cultural system, and the formulation of foreign policy'[100] but may nevertheless constitute a use of force in the territory of another State.

The final argument that a 'use of force' requires a coercive intent is based on the object and purpose of article 2(4). As discussed in Chapter 4, the main objects of article 2(4) are protecting State sovereignty (also protected by the non-intervention principle) and the maintenance of international peace and security. The protection of State sovereignty by article 2(4) is further supported by the principles of sovereign equality and non-intervention set out in articles 2(3) and 2(7) (although it is important to note that article 2(7) does not actually prohibit intervention by States in the internal affairs of other States; as mentioned earlier, the non-intervention principle is found in customary international law and not directly in the UN Charter itself). Considering this purpose behind the prohibition in article 2(4), it would make sense to interpret it as prohibiting conduct that is employed to bring about coercion/interference with the sovereign equality of States.

With respect to the second object and purpose of article 2(4) – to maintain international peace and security – one of the propositions Stürchler tests is that article 2(4) can be read together with article 2(3) to imply a positive obligation to achieve peaceful settlement of disputes without recourse to threats to use force.[101] This idea could be applied to the interpretation of a 'use of force' in article 2(4) to argue that the prohibition of the use of force is directed towards uses of force in contradistinction to the obligation of peaceful settlement of disputes (which Stürchler notes was recognised by the ICJ as a positive obligation in the *North Sea Continental Shelf* cases[102]). In other words, it could be argued that only those minimal uses of force that are used as a tool for foreign policy (i.e. accompanied or motivated by an element of coercion) would violate the prohibition. This would also reflect the notion of 'use of force' as a broader concept but in many ways a continuation of the old concept of 'war' from the preceding treaty, the Kellogg–Briand Pact, which condemns 'recourse to war for the solution of international controversies' and embodies its renunciation 'as an instrument of national policy'.[103] The

[100] *Nicaragua* case, *ibid.*, para. 205.
[101] Stürchler, n. 54, 53.
[102] *North Sea Continental Shelf (Federal Republic of Germany/Denmark; Federal Republic of Germany/Netherlands) Judgment, Merits* (1969) ICJ Reports 3 (20 February 1969) at paras. 83–101.
[103] *Ibid.*, art. 1.

Principle set out in article 2(3) of the UN Charter that '[a]ll Members shall settle their international disputes by peaceful means in such a manner that international peace and security, and justice, are not endangered' is a continuation of this aim to prevent the settlement of international disputes by force.[104] This also connects to the term 'international relations' in article 2(4);[105] as Chapter 8 will show, the elements of 'international relations', gravity and intention are interrelated.

A requirement of coercive intent may also play a role in determining whether an act falls within the scope of the *jus contra bellum* or another legal framework applicable within a particular domain, such as law of the sea. With respect to the location of the forcible act, as noted earlier in the discussion about gravity, the domain in which it occurs may impact on the legal characterisation of the act due to the sovereign rights and applicable legal framework within that space as well as the different nature of the perceived security threat. Measures which may be governed by another legal framework (such as the exercise of law enforcement jurisdiction at sea) could fall within or outside the scope of article 2(4) of the UN Charter, depending on a number of factors – including the element of a hostile or coercive intention vis-à-vis another State (in this case, the flag State of the vessel) – which may bring an act of purported maritime law enforcement within the realm of 'international relations' and thus a prohibited 'use of force' under article 2 (4) of the UN Charter. Interestingly, legal clarity over certain types of acts as definitely constituting unlawful uses of force may relate to intention. For example, as discussed in Chapter 5, the listed acts of aggression in the 1974 GA Definition of Aggression constitute a 'subsequent agreement' by UN Member States that those acts are unlawful 'uses of force' in violation of article 2(4). Thus, if a State commits one of these acts, it is highly likely that it had a hostile intent, since the act is unambiguously unlawful.

Evidence of Hostile Intent

If a hostile intent (however defined) is required for an act to be an unlawful 'use of force' under article 2(4), this raises questions of what kind of evidence counts and the required standard of proof. A problem with hostile intent is that intention is a subjective standard requiring a particular mental state, as opposed to an objective standard in which only the action or omission is

104 Kreß, n. 8, 432 footnote 93, citing Kirsten Sellars, *Crimes against Peace and International Law* (Cambridge University Press, 2013), 25.
105 See discussion in Chapter 5.

relevant for the prohibition to be engaged.[106] The problem of subjectivity is addressed by Ruys by adding the term 'manifest' to allow for an objective assessment of intention behind the act.[107] But on another view, manifest hostile intent relates to an 'armed attack', for example, to determine the necessity of using force in response.

Indicators that have been suggested for a hostile intent include 'the gravity or magnitude of the attack';[108] for less grave acts, States take into account other factors to determine intent, such as geopolitical context, repeated nature, location, nature of units, and specific indications related to weapons being fired up.[109] Corten provides six criteria that indicate gravity and intention (which in his view are interrelated): (1) where the act was carried out, (2) the context, (3) who decided on it and who conducted it, (4) the target, (5) whether 'the military operation [has] given rise to confrontation between the agents of two States' and (6) 'the scope of the means implemented by the intervening State'.[110] The Independent International Fact-Finding Mission on the Conflict in Georgia also set out indicators of hostile intent:

> According to State practice ... not all militarised acts amount to a demonstration of force and thus to a violation of Art. 2(4) of the UN Charter. Many are routine missions devoid of any hostile intent and are meaningless in the absence of a sizeable dispute. But as soon as they are non-routine, suspiciously timed, scaled up, intensified, geographically proximate, staged in the exact mode of a potential military clash, and easily attributable to a

[106] ILC Draft Articles, n. 53, commentary to article 2, at para. 3:

> Whether there has been a breach of a rule may depend on the intention or knowledge of relevant State organs or agents and in that sense may be 'subjective'. ... In other cases, the standard for breach of an obligation may be 'objective', in the sense that the advertence or otherwise of relevant State organs or agents may be irrelevant. Whether responsibility is 'objective' or 'subjective' in this sense depends on the circumstances, including the content of the primary obligation in question. The articles lay down no general rule in that regard. The same is true of other standards, whether they involve some degree of fault, culpability, negligence or want of due diligence. Such standards vary from one context to another for reasons which essentially relate to the object and purpose of the treaty provision or other rule giving rise to the primary obligation. Nor do the articles lay down any presumption in this regard as between the different possible standards. Establishing these is a matter for the interpretation and application of the primary rules engaged in the given case.

[107] Ruys, n. 27, 189.

[108] Henderson, n. 7, 78; Ruys, n. 27, 175.

[109] Ruys, n. 27, 175–6.

[110] Corten, n. 26, 91–2.

> foreign-policy message, the hostile intent is considered present and the demonstration of force manifest.[111]

There thus appears to be a connection between these objective indicators of a subjective hostile intent and the elements of gravity and international relations. The relationship between these elements is explored further in Part III.

Conclusion

Ultimately, whether or not intention is required for a prohibited use of force under article 2(4) cannot be definitively resolved at the level of textual analysis. It is possible that hostile intent is an indicative factor that can turn a forcible act that would otherwise not meet various criteria, such as gravity or if the harm is only potential but unrealised, into a 'use of force'. This discussion about the interrelationship between different elements of a 'use of force' (including the relationship between intention, gravity and international relations with respect to maritime law enforcement versus 'use of force') is continued in Part III.

CONCLUSION

The above textual analysis of article 2(4) of the UN Charter supports the following conclusions regarding the interpretation of the term 'use of force':

- ***Effects:***
  - *Physical effects*: Usually required but with some notable exceptions (discussed in Chapter 7).
  - *Object/target*: There is nothing explicit in the text of article 2(4) itself that restricts its scope to certain objects of harm, i.e. harm to physical property or persons. However, abstract forms of harm are probably excluded from the scope of an unlawful 'use of force'.
  - *Directness*: The relevant harmful effects must have sufficient proximity to the application of force. This refers to the intermediate steps between the act and its result, not how long it takes for the harm to manifest.

[111] 'Independent International Fact-Finding Mission on the Conflict on Georgia, Report' (2009), available at www.mpil.de/en/pub/publications/archive/independent_international_fact.cfm, para. 232.

  - *Permanent versus temporary*: The text of article 2(4) is not conclusive on this point. More State practice is required to determine whether it will reveal their agreement regarding this interpretation.
  - *Actual versus potential*: It is textually ambiguous whether any physical effect (i.e. harm) must actually ensue from such acts for them to fall within the scope of the prohibition, or if it is sufficient if there is merely a potential for physical effects/harm to result.
- ***Gravity of effects***: Although this work takes the position that there is no *de minimis* gravity threshold for a 'use of force' under article 2(4), gravity is relevant to the contextual element of 'international relations' (e.g. as an indicator of intention), and is a relevant factor to whether the act constitutes a 'use of force' for acts that may otherwise not meet the required threshold of the definition, for instance, because its effects are temporary, or only potential.
- ***Hostile intent***: The text of article 2(4) strongly indicates that at the very least, an intended *action* is required. The text does not explicitly require or exclude an intended *effect*, although State practice indicates that mistaken forcible acts are usually not treated as violating the prohibition of the use of force. There is textual support for the position that a coercive intent is required under article 2(4), due to the relationship between the prohibition of threats and uses of force, the relationship of the non-intervention principle and the principle of the non-use of force, and the object and purpose of the prohibition of the use of force in article 2 (4). However, such textual support is not definitive and the argument can be made both ways. It is possible that hostile intent is an indicative factor that can turn a forcible act that would otherwise not meet various criteria (such as gravity or if the harm is only potential but unrealised) into a 'use of force'.

However, it is clear that some 'uses of force' that are widely accepted as such; for instance an unopposed invasion or military occupation does not contain some of the elements identified above, particularly physical means or a physical effect. These examples challenge the conventional understanding of a prohibited 'use of force' as displaying the elements identified in this and the preceding chapter. How are these accepted forms of 'use of force' to be reconciled with the above analysis? This is the subject of Part III.

PART III

Defining Prohibited Force

7

Anomalous Examples of 'Use of Force' and Non-'Use of Force' under Article 2(4) of the UN Charter

INTRODUCTION

The conclusions drawn in Part II regarding the meaning and elements of a 'use of force' under article 2(4) of the UN Charter are supported by the principles of treaty interpretation. But there is an interesting and important problem: there are several well-known and accepted 'uses of force' that violate the prohibition in article 2(4) but do not conform to all of the criteria set out above. Conversely, there are also some acts that *do* use physical means or have physical effects but are still not regarded as violating article 2(4). This chapter will set out some of these anomalous examples and then put forward some possible explanations and the implications for the interpretation of a prohibited 'use of force' under article 2(4).

ANOMALOUS EXAMPLES OF 'USE OF FORCE'

Subsequent Agreements Regarding Anomalous Categories of 'Use of Force': The 1974 Definition of Aggression

It is instructive to examine anomalous acts which States agree fall within the scope of article 2(4). For this purpose, the 1974 Definition of Aggression serves as a key example.[1] As explained in Chapter 5, the 1974 Definition is a subsequent agreement on the interpretation of the prohibition of the use of force in article 2(4) of the UN Charter under article 31(3)(a) of the Vienna Convention on the Law of Treaties (VCLT). Some of the acts of aggression (and therefore 'uses of force') referred to in the 1974 Definition of Aggression

[1] UN General Assembly, 'Definition of Aggression' (14 December 1974), GA Res 3314 (XXIX).

are not strictly 'armed' or kinetic forms of force. Article 2 of the 1974 Definition of Aggression provides that:

> The first use of armed force by a State in contravention of the Charter shall constitute *prima facie* evidence of an act of aggression although the Security Council may, in conformity with the Charter, conclude that a determination that an act of aggression has been committed would not be justified in the light of other relevant circumstances, including the fact that the acts concerned or their consequences are not of sufficient gravity.

Article 3 lists acts which may qualify as acts of aggression and is set out and discussed later in the chapter. It provides that: 'Any of the following acts, regardless of a declaration of war, shall, subject to and in accordance with the provisions of article 2, qualify as an act of aggression'. Article 4 notes that '[t]he acts enumerated [in article 3] are not exhaustive and the Security Council may determine that other acts constitute aggression under the provisions of the Charter'. Since articles 1 and 2 of the Definition refer to 'armed force', the acts listed in article 3 must all only relate to *armed* force. As some of the listed acts do not conform to a normal understanding of 'force' and do not exhibit all the elements identified in the preceding chapters, it is helpful to examine those acts to assist in the interpretation of the term 'use of force' in article 2(4) of the UN Charter. The relevant acts that will be analysed are invasion and military occupation (article 3(a)), blockade (article 3(c)), mere presence in violation of a Status of Forces Agreement (SOFA) (article 3(e)) and indirect use of force either through inter-State assistance (article 3(f)) or through non-State armed groups (article 3(g)).

Article 3(a) The invasion or attack by the armed forces of a State of the territory of another State, or any military occupation, however temporary, resulting from such invasion or attack, or any annexation by the use of force of the territory of another State or part thereof

Ian Brownlie has noted that '[i]nvasion and unopposed military occupation following a threat of force, as in the case of the German occupations of the Czechoslovakian territories Bohemia and Moravia in March 1939, are usually regarded as a case of actual resort to force.'[2] However, the inclusion of military occupation in itself (as opposed to the preceding invasion or attack) as an act of aggression in the 1974 Definition (and therefore an illegal use of force under article 2(4) of the UN Charter) is anomalous because occupation may

2 Ian Brownlie, *International Law and the Use of Force by States* (Clarendon, 1963), 365, footnote omitted.

follow from either a lawful or an unlawful use of force and is not unlawful in itself under the *jus contra bellum*. Article 42 of the 1907 Hague Regulations defines a territory as occupied 'when it is actually placed under the authority of the hostile army. The occupation extends only to the territory where such authority has been established and can be exercised'.[3] The lawfulness of an occupation is determined under the *jus contra bellum*, but once it is factually in place then an occupation is regulated by the laws of occupation, including the 1907 Hague Regulations,[4] the Fourth Geneva Convention 1949[5] and customary international humanitarian law.[6] As with an unresisted invasion, an occupation may also meet with no armed resistance and may therefore involve no physical means or physical effects in terms of damage to persons or property.

In the *Armed Activities* case, the International Court of Justice (ICJ) held that the illegal occupation of Ituri by Uganda constituted a violation of the principle of the non-use of force.[7] However, this characterisation of the occupation of Ituri was criticised by Judge Pieter Kooijmans since it undermines the separation of the *jus contra bellum* (which prohibits aggression) and the *jus in bello* (which sets out the regime governing military occupation and makes no distinction 'between an occupation resulting from a lawful use of force and one which is the result of aggression').[8] Judge Kooijmans argued that article 3(a) of the 1974 Definition of Aggression 'lent credibility' to the impression of Governments that '"occupation" has become almost synonymous with aggression and oppression', and held: '[t]his resolution, as important as it may be from a legal point of view, does not in all its terms reflect customary law. The reference to military occupation as an act of aggression is in my opinion less than felicitous.'[9] As Bengt Broms has stated: 'it could be argued in view of the way in which the paragraph has been construed that the

3 *Regulations Respecting the Laws and Customs of War on Land, Annex to Hague Convention Respecting the Laws and Customs of War on Land* 1907 (adopted 18 October 1907, entered into force 26 January 1910). There is debate over when the laws of occupation begin to apply: see Marten Zwanenburg, Michael Bothe, and Marco Sassòli, 'Is the Law of Occupation Applicable to the Invasion Phase?' (2012) 94 *International Review of the Red Cross* 29.

4 *Regulations Respecting the Laws and Customs of War on Land, Annex to Hague Convention Respecting the Laws and Customs of War on Land* 1907, n. 3.

5 *Geneva Convention (IV) Relative to the Protection of Civilian Persons in Time of War* 1949 (adopted 12 August 1949, entered into force 21 October 1950), 75 UNTS 287.

6 See ICRC, *Customary IHL Database*, https://ihl-databases.icrc.org/customary-ihl/eng/docs/v1_rul.

7 *Armed Activities on the Territory of the Congo (Democratic Republic of the Congo v Uganda)* (2005) ICJ Reports 168, para. 345 ('*Armed Activities* case').

8 *Ibid.*, Separate Opinion of Judge Kooijmans, paras. 56, 58–63.

9 *Ibid.*, para. 63, footnote omitted.

military occupation or the annexation presupposes the existence of an act of aggression in the form of an invasion or attack and that it would therefore not have been necessary to include them separately in this paragraph.'[10] The inclusion in article 3(a) of military occupation as an act of aggression (and therefore a 'use of force') is therefore controversial. Nevertheless, since it is a listed act in the 1974 Definition of Aggression, it may be considered that States have made a subsequent agreement under article 31(3)(a) of the VCLT that it is a 'use of force' in a violation of article 2(4) of the UN Charter.

Article 3(c) The blockade of the ports or coasts of a State by the armed forces of another State;

A blockade is

> a belligerent operation to prevent vessels and/or aircraft of all nations, enemy and neutral, from entering or exiting specified ports, airports, or coastal areas belonging to, occupied by, or under the control of an enemy nation. The purpose of establishing a blockade is to deny the enemy the use of enemy and neutral vessels or aircraft to transport personnel and goods to or from enemy territory.[11]

For a blockade to be binding under treaty and customary international law, it must meet certain requirements, including that it be effective[12] and 'applied impartially to the vessels and aircraft of all States'.[13] A blockade is an anomalous example of an illegal use of force because until it is challenged and enforced, there is a lack of employment of physical means or physical effects – only an expressed intention to use force under certain circumstances (when

[10] 'The Definition of Aggression' (1977) 154 *Recueil des cours* 348, cited by Judge Kooijmans, Separate Opinion, n. 7, para. 63 at footnote 12.

[11] Wolff Heintschel von Heinegg, 'Blockade', *Max Planck Encyclopedia of Public International Law* (Oxford University Press, October 2015), http://opil.ouplaw.com/view/10.1093/law:epil/9780199231690/law-9780199231690-e252, para. 1. On the law of blockade generally, see further Lassa Oppenheim and Hersch Lauterpacht (eds), *International Law, vol. II: Disputes, War and Neutrality* (Longman, 7th ed, 1952), 768–97; Robert W Tucker, *The Law of Neutrality at Sea* (United States Government Printing Office, 1957, reprinted 2006 and 2008).

[12] Heintschel von Heinegg, n. 11, para. 33; *Declaration Respecting Maritime Law between Austria, France, Great Britain, Prussia, Russia, Sardinia and Turkey* (signed and entered into force 16 April 1856) (1856) 115 CTS 1 ('Paris Declaration'), para. 4; *Déclaration relative au droit de la guerre maritime* [Declaration concerning the Laws of Naval War] (26 February 1909, not entered into force) (1909) 208 CTS 338 ('London Declaration'), art. 2; San Remo Manual on International Law Applicable to Armed Conflicts at Sea (adopted 12 June 1994) reproduced in Louise Doswald-Beck (ed), *San Remo Manual on International Law Applicable to Armed Conflicts at Sea* (Cambridge University Press, 1995), para. 95.

[13] Heintschel von Heinegg, n. 11, para. 44; London Declaration, n. 12, art. 5.

the blockade is challenged). According to Brownlie, 'a naval blockade involves an unlawful use of force, although the tactical posture is passive, since its actual enforcement includes the use of force against vessels of the coastal state'.[14]

Article 3(c) of the 1974 Definition of Aggression does not specify that a blockade must actually be enforced in order to qualify as an act of aggression. An unchallenged blockade could be considered an act of aggression and therefore a 'use of force' because it is an act of warfare that confers a military advantage and is usually employed in conjunction with other forms of force as part of a broader military operation against the armed forces of the blockaded State.[15] However, as with the example to be discussed later of overstaying a Status of Forces agreement, it is not clear if a blockade that is unchallenged may really amount to a 'use of force' under article 2(4) of the UN Charter.[16] Nevertheless, an unchallenged blockade constitutes a 'threat of force' against the blockaded State and may therefore still violate article 2(4) of the UN Charter.

If a neutral warship or military aircraft attempts to or does breach a blockade, the neutral State commits a violation of the law of neutrality, but the blockading State does not have a right to attack it unless in the exercise of the right of self-defence.[17] But a more interesting legal issue is raised when it comes to the enforcement of a blockade against a neutral merchant vessel on the high seas. Under the *jus contra bellum*, the enforcement of a blockade against a ship flagged to a neutral State may amount to a use of force within the meaning of article 2(4) and violate the prohibition of the use of force unless justified by one of the recognised exceptions, that is, self-defence. This view is supported by State practice, for example, the position taken by the UK during the Gulf War, when it claimed that Iran's visit of a British-flagged merchant vessel on the high seas was justified as a measure of self-defence under article 51 of the UN Charter.[18] This implies the legal view that stopping and searching a foreign-flagged merchant vessel on the high seas would otherwise constitute an unlawful use of force in violation of article 2(4) of

[14] Brownlie, n. 2, 365–6, footnote omitted.

[15] Heintschel von Heinegg, n. 11, para. 1.

[16] This is noted by Mary Ellen O'Connell, 'The Prohibition of the Use of Force' in Nigel D White and Christian Henderson (eds), *Research Handbook on International Conflict and Security Law:* Jus ad Bellum, Jus in Bello *and* Jus post Bellum (Elgar, 2013), 89, 111.

[17] Heintschel von Heinegg, n. 11, para. 48.

[18] Statement by the Minister of State, Foreign and Commonwealth Office, 28 January 1986, House of Commons Debates, vol. 90, col. 426, printed in 57 *British Year Book of International Law* 583 (1986).

the UN Charter – that is, that it would not be justified by the law of neutrality.[19] It is not the blockade itself that transforms the capture or attack of the neutral ship into a use of force – due to the principle of exclusive flag State jurisdiction, such interference with a vessel flagged to a third State on the high seas takes place in 'international relations' and is arguably itself a use of force unless the capturing/attacking State has lawful grounds for the exercise of jurisdiction over the vessel, for example, under article 110 of the UN Convention on the Law of the Sea.[20]

But under the laws of naval warfare (*jus in bello*), 'since neutral merchant vessels and civilian aircraft are obliged to respect a blockade that conforms to the legal requirements of publicity and effectiveness they become liable to interception and capture if they act in violation of the legitimate right of the blockading power to prevent egress from, or ingress to, the blockaded area'.[21] Under the *jus in bello*, neutral merchant vessels and civilian aircraft are liable to be attacked if they are clearly resisting interception and capture, because such an act leads to loss of civilian status and renders the vessel or aircraft a legitimate military objective.[22] However, these rules apply under the laws of neutrality and armed conflict, not under the *jus contra bellum*. The law of blockade and *jus in bello* do not prohibit the attack, but neither do they justify it under the *jus contra bellum*. Therefore, attacking a merchant vessel attempting to resist intercept and capture by the blockading State in these circumstances would be an unlawful use of force unless justified by self-defence.

This raises the question of whether the law of neutrality and these rights of blockade continue to apply in the post-Charter era in the traditional way of providing a full justification for certain forcible action. On one view, belligerent rights and the traditional law of neutrality continue to exist in the post-Charter era, which means that the impairment of the rights of third States must be accepted.[23] On another view, the law of neutrality was abolished by the UN Charter and either belligerent rights no longer exist, or they have

19 This legal position has been criticised by Wolff Heintschel von Heinegg as not reflective of State practice and irreconcilable with the equal application of the *jus in bello*: '"Benevolent" Third States in International Armed Conflicts: The Myth of the Irrelevance of the Law of Neutrality' in MN Schmitt and J Pejic (eds), *International Law and Armed Conflict: Exploring the Faultlines* (Koninklijke Brill BV, 2007), 562–3.

20 See discussion of maritime law enforcement against foreign-flagged vessels with no basis for jurisdiction later in this chapter for a further discussion of this point.

21 Heintschel von Heinegg, n. 11, para. 42.

22 *Ibid.*, para. 47.

23 Heintschel von Heinegg argues in the affirmative, n. 19, 543–68.

continued in a modified form under the rubric of self-defence.[24] As Stephen Neff notes, there are serious difficulties with each position,[25] and this controversial question remains open. Even if one takes the position that these belligerent rights continue to exist but have been modified by the modern *jus contra bellum*, a further question would be raised of whether the very imposition of a blockade remains a lawful instrument even for a State acting in self-defence, since the principle of effectiveness requires that the blockading State enforce the blockade against neutral vessels resisting interception and capture – in other words, that the blockading State use force against the vessels of third States.[26]

Article 3(e) The use of armed forces of one State which are within the territory of another State with the agreement of the receiving State, in contravention of the conditions provided for in the agreement or any extension of their presence in such territory beyond the termination of the agreement;

This is an anomalous example of a 'use of force' because *mere continuing presence* of the armed forces of one State within the territory of another State in contravention of a Status of Forces Agreement, even without the actual employment of physical means or the producing of physical effects, may suffice under article 3(e) of the 1974 Definition of Aggression to constitute an act of aggression (and therefore a 'use of force' in violation of article 2(4) of the UN Charter), although this is a controversial proposition. Thomas Bruha observes that:

24 For a discussion of the scope of application of the laws of war and the law of neutrality in the post-Charter era with respect to the enforcement of blockades against neutral vessels, see Douglas Guilfoyle, 'The Mavi Marmara Incident and Blockade in Armed Conflict' (2011) 81 (1) *British Yearbook of International Law* 171, 177, with further references. See further Michael Bothe, 'Neutrality in Naval Warfare: What Is Left of the Traditional Law?', in Astrid JM Delissen and Gerard J Tanja (eds), *Humanitarian Law of Armed Conflict, Challenges Ahead* (Martinus Nijhoff, 1991), 387; Dietrich Schindler, 'Transformations in the Law of Neutrality since 1945' in Delissen and Tanja, *ibid.*, 367.

25 See Stephen C Neff, 'Towards a Law of Unarmed Conflict: A Proposal for a New International Law of Hostility' (1995) 28(1) *Cornell International Law Journal* 1 for a critique of the different schools of thought on this question.

26 James Farrant ('Modern Maritime Neutrality Law' (2014) 90 *International Law Studies* 198, 200–307) argues for policy reasons that the requirement of impartiality should be removed from the law of blockade, so that the blockading belligerent is not required to enforce the blockade against neutral shipping. For an original proposal to overcome the associated legal and policy issues with belligerent rights in the post-Charter era, see Neff, n. 25.

> The mere continuance of the presence of armed forces in the territory of another state in violation of, or after the termination of the agreement concluded with it, does not necessarily entail the use of armed force in the ordinary sense of the word. . . . even if one considers the continued stationing of armed forces 'within' another state as a *special case of non–transfrontier* use of armed force comparable to occupation, it leaves many questions open: what degree of violation of the agreement is required? Must the continued presence of the armed forces in the host state be enforced with threats or other manifestations of the use of armed force?[27]

The ICJ dealt with this point in the *Armed Activities* case. In that case, the Court found that Uganda's actions were not justified by consent or self-defence and that they were a violation of the prohibition of the use of force. The Court acknowledged the Democratic Republic of the Congo (DRC) had previously consented to the presence of Ugandan troops on its territory for a limited purpose of responding to cross-border attacks but that the DRC had a right to unilaterally withdraw this consent without any formalities required.[28] The Court found that the DRC had at least by 8 August 1998 withdrawn its consent to the presence of Ugandan troops on its territory.[29] The Lusaka Agreement provided for the withdrawal of Ugandan troops from the DRC within a particular timeframe, but the Court found that this did not constitute consent by the DRC to the presence of the Ugandan troops during the withdrawal period[30] and that such presence could only be justified, if at all, on the basis of self-defence.[31] A more recent example is provided by Bruha with respect to

> [t]he involvement of units of the Russian Black Sea forces stationed in the Ukraine harbour of Sevastopol in the interventionist activities of Russia leading to the illegal annexation of the Crimea . . . *even if no use of armed force was involved*, these activities may be considered as aggression according

27 Thomas Bruha, 'The General Assembly's Definition of the Act of Aggression' in Claus Kreß and Stefan Barriga (eds), *The Crime of Aggression: A Commentary* (Cambridge University Press, 2017), 142, 163.

28 *Armed Activities* case, n. 7, para. 47.

29 *Ibid.*, para. 53.

30 *Ibid.*, para. 99. This finding was contested by Judge Parra-Aranguren (Separate Opinion, paras. 3–20) and Judge *ad hoc* Kateka (Dissenting Opinion, para. 22).

31 *Ibid.*, para. 112; cf Claus Kreß, 'The State Conduct Element' in Claus Kreß and Stefan Barriga (eds), *The Crime of Aggression: A Commentary* (Cambridge University Press, 2017), 412, 445, who argues that 'the ICJ refrained from characterising as a use of force the unlawful presence of Ugandan troops during the withdrawal period' on the basis of paragraph 99 in conjunction with paragraph 345(1) and draws from this the implication of the 'requirement that the armed forces of the aggressor state adopt a hostile intent' (footnote omitted).

to article 3(e) of the Definition, because they were instrumental to and occurred in the context of aggressive activities of Russia against Ukraine.[32]

Article 3(f) The action of a State in allowing its territory, which it has placed at the disposal of another State, to be used by that other State for perpetrating an act of aggression against a third State;

This 'use of force' is also characterised by its lack of physical means or direct physical effects, unless one considers purely indirect means. This form of act of aggression is distinct from the other acts in that it appears to be either a new form of attribution or a broad understanding of the concept of 'force'.[33] This is because the conduct referred to in article 3(f) is more 'properly characterised as *aid or assistance* in the commission of an unlawful use of force by another State within the meaning of Article 16 of the International Law Commission (ILC) Articles on State Responsibility and customary international law'.[34] The analysis of article 3(f) by Claus Kreß[35] observes that paragraph 8 of the ILC commentary is ambiguous on this point because it characterises the conduct of the assisting State firstly as a breach of the obligation not to use force but in the same paragraph also discusses the Federal Republic of Germany's acceptance 'that the act of a State in placing its own territory at the disposal of another State in order to facilitate the commission of an unlawful use of force by that other State was itself an internationally wrongful act'. Kreß observes that:

> While the first formulation suggests that the ILC believes that the state conduct described in *littera* (f) constitutes as such a use of force, the second rather suggests that the ILC characterises such aid and assistance in the commission of an unlawful use of force by another state as an internationally wrongful act related to but distinguishable from a use of force. In any event, the ILC has emphasised that 'the assisting State is responsible for its own act in deliberately assisting another State to breach an international obligation by which they are both bound' and that 'it is not responsible, as such, for the act of the assisted State'.[36]

If the internationally wrongful act of the assisting State is not a result of the attribution of the act of aggression of the acting State to it but is an unlawful

[32] Bruha, n. 27, 163, footnote 145 (emphasis added).

[33] Kreß, n. 31, 446. Kreß notes (446, footnote 167) that the 1970 Friendly Relations Declaration does not contain a similar provision.

[34] Kreß, *ibid.*, 446, citations omitted.

[35] *Ibid.*, 446.

[36] *Ibid.*, footnotes omitted.

act in its own right, then because of the wording of the 1974 Definition the conduct described in article 3(f) must be considered a 'use of force' even though it does not conform to a normal understanding of this term.

This unique form of a prohibited 'use of force' requires that the assisting State place its territory at the disposal of another State, that the other State use the territory to perpetrate an act of aggression and that the assisting State 'allowed' the use of its territory for this purpose. In terms of the acting State 'making use of' the territory of the assisting State for perpetrating an act of aggression, Kreß notes that this occurs 'if its armed forces or the weapons that are used in the act of aggression are located on that territory' but that article 3 (f) does not require a direct territorial connection with the act of aggression.[37] Examples of use of territory falling within the scope of article 3(f) would thus include 'a command-and-control facility through which the act of aggression is being directed, or a military base from which targeting information for use in the course of the act of aggression is provided'.[38] The required degree of involvement of the aggressor (assisting) State within the meaning of article 3 (f) requires something approaching 'active collusion' rather than 'mere acquiescence' or a failure to prevent the use of its territory for perpetrating an act of aggression.[39] This degree of involvement therefore requires that the assisting State foresee the misuse of its territory and have 'knowledge of the circumstances' of the acts concerned[40] but does not require that the assisting State place its territory at the disposal of the acting State with the intention that the acting State use it for the purpose of carrying out an act of aggression.[41]

An example of inter-State assistance in which article 51 was invoked is Germany's assistance to the coalition's use of force in Syria and Iraq in 2015. The German parliament approved the military measures against IS in Iraq and Syria on the basis of article 51 of the UN Charter, article 42(7) of Treaty of the European Union and Security Council Resolutions 2170 (2014), 2199 (2015) and 2249 (2015).[42] Germany notified the UN Security Council under article 51 of the UN Charter that it had 'initiated military measures against the

37 *Ibid.*, 447.
38 *Ibid.*
39 Bruha, n. 27, 164.
40 *Ibid.*
41 Kreß, n. 31, 446.
42 Antrag der Bundesregierung, Drucksache 18/6866 (1 December 2015), Einsatz bewaffneter deutscher Streitkräfte zur Verhütung und Unterbindung terroristischer Handlungen durch die Terrororganisation IS auf Grundlage von Artikel 51 der Satzung der Vereinten Nationen in Verbindung mit Artikel 42 Absatz 7 des Vertrages über die Europäische Union sowie den Resolutionen 2170 (2014), 2199 (2015), 2249 (2015) des Sicherheitsrates der Vereinten Nationen.

terrorist organization Islamic State in Iraq and the Levant (ISIL)' 'in the exercise of the right of collective self-defence', and that '[e]xercising the right of collective self-defence, Germany will now support the military measures of those States that have been subjected to attacks by ISIL'.[43] Germany's invocation of article 51 could be evidence of a belief that the acts being justified would otherwise violate article 2(4), namely, support of coalition forces through the provision of intelligence, aerial refuelling and weapons delivery to coalition States. But the legal reasons for invoking article 51 were not explained and despite article 3(f) of the 1974 Definition of Aggression, there is a lack of clear subsequent practice of the parties to the UN Charter demonstrating their agreement that the term 'use of force' in article 2(4) includes such forms of inter-State assistance.

Article 3(g) The sending by or on behalf of a State of armed bands, groups, irregulars or mercenaries, which carry out acts of armed force against another State of such gravity as to amount to the acts listed above, or its substantial involvement therein

Similar to article 3(f), article 3(g) of the 1974 Definition of Aggression relates to forms of indirect aggression in which a State facilitates the unlawful use of force by another actor, in this case, by non-State actors. According to the ICJ in the *Nicaragua* case, the description in article 3(g) applies to the concept of 'armed attack' and is customary international law.[44]

There is debate about whether the State's 'substantial involvement' must relate to 'sending' or to the acts of armed force of the armed bands.[45] Kreß

[43] *Letter Dated 10 December 2015 from the Chargé d'affairs a.i. of the Permanent Mission of Germany to the United Nations Addressed to the President of the Security Council*, UN Doc S/2015/946 (10 December 2015), paras. 1 and 3.

[44] *Case concerning Military and Paramilitary Activities in and against Nicaragua (Nicaragua v United States of America), Merits, Judgment* (1986) ICJ Reports 14 ('*Nicaragua* case'), para. 195:

> The Court sees no reason to deny that, in customary law, the prohibition of armed attacks may apply to the sending by a State of armed bands to the territory of another State, if such an operation, because of its scale and effects, would have been classified as an armed attack rather than as a mere frontier incident had it been carried out by regular armed forces. But the Court does not believe that the concept of 'armed attack' includes not only acts by armed bands where such acts occur on a significant scale but also assistance to rebels in the form of the provision of weapons or logistical or other support. Such assistance may be regarded as a threat or use of force, or amount to intervention in the internal or external affairs of other States.

[45] Bruha, n. 27, 165.

points out that the French version is unambiguous that substantial involvement refers to substantial involvement in the sending:

> L'envoi par un Etat ou en son nom des bandes ou de groupes armés, de forces irrégulières ou de mercenaires qui se livrent à des actes de force armée contre un autre Etat d'une gravité tel qu'ils équivalent aux actes énumérés ci-dessus, ou le fait de s'engager d'une manière substantielle dans *une telle action*.[46]

There is also some debate about whether 'substantial involvement' is an alternative to or an application of the attribution test (direction or control); in other words, whether the conduct described is a form of 'indirect force' by the State itself or a form of attribution of the use of force by the armed group to the State. Article 3(g) of the 1974 Definition of Aggression must be read together with the chapeau of article 3 and article 2 of the Definition of Aggression, which refers to the first use of force by a State. Later ICJ judgments also discuss article 3(g) in terms of attribution.[47] Dapo Akande and Antonios Tzanakopolous[48] argue that article 3(g) reflects a customary rule for the attribution of acts by non-State actors to a State. Their position is that article 3(g) is merely an application of the direction or control test and that this is how the ICJ has interpreted it in *Nicaragua* and in the *Armed Activities* case.

Kreß argues that the test of attribution as set out in article 8 of the ILC Draft Articles should be applied to interpret the term 'sending', which according to the ICJ 'requires *effective* control over the specific acts in question, which is a very demanding threshold'.[49] But he goes on to discuss the 'alternative of the *substantial involvement* of a state *in the sending*', suggesting that this 'should, at the present stage of the legal development at least, be confined to the exercise of *overall* control by the aggressor state over the persons concerned, within the meaning of the case law of the international criminal courts, as initiated by the International Criminal Tribunal for the former Yugoslavia' in the *Tadic* case.[50] Kreß's argument is that it is controversial whether the overall control test of attribution forms part of customary international law (the ICJ has held that it does not). If we follow the ICJ, then 'the substantial involvement-limb of article 3(g) of the Annex to 1974 GA Resolution

46 Kreß, n. 31, 448 (emphasis on the singular added by Kreß).

47 For example, the *Armed Activities* case, n. 7, para. 146.

48 'The International Court of Justice and the Concept of Aggression' in Kreß and Barriga, n. 31, 214, 223–4.

49 Kreß, n. 31, 449, footnote omitted.

50 *Ibid.*, 449, referring to *Prosecutor v Duško Tadic*, ICTY Appeals Chamber Judgment of 15 July 1999, para. 145.

3314 should perhaps best be considered as the articulation of a *lex specialis* on attribution in the legal context of the prohibition of the use of force', especially considering that the ICJ has not elaborated on the meaning of 'substantial involvement in the sending'.[51] But if one adopts this interpretation, the result is that the 'substantial involvement' alternative in article 3(g) is rendered 'entirely redundant'.[52]

Kreß acknowledges that '[t]he ordinary meaning of "substantial involvement" is even wide enough to cover, beyond the exercise of overall control by a state over violent non-state actors, the (mere) toleration by a state of acts of armed force carried out by non-state actors from the territory of that state against another state'.[53] But he argues against this broad interpretation since the negotiations on the 1974 resolution do not show consensus on this point, the ICJ has not adopted this interpretation and since the lack of general acceptance of the US attempt to establish a 'harbouring doctrine' after the 9/11 terror attacks does not support a new customary international law rule on attribution.[54] Other scholars, such as Raphaël van Steenberghe interpret the ICJ case law and article 3(g) of the 1974 Definition differently and address the issue in terms of State 'substantial involvement' as an alternative to attribution.[55]

In the end, the interpretation of the term 'substantial involvement' in article 3(g) affects the scope of article 2(4) (as well as article 51). If one accepts that 'substantial involvement' is an alternative to the standard attribution test, the scope of articles 2(4) and 51 may be slightly broader and cover more State forms of involvement in attacks by non-State armed groups. In any case, this unlawful use of force is anomalous because, like the other form of indirect use of force under article 3(f) of the 1974 Definition, it is characterised by its lack of physical means or direct physical effects, unless one considers purely indirect means.

Conclusion

Although articles 1 and 2 of the 1974 Definition refer to 'armed force', the acts in article 3 listed earlier do not correspond to a normal understanding of 'force'. This shows that UN Member States interpret the concept of 'force' to include particular acts which do not correspond with the general definition of

51 Kreß, n. 31, 449.
52 *Ibid.*, 449.
53 *Ibid.*, 450, footnote omitted.
54 *Ibid.*
55 Raphaël van Steenberghe, *La légitime défense en droit international public* (Larcier, 2012), 319–22.

this term because they lack physical means and/or (direct) physical effects. Some explanations for this are considered at the end of this chapter.

Lower Gravity Anomalous Examples of 'Use of Force'

In addition to the acts set out in the 1974 Definition, there are other anomalous examples of acts characterised by States as a prohibited 'use of force' despite a lack of certain elements such as 'use' of physical force or a lack of physical effects. These include the following:

Intentionally Crossing a Border Bearing Arms with an Intention to Use Them Even before Any Weapons Are Fired

The mere crossing of a border by armed forces has sometimes been treated by States as a violation of the prohibition of the use of force, despite a lack of employment of physical means or of physical effects. For example, in the case of the *Temple of Preah Vihear*, Cambodia argued that Thailand committed a 'flagrant violation of Article 2, paragraph 4 of the Charter'[56] when it sent detachments of its armed forces to territory claimed by Cambodia in 1954 but subject to a border dispute between those two States, despite a lack of armed confrontation.[57] Similarly, in September 1964, Malaysia complained to the UN Security Council that Indonesia had committed 'blatant and inexcusable aggression' when it sent heavily armed paratroopers into Malaysian territory in the context of a broader political dispute.[58] The practice is however not clear-cut. For example, when Israeli commandos assassinated Khalil al-Wazir in Tunis on 16 April 1988, the UN Security Council adopted Resolution 611 (1988) condemning 'the aggression ... against the sovereignty and territorial integrity of Tunisia in flagrant violation of the Charter of the United Nations, international law and norms of conduct'.[59] However, it is unclear from the international response to this incident whether the mere act of *sending* Israeli armed forces into Tunisia for the purpose of carrying out the assassination (as opposed to the actual assassination itself) was sufficient in itself to constitute a

[56] *Temple of Preah Vihear, Application Instituting Proceedings, 30 September 1959, Pleadings, Oral Arguments, Documents* (1962) ICJ Reports vol. 1, 15.

[57] See also Olivier Corten, *The Law against War: The Prohibition on the Use of Force in Contemporary International Law* (Hart Publishing, 2010), 83.

[58] *Letter Dated 3 September 1964 from Representative of Malaysia to the President of the Security Council*, UN Doc S/5930 (17 September 1964), S/5930, OR, 19th year, Suppl. for July–September 1964, 263. See also Corten, *ibid.*, 78.

[59] UN Security Council, *Resolution 611* (25 April 1988) UN Doc S/RES/611.

prohibited 'use of force', having regard to the fact that no direct combat took place between the Israeli commando unit and Tunisian armed forces.[60]

Aerial Incursion

Similarly, there have been numerous instances of aerial incursion that States have treated as violations of the prohibition of the use of force, and in some cases, as an armed attack under article 51 of the UN Charter giving rise to a right to self-defence *despite the lack of employment of physical force and lack of physical effects*. For instance, Iraq, Lebanon and Libya have issued complaints to the UN Security Council regarding recurrent US incursions into their airspace, invoking the right of self-defence.[61] Likewise, the attempted US hostage rescue operation in Tehran on 24 April 1980 was characterised by both the United States (due to its invocation of article 51)[62] and Iran[63] as 'force' despite the relatively short period of the incursion and lack of any direct encounter with Iranian forces.[64] But the practice is mixed, since in similar cases of aerial incursion, article 2(4) or article 51 were not invoked. In the *Nicaragua* case, unauthorised overflight of territory was treated as a violation of sovereignty and was not characterised as a use of force.[65]

In the *Nicaragua* case, the ICJ held that '[t]he principle of respect for territorial sovereignty is . . . directly infringed by the unauthorized overflight of a State's territory by aircraft belonging to or under the control of the government of another State'.[66] However, the practice surveyed earlier demonstrates that States sometimes treat aerial incursion as an unlawful 'use of force' and not only a violation of sovereignty. If one considers that aerial incursion may

60 For a detailed legal analysis of this incident, see Erin Pobjie, Fanny Declercq, and Raphaël van Steenberghe, 'The Killing of Khalil Al-Wazir by Israeli Commandos in Tunis – 1988' in Tom Ruys and Olivier Corten (eds), *The Use of Force in International Law: A Case-Based Approach* (Oxford University Press, 2018), 403.

61 Tom Ruys, 'The Meaning of "Force" and the Boundaries of the *Jus Ad Bellum*: Are "Minimal" Uses of Force Excluded from UN Charter Article 2 (4)?' (2014) 108(2) *American Journal of International Law* 159, 184.

62 *Letter Dated 25 April 1980 from the Permanent Representative of the United States of America to the United Nations Addressed to the President of the Security Council*, UN Doc S/13908 (25 April 1980).

63 *Note Verbale Dated 28 April 1980 from the Permanent Representative of Iran to the United Nations Addressed to the Secretary-General*, UN Doc S/13915 (29 April 1980).

64 For an overview of the facts and the positions taken by the main protagonists and third States, see Mathias Forteau and Alison See Ying Xiu, 'The US Hostage Rescue Operation in Iran – 1980' in Ruys and Corten, n. 60, 306.

65 *Nicaragua* case, n. 44, Dispositif para. 5 and paras. 87–92, referring to Nicaragua's claims of high-altitude reconnaissance flights and low-altitude flights which caused 'sonic booms'.

66 *Ibid.*, para. 251.

indeed constitute an unlawful use of force, then the interesting question is raised of why this should be so, even when there is no application of physical force or physical effects. Note that this differs slightly from the issue of the legal regime governing the territorial State's response to such incursion, which is discussed later in the context of anomalous *non*-uses of force.

Conclusion

The anomalous examples of 'use of force' discussed earlier seem to be characterised by no use of weapon or no physical effects but an interference with sovereignty. The first category involves *military incursion without recourse to the use of weapons*, for example: unopposed invasion and unopposed military occupation, intentionally crossing a border bearing arms with an intention to use them even before any weapons are actually fired and aerial incursion into sovereign airspace. Other examples involve *unconsented mere presence* in territory, such as an unchallenged blockade and overstaying a Status of Forces Agreement. Another category of anomalous examples relates to the *indirect use of force* through assisting another State or non-State armed groups in their use of force.

ANOMALOUS EXAMPLES OF NON-'USE OF FORCE'

In addition to the above anomalous accepted instances of 'use of force' that do not correspond to the general interpretation of this term, there are also anomalous examples of forcible acts that appear to meet the key criteria of a 'use of force' but are nevertheless *not* characterised as illegal uses of force under article 2(4) of the UN Charter. This part will discuss anomalous examples of non-use of force in the air and at sea.

Forcible Response to Aerial Incursion

The previous analysis discussed State practice regarding aerial incursion into sovereign airspace and its characterisation as a 'use of force' in some instances. A related anomaly is the legal characterisation of forcible response to such incursion, such as shooting down the aircraft, as *not* a 'use of force' and therefore falling outside the scope of the *jus contra bellum*. For instance, in 1983, the Korean aircraft KAL flight 007 was mistaken for a spy plane and shot down by fighters in Soviet airspace. This was widely condemned but article 2 (4) was not invoked; instead, the shooting down of the aircraft was condemned as inhumane and disproportionate and in violation of Annex 2 of the Chicago Convention on International Civil Aviation ('Chicago Convention') regarding interception of civilian aircraft.[67] In 1996, the Cuban Air Force shooting down two civil aircraft was widely condemned as a violation of article 3bis of the Chicago Convention and resulted in UN Security Council Resolution 1067 (1996) condemning it without mentioning article 2(4) of the UN Charter.[68]

Scholars are divided over the question of whether the use of force by a State against intruding military aircraft in its own territory is governed by the *jus contra bellum*, or law enforcement/air law.[69] For example, Olivier Corten argues that the shooting down of a single military aircraft intruding in airspace is governed by air law rather than the *jus contra bellum*: 'if the measures taken against an intruding aircraft are considered police measures for air security, we are referred on to other conditions of lawfulness: prior warning, unless there is a manifest hostile intent, necessary and proportionate measure, or riposte in self-defence'.[70] In Corten's view, air law and the *jus contra bellum* have 'two separate domains of application'.[71] In support of this view, he cites articles 1 and 3bis(a) of the Chicago Convention (the latter which however states that '[t]his provision shall not be interpreted as modifying in any way the rights and obligations of States set forth in the Charter of the United Nations'). Corten also notes the International Law Commission's discussion of circumstances precluding wrongfulness uses the example of an aircraft in distress entering airspace unauthorised as being justified as *force majeure* or distress. Since the ILC regards article 2(4) as a peremptory norm, this aircraft example must not fall under the *jus contra bellum* but under aviation rules since violations of *jus cogens* cannot be justified by circumstances precluding wrongfulness and *lex specialis* is not applicable to such norms.[72] According to Corten, the way to determine which body of rules is applicable depends 'on the type of action in question, whether a simple police measure in the first instance, or an act of force in international relations in the second'.[73]

In contrast to Corten, Tom Ruys argues:

[67] This led to the drafting of article 3bis with specific rules for intercepting civilian aircraft (considered customary international law). For a discussion of this incident, see Corten, n. 57, 61–2.

[68] Ruys, n. 61, 204, footnotes 275–8, 207 at footnote 299; Corten, n. 57, 62–3. See also Corten, n. 57, 63–4 for a discussion of other aerial incidents in which article 2(4) was not invoked.

[69] See discussion in Chapter 4, 'International Relations', on whether this falls under the scope of the prohibition, or if the response is governed by law enforcement jurisdiction.

[70] Corten, n. 57, 60.

[71] *Ibid.*, 61, citing K-G Park.

[72] *Ibid.*, 64–5.

[73] *Ibid.*, 65.

> One cannot rely on the argument that 'minimal' use of armed force by way of enforcement measures within a state's own territory would somehow find its legal basis in 'particular (and mainly conventional) legal regimes on land (such as the Schengen convention), at sea (such as the Montego Bay convention), or in the air (such as the Chicago convention).' None of the conventions cited provides a legal basis for forcible action against unlawful territorial incursions by military or police forces of another state.[74]

He concludes that: 'whenever state A deliberately uses (potentially) lethal force within its own territory – including its territorial sea and its airspace – against military or police units of state B acting in their official capacity, that action by state A amounts to the interstate use of force in the sense of UN Charter Article 2(4).'[75]

A more recent incident raising this issue concerned the shooting down of a Russian fighter jet by Turkey on 24 November 2015. The jet was in the region as part of Russia's ongoing operation in Syria fighting the opposition with the consent of the Assad government. Russia disputes that its jet crossed the Turkish border, but Turkey claimed that:

> 2 SU-24 planes, the nationality of which are unknown have approached Turkish national airspace in Yayladaga/Hatay region. The planes in question have been warned 10 times during a period of 5 minutes via 'Emergency' channel and asked to change their headings south immediately. Disregarding these warnings, both planes, at an altitude of 19.000 feet, violated Turkish national airspace to a depth of 1,36 miles and 1,15 miles in length for 17 seconds from 9.24′.05″ local time. Following the violation, plane 1 left Turkish national airspace. Plane 2 was fired at while in Turkish national airspace by Turkish F-16s performing air combat patrolling in that area in accordance with the rules of engagement. Plane 2 crashed onto the Syrian side of the Turkish-Syrian border.[76]

Russia strongly protested against the shooting down of its jet and claimed that at the time it was shot down, it was 4 km within Syrian territory. It is clear that if Russia's aerial incursion was an armed attack, Turkey would have the right to use force in self-defence under article 51 of the UN Charter. Under the *jus contra bellum*, Turkey's response would be governed by the conditions of necessity and proportionality.[77] If it is proportionate to the goal of halting the

[74] 'Ibid'.

[75] Ruys, n. 61, 181–8, footnote omitted.

[76] *Letter Dated 24 November 2015 from the Permanent Representative of Turkey to the United Nations Addressed to the President of the Security Council.*

[77] *Nicaragua* case, n. 44, para. 176; *Legality of the Threat or Use of Nuclear Weapons, Advisory Opinion* (1996) ICJ Reports 226 ('*Nuclear Weapons* Advisory Opinion'), para. 41.

attack,[78] then the plane may be shot down. The key issue would then be when the right to self-defence arises – that is, when an 'armed attack' 'occurs'. There are different views regarding when the right to self-defence arises: for example, 'interceptive self-defence'[79] or imminence.[80] But if such an aerial incursion does not constitute an armed attack, then there is difficulty with explaining the legal basis for response to those small-scale incidents due to the 'gap' between a prohibited 'use of force' under article 2(4) and the higher gravity threshold of an 'armed attack' under article 51.

It remains disputed whether there is a right to use force against intruding military aircraft unless in self-defence.[81] But since it is very restrictive to hold that States can only respond to aerial incursions by military aircraft within their territory with force in the event of a strictly construed armed attack, there are three legal possibilities to address this. Firstly, one can interpret a lower threshold for 'armed attack' giving rise to a right of self-defence. Secondly, one can find an exception to the prohibition of the use of force outside article 51 self-defence and Chapter VII enforcement action – for example, 'proportionate defensive action against incipient attack',[82] or forcible countermeasures by the victim State to acts violating article 2(4) but falling short of article 51 armed attack[83] (however, this view is firmly in the minority position since it is widely

78 David Kretzmer, 'The Inherent Right to Self-Defence and Proportionality in *Jus Ad Bellum*' (2013) 24(1) *European Journal of International Law* 235.

79 Yoram Dinstein, *War, Aggression and Self-Defence* (Cambridge University Press, 5th ed, 2011), 204–5: 'Interceptive self-defence is lawful, even under Article 51 of the Charter [fn], for it takes place after the other side has committed itself to an armed attack in an ostensibly irrevocable way. . . . an interceptive strike counters an armed attack which is already in progress, even if it is still incipient.'

80 On the requirement of imminence, see Noam Lubell, 'The Problem of Imminence in an Uncertain World' in Marc Weller (ed), *The Oxford Handbook of the Use of Force in International Law* (Oxford University Press, 2015), 697.

81 See discussion in Chapter 4.

82 Ruys, n. 61, 176.

83 *Oil Platforms (Islamic Republic of Iran v United States of America), Judgment* (2003) ICJ Reports 161 ('*Oil Platforms*'), Separate Opinion of Judge Simma, para.13:

> To sum up my view on the use of force/self-defence aspects of the present case, there are two levels to be distinguished: there is, first, the level of 'armed attacks' in the substantial, massive sense of amounting to 'une agression armée', to quote the French authentic text of Article 51. Against such armed attacks, self-defence in its not infinite, but still considerable, variety would be justified. But we may encounter also a lower level of hostile military action, not reaching the threshold of an 'armed attack' within the meaning of Article 51 of the United Nations Charter. Against such hostile acts, a State may of course defend itself, but only within a more limited range and quality of responses (the main difference being that the possibility of collective self-defence does not arise, cf. Nicaragua) and bound to necessity, proportionality and immediacy in time in a particularly strict way.

accepted that since the advent of the UN Charter, forcible countermeasures, that is armed reprisals,[84] are unlawful).[85] The third possibility – which would constitute an anomalous example of non-use of force – is to interpret the prohibition of the use of force as not applying to a State's use of force against incursions by the military of another State within its own territory. This could either be on the basis that the contextual requirements of article 2(4) are not met, since the forcible act is not 'in international relations' or against the territorial integrity or sovereignty of another State or against the purposes of the United Nations, or on the basis that the act does not constitute a 'use of force'.

Maritime Law Enforcement against Foreign-Flagged Vessels with No Basis for Jurisdiction

A further example of forcible acts that appear to meet the criteria for a 'use of force' but are not consistently characterised as such relates to maritime law enforcement against foreign-flagged vessels that is without lawful basis. The use of force at sea is a complex issue, because it is governed by a parallel legal regime: the law of the sea. The law of the sea as embodied in the UN Convention on the Law of the Sea (UNCLOS)[86] recognises different legal spaces at sea and strikes a balance between the rights of coastal States and the general interest of all States to freedom of navigation and peaceful uses of the sea. The resulting regime can result in multiple States having enforcement jurisdiction over the same physical space because of the principle of exclusive flag State jurisdiction, territorial sovereignty of the coastal State over internal waters and the territorial sea (with the territorial sea subject to certain rights of other States such as innocent passage), a customs and immigration enforcement area within the contiguous zone but outside territorial waters, and the exclusive economic rights of the coastal State within its Exclusive Economic Zone (subject to freedoms of the high seas such as navigation, overflight and laying of cables). This is the most fraught zone of the seas, because it is here that there is a complex balance between the rights of the coastal State and the rights of all other States; this is a result of a compromise to create a new zone,

84 Claus Kreß, 'The International Court of Justice and the Non-Use of Force' in Weller, n. 79, 561, 593.

85 *Nuclear Weapons* Advisory Opinion, n. 76, para.46; ILC, 'Draft Articles on Responsibility of States for Internationally Wrongful Acts, with Commentaries, in Report of the International Law Commission on the Work of Its Fifty-Third Session' UN Doc A/56/10 (2001), art. 50.

86 *United Nations Convention on the Law of the Sea* 1982 (adopted 10 December 1982, entered into force 16 November 1994), 1833 UNTS 397.

the Exclusive Economic Zone of 200 nautical miles, while preserving other rights of third States. Not all rights are assigned within this area, so there remains uncertainty over the legal rights that the coastal State and other States are entitled to exercise within this zone. UNCLOS also recognises other maritime spaces such as transit straits, archipelagic seas and the high seas (subject to freedom of navigation and peaceful uses).[87]

In respect of purported maritime law enforcement with no basis for jurisdiction, despite the presence of elements of a 'use of force' identified in Part II, States do not always characterise such acts as a violation of article 2(4) of the UN Charter. The following section will discuss two examples of anomalous non-uses of force: response to non-innocent passage through the territorial sea by submerged submarines and unlawful attempts to exercise law enforcement jurisdiction on the high seas against foreign vessels (which has no legal basis outside certain recognised exceptions under customary international law and treaty, e.g. article 110 of UNCLOS).

An anomalous example of forcible acts which are not usually characterised as an unlawful 'use of force' is the forcible response to non-innocent passage of submerged submarines through the territorial waters of another State. The coastal State has sovereignty over the territorial sea, which may extend twelve nautical miles from the baseline.[88] Foreign vessels, including warships and submarines, have a right of innocent passage through the territorial sea.[89] According to article 19(1) of UNCLOS, '[p]assage is innocent so long as it is not prejudicial to the peace, good order or security of the coastal State. Such passage shall take place in conformity with this Convention and with other rules of international law'. Article 19(2) of UNCLOS specifies acts which render passage not innocent, including '(a): any threat or use of force against the sovereignty, territorial integrity or political independence of the coastal State, or in any other manner in violation of the principles of international law embodied in the Charter of the United Nations'. Article 20 states that: '[i]n the territorial sea, submarines and other underwater vehicles are required to navigate on the surface and to show their flag'. Furthermore, according to article 25(1): '[t]he coastal State may take the necessary steps in its territorial sea to prevent passage which is not innocent'. Under customary international law, foreign government vessels such as warships and submarines have

87 For an overview of maritime zones and the implications for maritime security, see Natalie Klein, *Maritime Security and the Law of the Sea* (Oxford University Press, 2011), 62–146. See also Francesco Francioni, 'Peacetime Use of Force, Military Activities, and the New Law of the Sea' (1985) 18 *Cornell International Law Journal* 203.

88 UNCLOS, note 86, arts. 2 and 3.

89 *Ibid.*, art.17.

sovereign immunity from the jurisdiction of any State except their flag State.[90] UNCLOS is silent on the measures that may be taken in response to non-innocent passage, and its article 25 does not explicitly authorise a forcible response to non-innocent passage. Thus, it is unclear which legal regime governs the forcible response of the coastal State to non-innocent passage by foreign government vessels.

This issue comes to the fore in instances of submerged submarines entering the territorial waters of another State in violation of article 20 of UNCLOS. For example, in 1982,

> Sweden utilized depth charges and mine detonations in its efforts to force a submarine that was near one of its naval bases to the surface, and further threatened to sink foreign submarines if they refused to surface and leave Sweden's waters. This threat was generally tolerated by other states, and could thus be indicative of what responses may lawfully be taken to respond to this particular security concern.[91]

A similar issue was raised in 2004 when a submerged submarine which was later identified as Chinese entered Japan's territorial sea. '[A] "maritime security operation" (*kaijo-keibi-kodo*) was ordered to the Commander of the Japan Maritime Self-Defense Force (JMSDF) Fleet, and patrol helicopters and vessels of the JMSDF joined the operation.'[92] The incident was framed by Japan as a violation of international law (specifically of article 20 of UNCLOS to which Japan and China are party). There was no invocation of the language of article 2(4) or article 51 of the UN Charter. Japan demanded an apology, explanation and assurance of non-repetition. Despite calls in the Japanese Diet for greater clarity over the measures that may be taken against submerged submarines in such situations, the government response plan does not address what measures it believes a State may take in response to violations of article 20.[93]

[90] Klein, n. 86, 64; UNCLOS, n. 87, art. 32: 'With such exceptions as are contained in subsection A and in articles 30 and 31, nothing in this Convention affects the immunities of warships and other government ships operated for non-commercial purposes.'

[91] Klein, n. 86, 41, footnotes omitted. For a discussion of the international response to this incident, see Corten, n. 57, 118–19 and Romana Sadurska, 'Foreign Submarines in Swedish Waters: The Erosion of an International Norm' (1984) 10 *Yale Journal of International Law* 34.

[92] Yukiya Hamamoto, 'The Incident of a Submarine Navigating Underwater in Japan's Territorial Sea' (2005) 48 *The Japanese Annual of International Law* 123, 123.

[93] See further Tomohiro Mikanagi and Hirohito Ogi, 'The Japanese View on Legal Issues Related to Security' (2016) 59 *Japanese Yearbook of International Law* 360, 367–9 for extracts of parliamentary question and answer sessions relating to measures against foreign government ships conducting non-innocent navigation inside the territorial sea:

These examples are anomalous because a coastal State may not exercise law enforcement jurisdiction over a foreign warship or submarine, since foreign government vessels enjoy sovereign immunity. Thus, a use of force against submerged submarines in the territorial sea in an attempt to bring them to the surface and require them to leave the territorial sea is not authorised by UNCLOS nor customary international law. 'To the extent that any maritime security threats or breaches are state sponsored, law enforcement powers against sovereign immune vessels are not available. Instead, questions involving the threat or use of force may arise and diplomatic or other avenues for dispute settlement must be pursued.'[94] In the absence of a basis for the exercise of jurisdiction against such vessels, a use of force against them would appear to be in international relations and fall within the ambit of the prohibition of the use of force under article 2(4) of the UN Charter, so it is curious that States do not always invoke self-defence to respond to submerged submarines in territorial waters. However, omitting to invoke article 2(4) or article 51 does not necessarily indicate an *opinio juris* that such incidents definitively fall outside the scope of article 2(4), since it could be motivated by other considerations (such as political) and also due to uncertainty over the applicable legal framework.

With respect to attempted law enforcement against foreign-flagged vessels on the high seas, this is sometimes but not always characterised as an unlawful use of force under the *jus contra bellum*. On the high seas, the principle of *mare liberum* and exclusive flag State jurisdiction with only few exceptions applies. This was affirmed by the Permanent Court of International Justice in the SS *Lotus* case: 'It is certainly true that – apart from certain special cases which are defined by international law – vessels on the high seas are subject to no authority except that of the State whose flag they fly.'[95] Exceptions to sole flag State jurisdiction on the high seas include the right of hot pursuit, plus 'the right of visit in relation to piracy, slave trading, drug trafficking, people

Regarding the following question, Deputy Commandant of the Japan Coast Guard Kunio Kishimoto explained as follows:

'(Question asked by Member of the House of Councilors Masahisa Sato) The Japan Coast Guard can take necessary steps to require foreign government ships to leave the territorial sea which are permitted under Article 25 of the United Nations Convention on the Law of the Sea. While it cannot conduct forcible boarding or arrest, I think that in certain circumstances, it can take forcible steps to require foreign government ships to leave the territorial sea, including ramming and the use of water cannons, as an exercise of police power. I would like to ask the view of the Coast Guard.'

[94] Klein, n. 86, 65.

[95] *SS Lotus Case (France v Turkey)* [1927] PCIJ Series A No 10 (7 September) 25.

smuggling, and unauthorized broadcasting'.[96] Therefore, attempts by a State to exercise jurisdiction against a foreign vessel on the high seas outside of these recognised exceptions or on the basis of a specific treaty (such as the 1995 Fish Stocks Agreement[97]) have no legal basis. With respect to interdiction (unilateral boarding and arrest of a vessel) by the non-flag State on the high seas, Douglas Guilfoyle argues that such unauthorised interference is 'a clear attack on a State's sole means of exercising a fundamental right'.[98]

A prominent example of high-gravity employment of force in purported law enforcement on the high seas without lawful basis is the 1967 bombing of a Liberian-flagged oil tanker, *Torrey Canyon*, by the United Kingdom to prevent marine pollution after it ran aground on the high seas outside British territorial waters.[99] 'The operation, conducted by the RAF, lasted several days with napalm bombs being dropped on the wreck to release and burn the oil remaining in the ship's tanks.'[100] The legal debate following the incident turned around the lawfulness of police measures on the high seas to prevent the risk of pollution, including the possibility of invoking necessity as a ground precluding wrongfulness.[101] Although the UK had no grounds for exercising law enforcement jurisdiction over the Liberian-flagged vessel on the high seas, and despite the high gravity of means and physical effects, the incident was not characterised as a 'use of force' under article 2(4) of the UN Charter. Corten argues that this precedent confirms that two separate legal frameworks can apply to the use of force at sea: one relating to police measures based on treaty or customary rules of the law of the sea, and the other governed by the *jus contra bellum*.[102] However, due to the lack of legal grounds for exercising law enforcement jurisdiction in this case, this argument is not convincing and the reasoning may lie elsewhere.[103]

[96] Klein, n. 86, 108; see UNCLOS, n. 87, arts. 99–111.

[97] *United Nations Agreement for the Implementation of the Provisions of the United Nations Convention on the Law of the Sea of 10 December 1982 Relating to the Conservation and Management of Straddling Fish Stocks and Highly Migratory Fish Stocks* 1995 (adopted 4 August 1995, entered into force 11 December 2001), 2167 UNTS 88, art. 21(14), discussed in Klein, n. 86, 78.

[98] Douglas Guilfoyle, 'Interdicting Vessels to Enforce the Common Interest: Maritime Countermeasures and the Use of Force' (2007) 56(1) *The International and Comparative Law Quarterly* 69, 80.

[99] See Ruys, n. 61, 203, footnote 271; Corten, n. 57, 58–9.

[100] Corten, n. 57, 59, citing Keesing's Contemporary Archives (1967) 22.003.

[101] *Ibid.*, 59.

[102] *Ibid.*

[103] This case is discussed further in Chapter 8.

The *Fisheries Jurisdiction (Spain v Canada)* case[104] before the ICJ is also sometimes cited in support of the argument that there is a *de minimis* gravity threshold that divides a '"minimum use of force", that can be ascribed to simple police measures, and a more serious use, that might come within the ambit of article 2(4)'.[105] In this case, Canada had entered a reservation to its acceptance of the Court's compulsory jurisdiction excluding the Court's jurisdiction over 'disputes arising out of or concerning conservation and management measures taken by Canada with respect to vessels fishing in the NAFO Regulatory Area, as defined in the Convention on Future Multilateral Co-operation in the Northwest Atlantic Fisheries, 1978, and the enforcement of such measures'. On the same day, Canada introduced domestic legislation regarding conservation and management measures over parts of the high seas. Canada then later enforced that legislation on the high seas 245 miles from the Canadian coast against a Spanish fishing vessel, the *Estai*, by boarding, inspecting and seizing the vessel. Spain protested and claimed that this was an unlawful use of force in violation of article 2(4). Canada argued that the Court had no jurisdiction to hear the dispute, since it fell within the scope of its reservation. Spain argued that since the acts complained of were unlawful under the UN Charter, they could not be regarded as falling within the scope of the Canadian reservation. Consequently, the case ultimately concerned whether the matter was a 'dispute[] arising out of or concerning conservation and management measures taken by Canada with respect to vessels fishing in the NAFO Regulatory Area, as defined in the Convention on Future Multilateral Co-operation in the Northwest Atlantic Fisheries, 1978, and the enforcement of such measures'.

The Court found that it had no jurisdiction because the measures taken against the *Estai* fell within the scope of Canada's reservation. In particular, it stated:

> Boarding, inspection, arrest and minimum use of force for these purposes are all contained within the concept of enforcement of conservation and management measures according to a 'natural and reasonable' interpretation of this concept.[106]

This statement has been relied upon by Corten to support his position regarding a *de minimis* gravity threshold distinguishing law enforcement

[104] *Fisheries Jurisdiction Case (Spain v Canada), Jurisdiction of the Court, Judgment* (1998) ICJ Reports 432.
[105] Corten, n. 57, 172, footnote omitted.
[106] *Spain v Canada*, n. 103, para. 84.

measures from a 'use of force' at sea. However, a close reading of the judgment shows that the Court was not drawing a boundary between 'use of force' under article 2(4) and the enforcement of conservation and management measures at sea. In fact, the Court explicitly declined to scrutinise the legality of the measures under international law (including article 2(4) of the UN Charter) since it did not have jurisdiction to do so.[107] The Court confined itself to interpreting 'conservation and management measures' in a technical sense (to see if the acts fell within the scope of Canada's reservation from its acceptance of the Court's jurisdiction) and was careful to distinguish this from the legality of the measures under international law. It was therefore left unsettled whether the enforcement measures violated article 2(4). This case therefore provides no support either in favour or against a gravity threshold that distinguishes law enforcement measures and a 'use of force' under article 2(4).

Conclusion

An analysis of anomalous examples of non-'use of force' such as forcible response to aerial and maritime incursion and purported maritime law enforcement may further clarify the complex relationship between competing applicable legal frameworks and where the boundaries between them lie, as well as indicate which elements of a 'use of force' are necessary and the relationship between those elements. The next section will discuss possible legal explanations for these anomalous 'uses of force' and non-'uses of force' under article 2(4) of the UN Charter.

POSSIBLE EXPLANATIONS

The problem remains of how to reconcile these seemingly anomalous examples with a coherent definition of a prohibited 'use of force' under article 2(4) of the UN Charter. There are several possible explanations for these anomalous examples of 'use of force' and non-'use of force', namely, that these are agreed exceptions to the general interpretation of a 'use of force' under article 2(4), the concept of 'use of force' is broader than generally understood or that a 'use of force' is characterised not by a checklist of essential elements

[107] There was disagreement between the judges over this approach. See Dissenting Opinion of Judge Torres Bernárdez, paras. 343 and 345; and Dissenting Opinion of Vice-President Weeramantry, para. 23 ff.

but of a basket of elements to be weighed and balanced. Each of these interpretive possibilities are canvassed further in the following sections.

1. *These Are Agreed Exceptions to the General Interpretation of Article 2(4)*

One possibility is that these anomalous examples are merely agreed exceptions to the general interpretation of a 'use of force' under article 2(4) and customary international law. This possibility is not excluded but would need to be strongly supported by subsequent agreement or evidence of subsequent practice demonstrating the parties' agreement to this interpretation. If one considers 1974 GA Resolution 3314 as a subsequent agreement regarding the interpretation of article 2(4) of the UN Charter,[108] an argument could be constructed to support recognised exceptions to the general interpretation of this term, as set out in the preceding section, namely: military occupation (as distinct from the invasion or armed attack preceding it) (article 3(a)), an unenforced blockade (article 3(c)), mere continuing presence in contravention of SOFA (article 3(e)) and indirect aggression either through '[t]he action of a State in allowing its territory, which it has placed at the disposal of another State, to be used by that other State for perpetrating an act of aggression against a third State' (article 3(f)) or '[t]he sending by or on behalf of a State of armed bands, groups, irregulars or mercenaries, which carry out acts of armed force against another State of such gravity as to amount to the acts listed above, or its substantial involvement therein' (article 3(g)). In this case, the general definition of a prohibited 'use of force' would apply, requiring the presence of the identified elements of a 'use of force', unless an act fell within the scope of an agreed special case.

This is of course possible, but there are two issues with this explanation. The first is that it would be preferable to find a solution that results in a consistent interpretation of this provision. This is not an insurmountable objection, since it may be that this is the situation *lex lata* even though it may not be the preferred interpretive outcome as a matter of legal policy. The second and more important issue with this explanation is that, although it explains certain anomalous examples of 'use of force' that do not display the usual elements (such as physical means or physical effects), it does not fully explain the phenomena in question. For instance, it does not explain anomalous examples of non-use of force discussed earlier (although of course, these could also be subsequent agreements regarding acts that fall outside the scope

[108] See Chapter 5.

of the prohibition). It also does not provide a satisfactory definition of an unlawful 'use of force' for acts that do not fall within subsequently agreed special exceptions to the general definition. As will be argued in more detail in the following chapter, a prohibited 'use of force' (even one that is a 'standard' type of force and not a special case such as unresisted invasion) is not characterised by a checklist of essential elements. The theory of subsequently agreed special types of 'use of force' therefore does not provide a full explanation of how to identify whether certain acts fall within the general definition.

2. *The Interpretation of 'Use of Force' Is Broader than Generally Understood*

An alternative explanation for these anomalous uses of force and non-uses of force is that the definition of a prohibited 'use of force' is broader than previously understood and encompasses acts which do not conform with the typical understanding of 'force' as derived in Part II. The 1974 Definition of Aggression could be regarded as a subsequent agreement that shows that UN Member States share a broader understanding of the concept of 'armed force'. The majority of the acts listed (articles 3(a)–(d)) involve classical acts of inter-State warfare, namely, invasion, military occupation, bombardment, blockade and attacks on the armed forces of a State or its marine and air fleets. The remainder of listed acts involve a special case of violation of sovereignty that could be (at a broad level) considered similar to military occupation due to the unconsented to and thus unlawful presence of the armed forces of another State within a State's territory (in the case of article 3(e)), and as closing loopholes in unlawful conduct by enclosing forms of indirect aggression such as certain forms of assistance to another State to commit aggression (article 3 (f)) or through sending/substantial involvement in the armed attack against a State by a non-State armed group (article 3(g)). All of these acts (including the case of attacks against the marine or air fleets of a State, due to the nexus to the State demanded by the scale of the attack, as denoted by the term 'fleets') share in common a violation of the territorial integrity, sovereignty and political independence of the victim State and serve to protect these interests. Therefore, in this sense it could be hypothesised that an unlawful use of force is something broader than the application of violence between States and encompasses any significant injury to the fundamental rights of State sovereignty and political independence.

This is more satisfactory than the previous hypothesis, because it provides a coherent (if presently vague) definition of a 'use of force'. But it is also problematic because like the first hypothesis, it does not fully explain *why* some acts fall within or outside the definition. Why is it that these acts should still be considered a 'use of force' under article 2(4) despite lacking certain elements, such as physical means or physical effects? Does it mean that those elements are not really necessary for an act to constitute a prohibited 'use of force'? How is this to be reconciled with the fact that most uses of force *do* display these elements? And, even more problematically, the possibility under consideration does not explain why other acts which may very well violate the territorial integrity, sovereignty and political independence of the victim State are *not* characterised as prohibited 'uses of force', such as certain forms of support for armed non-State groups. To conclude that the anomalous examples discussed earlier are explained by a broader understanding of 'use of force' is also unsatisfactory because it risks giving the prohibition of the use of force an overreach.

3. *'Use of Force' as a Type Rather than a Concept*

The third and arguably more convincing hypothesis is that these anomalous examples of use of force and non-use of force may be reconciled with a consistent interpretation of 'use of force' if it is accepted that a 'use of force' under article 2(4) of the UN Charter is a type rather than a concept. In other words, it may be that not all of the elements identified in Part II are necessary, although in particular combinations they may be sufficient, to constitute a 'use of force'. This hypothesis is explored in more detail in Chapter 8.

8

The Meaning of Prohibited 'Use of Force' in International Law

INTRODUCTION

This chapter proposes a framework for the definition of a prohibited 'use of force' that incorporates the elements identified in Part II and reconciles the anomalous examples of 'use of force' and non-'use of force' discussed in Chapter 7. It argues that a prohibited 'use of force' under article 2(4) of the UN Charter and customary international law is not a single category in which essential elements must all be present in order for an act to fall within the definition but rather that there are different 'types' of 'use of force' in relation to which these elements may be present in different combinations and must be weighed and balanced to determine if they meet a particular threshold. The theory of 'type' is firstly set out before explaining how it applies to the prohibition of the use of force between States in international law, with illustrative examples from State practice and two case studies. These case studies will apply type theory to two very different potential 'uses of force': the attempted killing of Sergei Skripal in the UK in 2018 with the nerve agent Novichok, and the use of force in outer space, to demonstrate how to apply type theory in practice to assess whether an act is a prohibited 'use of force'. Finally, this chapter proposes a general framework to identify an unlawful 'use of force' according to this theory.

WHAT IS A TYPE?

In the sense employed here, type denotes a category (here: 'use of force') which contains certain conditions (elements, such as physical means, physical effects etc.), not all of which are necessary or sufficient but which must be weighed and balanced to determine whether the threshold for the definition is met. A type is to be distinguished from a concept, in which an object (e.g. a forcible act) belongs to the set ('use of force') only if the shared group of necessary conditions are met (i.e. the conditions are all necessary and are jointly sufficient). A typical example of a concept is the definition of crimes: due to the requirements of *nullum crimen sine lege*, crimes under domestic and international law are typically defined by elements which must all be met in order for a particular act to fall within the definition. An example for illustrative purposes is the war crime of wilful killing, which has the following elements under article 8(2)(a) of the Rome Statute of the International Criminal Court (Elements of Crimes, footnotes omitted):

Elements

1. The perpetrator killed one or more persons.
2. Such person or persons were protected under one or more of the Geneva Conventions of 1949.
3. The perpetrator was aware of the factual circumstances that established that protected status.
4. The conduct took place in the context of and was associated with an international armed conflict.
5. The perpetrator was aware of factual circumstances that established the existence of an armed conflict.

Under this definition, each of the aforementioned elements is necessary and when these elements are all fulfilled, then they are also jointly sufficient for meeting the definition of the crime.

In contrast, it is proposed that a prohibited 'use of force' between States within the meaning of article 2(4) of the UN Charter is defined by a basket of elements, not all of which are necessary conditions; these elements do not all have to be present for an act to meet the definition. Instead, these elements are identified and weighed up to determine whether the threshold of the definition is met. In other words, individually each of these elements may not be necessary, but in a given case a particular combination of them may be jointly sufficient to constitute a prohibited 'use of force'. Conversely, if *none* of the elements are present, although they are not individually necessary, then the act will not constitute a prohibited 'use of force'.

The crime of *Nötigung* (coercion) under German criminal law provides an instructive illustration of the idea of type. *Nötigung* is a catch-all provision in section 240 of the German Criminal Code which criminalises the threat or use of force to coerce another person to carry out, suffer or refrain from an act.[1] The crime is defined as follows:

[1] I am grateful to Christian Kaerkes for his invaluable assistance with this topic.

Section 240 of the Strafgesetztbuch (German Criminal Code)[2]

Using threats or force to cause a person to do, suffer or omit an act

(1) Whosoever unlawfully with force or threat of serious harm causes a person to commit, suffer or omit an act shall be liable to imprisonment not exceeding three years or a fine.
(2) The act shall be unlawful if the use of force or the threat of harm is deemed inappropriate for the purpose of achieving the desired outcome.
(3) The attempt shall be punishable.
(4) In especially serious cases the penalty shall be imprisonment from six months to five years. An especially serious case typically occurs if the offender
   1. causes another person to engage in sexual activity;
   2. causes a pregnant woman to terminate the pregnancy; or
   3. abuses his powers or position as a public official.[3]

The definition of the crime of *Nötigung* requires that the behaviour be unlawful. This is essentially a means-ends analysis, as set out in sub-section (2). However, it can also be unlawful under this analysis to achieve a lawful outcome with a lawful act if the means (the use of force or the threat of harm) 'is deemed inappropriate' for that purpose. For example, this is usually discussed in relation to making threats to lodge a legitimate criminal complaint with the authorities in cases where the desired outcome of the threat (for instance, repaying a debt) is not connected with the criminal complaint itself (i.e. a case of blackmail). Other examples of *Nötigung* include (a) locking up a person;[4] (b) preventing a person from entering a building;[5] (c) 'unwanted' anaesthesia;[6] (d) turning off the heating of a property to compel the tenant to pay the rent;[7] and (e) tailgating in traffic.[8]

What is interesting about the crime of *Nötigung* for our purposes is that the German courts have interpreted this crime as comprising a number of factors which must be weighed up and which do not all have to be present for a

2 Criminal Code in the version promulgated on 13 November 1998, Federal Law Gazette [Bundesgesetzblatt] I p. 3322, last amended by article 1 of the Law of 24 September 2013, Federal Law Gazette I p. 3671 and with the text of article 6(18) of the Law of 10 October 2013, Federal Law Gazette I p. 3799.

3 Translation of the German Criminal Code provided by Prof. Dr. Michael Bohlander, available at www.gesetze-im-internet.de/englisch_stgb/englisch_stgb.html#p2015.

4 BGHSt 20, 194.

5 OLG Düsseldorf, NJW 1986, 942, 943.

6 BGH, NJW 1953, 351.

7 OLG Hamm, NJW 1983, 1505, 1506.

8 BGHSt 19, 263, 265 ff.

particular act to be 'deemed inappropriate' under section 240(2) and thus fall within the scope of the crime. Under the current definition of 'use of force' with respect to *Nötigung*, two elements of 'force' must be present: 'force' is defined as any physical action that produces a physical effect on the victim (to break his or her (expected) resistance).[9] However, the threshold of these requirements is extremely low; the mere act of sitting down or turning a key meets the requirements for a physical action, and a physical reaction (such as perspiring) can suffice to meet the requirements for a physical effect. There is one minor limitation to this, however: force against objects is usually not enough unless it also indirectly impacts on a person (e.g. destroying windows of a building in the winter so that the residents must vacate the premises).

In order to meet the elements of the crime of *Nötigung*, all relevant factors must be considered, although their specific requirements are debatable, including:

- lawfulness, weight and acceptability of the desired outcome;
- the intensity of the force;
- motivation;
- the weight of the encroachment on the freedom of the recipient of the use of force;
- a greater than insignificant effect on the receiver;
- priority of public authority (i.e. no vigilantism);
- internal connection between the act and desired outcome;
- effect on constitutional rights;
- legally relevant (not merely morally questionable) actions;
- individual autonomy (it is not unlawful if the act is considered an autonomous decision and is not required by the law);
- the factors listed in sub-section (4) are considered especially grave; and
- the context of the action/circumstances of the case.
- It is controversial whether long-term objectives of an act (e.g. environmental protection in violent demonstration cases) are legally relevant to determining if the definition of the crime is met; the majority does not consider them.[10]

Once the definition of 'force' is met, then one must weigh up the relevant factors against each other to determine whether the 'force' is unlawful under section 240. Each of the factors set out earlier may not be individually

[9] BverfGE 92, 1.

[10] For a discussion of these factors, see Claus Roxin, 'Verwerflichkeit und Sittenwidrigkeit als unrechtsbegründende Merkmale im Strafrecht' (1964) *JuS* 373.

sufficient or even necessary conditions for an act to meet the definition of *Nötigung*. To give some examples of the way that this balancing act has been carried out by the German courts:[11]

- Loading and aiming a gun to scare people away constitutes 'force'. It is unlawful if one could have requested assistance from the police in time (priority of public authority). Another factor is the potential danger of a gun and the violation of the law which forbids the possession of firearms.[12]
- Turning off the heating of an apartment can be an unlawful use of force or threat of harm. It is to be considered that cold temperatures can have deleterious effects on health and make the apartment uninhabitable. Another relevant aspect is whether or not the claim (here, the rent) is disputed.[13]
- With respect to a sit-in protest: To determine lawfulness, it is to be considered whether the protest is protected by the right to freedom of speech and/or freedom of assembly. Furthermore, a road blockade which only lasts for one minute is of such a short duration that it may not be punishable. Another factor is whether all or only some entrances are affected. It was also considered that the only people affected were those against whom the protest was directed.[14]
- A 'tailgating-case': Here, the court considered the danger of the behaviour with respect to important legal rights (i.e. possible traffic accident, because the car probably could not stop in time). The motive of the tailgating (to be able to drive slightly faster) was unreasonable. Another factor was again the duration of the dangerous act.[15]

In each of these cases, the factors identified earlier are not explicitly weighed up against each other in detail. Rather, the relevant factors in the specific case are identified, and the court determines whether these factors are sufficient to meet the requirements for an unlawful use of force for the crime of *Nötigung*.

TYPE THEORY AND 'USE OF FORCE'

It is proposed that a prohibited 'use of force' between States within the meaning of article 2(4) of the UN Charter is a type rather than a

[11] For key German jurisprudence regarding *Nötigung*, see BVerfGE 92, 1; BGHSt 23, 46 and BGHSt 37, 350.

[12] BGH, NJW 1993, 1869, 1870.

[13] OLG Hamm, NJW 1983, 1505, 1506 f.

[14] BayObLG, NJW 1993, 213, 214.

[15] BGHSt 19, 263, 265 ff.

concept; that is, it is characterised by a basket of elements, not all of which must necessarily be present for an act to meet the definition. Instead, these elements are identified and weighed up to determine whether the threshold of the definition of 'use of force' is met. In other words, individually each of these elements may not be necessary, but in a given case a particular combination of them may be jointly sufficient to constitute a prohibited 'use of force'. If some elements are weak, but other elements are of a higher gravity/intensity, then the balancing of the elements under the particular circumstances may result in an act meeting the definition of an unlawful 'use of force' under article 2 (4). As with the crime of *Nötigung*, there are two kinds of elements to weigh up to determine whether an act constitutes an unlawful 'use of force' under article 2(4): firstly, those relating to whether an act is a 'use of force', and, secondly, contextual elements that must be present for that 'use of force' to fall within the scope of article 2(4) and thus be unlawful under that provision.

Accordingly, if a 'use of force' is a type, then all 'uses of force' share elements in common; however, for an act to fall within the definition of 'use of force', it does not have to display *all* elements. The consequence of this is that there will be several different types of 'use of force', for example, classical uses of force employing armed force of a high gravity (bombardment, invasion against opposition), as well as uses of force that do not employ physical/armed force, such as an unresisted invasion or occupation. This theory is supported by the analysis of anomalous examples of 'use of force' and non-'use of force' in Chapter 7, which has demonstrated that each of the elements of a 'use of force' must not always be present for an act to constitute an unlawful 'use of force'. Putting it all together, it is apparent that none of the elements of a 'use of force' identified in Part II are strictly necessary for an act to meet the definition, except for the object/target of the use of force (as explained in Chapter 4 with respect to 'international relations', a nexus is probably required between the object or target of the 'use of force' and another State). The examples of 'use of force' which disprove the necessity of each of the elements of a prohibited 'use of force' are summarised as follows:

- *Physical force*: Military incursion without recourse to the use of weapons, unresisted invasion or military occupation, unconsented mere presence. Controversial: cyber operations, non-kinetic non-cyber operations.
- *Physical effects*: As earlier. Although there are 'uses of force' which do not have any physical effects, to be legally relevant to the equation of whether an act is a 'use of force', any effects must be physical and direct (no intermediate steps between the act and its result). In other words, although a physical effect is not necessary for an act to constitute an

unlawful 'use of force', non-physical and non-direct effects will not be relevant to the calculation. As discussed in Chapter 6, it is legally uncertain whether the physical effects must actually ensue (as opposed to merely potential effects), and if they must be permanent.

- *Gravity*: As discussed in Chapter 6, it is legally uncertain if there is a lower gravity threshold for an act to fall within the scope of the *jus contra bellum*. However, since even a single shot fired across the border by the military of one State could be considered an unlawful 'use of force', this appears to negate the argument that there is a gravity threshold for a prohibited 'use of force' under article 2(4).
- *Intent*: As discussed in Chapter 6, although it is legally uncertain, it seems that even an accidental use of force could be considered a violation of article 2(4) of the UN Charter under certain circumstances, such as 'the accidental projection of armed force . . . across a border' (e.g. shots or shells fired).[16]

This disproves the null hypothesis (the commonly accepted position which, if proven, would disprove the alternative hypothesis) that a 'use of force' is not a type but a concept, for which there is a checklist of fixed elements that must always be present for the definition to be met. Rather, determining that an act meets the definition of a 'use of force' is not a matter of going through a checklist of elements to see whether every element is present. Instead, it is an equation that must be weighed up.

On the basis of this type hypothesis, two kinds of elements are proposed that indicate an unlawful 'use of force' under article 2(4): firstly, elements relevant to whether the act is a 'use of force', and, secondly, contextual elements that are required to bring the 'use of force' within the scope of article 2(4) and render it unlawful. Since the latter are fundamental requirements, they are dealt with first:

(1) **Fundamental requirements (contextual elements)**: These are the necessary (but insufficient) contextual elements to bring a 'use of force' within the scope of article 2(4). These elements must always be present for an act to constitute an unlawful 'use of force' in violation of article 2(4), but on their own they will not suffice for an act to violate that provision (since it must also meet the definition of 'use of force'). 'Threat of force' is not considered here, but in respect of 'threats of force' under article 2(4), the

[16] Tom Ruys, 'The Meaning of "Force" and the Boundaries of the *Jus Ad Bellum*: Are "Minimal" Uses of Force Excluded from UN Charter Article 2 (4)?' (2014) 108(2) *American Journal of International Law* 159, 191.

same framework of analysis would apply with respect to the contextual elements.[17] These fundamental requirements follow explicitly from the text of article 2(4) itself, such as:

- two or more States;
- international relations;
- 'against the territorial integrity or political independence of any state or in any other manner inconsistent with the Purposes of the United Nations'.

Each of these elements is discussed in further detail in Chapter 4.

(2) **Elements that indicate that an act is a 'use of force'**: These relate to the meaning of 'use of force' rather than to the other terms of article 2(4). These elements are more likely to be based on subsequent agreement or subsequent practice (rather than the contextual requirements which are more likely to be text-based), since they do not come from a plain reading of the text of article 2(4) (or are not explicit) but are the result of a shared understanding of the parties to the UN Charter. These may include the following elements identified in Chapters 5 and 6:

- *Means*: Physical force
- *Physical Effects*:
  - Direct physical effects
  - Permanent versus temporary
  - Actual versus potential
- *Object/target*: In particular, the required nexus to a State. For non-State objects/targets that do not have a close association with a State, more will be required to bring the act within the scope of article 2(4), such as the presence of other factors including possibly the gravity of the (potential) effects, a pre-existing dispute between States or a coercive intent against a State.
- *Gravity of effects*: Noting again that the question of whether there is a *de minimis* gravity threshold is not solved by the text of article 2(4), which neither specifies nor excludes a gravity threshold for a use of force to fall within the scope of the prohibition. As discussed in Chapter 7, any such threshold may also differ by domain.
- *Hostile intent*: The text of article 2(4) strongly indicates that at the very least, an intended *action* is required. The text does not explicitly require

[17] The concept of 'threat of force' in article 2(4) is significantly less explored; see Nikolas Stürchler, *The Threat of Force in International Law* (Cambridge University Press, 2009) for an innovative analysis.

or exclude an intended *effect*, although State practice indicates that mistaken forcible acts are usually not treated as violating the prohibition of the use of force. There is textual support for the position that a coercive intent is required under article 2(4), due to the relationship between the prohibition of threats and uses of force; the relationship of the non-intervention principle and the principle of the non-use of force; and the object and purpose of the prohibition of the use of force in article 2(4).

Other relevant indicative factors that may relate to one or more of the aforementioned elements are:

- *Type of weapon:* The type of weapon employed could be relevant to the gravity of the (potential) effects and also to whether the 'use of force' is perceived to be in 'international relations', since certain sophisticated weapons could only have been developed by States and are not easily available to other actors, thus making it more likely for the victim State to conclude attribution and hostile intent. An example is the use of the chemical weapon Novichok in the Skripal assassination attempt, discussed in Chapter 6 and later in this chapter.
- *Political context*: As discussed in Chapter 4, the political context of a forcible act, such as whether there is a pre-existing political dispute, influences its characterisation as a violation of article 2(4). This relates to the contextual elements of prohibited force since the presence of a political dispute may bring an act within the realm of international relations and a use of force between States. It may also relate to elements relevant to whether the act is a 'use of force', such as gravity (e.g. by increasing the perceived level of security threat to the State) and intention (by demonstrating a hostile/coercive intention, or at the very least, an intention to influence or resolve a political dispute using force).
- *Who carries out the forcible act*: It is relevant whether the forcible act is carried out by military or police/other traditional law enforcement bodies, for example, the coast guard.[18] This is relevant not only in terms of attribution but also to the perception by the other State with respect to the perceived military nature of the act, and may also be relevant to the assessment of gravity and intent. Due to grey zone operations, this could

[18] See Ruys, n. 16, 207, who notes that 'forcible acts by military units are more likely to trigger Article 2(4) than forcible acts by police units'.

become increasingly relevant, for example, the use of maritime militia in the South and East China Seas.[19]

- *Location of forcible act:* It is also relevant to the assessment of whether an act constitutes a prohibited 'use of force'; whether the conduct and/or its effects occur within or outside a State's own territory (on land, sea or air respectively); within a third State's territory (land, sea or air); in disputed territory or in zones to which special legal rules apply such as a State's Exclusive Economic Zone, the high seas, international airspace, outer space or *terra nullius*. This is relevant not only to the applicable legal framework and jurisdiction but also to the 'international relations' aspect of the article 2(4) prohibition, and potentially also gravity (due to differences in potential threat or the type of force that is possible in each domain).

According to the type theory proposed here, the aforementioned elements must be identified, weighed and balanced to determine whether an act is a prohibited 'use of force' under article 2(4) and may be combined in different permutations to produce different *types* of 'use of force' which may not share all of the same elements. Part of such a balancing and weighing exercise implies that the weaker certain elements are, the higher the number or gravity/intensity of the other elements must be in order for the act to constitute a prohibited 'use of force'.

APPLYING TYPE THEORY TO ANOMALOUS EXAMPLES OF 'USE OF FORCE'

As discussed in detail in Chapter 7, there are several well-known and accepted 'uses of force' that violate the prohibition in article 2(4) but do not conform to all of the criteria normally associated with a 'use of force', namely, physical means and/or physical effects. These examples, taken from the 1974 Definition of Aggression,[20] include invasion and military occupation (article 3(a)), blockade (article 3(c)), mere presence in violation of a Status of Forces Agreement (SOFA) (article 3(e)) and indirect use of force either

[19] See Junichi Fukuda, 'A Japanese Perspective on the Role of the U.S.-Japan Alliance in Deterring – Or, if Necessary, Defeating – Maritime Gray Zone Coercion' in Scott W Harold et al (eds), *The U.S.-Japan Alliance and Deterring Gray Zone Coercion in the Maritime, Cyber, and Space Domains* (RAND Corporation, 2017), 23–41, which discusses the Japanese legal framework for response to various types of maritime incidents.

[20] UN General Assembly, 'Definition of Aggression' (14 December 1974), GA Res 3314 (XXIX). As explained in further detail in Chapter 5, this document is a subsequent agreement on the interpretation of the prohibition of the use of force in article 2(4) of the UN Charter under article 31(3)(a) of the Vienna Convention on the Law of Treaties.

through inter-State assistance (article 3(f)) or through non-State armed groups (article 3(g)). Other, lower gravity, examples discussed in Chapter 7 include intentionally crossing a border bearing arms with an intention to use them even before any weapons are actually fired and aerial incursion. Applying the type theory framework to these anomalous examples of 'use of force' helps to identify and explain why these are indeed unlawful 'uses of force'. The analysis results in the following two types of 'use of force' which display a different combination of elements, and highlights a unique third category of 'use of force' that is the result of subsequent agreement.

1. *Military Incursion without Recourse to the Use of Weapons*

Examples: unresisted invasion, military occupation (article 3(a) of the 1974 Definition of Aggression), intentionally crossing a border bearing arms with an intention to use them even before any weapons are actually fired, aerial incursion.

Contextual elements:

- Political context: In clear-cut cases (such as invasion and military occupation), the use of force occurs in the context of a political dispute and is clearly in 'international relations'.

Elements of 'use of force'/indicative factors:

- Lack of physical means.
- Lack of physical effects but high potential effects if escalation occurs.
- Actor: Military units, indicating a clearly implied intention to use force if resisted (hostile intent, possibly coercive intent depending on context).
- Location: Within the territory (including airspace) of another State, constituting a violation of sovereignty and territorial integrity and a high threat of escalation to physical means and physical effects on the territorial State.

2. *Unconsented Presence in Territory*

Examples: the blockade of the ports or coasts of a State by the armed forces of another State (article 3(c) of the 1974 Definition of Aggression); the use of armed forces of one State which are within the territory of another State with the agreement of the receiving State, in contravention of the conditions provided for in the agreement or any extension of their presence in such territory beyond the termination of the agreement (article 3(e) of the 1974 Definition of Aggression).

Contextual elements:

- Political context: In clear-cut cases (blockade), the use of force occurs in the context of a political dispute and is clearly in 'international relations'. In the less clear-cut case of overstaying in violation of a Status of Forces Agreement, the political context may be a decisive factor in the characterisation of the act as a prohibited 'use of force' by indicating if the act is one in 'international relations' and if there is a hostile/coercive intent.

Elements of 'use of force'/indicative factors: As in the previous example, there is a lack of physical means and physical effects, but the following elements and indicative factors are present:

- Actor: Military units, indicating an implied intention to use force if resisted (hostile intent, possibly coercive intent depending on context).
- Location: Within the territory (including airspace) of another State, constituting a violation of sovereignty and territorial integrity and a threat of escalation to physical means and physical effects on the territorial State.

3. *Special Case: Indirect Use of Force*

Examples: The action of a State in allowing its territory, which it has placed at the disposal of another State, to be used by that other State for perpetrating an act of aggression against a third State (article 3(f) of the 1974 Definition); the sending by or on behalf of a State of armed bands, groups, irregulars or mercenaries, which carry out acts of armed force against another State of such gravity as to amount to the acts listed earlier, or its substantial involvement therein (article 3(g) of the 1974 Definition).

Unlike the previous examples, due to the lack of both direct physical means or direct physical effects, this category of unlawful 'use of force' appears to really be an agreed special case rather than meeting the definition through a combination of elements that reaches a particular threshold. Thus, indirect force, unlike the other types of force discussed in this chapter, is a result of subsequent agreement between States regarding the interpretation of article 2 (4) of the UN Charter to cover certain forms of indirect force.

ILLUSTRATIVE EXAMPLES OF BALANCING THE ELEMENTS OF A 'USE OF FORCE'

Applying type theory to specific instances of inter-State 'use of force' further illustrates the notion of weighing the various elements of a prohibited 'use of force' to determine why some of these incidents were characterised by States as an unlawful 'use of force' and other similar incidents were not. Here, we will focus on the object/target of a use of force to explain why one attempted killing – that is, a forcible act with potential but unrealised effects (the attempted killing of George Bush) – was regarded by several States as an unlawful use of force but another (Sergei Skripal) was not. We will also examine excessive or unlawful maritime law enforcement to identify why some incidents (the *Mayaguez* incident, the *Germany/Iceland Fisheries Jurisdiction* case and *Guyana/Suriname*) were characterised as an unlawful 'use of force' whereas similar incidents (*Red Crusader*, *Torrey Canyon*, *Rainbow Warrior* and *M/V Saiga (No. 2)*) were not. As well as their explanatory purpose to show how type theory can help to clearly identify *why* particular incidents are or are not an unlawful 'use of force', these examples highlight the relationship between particular elements of a 'use of force'.

Potential Effects, Object/Target and Intention

A use of force with only potential but unrealised effects may require a higher level of (potential) gravity, intention, or an object/target that has a particularly close connection to another State (such as Foreign Minister/President) in order to be characterised as unlawful under article 2(4) of the UN Charter. Although these elements are elements of a 'use of force', they may also relate to the contextual element of whether the act is in 'international relations'. This is illustrated through the juxtaposition of States' legal characterisation of two attempted killings: that of former US President George Bush in 1993 and of the former Russian intelligence officer Sergei Skripal in England in 2018.

In the first incident, the Iraqi Intelligence Service (IIS) allegedly directed and carried out an attempted assassination of former US President George Bush by planning to explode a car bomb next to his motorcade on a visit to Kuwait from 14 to 16 April 1993.[21] In response, from 26 to 27 June 1993, the United States retaliated by launching twenty-three Tomahawk missiles against the headquarters of the IIS in Baghdad, destroying the building, killing at least six civilians and injuring twenty others. To justify the strike, the United States referred to article 51 of the UN Charter and stated that it was exercising the 'right to self-defence by responding to the Government of Iraq's unlawful attempt to murder the former Chief Executive of the United States

[21] For an explanation of the facts, reaction of States and legal analysis of this incident, see Paulina Starski, 'The US Airstrike against the Iraqi Intelligence Headquarters – 1993' in Tom Ruys and Olivier Corten (eds), *The Use of Force in International Law: A Case-Based Approach* (Oxford University Press, 2018), 504.

Government, President George Bush'.[22] The international response to the US action was mixed.[23] However, some States that expressed support or understanding for the US action referred expressly to the nature of the target of the assassination attempt, including Japan, Brazil, New Zealand and Spain.[24] In particular, New Zealand asserted that 'any nation that seeks to assassinate the Head of State or a member of the senior political leadership of another State commits an act of aggression. Such actions are at the most serious end of the scale because Heads of State symbolize the sovereignty and integrity of their country'.[25] Some scholars also 'emphasized that the protection of a state's elected officials would be an essential attribute of state sovereignty, especially taking into account the destabilizing effects that an assassination of a Head of State could have on the nation'.[26] Thus, although the international response to the incident was 'not unanimous and in most cases not unequivocal'[27] regarding the US self-defence claim, what matters for our purposes is the characterisation of the attempted killing itself as an unlawful use of force on the basis of the close nexus between the target and the victim State even though the intended harmful effect did not materialise.

In contrast, the attempted killing of Sergei Skripal in the UK by suspected Russian agents shows that when there is a relatively low nexus with the territorial State, the attempted killing of an individual by foreign State agents is not enough on its own for States to widely characterise the incident as an unlawful 'use of force' in violation of article 2(4). Mr Skripal (apparently a dual Russian/UK national and former double agent)[28] and his daughter Yulia

[22] *Letter Dated 26 June 1993 from the Permanent Representative of the United States of America to the UN Addressed to the President of the Security Council*, UN Doc S/26003 (26 June 1993).

[23] Starski (n. 21, 505, footnotes omitted) notes that '[q]uite a few scholars discussing the 1993 raid find that the legality of the US riposte was viewed largely favourably by the international community and met only with little opposition. This finding does not appear to be entirely accurate if the statements of relevant actors are analysed closely.' For a close analysis of the reaction of the international community, see *ibid.*, 507–9; see also Christine Gray, *International Law and the Use of Force* (Oxford University Press, 3rd ed, 2008), 196 ff.

[24] See Starski, n. 21, 507–9.

[25] UN Security Council, *Provisional Verbatim Record of the 3245th Meeting* (27 June 1993) UN Doc S/PV.3245, 23 (New Zealand).

[26] Starski, n. 21, 512, citing Alan D Surchin, 'Terror and the Law: The Unilateral Use of Force and the June 1993 Bombing of Baghdad' (1995) 5 *Duke Journal of Comparative and International Law* 457, 474 and Robert F Teplitz, 'Taking Assassination Attempts Seriously: Did the United States Violate International Law in Forcefully Responding to the Iraq Plot to Kill George Bush?' (1995) 28 *Cornell International Law Journal* 569, 609.

[27] Starski, n. 21, 507.

[28] Bill Chappell, 'Former Spy Sergei Skripal Released from Hospital, Recovering from Exotic Nerve Agent', *NPR* (18 May 2018), www.npr.org/sections/thetwo-way/2018/05/18/612259535/former-spy-sergei-skripal-released-from-hospital-recovering-from-exotic-nerve-ag.

were found unconscious on a bench in Salisbury and later hospitalised in serious condition together with an attending police officer. The United Kingdom alleged that a military-grade Novichok nerve agent of a type developed by Russia was used in the attack and accused Russia of being responsible for carrying out the attack. The Russian government denied any involvement.[29] Despite the use of a chemical weapon allegedly by Russian agents on the territory of the United Kingdom, the attempted killing was not widely denounced as a violation of article 2(4), possibly because of the lack of a particularly close connection between Mr Skripal and the territorial State. For such targets that do not have a close association with a State, other elements of a 'use of force' must be more serious to bring the act within the scope of article 2(4), such as the gravity of the (potential) effects, a pre-existing dispute between States or a coercive or hostile intent against a State. In this case, the UK emphasised the gravity of the potential effects of the chemical weapon on the wider public when claiming that the attack on Mr Skripal was an unlawful use of force in violation of article 2(4).[30] This incident is analysed in more detail as a case study to illustrate the application of type theory later in this chapter.

'International Relations', Gravity and Intention

As argued in Chapter 6, the elements of 'international relations', gravity and intention are interrelated. This is illustrated in the following case study on excessive or unlawful maritime law enforcement and 'use of force'. With respect to excessive maritime law enforcement, there is mixed practice in this regard. First of all, why would a use of force against a civilian vessel registered to another State be considered 'force' under article 2(4) at all? The reason is the principle of exclusive flag State jurisdiction – a use of force against a civilian vessel by a non-flag State is the exercise of enforcement jurisdiction within a domain subject to the exclusive jurisdiction of another State. It may therefore under certain circumstances fall under 'international relations' and

29 'Russian Spy: What Happened to the Skripals?', *BBC News* (18 April 2018), www.bbc.com/news/uk-43643025.

30 'The Russian State Was Responsible for the Attempted Murder … and for Threatening the Lives of Other British Citizens in Salisbury: Statement by Ambassador Jonathan Allen, Chargé d'Affaires, at a UN Security Council Briefing on a Nerve Agent Attack in Salisbury' (14 March 2018), www.gov.uk/government/speeches/the-russian-state-was-responsible-for-the-attempted-murderand-for-threatening-the-lives-of-other-british-citizens-in-salisbury.

be considered to be against the sovereignty of another State (i.e. the flag State). It is important to note that different international law principles apply to use of force in law enforcement versus a use of inter-State force under the *jus contra bellum*.[31] Patricia Jiminez Kwast makes the important point that there are two separate issues: which legal category applies (law enforcement or use of force), and whether the act complies with the lawful requirements of that category – just because law enforcement action is unlawful under that framework does not automatically render it a violation of the prohibition of the use of force.[32] Tom Ruys posits that

> [a]n argument could therefore be developed that enforcement action undertaken by the territorial state within its territory or, by extension, against merchant vessels in relation to a coastal state's Exclusive Economic Zone or continental shelf – even if the action is tainted by illegality – is presumed not to affect the international relations between those states and accordingly remains beyond the reach of Article 2(4). Only if it appears from the circumstances of the case that the force used 'directly arises from a dispute between sovereign States' will this presumption be rebutted.[33]

In light of the increasing constabulary role of navies, especially in the South and East China Seas, the distinction between these two applicable legal frameworks and their boundary is of particular relevance.[34]

State practice shows that States do sometimes consider purported maritime law enforcement to be a use of force. There are numerous examples in State practice where forcible acts at sea were characterised by States as a violation of article 2(4): the 1975 *Mayaguez* incident (self-defence); the *Germany/Iceland Fisheries Jurisdiction* case (Germany claimed a violation of article 2(4), although the Court did not rule on this point); the *Canada/Spain Fisheries*

[31] For an overview of the jurisprudence regulating use of force in maritime law enforcement, see Matteo Tondini, 'The Use of Force in the Course of Maritime Law Enforcement Operations' (2017) 4(2) *Journal on the Use of Force and International Law* 253; with respect to international human rights law principles applicable to the use of force in law enforcement, see Nigel Rodley and Matt Pollard, *The Treatment of Prisoners under International Law* (Oxford University Press, 3rd ed, 2009), 246–78.

[32] Patricia Jiminez Kwast, 'Maritime Law Enforcement and the Use of Force: Reflections on the Categorisation of Forcible Action at Sea in the Light of the Guyana/Suriname Award' (2008) 13(1) *Journal of Conflict and Security Law* 49.

[33] Ruys, n. 16, 206.

[34] See Tondini, n. 31; Ivan T Luke, 'Naval Operations in Peacetime: Not Just "Warfare Lite"' (2013) 66(2) *Naval War College Review* 11, 13; Harold et al, n. 19.

Jurisdiction case (Spain claimed a violation of article 2(4), but the Court held it had no jurisdiction – discussed in Chapter 7); and the *Guyana/Suriname* arbitration. However, State practice is not consistent and numerous similar incidents have not been characterised as an unlawful use of force under article 2(4). These include the 1962 *Red Crusader* (Denmark/UK) case, the 1967 *Torrey Canyon* incident, the 1985 *Rainbow Warrior* incident and the 1997 *M/V Saiga (No. 2)* incident. It is therefore instructive to examine these incidents through the lens of type theory (i.e. the identification and balancing of the elements of a 'use of force') to see why only some of these incidents were characterised as an unlawful 'use of force'.

Excessive Maritime Law Enforcement

The *Mayaguez* incident in 1975 occurred in the context of the Vietnam War and the recent ousting of the US-backed Khmer Republic by the Khmer Rouge. The US-flagged container ship the *Mayaguez* and its crew were seized by Cambodian naval forces within Cambodian territorial waters, although the United States disputed the twelve nautical mile rule at the time. During the seizure of the vessel, the Khmer Rouge naval vessel fired a machine gun and then a rocket-propelled grenade across the bow of the ship before boarding and seizing the vessel.[35] The United States launched a rescue operation, citing article 51 of the UN Charter.[36] The seizure of the *Mayaguez* was thus considered an unlawful 'use of force' (and 'armed attack') by the United States, giving rise to a right to self-defence. In this incident, the target of the use of force had a strong connection to the victim State (given the political context) and due to the surrounding events, the forcible act evinced a hostile intent and was clearly in the 'international relations' between the two States concerned. Thus, the contextual elements of an unlawful 'use of force' were present. In terms of elements of 'use of force', the gravity of the physical means was moderate, as was the gravity of the physical effects (the seizure of the vessel and its crew).

[35] Ralph Wetterhahn, *The Last Battle: The Mayaguez Incident and the End of the Vietnam War* (Plume, 2002); for a legal analysis of the incident, see Natalino Ronzitti, 'The Mayaguez Incident – 1975' in Tom Ruys and Olivier Corten (eds), *The Use of Force in International Law: A Case-Based Approach* (Oxford University Press, 2018), 213.

[36] *Letter Dated 14 May 1975 from the Permanent Representative of the United States of America to the United Nations Addressed to the President of the Security Council*, UN Doc S/11689 (15 May 1975).

In contrast, in the *Red Crusader* incident in 1962, maritime law enforcement was found to be excessive and unlawful but was not characterised as a violation of article 2(4) of the UN Charter. In that incident, Danish authorities arrested a British-flagged vessel in Danish territorial waters and fired shots at the vessel without warning. The International Commission of Inquiry found:[37]

> In opening fire at 03.22 hours up to 03.53 hours, the commanding officer of the Niels Ebbeen exceeded legitimate use of armed force on two counts: (a) firing without warning of solid gun-shot; (b) creating danger to human life on board the Red Crusader without proved necessity, by the effective firing at the Red Crusader after 03.40 hours.[38]

Similarly, in the 1997 *M/V Saiga (No. 2)* incident, maritime law enforcement was found to be excessive but not an unlawful 'use of force' under article 2(4) of the UN Charter. In that incident, Guinea arrested a vessel flagged to St Vincent and the Grenadines within the Exclusive Economic Zone of Guinea, injuring at least two crew members. St Vincent and the Grenadines did not claim that it was a violation of article 2(4) but of the UN Convention on the Law of the Sea[39] (UNCLOS) articles 56(2) and 58, 111, 292 (freedom of navigation, violation of hot pursuit conditions and prompt release). The International Tribunal for the Law of the Sea also did not raise article 301 of UNCLOS nor article 2(4) of the UN Charter. The Tribunal instead applied the requirements for lawfulness of use of force in law enforcement measures:[40]

> In considering the use of force used by Guinea in the arrest of the Saiga, the Tribunal must take into account the circumstances of the arrest in the context of the applicable rules of international law. Although the Convention does not contain express provisions on the use of force in the arrest of ships, international law, which is applicable by virtue of article 293 of the Convention, requires that the use of force must be avoided as far as possible and, where force in unavoidable, it must not go beyond what is

[37] *Judgment of 23 May 1962* (1967) 35 International Law Reports 499.

[38] See Olivier Corten, *The Law against War: The Prohibition on the Use of Force in Contemporary International Law* (Hart Publishing, 2010), 58, who states that '[w]hen the "use of armed force" is applied here, there is plainly no question of applying article 2(4) of the UN Charter'.

[39] *United Nations Convention on the Law of the Sea* 1982 (adopted 10 December 1982, entered into force 16 November 1994), 1833 UNTS 397.

[40] *M/V 'Saiga' (No. 2) (St. Vincent v Guinea)*, ITLOS Case No. 2, Merits (1 July 1999), paras. 155–6.

> reasonable and necessary in the circumstances. Considerations of humanity must apply in the law of the sea, as they do in other areas of international law. These principles have been followed over the years in law enforcement operations at sea.

In the *Red Crusader* and *M/V Saiga (No. 2)* incidents, it is not apparent that the vessels were targeted due to their nationality nor in the context of a political dispute between the States concerned. There was no apparent coercive or hostile intent against the flag State, given that Denmark and Guinea respectively were enforcing domestic laws within their own territorial sea (in the case of the *Red Crusader*) or Exclusive Economic Zone (in the case of the *M/V Saiga (No. 2)*. As the forcible act did not occur in the international relations between the States concerned, the contextual elements of an unlawful 'use of force' are missing. In terms of elements of 'use of force', the physical means employed and their physical effects were of relatively low gravity. This coupled with a low nexus and a lack of hostile intent against another State results in an insufficient combination of elements of a 'use of force' including their relative weight. Accordingly, these two incidents were deemed to fall within the realm of law enforcement rather than the *jus contra bellum*.

Maritime Law Enforcement with No Basis for Jurisdiction

In contrast to the previous incidents which involved excessive maritime law enforcement, the following category of incidents involved the purported exercise of law enforcement against foreign-flagged vessels with no (or a disputed) basis for jurisdiction because it took place in the territorial waters of another State, on the high seas or in a disputed maritime zone.

In the incidents of the *Fisheries Jurisdiction case (Germany v Iceland)* and the *Guyana v Suriname* arbitration, the purported maritime law enforcement by Iceland and Suriname respectively were characterised by the 'victim' State as either an unlawful use or threat of force. These incidents both occurred in disputed maritime zones. In the former case, Iceland sought to unilaterally extend its fisheries jurisdiction to fifty miles from the baseline. Germany challenged this and claimed that Iceland's actions in enforcing this extended fisheries jurisdiction zone against German fishing vessels by cutting their nets and firing warning shots and live rounds was a violation of article 2(4) of the UN Charter.[41] The International Court of Justice (ICJ) did not analyse

[41] Part V of Germany's memorial and Annexes G, H, I, K and L.

Germany's submission regarding use of force in substance. Instead, it made a finding on procedural grounds that it was unable to accede to the submission, since it was not put in concrete terms seeking specific damages with evidence to support each claim.[42] In the case of *Guyana v Suriname* in 2007, Guyana claimed that the Surinamese navy had violated article 2(4) of the UN Charter by ordering an oil rig and drill ship operating under licences issued by Guyana to leave the disputed maritime zone in which they were operating.[43] The tribunal held that 'the action mounted by Suriname on 3 June 2000 seemed akin to a threat of military action rather than a mere law enforcement activity'.[44]

Applying type theory to these incidents, they were each characterised by the other State (and by the arbitral tribunal in *Guyana v Suriname*) as a use or threat of force despite the relatively low gravity of each incident in terms of their physical means and effects. One explanation is that since each incident took place within a disputed maritime zone and as a means of enforcing the State's claim to that zone, it was a coercive measure in the 'international relations' between the respective States. Thus, even incidents of low gravity in physical means and physical effects may suffice to meet the definition of unlawful use or threat of force when combined with a clear coercive intent and when the incident clearly takes place within 'international relations'.

In contrast, the incident of the *Torrey Canyon* in 1967, in which the British RAF dropped napalm bombs on a Liberian-flagged oil tanker which ran aground on the high seas (discussed in the Chapter 7), was not characterised as an unlawful 'use of force' despite the lack of legal grounds for the UK to exercise law enforcement jurisdiction against the vessel to prevent marine pollution under either treaty or customary international law. Clearly, a high gravity of physical means and physical effects were present in this case. One basis for the lack of any invocation of article 2(4) in relation to this incident could be that the contextual requirement of 'international relations' was missing. Given that the UK had a clear and limited intention to release and burn the remaining oil in the vessel's tanks to prevent marine pollution on the high seas (an intention that was accepted as legitimate by the international

[42] *Ibid.*, para. 76. This reasoning was criticised by some of the judges, for example, Declaration of Judge Dillard, 207–8; Separate Opinion of Judge Waldock, para. 13; Dissenting Opinion of Judge Onyeama, 250–1.

[43] *Arbitral Tribunal Constituted Pursuant to Article 287, and in Accordance with Annex VII of the UN Convention on the Law of the Sea (Guyana and Suriname)* (17 September 2007), para. 151 ff. See also Corten, n. 38, 72–3 and Ruys, n. 16, 205.

[44] *Arbitral Tribunal, Ibid.*, paras. 443–4.

community as a whole, as demonstrated by the subsequent adoption of the International Convention on Intervention on the High Seas in Cases of Oil Pollution Casualties[45] to permit this type of action), and the application of force, though deliberate, was not coercive or hostile with respect to the flag State, it was not regarded by any State to engage the 'international relations' between the UK and the flag State of the vessel, Liberia, or any other State.[46]

In the *Rainbow Warrior* affair, on 10 July 1985, on official orders, French secret service agents carried out an attack against a British-flagged civilian (Greenpeace) vessel moored in the internal waters of New Zealand. Two high explosive devices detonated and sunk the vessel, killing a Dutch citizen who was on board.[47] The New Zealand government argued that the attack against the *Rainbow Warrior* was a 'serious violation of basic norms of international law . . . specifically, it involved a serious violation of New Zealand sovereignty and of the Charter of the United Nations' and sought reparations.[48] However, New Zealand did not allege a violation of article 2(4). Olivier Corten argues that this is probably because the operation was limited in scope and was not ordered by 'the highest echelons of the State'.[49] Applying type theory analysis to this incident, we can see that the attack clearly took place in the 'international relations' between the two States since it was officially ordered and carried out by French government agents and constituted a serious violation of the sovereignty of New Zealand. However, there was no hostile or coercive intention vis-a-vis New Zealand and although the physical means employed were of relatively high gravity, the physical effect on the 'victim' State

45 Adopted 29 November 1969, entered into force 6 May 1975, 970 UNTS 221; see also (the subsequently adopted) UNCLOS article 221, which also authorises States to 'take and enforce measures beyond the territorial sea proportionate to the actual or threatened damage to protect their coastline or related interests, including fishing, from pollution or threat of pollution following upon a maritime casualty or acts relating to such a casualty, which may reasonably be expected to result in major harmful consequences'.

46 This kind of limited intention negating the 'international relations' contextual element and resulting in a 'use of force' falling outside the scope of article 2(4) is to be distinguished from other claims of limited purpose to legally justify a 'use of force', such as humanitarian intervention, since the latter is less unambiguously to be regarded as occurring within 'international relations' and is also not universally regarded as a legitimate (as evidenced by the continuing heated controversy surrounding its morality and legality).

47 *Memorandum of the Government of New Zealand to the Secretary-General of the United Nations* (6 July 1986) Reports of International Arbitral Awards, vol. XIX, 201.

48 *Ibid.*, 201–2.

49 Corten, n. 38, 86.

(New Zealand) was confined to a violation of sovereignty, since the vessel was British-flagged and the person killed in the attack was of Dutch nationality. As such, New Zealand did not treat the matter as an unlawful 'use of force' against it but as a domestic crime (by the secret service agents who carried out the attack) and a violation of its sovereignty by France.

This conclusion has implications for a wider debate under *jus in bello* regarding whether 'non-consensual force against a non-State actor on the territory of another State is always an [International Armed Conflict (IAC)], as opposed to those who say it is only sometimes an IAC, depending on the circumstances'.[50] The classification of conflict under *jus in bello* is a separate question to whether an act is a prohibited 'use of force' under *jus contra bellum* and is relevant to whether (and which) rules of international humanitarian law (IHL) apply to the conduct of hostilities. The International Committee of the Red Cross (ICRC) appears to take the first position set out earlier, stating that an IAC 'arises between the territorial State and the intervening State when force is used on the former's territory without its consent'.[51] The benefit of this approach is that it provides legal certainty regarding the classification of conflict and applicability of IHL rules to ensure protection. Others such as Noam Lubell point out the absurdity of applying this approach to incidents such as the sinking of the *Rainbow Warrior* since this would lead to the conclusion that there was an IAC between France and New Zealand, which 'would ... seem incongruous with the notion of IAC' and lead to inappropriate application of IHL rules to the situation.[52] The conclusion of the type theory analysis in this chapter that the sinking of the *Rainbow Warrior* was not a 'use of force' under article 2(4) of the UN Charter allows a way out of the impasse and has the potential to provide clarity to the debate on classification of conflict under *jus in bello* when States use force against non-State actors on the territory of another State. A more detailed analysis of the relationship between 'use of force' under *jus contra bellum* and classification of conflict under *jus in bello* is beyond the scope of this book.

[50] See Noam Lubell, 'Fragmented Wars: Multi-Territorial Military Operations against Armed Groups' (2017) 93 *International Law Studies* 215, 231–8, with further references to scholarship on both sides of the debate at footnote 42.

[51] International Committee of the Red Cross, *Commentary to the Geneva Convention I for the Amelioration of the Condition of the Wounded and Sick in the Armed Forces in the Field* (2nd ed, 2016), 262. See also Dapo Akande, 'Classification of Armed Conflicts: Relevant Legal Concepts' in Elizabeth Wilmshurst (ed), *International Law and the Classification of Conflicts* (Oxford University Press, 2012), 32, 70–9.

[52] Lubell, n. 50, 234.

CASE STUDY: THE ATTEMPTED KILLING OF SERGEI SKRIPAL

The final part of this chapter sets out a detailed analysis of two illustrative examples in order to demonstrate how to apply type theory to a specific incident. The first case study that will be analysed is the killing of Sergei Skripal in the UK in 2018. The second case study concerns the use of force in outer space. This exercise will show the usefulness of type theory for analysing controversial or borderline incidents and demonstrate how to apply it in concrete cases, as well as highlighting the open questions and challenges involved.

Facts and Legal Claim

As briefly discussed earlier in this chapter, Mr Skripal, a former Russian double agent,[53] was the subject of an attempted assassination in Salisbury in the United Kingdom in 2018 using a military-grade nerve agent, Novichok. Traces of the nerve agent Novichok were later discovered at nine sites around Salisbury, with the highest concentration on the door-knob of Mr Skripal's home.[54] A UK police investigation identified two Russian military intelligence officers as the main suspects in the attack on Mr Skripal.[55] The United Kingdom accused Russia of the attempted killing, with the Russian government denying involvement in the attack.

In a statement to the House of Commons on 14 March 2018, UK Prime Minister Theresa May said that the UK government had given Russia one day to account for the incident and stated: 'Should there be no credible response, we will conclude that this action amounts to an unlawful use of force by the Russian State against the United Kingdom. … this attempted murder using a weapons-grade nerve agent in a British town was … an indiscriminate and reckless act against the United Kingdom, putting the lives of innocent civilians at risk.'[56] On 14 March 2018, the UK

[53] 'Sergei Skripal: Who Is the Former Russian Intelligence Officer?' *BBC News* (29 March 2018), www.bbc.com/news/world-europe-43291394.

[54] 'Russian Spy: What Happened to the Skripals?', n. 29.

[55] Gordon Corera, 'Salisbury Poisoning: What Did the Attack Mean for the UK and Russia?' *BBC News* (4 March 2020), www.bbc.com/news/uk-51722301.

[56] UK Government, 'PM Commons Statement on Salisbury Incident Response: A Statement to the House of Commons by Prime Minister Theresa May following the Salisbury Incident' (14 March 2018), www.gov.uk/government/speeches/pm-commons-statement-on-salisbury-incident-response-14-march-2018. See also the UK's briefing to the North Atlantic Council in

Ambassador Jonathan Allen, in a briefing to the UN Security Council, stated that the UK 'conclude[d] that the Russian State was responsible for the attempted murder of Mr Skripal and his daughter, and Police Officer Nick Bailey, and for threatening the lives of other British citizens in Salisbury' and described it as 'an unlawful use of force – a violation of article two of the United Nations charter, the basis of the international legal order'.[57]

Applying type theory to the Skripal incident shows that the contextual elements in this incident are factually contentious, whereas the elements of a 'use of force' are legally contentious. The systematic application of type theory highlights that the crux of the matter is whether the potential effects of the purported use of force suffice to render the act a violation of *jus contra bellum*.

Contextual Elements

- *Two or more States*: If, as the UK claimed, Russia was responsible for the attack, then this contextual element is fulfilled. Of course, this would need to be substantiated by evidence and fulfil the attribution requirements under international law.[58] For the purposes of this analysis, we will leave these aside in order to focus on the legally contentious aspects of the incident.
- *In their 'international relations'*: Again, proceeding on the assumption that the attack is attributable to Russia, the use of a prohibited nerve agent on the territory of another State to carry out a targeted killing is clearly in 'international relations'.
- *'[A]gainst the territorial integrity or political independence of any state or in any other manner inconsistent with the Purposes of the United Nations'*: A targeted killing by a State on the territory of another State violates the territorial integrity of that State. It is also inconsistent with

which it described the incident as an 'indiscriminate and reckless attack against the United Kingdom, putting the lives of innocent civilians at risk.' NATO, 'Statement by the North Atlantic Council on the Use of a Nerve Agent in Salisbury' (14 March 2018), www.nato.int/cps/en/natohq/news_152787.htm.

57 'The Russian State Was Responsible for the Attempted Murder … and for Threatening the Lives of Other British Citizens in Salisbury', n. 30.

58 ILC, 'Draft Articles on Responsibility of States for Internationally Wrongful Acts, with Commentaries, in Report of the International Law Commission on the Work of Its Fifty-Third Session' UN Doc A/56/10 (2001) ('ILC Draft Articles'), chapter II.

the Purposes of the United Nations (namely, respect for human rights: Article 1(3) of the Charter).

Accordingly, if the attack is attributable to Russia, all contextual elements of a prohibited 'use of force' are fulfilled.

Elements of Prohibited Force

- *Means*: No physical force was employed, but the weapon used was a prohibited military-grade chemical nerve agent, Novichok.
- *Physical effects*: The Novichok attack had direct physical effects on at least four people who fell critically or seriously ill: Sergei Skripal, his daughter Yulia Skripal and two police officers involved in the investigation of the attack. Months after the attack, two more individuals in Salisbury suffered physical effects after coming into contact with the container used to carry the nerve agent, one of whom died.[59] In addition to the direct physical effects, the use of the highly toxic chemical weapon Novichok carried a risk of potential harm to the wider public due to nature of the weapon, which was used in a public location and can reportedly persist for long periods.[60]

  The UK emphasised the potential effects of the attack at the UN Security Council, namely, that 'British Police Officer Nick Bailey, was ... exposed and remains in hospital in a serious condition. Hundreds of British citizens have been potentially exposed to this nerve agent in what was an indiscriminate and reckless act against the United Kingdom.'[61] Marc Weller argues that the UK's position is implicitly that 'any use of toxins would amount to a use of force, due to their potential (rather than actual) widespread and indiscriminate effects'.[62]

59 Simon Murphy, 'Met Confirms Second Police Officer Was Victim of Salisbury Attack', *The Guardian* (15 August 2019), www.theguardian.com/uk-news/2019/aug/15/met-confirms-second-police-officer-was-victim-of-salisbury-attack.

60 'Russian Spy: What Are Nerve Agents and What Do They Do?', *BBC News* (12 March 2018), www.bbc.com/news/health-43328976.

61 'The Russian State Was Responsible for the Attempted Murder ... and for Threatening the Lives of Other British Citizens in Salisbury', n. 30.

62 'An International Use of Force in Salisbury', *EJIL Talk* (14 March 2018), www.ejiltalk.org/an-international-use-of-force-in-salisbury/.

- *Object/target*: The attack took place in the United Kingdom town of Salisbury. The target of the forcible act, Sergei Skripal, was a Russian double agent convicted of spying for the United Kingdom and relocated there in 2010 as part of a prisoner swap, later gaining UK citizenship.[63]
- *Gravity of effects*: The actual effects were relatively low in gravity but there was a potential for high gravity of effects, as set out earlier.
- *Hostile intent*: There is no evidence that the attack manifested a hostile intent *against the United Kingdom* rather than against the individual target of the attack due to his prior conviction in Russia of spying.

Conclusion

Assuming that the attack was attributable to Russia, then the contextual elements are present which would bring the attack within the scope of article 2(4) of the UN Charter. The following elements of a 'use of force' are present: means (prohibited chemical weapon), direct physical effects with low gravity but very grave potential effects. Conversely, the target of the attack, Mr Skripal, did not have close ties to the territorial State; the actual gravity of the attack was relatively low and there was no evidence of a hostile intent by Russia against the United Kingdom. For the United Kingdom (the only State to characterise the attempted killing as a prohibited use of force), it appears that the decisive element was the use of a prohibited chemical weapon on its territory which carried a risk of grave harm to the wider public. This characterisation is plausible, but it is a borderline case because none of the other elements of a 'use of force' were particularly pronounced. In the absence of a closer connection between the target of the forcible act and the territorial State, a hostile intent or more widespread harm directly caused by the nerve agent, in this author's view, the attempted killing of Sergei Skripal was not a prohibited use of force against the United Kingdom. Nevertheless, this incident provides an illustration of how the type of weapon and potential harm may be considered as relevant factors in an assessment of legality under article 2(4).

[63] 'Sergei Skripal: Who Is the Former Russian Intelligence Officer?', n. 53.

CASE STUDY: USE OF FORCE IN OUTER SPACE

The second case study to demonstrate how to apply type theory and its utility concerns the use of force in outer space. Outer space has been militarised since the late 1950s and is becoming an increasingly important military domain. In 2019 NATO declared outer space to be an operational domain,[64] and a growing number of States have since established a military space force or expanded existing military branches to cover outer space.[65] Space capabilities have important military functions, including for navigation, surveillance, communications, situational (battlefield) awareness and targeting.[66] Military uses of outer space at present principally concern satellites, which are potentially threatened by the testing and use of anti-satellite (ASAT) and other space weapons and their stationing (potentially, in some instances) in outer space. The Gulf War is regarded as the first space war due to the heavy reliance by Allied States on space-based military assets against Iraq.[67] Critical civilian infrastructure and services also increasingly rely on space systems, including infrastructure essential for food production, health care, disaster relief, transport, communication, energy and trade, environmental science and the global navigation satellite systems such as GPS, which themselves underpin global communication networks, banking and financial markets and energy grids.[68] At the 2021 Brussels Summit, NATO leaders recognised that 'attacks to, from, or within space present a clear challenge to the security of the Alliance, the impact of which could threaten national and Euro-Atlantic prosperity, security, and stability, and could be as harmful to modern societies as a conventional attack'.[69]

[64] NATO, 'NATO's Approach to Space' (2 December 2021), www.nato.int/cps/en/natohq/topics_175419.htm.

[65] These include the United States Space Force (established 2019), United Kingdom Space Command (formed in 2021), the French Air and Space Force (renamed in 2020), the Spanish Air and Space Force (renamed in 2022), the German Weltraumkommando der Bundeswehr (established in 2021) and the Australian Defence Space Command (established in 2022).

[66] United States and Defense Intelligence Agency, *Challenges to Security in Space: Space Reliance in an Era of Competition and Expansion* (2022), 2, www.dia.mil/Portals/110/Documents/News/Military_Power_Publications/Challenges_Security_Space_2022.pdf.

[67] Isavella Maria Vasilogeorgi, 'Military Uses of Outer Space: Legal Limitations, Contemporary Perspectives' (2014) 39(2) *Journal of Space Law* 379, 408 with further references.

[68] ICRC, *The Potential Human Cost of the Use of Weapons in Outer Space and the Protection Afforded by International Humanitarian Law* (9 April 2021) ('ICRC Position Paper'), 2.

[69] NATO, *Brussels Summit Communiqué Issued by NATO Heads of State and Government (2021)* (14 June 2021), para. 33.

The prohibition of the threat or use of force in article 2(4) of the UN Charter applies in outer space. The applicability of international law, including the UN Charter, to activities in outer space is recognised in article III of the Outer Space Treaty[70] (OST) as well as article 3(2) of the Moon Agreement,[71] and in relevant UN General Assembly resolutions.[72] Article III of the OST provides: 'States Parties to the Treaty shall carry on activities in the exploration and use of outer space, including the moon and other celestial bodies, in accordance with international law, including the Charter of the United Nations, in the interest of maintaining international peace and security and promoting international co-operation and understanding.' Article 3(2) of the Moon Agreement is more explicit and provides: 'Any threat or use of force or any other hostile act or threat of hostile act on the moon is prohibited. It is likewise prohibited to use the moon in order to commit any such act or to engage in any such threat in relation to the earth, the moon, spacecraft, the personnel of spacecraft or man-made space objects.'[73] However, as on Earth, there is no agreed definition of a prohibited use of force in space.[74] The application of the prohibition of the use of force in outer space faces special challenges due to the unique environment of outer space and the types of

70 *Treaty on Principles Governing the Activities of States in the Exploration and Use of Outer Space, Including the Moon and Other Celestial Bodies* 1967 (adopted 27 January 1967, entered into force 10 October 1967), 610 UNTS 205.

71 *Agreement Governing the Activities of States on the Moon and Other Celestial Bodies* 1979 (opened for signature 18 December 1979, entered into force 11 July 1984), 1636 UNTS 3.

72 For example, UN General Assembly, *Resolution* 75/36 (16 December 2020), UN Doc A/RES/75/36, preambular para. 1.

73 Under article 1(1) of the Moon Agreement, reference to the moon in the agreement also includes reference to other celestial bodies within the solar system other than the earth. For a concise overview of the international legal framework relevant to space security, see United Nations Institute for Disarmament Research (UNIDIR), *Existing Legal and Regulatory Frameworks concerning Threats Arising from State Behaviours with Respect to Outer Space (Advance Unedited Version)* (No A/AC.294/2022/WP.1, 5 May 2022).

74 Recent concrete proposals for regulating military uses of outer space include a draft treaty sponsored by Russia and China on the Prevention of the Placement of Weapons in Outer Space, the Threat or Use of Force against Outer Space Objects (PPWT) in 2008 and revised in 2014; an EU-led International Code of Conduct for Outer Space Activities in 2010, measures proposed by the UN Group of Governmental Experts (GGE) on transparency and confidence building measures (TCBMs) in 2013 and further practical measures for the prevention of an arms race in outer space (PAROS) in 2018–19.

'use of force' that can be employed there. These challenges include issues of attribution, wide-spread dual use of objects for military and civilian purposes, difficulties with identifying hostile intent and whether attacks with temporary and reversible effects (such as dazzling satellites through directed energy attacks, i.e., temporarily blinding an imaging satellite by using a laser to interfere with its sensor or jamming of GPS signals) would meet the threshold of prohibited force under *jus contra bellum*. As such, the use of force in outer space makes for an apt case study to demonstrate how the type framework can be applied to an emerging domain to analyse whether certain acts constitute an unlawful use of force or not. We will focus on a current counterspace capability that has already been demonstrated, namely, direct-ascent ASAT (DA-ASAT) tests.

DA-ASAT Tests

Due to their visibility, predictable paths, limited manoeuvrability, fragility and low defensibility, satellites are highly vulnerable to attack and other forms of interference.[75] The high speed of satellites (about 17,500 km/hr in low Earth orbit) also renders them vulnerable to destruction by collision with small objects on different orbits.[76] Forms of attack on satellites include kinetic attacks such as direct-ascent ASAT weapons (e.g. anti-ballistic missiles which can also kill satellites) and on-orbit ASAT weapons (e.g. a satellite releasing an object which will collide with another satellite). Several States, including the United States, Russia, China and India, have already developed counterspace capabilities, including anti-satellite weapons.[77] On 15 November 2021, Russia launched an unannounced DA-ASAT missile test to destroy one of its own defunct satellites. The destructive impact forced astronauts and cosmonauts aboard the International Space Station to seek shelter in their hardened Crew Dragon and Soyuz capsules from thousands of trackable pieces of space debris, many of which will remain in orbit for

[75] David Wright, Laura Grego and Lisbeth Gronlund, *The Physics of Space Security: A Reference Manual* (American Academy of Arts and Sciences, 2005), 109.

[76] *Ibid.*

[77] Brian Weedon and Victoria Samson (eds), *Secure World Foundation Global Counterspace Capabilities Report* (April 2022), viii–xxii.

months or years.[78] In addition to the trackable space debris, there will be tens of thousands of untrackable but still lethal debris created that, because they are untracked, cannot be avoided through manoeuvres. This is not the first kinetic DA-ASAT test creating long-lasting debris: notoriously, China conducted such a test in 2007, blowing up one of its own weather satellites and creating several thousand trackable pieces of debris.[79] The United States conducted a kinetic DA-ASAT test in 2008, creating 400 pieces of trackable debris,[80] as did India in 2019, creating a similar amount of trackable debris.[81]

A major issue with kinetic ASAT weapons is the side effect of creating space debris, with even small pieces able to destroy other space objects due to the often high relative velocities of objects in orbit.[82] Risks from space debris are increasing due to a rapidly changing orbital environment characterised by higher congestion including from abandoned rocket bodies and satellite mega-constellations.[83] In the worst case, space debris can trigger the Kessler syndrome, a collisional cascade that could make some orbits unsafe to access and use for decades. The clear dangers of space debris have led to calls for a treaty banning kinetic ASAT testing[84] and unilateral declarations by a growing number of States including the United States,[85] Canada,[86] Germany,[87]

78 Joey Roulette, 'Debris from Test of Russian Antisatellite Weapon Forces Astronauts to Shelter', *The New York Times* (16 November 2021), www.nytimes.com/2021/11/15/science/russia-anti-satellite-missile-test-debris.html.

79 Weedon and Samson, n. 77, 03–11.

80 *Ibid.*, 01–15.

81 *Ibid.*, 04–03.

82 See Christos Kypraios and Elena Carpanelli, 'Space Debris' in Rüdiger Wolfrum (ed), *Max Planck Encyclopaedia of Public International Law* (Oxford University Press, 2018).

83 Aaron C Boley and Michael Byers, 'Satellite Mega-Constellations Create Risks in Low Earth Orbit, the Atmosphere and on Earth' (2021) 11(1) *Scientific Reports* 10642.

84 'International Open Letter Re: Kinetic ASAT Test Ban Treaty', Letter from Outer Space Institute to the President of the UN General Assembly (2 September 2021) https://outerspaceinstitute.ca/docs/OSI_International_Open_Letter_ASATs_PUBLIC.pdf.

85 The White House, *Vice President Harris Advances National Security Norms in Space* (19 April 2022), www.whitehouse.gov/briefing-room/statements-releases/2022/04/18/fact-sheet-vice-president-harris-advances-national-security-norms-in-space/.

86 Permanent Mission of Canada to the United Nations in Geneva, Tweet posted 9 May 2022 at 4:25 PM, https://twitter.com/CanadaGeneva/status/1523685496399966209.

87 *Statement by Germany in the Open-Ended Working Group on Reducing Space Threats through Norms, Rules and Principles of Responsible Behaviours* (13 September 2022), https://documents.unoda.org/wp-content/uploads/2022/09/220913-Statement-by-Germany-on-13-September.pdf.

New Zealand,[88] the UK,[89] Japan[90] and Australia[91] committing to refrain from such testing.

In the absence of physical effects on another State, the use by a State of a DA-ASAT weapon against its own satellite is not a prohibited use of force, because the contextual requirements are missing. But what if the DA-ASAT test creates debris which causes physical damage to or destruction of another State's space object?[92] We shall apply the type theory framework to assess this question. The scenario in question is the use of a DA-ASAT missile strike that targets and destroys a State's own satellite, creating debris which permanently damages or destroys another State's satellite.

Contextual Elements

Whether the contextual elements of article 2(4) of the UN Charter are met in this scenario primarily depends on whether the incident is regarded by States as taking place in their 'international relations'. As argued in Chapter 4, the text of article 2(4) and its object and purpose do not exclude an interpretation that encompasses a use of force that is in 'international relations' outside the context of State damage, such as malicious destruction of parts of Antarctica, the Moon or other celestial bodies as *terra nullius*, if it is 'inconsistent with the Purposes of the United Nations'.

88 New Zealand Foreign Minister Nanaia Mahuta, 'Otago Foreign Policy School, Opening Address', New Zealand Government (1 July 2022), www.beehive.govt.nz/speech/otago-foreign-policy-school-opening-address.

89 UK Foreign, Commonwealth & Development Office and UK Space Agency, *Responsible Space Behaviours: The UK Commits Not to Destructively Test Direct Ascent Anti-Satellite Missiles* (3 October 2022), www.gov.uk/government/news/responsible-space-behaviours-the-uk-commits-not-to-destructively-test-direct-ascent-anti-satellite-missiles.

90 Ministry of Foreign Affairs of Japan, *Decision Not to Conduct Destructive, Direct-Ascent Anti-Satellite Missile Testing* (13 September 2022), www.mofa.go.jp/press/release/press3e_000451.html.

91 Australian Government, *Australia Advances Responsible Action in Space: Joint Media Release of the Minister for Foreign Affairs, Minister for Defence and Minister for Industry and Science* (27 October 2022), www.foreignminister.gov.au/minister/penny-wong/media-release/australia-advances-responsible-action-space?utm_source=nationaltribune&utm_medium=nationaltribune&utm_campaign=news.

92 In addition to physical damage, debris created by a DA-ASAT test could potentially cause the loss of safe access to valuable orbits or the premature exhaustion of thruster fuel because of the need to engage in frequent collision-avoidance manoeuvres. This is beyond the scope of the present analysis. For a discussion, see Michael Byers and Aaron Boley, *Who Owns Outer Space? International Law, Astrophysics, and the Sustainable Development of Space* (Cambridge University Press, 2023).

This is as yet untested in State practice. In any case, our case study is concerned with the creation of debris which damages or destroys another State's satellite.

Whether such damage is considered to be in 'international relations' will be influenced by the perceived intent of the State conducting the DA-ASAT test and the degree of recklessness in carrying out the strike. Intent is discussed later in the chapter as an element of 'use of force'. An assessment of whether the incident occurs in 'international relations' will of course also depend on the relations between the States concerned. Damage to another State's satellite caused by debris generated by a DA-ASAT test is more likely to be perceived to be in 'international relations' if there is already a heightened state of tension between the two States – for example, between Russia and the United States. Alternatively, it could be considered that all such incidents are in 'international relations' because they take place in the context of the Outer Space Treaty and negatively affect the freedom for exploration and use by all States guaranteed in article I.

In addition to being in 'international relations', to meet the contextual elements of article 2(4) and fall within the scope of the prohibition, a use of force in space must also be 'against the territorial integrity or political independence of any state, or in any other manner inconsistent with the Purposes of the United Nations'. States may not assert sovereignty over celestial bodies (article II OST). Nevertheless, State practice and subsequent agreement regarding the interpretation of the UN Charter confirm that uses of force against objects or persons with a certain nexus to a State may fall within the scope of article 2(4), for example, uses of force against private vessels and aircraft registered to another State.[93] Similar to flag ship jurisdiction, under article VIII of the OST, '[a] State Party to the Treaty on whose registry an object launched into outer space is carried shall retain jurisdiction and control over such object, and over any personnel thereof, while in outer space or on a celestial body'.[94] With respect

93 See article 3(g) of the Annex to 1974 General Assembly Resolution 3314 which lists as an act of aggression an 'attack by the armed forces of a State on the ... marine and air fleets of another State'.

94 See also *Convention on Registration of Objects Launched into Outer Space* 1975 (opened for signature 14 January 1975, entered into force 15 September 1976), 1023 UNTS 15.

to space objects, it is as yet unclear if registration would suffice for a use of force against the object to be considered 'against the territorial integrity or political independence of any state, or in any other manner inconsistent with the Purposes of the United Nations' or if a more specific nexus with the State is required. The function of the space object (military/civil vs commercial) will be relevant to this determination – an assessment that overlaps with the element of 'force' of effects (discussed later). Other factors that may be relevant to determining if the required nexus is met are the number of satellites struck[95] and the value of the satellite, financially or in terms of the importance of its functions to the State.[96]

Elements of 'Use of Force'

- ***Means:*** A DA-ASAT missile is a kinetic weapon and thus employs physical means.
- ***Effects:*** The direct physical effects of debris generated by a DA-ASAT test colliding with another State's satellite could well be catastrophic damage to or destruction of the satellite due to the high relative velocity that would likely be involved.[97] An issue is whether this effect is sufficiently proximate to the ASAT test since it is a secondary effect. A factor which may come into play in this assessment is the known risk that debris generated by a DA-ASAT test will collide with other States' space objects. For example, even an ASAT test carried out at low altitude in an effort to minimise long-lived debris, such as the test conducted by India in 2019, has 'the potential to affect a busy, near-future orbital environment that includes at least four planned "mega-constellations" from different countries: SpaceX's Starlink with 42,000 satellites and Amazon's Kuiper with 3236 satellites, both from the United States; OneWeb with 7000 satellites

95 For instance, there would seem to be a difference between an attack on a single merchant vessel and a fleet of merchant vessels, at least with respect to an act of aggression: article 3(g) of the 1974 General Assembly Definition of Aggression (discussed in Chapter 4).

96 An extreme example would be a billion dollar Earth imaging satellite essential for food production versus a CubeSat ('a square-shaped miniature satellite (10 cm × 10 cm × 10 cm – roughly the size of a Rubik's cube), weighing about 1 kg': Canadian Space Agency, 'CubeSats in a Nutshell' (6 May 2022) www.asc-csa.gc.ca/eng/satellites/cubesat/what-is-a-cubesat.asp.

97 Wright et al, n. 75, 109.

from the United Kingdom; and Guo Wang's StarNet with 12,992 satellites from China.'[98]

If a collision of space debris from an ASAT test destroys another State's satellite, there may be further serious effects. Damage to or destruction of a satellite may adversely affect critical military functions such as 'ISR, meteorology, communications, PNT, and SSA [space situational awareness]', which are of particular importance for co-ordinating forces in distant theatre conflicts.[99] The use of force in space could also have significant non-military effects. Disabling, damaging, or destroying such satellites, including through missile attacks, could have 'wide-reaching consequences for civilians on earth'.[100] Canada's submission to the UN Open-Ended Working Group on Reducing Space Threats (OEWG) in May 2022 stated that:

> Actions that disrupt or impair the delivery of critical space-based services, resulting in serious risks for the safety and security of people or property are irresponsible and could be perceived as a threat. For example, actions that disrupt a satellite's ability to provide crucial information to the public, such as navigation information used by aircrafts to avoid collisions or data used by emergency responders to forecast and/or respond to major disasters. These effects and consequences are expected to increase as more terrestrial activities leverage space to deliver services.[101]

Similarly, there are potential secondary physical effects of the destruction of a satellite from space debris generated by an ASAT test.

> Due to the high impact energies involved, debris from a kinetic ASAT test often ends up on highly eccentric orbits that cross multiple satellite 'orbital shells' twice per revolution. If just one piece of debris from such a test collides with a satellite and causes a

98 'International Open Letter Re: Kinetic ASAT Test Ban Treaty', n. 84, 1.

99 Dean Cheng, 'Space Deterrence, the U.S.-Japan Alliance, and Asian Security: A U.S. Perspective' in Harold et al, n. 19, 74, 75: 'Given the distances encompassed within the Asia-Pacific theater, now extending even to the Indian Ocean as part of the "Indo-Pacific," space-based systems play a central and growing role in coordinating forces and creating a common situational picture. This reliance on space is especially great for U.S. forces, because they are typically conducting expeditionary operations far from the U.S. homeland.'

100 ICRC Position Paper, n. 68, 2.

101 Canada, *Canada's Views on Reducing Space Threats through Norms, Rules and Principles of Responsible Behaviour (Advanced Unedited Version)* (2022) UN Doc A/AC.294/2022/WP.7, 3.

major fragmentation event, this could lead to additional events affecting all States, which could include further fragmentations, satellite failures, or service disruptions.[102]

It is not clear how far such physical and non-physical secondary effects are relevant to a determination of a use of force as the effects are not direct; there are intermediate steps between the forcible act (the DA-ASAT test) and such effects, namely, the creation of debris and the collision of that debris with a satellite. Even if these secondary effects are legally relevant to an assessment of 'use of force', establishing causation between a DA-ASAT test and these secondary effects may be challenging and will only ever be possible with regard to trackable debris (noting that non-trackable debris poses just as great a risk, especially because it exists in far greater numbers and total surface area).

- **Gravity:** As already noted,[103] the gravity threshold of a prohibited use of force is controversial. This is all the more relevant in outer space due to the range of intensity of uses of force which are possible in outer space, as well as the dual-use nature of many space objects which may entail significant secondary effects of an attack, as discussed earlier. In the 2019 Report of the UN Group of Governmental Experts on Further Practical Measures for the Prevention of an Arms Race in Outer Space (GGE), '[i]t was considered that threats exist on a continuum from low intensity, characterized by reversible and disruptive impacts, to high intensity, characterized by irreversible and destructive impacts'.[104] Damage or destruction to another State's satellite by the creation of debris would fall into the highest level of intensity as assessed by the GGE. The gravity of the secondary effects (if legally relevant, as discussed earlier) will vary depending on the function of the damaged space object and could potentially be very high. The ICRC has noted the 'potentially significant human cost for civilians on earth of the use of weapons in outer space'.[105]

[102] 'International Open Letter Re: Kinetic ASAT Test Ban Treaty', n. 84, 1.
[103] See Chapter 6.
[104] *Report of the Group of Governmental Experts on Further Practical Measures for the Prevention of an Arms Race in Outer Space*, UN Doc A/74/77 (19 April 2019) ('GGE Report'), para. 35.
[105] ICRC Position Paper, n. 68, 4.

- **Intent:** As explained in Chapter 6, the text of article 2(4) and its *travaux préparatoires* do not indicate whether a 'use of force' must be motivated by a hostile intent or be intentional at all, in other words, whether mistaken or accidental uses of force also fall within the scope of the prohibition. However, emerging State practice gives early indications that only acts which deliberately cause damage to or interfere with space objects are likely to be perceived as a security threat and/or a use of force. Although none of the international efforts to define a 'use of force' in outer space have achieved consensus so far, it is notable that the draft treaty sponsored by Russia and China on the Prevention of the Placement of Weapons in Outer Space, the Threat or Use of Force against Outer Space Objects (PPWT) in 2008,[106] the revised definition in the 2014 Draft PPWT[107] and the 2019 Report of the GGE all share reference to *intentional* acts.[108] The US criticism of the definition of 'use of force' in the 2008 draft PPWT notably did not criticise the requirement that the action be 'hostile'.[109] This approach is also supported by Canada's submission to the OEWG in May 2022, which distinguishes between irresponsible behaviours, such as actions leading to damage to the space environment (e.g. debris creation), and actions which are security threats, such as

[106] *Letter Dated 2008/02/12 from the Permanent Representative of the Russian Federation and the Permanent Representative of China to the Conference on Disarmament Addressed to the Secretary-General of the Conference* transmitting the Russian and Chinese texts of the draft 'Treaty on Prevention of the Placement of Weapons in Outer Space and of the Threat or Use of Force against Outer Space Objects (PPWT)' introduced by the Russian Federation and China, UN Doc CD/1839 (29 February 2008). Article 1(e): 'the "use of force" or "threat of force" mean any hostile actions against outer space objects including, inter alia, those aimed at their destruction, damage, temporarily or permanently injuring normal functioning, deliberate alteration of the parameters of their orbit, or the threat of these actions.'

[107] Article 1(d):

> the terms 'use of force' or 'threat of force' mean, respectively, any intended action to inflict damage to outer space object under the jurisdiction and/or control of other States, or clearly expressed in written, oral or any other form intention of such action. Actions subject to special agreements with those States providing for actions, upon request, to discontinue uncontrolled flight of outer space objects under the jurisdiction and/or control of the requesting States shall not be regarded as use of force or threat of force.

[108] GGE Report, n. 104, para. 32.

[109] *Letter Dated 19 August 2008 from the Permanent Representative of the United States of America Addressed to the Secretary-General of the Conference Transmitting Comments on the Draft Treaty on Prevention of the Placement of Weapons in Outer Space and of the Threat or Use of Force against Outer Space Objects (PPWT) as Contained in Document CD/1839 of 29 February 2008*, UN Doc CD/1847 (26 August 2008), para. 5(i).

> '*deliberately* causing non-consensual interference' to space systems.[110] It therefore seems likely that States would consider intent as an essential element of a 'use of force' in outer space, whereas accidental, mistaken or recklessly caused damage will be perceived as irresponsible or unsafe behaviours.

The difficulty is that a deliberate or hostile intent is difficult to discern in outer space. It may be difficult or impossible to verify if acts which cause damage to or endanger space objects are intentional, such as collision of space objects and the creation of space debris. Since the risks of space debris creation (and collision) from DA-ASAT tests are known, such tests are at the very least reckless. One may well question whether deliberately ignoring the warnings of one's own scientists about the certainty of debris creation constitutes negligence or wilful blindness amounting to a deliberate act. However, in the absence of other evidence in a particular case, a DA-ASAT test is not likely to fulfil the element of an intention to damage or destroy other States' space objects.

Conclusion

The elements of 'use of force' that are present are thus physical means, physical effects and high gravity. The element which is missing in this hypothetical scenario is a hostile or deliberate intent. However, given the known dangers of space debris, deliberately creating debris which causes damage to another State's space object is unlikely to be seen as a mere accident or mistake, and at the very least as reckless. Does this combination of elements suffice to reach the threshold of a prohibited 'use of force'? Perhaps not. But if some of the elements are more heavily weighted in the scenario, such as secondary effects with a high gravity (e.g. if a satellite that carries out key military or civilian functions is destroyed by the debris) and the conduct evinces a particularly reckless or potentially hostile intent (e.g. the ASAT test is unannounced and conducted at high altitude and there are pre-existing tensions between the State conducting the ASAT test and the State whose satellite is destroyed by the debris), then all of these elements in combination could meet the threshold. Thus, in certain circumstances, the creation of debris by a State conducting a direct-ascent ASAT test which then damages or destroys the space object of another

[110] Canada, *Canada's Views on Reducing Space Threats through Norms, Rules and Principles of Responsible Behaviour (Advanced Unedited Version)*, n. 101, 2–3, emphasis added.

State could constitute a prohibited 'use of force' in violation of article 2(4) of the UN Charter and customary international law. Due to the rapidly escalating militarisation of outer space, the grave and widespread potential effects of uses of force in this domain and uncertainty over how to define a prohibited 'use of force' in outer space (particularly with respect to non-kinetic attacks and attacks with temporary effects), the application of type theory to the use of force in outer space acquires particular salience and demonstrates the potential utility of this framework.

REFLECTIONS

A key observation arising from the case studies in this chapter is the importance of the contextual element of 'international relations' for an act to fall within the scope of article 2(4) of the UN Charter and the implications this has for the significance of certain elements of a 'use of force', namely, object/target, gravity and intention. These three elements are relevant to the characterisation of an act as a 'use of force' and also contribute towards an assessment of whether the act meets the contextual requirement that the 'use of force' takes place in 'international relations'. This explains why the element of a hostile or coercive intent is present in each of the unlawful uses of force examined in this chapter; in the absence of a hostile or coercive intent, it is difficult to show that the contextual element of international relations is met and that the act falls within the scope of article 2(4). The relationship between intention and international relations is mutual, as an overtly hostile or coercive intent increases the likelihood that the act is in international relations and heightened tensions in the international relations of the two States concerned may signal a hostile intent behind a forcible act. As the examples in this chapter show, a hostile or coercive intention is not only relevant to the contextual element of 'international relations' but also to the determination of whether the act is a 'use of force'.

Similarly, the object/target of a forcible act and its gravity may indicate whether the act is in 'international relations' as well as being elements to weigh in assessing whether it is a 'use of force'. Unlike intention, the object or target of a use of force is not necessarily decisive, as a use of force can still be in international relations without a strong nexus between the target and another State (e.g. in the Skripal incident discussed earlier in this chapter).

International relations must definitely be present as a contextual element, whereas the object/target of the forcible act, its gravity and intention may be balanced with the other elements of means and effects to determine if it is a 'use of force'.

The examples analysed in this chapter illustrate how type theory can be applied to particular incidents to determine whether they are an unlawful 'use of force' in violation of article 2(4) of the UN Charter and customary international law. The utility of this approach is that it provides a framework for a systematic analysis of an incident to be able to assess whether it violates the prohibition of the use of force or not. The framework is helpful in breaking down the analysis of specific forcible incidents to be able to identify and weigh each element. Type theory is also useful for seeing how contextual elements shape whether an act is a prohibited use of force. This enables a meaningful discussion and debate about whether and why a particular incident is or is not a prohibited 'use of force'. In particular, the type theory framework is useful in borderline and novel cases, such as when the forcible act is at the low end of the gravity spectrum, there is a potentially applicable parallel legal framework (e.g. law enforcement), a kinetic weapon is not used (e.g. cyber operations) and in emerging military domains (e.g. outer space).

Conclusion

A Definition of Prohibited 'Use of Force'

Until now, it has often been implicitly assumed that the use of force is a concept, for which certain elements must always be present for the definition to be met. This has led to the rejection by scholars of particular elements as being relevant to the assessment of whether an act is a 'use of force' due to anomalous examples of 'use of force' which do not display that element.[1] The idea that a 'use of force' is a concept has been disproven in this work, by showing that for each element of a 'use of force', there are widely accepted examples of unlawful 'use of force' which do not contain this element. Therefore, none of the elements of a 'use of force' – including physical means or physical effects – is strictly necessary for the definition to be met. This work has argued that rather than a concept, a 'use of force' is a type, characterised by a basket of elements which do not all have to be present and which must be weighed and balanced to determine whether the threshold for the definition is met and an act is an unlawful 'use of force' under article 2(4) of the UN Charter.

The following framework for an unlawful 'use of force' under article 2(4) in accordance with type theory is proposed:

> A 'use of force' must take place within the context of the following fundamental requirements to fall within the scope of article 2(4):
>
> - Two or more States (including that the object/target of the 'use of force' has a sufficient nexus to another State)

[1] For example, Marco Roscini rejects directness as an element of 'use of force' on this basis. *Cyber Operations and the Use of Force in International Law* (Oxford University Press, 2014), 48.

- International relations
- 'Against the territorial integrity or political independence of any state or in any other manner inconsistent with the Purposes of the United Nations'

The following (non-essential) elements of a 'use of force' must be identified and weighed up to determine whether an act meets the threshold of the definition of a 'use of force':

- Physical force
- Direct physical effects (which may possibly be temporary and/or potential)
- Object/target
- Gravity
- Coercive or hostile intent

Each of these elements is explained in greater detail in Part II of this work.

It is an interesting question whether these are formal legal criteria, or 'merely factors that influence States making use of force assessments'.[2] In so far as these criteria are supported by principles of treaty interpretation including the subsequent agreement and subsequent practice of States in their application of article 2(4) of the UN Charter[3] (the approach taken in this work), they are legal and not merely political criteria, although the distinction may be a fine one in practice. This is due to the inherent connection between international law and political decision-making, which is recognised in the process of customary international law formation (through the requirements of State practice and *opinio juris*) as well as in principles of treaty interpretation (through the elements of subsequent agreement and subsequent practice of States). This close connection between international law and politics comes to the fore especially in matters close to the heart of State power, such as the prohibition of the use of force. However, in respect of the interpretation of the term 'use of force' in the UN Charter, a legal process of treaty interpretation applies, and it has been the purpose of this work to apply this process to identify legal criteria for identifying an unlawful 'use of force' under international law.

A related question is how the process of applying type theory relates to the general process of treaty interpretation regarding subsequent agreement and subsequent practice. This work has used the latter to interpret article 2(4) in

[2] This is the approach taken by the *Tallinn Manual* 2.0, Commentary to rule 69, para. 9.

[3] *Vienna Convention on the Law of Treaties*, art. 31(3)(b).

order to identify the elements of a 'use of force' and then proposed type theory to place those elements within a framework that can be applied to specific incidents to assess whether they constitute a prohibited use of force. Of course, the incidents being analysed may themselves contribute to subsequent practice under article 31(3) of the VCLT. The legal justification of the attacking State and the response of the victim State and international community are indeed relevant in assessing whether States regard the incident as a prohibited use of force and may contribute to subsequent practice in the interpretation of the treaty (and State practice and *opinio juris* regarding the scope of the customary rule). What type theory adds is criteria that States and scholars can use to themselves legally assess whether a particular act is a use of force and, importantly, to be able to articulate *why*.

Some may be sceptical of this framework, seeing it as artificial and not representing the process that States and legal scholars actually go through to determine whether a particular instance is a 'use of force' or not. But so far there is no generally shared framework or process for analysing potentially forcible incidents to determine if they fall within the scope of article 2(4) of the UN Charter or not. This theory is an attempt to develop such a language and shared framework and is offered as a potential tool of analysis. The alternative is a legal black box/rule of thumb approach, as with the distinction some claim between art and pornography: 'I know it when I see it'. The decision of whether or not to use potentially forcible measures, as well as how to respond to such measures (be it verbally or with other actions), have a real impact on the interpretation of this cornerstone provision, on international relations, but also on the ground, in terms of property and human life. For such a foundational rule of the international legal system, it is not satisfactory to apply vague, ad hoc standards. It is desirable to develop a language for talking about the use of force in concrete instances, if only to bring to light differences of opinion and method in interpreting and applying this term.

The identification of the elements of a prohibited 'use of force' and the proposal of type theory for the first time provides an analytical framework and shared language for analysing forcible incidents and assessing whether or not they meet the threshold for a 'use of force' between States under international law. Type theory sets out a systematic analytical framework that can be interrogated, debated, discussed and applied. Even if the particular elements, their relationship and their combined threshold are debated, at the very least, the benefit of type theory is that it provides a shared language and coherent framework for legal analysis and scholarly debate regarding the content of a prohibited 'use of force' between States under international law.

The framework of type theory has the potential to facilitate clearer analysis of 'uses of force' between States. It is hoped that this clarity will in turn lead to greater compliance with the prohibition of the use of force between States in their international relations and contribute to our shared endeavour of international peace and security.

Bibliography

BOOKS

Allen, Craig H, *Maritime Counterproliferation Operations and the Rule of Law* (Praeger Security International, 2007).
Arend, Anthony Clark and Robert J Beck, *International Law and the Use of Force* (Routledge, 2nd ed, 2008).
Barriga, Stefan and Claus Kreß (eds), *The Crime of Aggression: A Commentary* (Cambridge University Press, 2017).
(eds), *The Travaux Préparatoires of the Crime of Aggression* (Cambridge University Press, 2012).
Boddens Hosang, Hans FR, *The Handbook of the International Law of Military Operations* (Oxford University Press, 2010).
Brecher, Michael and Jonathan Wilkenfeld, *A Study of Crisis* (University of Michigan Press, 1997).
Brownlie, Ian, *International Law and the Use of Force by States* (Clarendon, 1963).
Byers, Michael and Aaron Boley, *Who Owns Outer Space? International Law, Astrophysics, and the Sustainable Development of Space* (Cambridge University Press, 2023).
Cannizzaro, Enzo and Paolo Pachletti (eds), *Customary International Law on the Use of Force: A Methodological Approach* (Martinus Nijhoff Publishers, 2005).
Cassese, Antonio (ed), *The Current Legal Regulation of the Use of Force* (Nijhoff, 1986).
Churchill, RR and V Lowe, *The Law of the Sea* (Juris Publishing, 3rd ed, 2007).
Constantinou, Avra, *The Right of Self-Defence under Customary International Law and Article 51 of the United Nations Charter* (Ant. N. Sakkoulas, 2000).
Corten, Olivier, *Le droit contre la guerre: L'interdiction du recours à la force en droit international contemporain* (Pedone, 2nd ed, rev. and expanded, 2014).
The Law against War: The Prohibition on the Use of Force in Contemporary International Law (Hart Publishing, 2010).
The Law against War: The Prohibition on the Use of Force in Contemporary International Law (Hart Publishing, 2nd ed, 2021).
Crawford, James Richard, *Chance, Order, Change* (Martinus Nijhoff Publishers, 2013).

Dinstein, Yoram, *War, Aggression and Self-Defence* (Cambridge University Press, 5th ed, 2011).
Doswald-Beck, Louise (ed), *San Remo Manual on International Law Applicable to Armed Conflicts at Sea* (Cambridge University Press, 1995).
Franck, Thomas M, *Fairness in International Law and Institutions* (Clarendon, 1997).
Recourse to Force: State Action against Threats and Armed Attacks (Cambridge University Press, 2003).
Gazzini, Tarcisio, *The Changing Rules on the Use of Force in International Law* (Manchester University Press, 2005).
The Use of Force in International Law (Ashgate, 2012).
Goldsmith, Jack L and Eric A Posner, *The Limits of International Law* (Oxford University Press, 2007).
Gray, Christine, *International Law and the Use of Force* (Oxford University Press, 3rd ed, 2008).
Green, James A, *The International Court of Justice and Self-Defence in International Law* (Hart Publishing, 2009).
(ed), *Cyber Warfare: A Multidisciplinary Analysis* (Routledge, 2015).
Gruber, Lloyd, *Ruling the World* (Princeton University Press, 2000).
Guilfoyle, Douglas, *Shipping Interdiction and the Law of the Sea* (Cambridge University Press, 2011).
Hannikainen, Lauri, *Peremptory Norms (Jus Cogens) in International Law* (Lakimiesliiton Kustannus, 1988).
Hart, HLA, *The Concept of Law* (Oxford University Press, 3rd ed, 2012).
Henderson, Christian, *The Use of Force and International Law* (Cambridge University Press, 1st ed, 2018).
Hilderbrand, Robert C, *Dumbarton Oaks: The Origins of the United Nations and the Search for Postwar Security* (University of North Carolina Press, 1990).
Kelsen, Hans, *The Law of the United Nations: A Critical Analysis of Its Fundamental Problems* (Stevens, 1950).
Klein, Natalie, *Maritime Security and the Law of the Sea* (Oxford University Press, 2011).
Kolb, Robert, *Ius contra bellum: Le droit international relatif au maintien de la paix: précis* (Helbing & Lichtenhahn, 2nd ed, 2009).
Peremptory International Law – Jus Cogens: A General Inventory (Bloomsbury Publishing, 2015).
Koskenniemi, Martti, *From Apology to Utopia: The Structure of International Legal Argument* (Cambridge University Press, 2005)
Krasner, Stephen D, *Sovereignty: Organized Hypocrisy* (Princeton University Press, 1999).
Lubell, Noam, *Extraterritorial Use of Force against Non-State Actors* (Oxford University Press, 2010).
Mazarr, Michael J, *Mastering the Gray Zone: Understanding a Changing Era of Conflict* (United States Army War College Press, December 2015).
Melzer, Nils, *Targeted Killing in International Law* (Oxford University Press, 2008).
Newton, Michael and Larry May, *Proportionality in International Law* (Oxford University Press, 2014).

Oppenheim, Lassa and Hersch Lauterpacht (eds), *International Law, vol. II Disputes, War and Neutrality* (Longmans, 7th ed, 1952).
Orakhelashvili, Alexander, *Peremptory Norms in International Law* (Oxford University Press, 2006).
Rodley, Nigel and Matt Pollard, *The Treatment of Prisoners under International Law* (Oxford University Press, 3rd ed, 2009).
Ronzitti, Natalino, *Rescuing Nationals Abroad through Military Coercion and Intervention on Grounds of Humanity* (Nijhoff, 1985).
Roscini, Marco, *Cyber Operations and the Use of Force in International Law* (Oxford University Press, 2014).
Rothwell, Donald and Tim Stephens, *The International Law of the Sea* (Hart Publishing, 2010).
Ruys, Tom, *'Armed Attack' and Article 51 of the UN Charter* (Cambridge University Press, 2010).
Ruys, Tom and Olivier Corten (eds), *The Use of Force in International Law: A Case-Based Approach* (Oxford University Press, 2018).
Schmitt, Michael N (ed), *Tallinn Manual 2.0 on the International Law Applicable to Cyber Operations* (Cambridge University Press, 2017).
Schofield, Clive H, *The Limits of Maritime Jurisdiction* (Martinus Nijhoff Publishers, 2014).
Sellars, Kirsten, *Crimes against Peace and International Law* (Cambridge University Press, 2013)
Simma, Bruno et al (eds), *The Charter of the United Nations: A Commentary* (Oxford University Press, 3rd ed, 2012).
Sloan, James, *The Militarisation of Peacekeeping in the Twenty-First Century* (Hart Publishing, 2011).
van Steenberghe, Raphaël, *La légitime défense en droit international public* (Larcier, 2012).
Stürchler, Nikolas, *The Threat of Force in International Law* (Cambridge University Press, Paperback ed, 2009).
Tanaka, Yoshifumi, *The International Law of the Sea* (Cambridge University Press, 2012).
Thirlway, Hugh WA, *The Sources of International Law* (Oxford University Press, 2014).
Tucker, Robert W, *The Law of Neutrality at Sea* (United States Government Printing Office, 1957, reprinted 2006 and 2008).
Waldock, Humphrey, *106 Collected Courses, Academy of International Law* (The Hague, 1962-II).
The Regulation of the Use of Force by Individual States in International Law (Hague Academy of International Law, 1953).
Weisburd, A Mark, *Use of Force: The Practice of States since World War II* (Pennsylvania State University Press, 1997).
Weller, Marc (ed), *The Oxford Handbook of the Use of Force in International Law* (Oxford University Press, 2015).
Westra, Joel H, *International Law and the Use of Armed Force* (Routledge, 2007).
de Wet, Erika, *Military Assistance on Request and the Use of Force* (Oxford University Press, 2020).

Wetterhahn, Ralph, *The Last Battle: The Mayaguez Incident and the End of the Vietnam War* (Plume, 2002).
White, Nigel D and Christian Henderson (eds), *Research Handbook on International Conflict and Security Law:* Jus ad Bellum, Jus in Bello *and* Jus post Bellum (Elgar, 2013).
Wright, David, Laura Grego and Lisbeth Gronlund, *The Physics of Space Security: A Reference Manual* (American Academy of Arts and Sciences, 2005).
Young, Margaret A (ed), *Regime Interaction in International Law: Facing Fragmentation* (Cambridge University Press, 2011).

CHAPTERS IN EDITED BOOKS

Akande, Dapo, 'Classification of Armed Conflicts: Relevant Legal Concepts' in Elizabeth Wilmshurst (ed), *International Law and the Classification of Conflicts* (Oxford University Press, 2012) 32.
Akande, Dapo and Antonios Tzanakopoulos, 'The International Court of Justice and the Concept of Aggression' in Claus Kreß and Stefan Barriga (eds), *The Crime of Aggression: A Commentary* (Cambridge University Press, 2017) 214.
Anderson, David H, 'Some Aspects of the Use of Force in Maritime Law Enforcement' in Nerina Boschiero et al (eds), *International Courts and the Development of International Law* (Springer, 2013) 233.
Archibugi, Daniele, Mariano Croce and Andrea Salvatore, 'Law of Nations or Perpetual Peace? Two Early International Theories on the Use of Force' in Marc Weller (ed), *The Oxford Handbook of the Use of Force in International Law* (Oxford University Press, 2015) 56.
Becker-Weinberg, Vasco and Guglielmo Verdirame, 'Proliferation of Weapons of Mass Destruction and Shipping Interdiction' in Marc Weller (ed), *The Oxford Handbook of the Use of Force in International Law* (Oxford University Press, 2015) 1017.
Blokker, Niels, 'Outsourcing the Use of Force: Towards More Security Council Control of Authorized Operations?' in Marc Weller (ed), *The Oxford Handbook of the Use of Force in International Law* (Oxford University Press, 2015) 202.
Bothe, Michael, 'Neutrality in Naval Warfare, What Is Left of the Traditional Law?' in Astrid JM Delissen and Gerard J Tanja (eds) *Humanitarian Law of Armed Conflict, Challenges Ahead* (Martinus Nijhoff, 1991), 387.
Bruha, Thomas, 'The General Assembly's Definition of the Act of Aggression' in Claus Kreß and Stefan Barriga (eds), *The Crime of Aggression: A Commentary* (Cambridge University Press, 2017) 142.
Chevalier-Watts, Juliet, 'The Right to Life and Law Enforcement Activities: The Appropriateness of a Military Response to the Problem of Terrorism' in Murray SY Bessette (ed), *Liberty and Security in the Age of Terrorism* (Commonwealth Security Studies Laboratory, 2011) 33.
Crawford, James and Rowan Nicholson, 'The Continued Relevance of Established Rules and Institutions Relating to the Use of Force' in Marc Weller (ed), *The Oxford Handbook of the Use of Force in International Law* (Oxford University Press, 2015) 96.

De Hoogh, André, '*Jus Cogens* and the Use of Armed Force' in Marc Weller (ed), *The Oxford Handbook of the Use of Force in International Law* (Oxford University Press, 2015) 1162.

Forteau, Mathias and Alison See Ying Xiu, 'The US Hostage Rescue Operation in Iran – 1980' in Tom Ruys and Olivier Corten (eds), *The Use of Force in International Law: A Case-Based Approach* (Oxford University Press, 2018) 306.

Francioni, Francesco, 'Use of Force, Military Activities, and the New Law of the Sea' in Antonio Cassese (ed), *The Current Legal Regulation of the Use of Force* (Nijhoff, 1986) 371.

Glennon, Michael J, 'The Limitations of Traditional Rules and Institutions Relating to the Use of Force' in Marc Weller (ed), *The Oxford Handbook of the Use of Force in International Law* (Oxford University Press, 2015) 79.

Grewe, Wilhelm G and Daniel-Erasmus Khan, 'Drafting History' in Bruno Simma et al (eds), *The Charter of the United Nations: A Commentary* (Oxford University Press, 2nd ed, 2002) vol. I, 1.

Guilfoyle, Douglas, 'The Use of Force against Pirates' in Marc Weller (ed), *The Oxford Handbook of the Use of Force in International Law* (Oxford University Press, 2015) 1057.

Harold, Scott W et al (eds), *The U.S.-Japan Alliance and Deterring Gray Zone Coercion in the Maritime, Cyber, and Space Domains* (RAND Corporation, 2017).

Heathcote, Vasco, 'Feminist Perspectives on the Law on the Use of Force' in Marc Weller (ed), *The Oxford Handbook of the Use of Force in International Law* (Oxford University Press, 2015) 114.

Heintschel von Heinegg, Wolff, '"Benevolent" Third States in International Armed Conflicts: The Myth of the Irrelevance of the Law of Neutrality' in MN Schmitt and J Pejic (eds), *International Law and Armed Conflict: Exploring the Faultlines* (Koninklijke Brill BV, 2007), 562.

'Blockades and Interdictions' in Marc Weller (ed), *The Oxford Handbook of the Use of Force in International Law* (Oxford University Press, 2015) 925.

'Maritime Interception/Interdiction Operations' in Terry D Gill (ed), *The Handbook of the International Law of Military Operations* (Oxford University Press, 2010) 375.

Kadelbach, Stefan, 'Interpretation of the Charter' in Bruno Simma et al (eds), *The Charter of the United Nations: A Commentary* (Oxford University Press, 3rd ed, 2012) vol. I, 71.

Klabbers, Jan, 'International Organizations in the Formation of Customary International Law' in Enzo Cannizzaro and Paolo Palchetti (eds), *Customary International Law on the Use of Force: A Methodological Approach* (Martinus Nijhoff Publishers, 2005) 179.

Kreß, Claus, 'The International Court of Justice and the Non-Use of Force' in Marc Weller (ed), *The Oxford Handbook of the Use of Force in International Law* (Oxford University Press, 2015) 561.

'The State Conduct Element' in Claus Kreß and Stefan Barriga (eds), *The Crime of Aggression: A Commentary* (Cambridge University Press, 2017) 412.

Kreß, Claus and Benjamin K Nußberger, 'The Entebbe Raid – 1976' in Tom Ruys and Olivier Corten (eds), *The Use of Force in International Law: A Case-Based Approach* (Oxford University Press, 2018) 220.

Krisch, Nico, 'Chapter VII Powers: The General Framework. Articles 39 to 43' in Bruno Simma et al (eds), *The Charter of the United Nations: A Commentary* (Oxford University Press, 3rd ed, 2012) vol. I, 1237.

Kypraios, Christos and Elena Carpanelli, 'Space Debris' in Rüdiger Wolfrum (ed), *Max Planck Encyclopaedia of Public International Law* (Oxford University Press, 2018).

Lesaffer, Randall, 'Too Much History: From War as Sanction to the Sanctioning of War' in Marc Weller (ed), *The Oxford Handbook of the Use of Force in International Law* (Oxford University Press, 2015) 35.

Lubell, Noam, 'The Problem of Imminence in an Uncertain World' in Marc Weller (ed), *The Oxford Handbook of the Use of Force in International Law* (Oxford University Press, 2015) 697.

Mann, FA, 'Reflections on the Prosecution of Persons Abducted in Breach of International Law' in Yoram Dinstein (ed), *International Law in a Time of Perplexity: Essays in Honour of Shabtai Rosenne* (Martinus Nijhoff Publishers, 1989) 411.

McDougall, Carrie, 'The Crimes against Peace Precedent' in Claus Kreß and Stefan Barriga (eds), *The Crime of Aggression: A Commentary* (Cambridge University Press, 2017) 49.

McMahon, Jeff, 'Unjust War and the Crime of Aggression' in Claus Kreß and Stefan Barriga (eds), *The Crime of Aggression: A Commentary* (Cambridge University Press, 2017) 1386.

Mégret, Frédéric, 'What Is the Specific Evil of Aggression?' in Claus Kreß and Stefan Barriga (eds), *The Crime of Aggression: A Commentary* (Cambridge University Press, 2017) 1398.

O'Connell, Mary Ellen, 'The Prohibition of the Use of Force' in Nigel D White and Christian Henderson (eds), *Research Handbook on International Conflict and Security Law: Jus ad Bellum, Jus in Bello and Jus post Bellum* (Elgar, 2013) 89.

'Taking *Opinio Juris* Seriously: A Classical Approach to International Law on the Use of Force' in Enzo Cannizzaro and Paolo Palchetti (eds), *Customary International Law on the Use of Force: A Methodological Approach* (Martinus Nijhoff Publishers, 2005) 9.

Orakhelashvili, Alexander, 'Changing *Jus Cogens* through State Practice? The Case of the Prohibition of the Use of Force and Its Exceptions' in Marc Weller (ed), *The Oxford Handbook of the Use of Force in International Law* (Oxford University Press, 2015) 157.

Palmisano, Giuseppe, 'Determining the Law on the Use of Force: The ICJ and Customary Rules on the Use of Force' in Enzo Cannizzaro and Paolo Palchetti (eds), *Customary International Law on the Use of Force: A Methodological Approach* (Martinus Nijhoff Publishers, 2005) 197.

Pobjie, Erin, Fanny Declercq and Raphaël van Steenberghe, 'The Killing of Khalil Al-Wazir by Israeli Commandos in Tunis – 1988' in Tom Ruys and Olivier Corten (eds), *The Use of Force in International Law: A Case-Based Approach* (Oxford University Press, 2018) 403.

Popovski, Vesselin, 'UNCLOS and the Peaceful Uses of the Sea' in Nong Hong, Shicun Wu and Mark Valencia (eds), *UN Convention on the Law of the Sea and the South China Sea* (Ashgate Publishing, 2015) 73.

Randelzhofer, Albrecht and Oliver Dörr, 'Article 2(4)' in Bruno Simma et al (eds), *The Charter of the United Nations: A Commentary* (Oxford University Press, 3rd ed, 2012) 200.

Rensmann, Thilo, 'Reform' in Bruno Simma et al (eds), *The Charter of the United Nations: A Commentary* (Oxford University Press, 3rd ed, 2012) vol. I, 25.

Röling, Bert VA, 'The Ban on the Use of Force and the UN Charter' in Antonio Cassese (ed), *The Current Legal Regulation of the Use of Force* (Nijhoff, 1986) 3.

Ronzitti, Natalino, 'The Legality of Covert Operations against Terrorism in Foreign States' in Andrea Bianchi (ed), *Enforcing International Law Norms against Terrorism* (Hart Publishing, 2004) 17.

'The Mayaguez Incident – 1975' in Tom Ruys and Olivier Corten (eds), *The Use of Force in International Law: A Case-Based Approach* (Oxford University Press, 2018) 213.

Schachter, Oscar, 'Entangled Treaty and Custom' in Yoram Dinstein (ed), *International Law at a Time of Perplexity: Essays in Honour of Shabtai Rosenne* (Martinus Nijhoff Publishers, 1989) 717.

Scheffer, David, 'Amending the Crime of Aggression under the Rome Statute' in Claus Kreß and Stefan Barriga (eds), *The Crime of Aggression: A Commentary* (Cambridge University Press, 2017) 1480.

Schindler, Dietrich, 'Transformations in the Law of Neutrality since 1945', in Astrid JM Delissen and Gerard J Tanja (eds), *Humanitarian Law of Armed Conflict: Challenges Ahead* (Martinus Nijhoff, 1991) 367.

Schmitt, Michael N, 'The Use of Cyber Force and International Law' in Marc Weller (ed), *The Oxford Handbook of the Use of Force in International Law* (Oxford University Press, 2015) 1110.

Schrijver, Nico, 'The Ban on the Use of Force in the UN Charter' in Marc Weller (ed), *The Oxford Handbook of the Use of Force in International Law* (Oxford University Press, 2015) 465.

Singh, Narinder, 'India' in Claus Kreß and Stefan Barriga (eds), *The Crime of Aggression: A Commentary* (Cambridge University Press, 2017) 1002.

Snyder, Glenn, 'The Balance of Power and the Balance of Terror', in Paul Seabury (ed), *The Balance of Power* (Chandler, 1965)

Starski, Paulina, 'The US Airstrike against the Iraqi Intelligence Headquarters – 1993' in Tom Ruys and Olivier Corten (eds), *The Use of Force in International Law: A Case-Based Approach* (Oxford University Press, 2018) 504.

Talmon, Stefan, 'Article 2 (6)' in Bruno Simma et al (eds), *The Charter of the United Nations: A Commentary* (Oxford University Press, 3rd ed, 2012) vol. I, 252.

Tsagourias, Nicholas, 'The Prohibition of Threats of Force' in Nigel D White and Christian Henderson (eds), *Research Handbook on International Conflict and Security Law: Jus ad Bellum,* Jus in Bello *and* Jus post Bellum (Elgar, 2013) 67.

Weller, Marc, 'Introduction: International Law and the Problem of War' in Marc Weller (ed), *The Oxford Handbook of the Use of Force in International Law* (Oxford University Press, 2015) 3.

Witschel, Georg, 'Article 108' in Bruno Simma et al (eds), *The Charter of the United Nations: A Commentary* (Oxford University Press, 3rd ed, 2012) vol. I, 2199.

Wolfrum, Rüdiger, 'Article 1' in Bruno Simma et al (eds), *The Charter of the United Nations: A Commentary* (Oxford University Press, 3rd ed, 2012) vol. I, 107.

'Preamble' in Bruno Simma et al (eds), *The Charter of the United Nations: A Commentary* (Oxford University Press, 3rd ed, 2012) vol. I, 45.

JOURNAL ARTICLES AND CONFERENCE PAPERS

Akande, Dapo and Antonios Tzanakopoulos, 'Legal: Use of Force in Self-Defence to Recover Occupied Territory' (2021) 32(4) *European Journal of International Law* 1299.

Allen, Craig H, 'Limits on the Use of Force in Maritime Operations in Support of WMD Counter-Proliferation Initiatives' [2006] (81) *International Law Studies* 77.

Baxter, RR, 'Multilateral Treaties as Evidence of Customary International Law' (1965) 41 *British Yearbook of International Law* 275.

'Treaties and Custom' (1970) 129 *Recueil des cours: Collected Courses of the Hague Academy of International Law* 25.

Benvenisti, Eyal and George W Downs, 'The Empire's New Clothes: Political Economy and the Fragmentation of International Law' (2007) 60 *Stanford Law Review* 595.

Bianchi, Andrea, 'The International Regulation of the Use of Force: The Politics of Interpretive Method' (2009) 22(4) *Leiden Journal of International Law* 651.

Boley, Aaron C and Michael Byers, 'Satellite Mega-Constellations Create Risks in Low Earth Orbit, the Atmosphere and on Earth' (2021) 11(1) *Scientific Reports* 10642.

Bridge, Robert L, 'International Law and Military Activities in Outer Space' (1979) 13 *Akron Law Review* 649.

Broms, Bengt, 'The Definition of Aggression' (1977) 154 *Recueil des cours* 348.

Brownlie, Ian, 'International Law and the Use of Force by States Revisited' (2002) 1 *Chinese Journal of International Law* 1.

Buchan, Russell, 'Cyber Attacks: Unlawful Uses of Force or Prohibited Interventions?' (2012) 17(2) *Journal of Conflict and Security Law* 212.

Butchard, Patrick M, 'Back to San Francisco: Explaining the Inherent Contradictions of Article 2(4) of the UN Charter' (2018) 23(2) *Journal of Conflict and Security Law* 229.

Cheng, Bin, 'United Nations Resolutions on Outer Space: "Instant" International Customary Law?' (1965) 5 *Indian Journal of International Law* 36.

Cheng, Dean, 'Space Deterrence, the U.S.-Japan Alliance, and Asian Security: A U.S. Perspective', in Scott W Harold et al, *The U.S.-Japan Alliance and Deterring Gray Zone Coercion in the Maritime, Cyber, and Space Domains* (RAND Corporation, 2017) 74.

Corten, Olivier, 'The Russian Intervention in the Ukrainian Crisis: Was *Jus Contra Bellum* "Confirmed Rather than Weakened"?' (2015) 2(1) *Journal on the Use of Force and International Law* 17.

Corthay, Eric Louis, 'Legal Bases for Forcible Maritime Interdiction Operations against Terrorist Threat on the High Seas' (2018) 31(2) *Australian and New Zealand Maritime Law Journal* 53.

Davis, John A, 'The U.S.-Japan Alliance and Deterrence in Cyberspace', in Scott W Harold et al, *The U.S.-Japan Alliance and Deterring Gray Zone Coercion in the Maritime, Cyber, and Space Domains* (RAND Corporation, 2017) 41.

Dev, Priyanka R, '"Use of Force" and "Armed Attack" Thresholds in Cyber Conflict: The Looming Definitional Gaps and the Growing Need for Formal UN Response' (2015) 50(2) *Texas International Law Journal* 2.

Dinstein, Yoram, 'The Interaction between Customary International Law and Treaties' (2006) 322 *Recueil des cours: Collected Courses of the Hague Academy of International Law* 243.

Farrant, James 'Modern Maritime Neutrality Law' (2014) 90 *International Law Studies* 198.

Ferencz, Benjamin B, 'The Illegal Use of Armed Force as a Crime against Humanity' (2015) 2(2) *Journal on the Use of Force and International Law* 187.

Ferreira-Snyman, Anel, 'Selected Legal Challenges Relating to the Military Use of Outer Space, with Specific Reference to Article IV of the Outer Space Treaty' (2015) 18(3) *Potchefstroom Electronic Law Journal/Potchefstroomse Elektroniese Regsblad* 487.

Focarelli, Carlo, 'Promotional *Jus Cogens*: A Critical Appraisal of *Jus Cogens*' Legal Effects' (2008) 77(4) *Nordic Journal of International Law* 429.

Ford, Stuart, 'Legal Processes of Change: Article 2(4) and the Vienna Convention on the Law of Treaties' (1999) 4(1) *Journal of Conflict and Security Law* 75.

Francioni, Francesco, 'Peacetime Use of Force, Military Activities, and the New Law of the Sea' (1985) 18 *Cornell International Law Journal* 203.

Franck, Thomas M, 'Legitimacy in the International System' (1988) 82(4) *American Journal of International Law* 705.

Fraser, Adeo, 'From the Kalashnikov to the Keyboard: International Law's Failure to Define a Cyber Use of Force Is Dangerous and May Lead to a Military Response to a Cyber Use of Force' (2016) 15 *Hibernian Law Journal* 86.

Fukuda, Junichi, 'A Japanese Perspective on the Role of the U.S.-Japan Alliance in Deterring – Or, if Necessary, Defeating – Maritime Gray Zone Coercion' in Scott W Harold et al (eds), The U.S.-Japan Alliance and Deterring Gray Zone Coercion in the Maritime, Cyber, and Space Domains (RAND Corporation, 2017) 23.

Gill, TD, 'The Forcible Protection, Affirmation and Exercise of Rights by States under Contemporary International Law' (1992) 23 *Netherlands Yearbook of International Law* 105.

Gilmore, William C, 'Narcotics Interdiction at Sea: UK–US Cooperation' [1989] *Marine Policy* 218.

Gleditsch, Nils Petter, Peter Wallensteen, Mikael Eriksson, Margareta Sollenberg and Håvard Strand, 'Armed Conflict 1946–2001: A New Dataset' (2002) 39(5) *Journal of Peace Research* 615.

Glennon, Michael J, 'How International Rules Die' (2005) 93(3) *Georgetown Law Journal* 939.

'Why the Security Council Failed' [2003] 82(3) (May/June 2003) *Foreign Affairs* 16.

Green, James A, 'Questioning the Peremptory Status of the Prohibition of the Use of Force' (2010) 32 *Michigan Journal of International Law* 215.

Guilfoyle, Douglas, 'Counter-Piracy Law Enforcement and Human Rights' (2010) 59 (1) *International and Comparative Law Quarterly* 141.

'Interdicting Vessels to Enforce the Common Interest: Maritime Countermeasures and the Use of Force' (2007) 56(1) *The International and Comparative Law Quarterly* 69.

'The Mavi Marmara Incident and Blockade in Armed Conflict' (2011) 81(1) *British Yearbook of International Law* 171.

Hamamoto, Yukiya, 'The Incident of a Submarine Navigating Underwater in Japan's Territorial Sea' (2005) 48 *The Japanese Annual of International Law* 123.

Harold, Scott W, 'Conclusion: Leveraging the U.S.-Japan Alliance to Deter Gray Zone Coercion in the Maritime, Cyber, and Space Domains' in Scott W Harold et al (eds), *The U.S.-Japan Alliance and Deterring Gray Zone Coercion in the Maritime, Cyber, and Space Domains* (RAND Corporation, 2017) 105.

Henry, Etienne, 'The Sukhoi Su-24 Incident between Russia and Turkey' (2016) 4(1) *Russian Law Journal* 8.

Hofer, Alexandra, 'The Developed/Developing Divide on Unilateral Coercive Measures: Legitimate Enforcement or Illegitimate Intervention?' (2017) 16(2) *Chinese Journal of International Law* 175.

Jones, Daniel M, Stuart A Bremer and J David Singer, 'Militarized Interstate Disputes, 1816–1992: Rationale, Coding Rules, and Empirical Patterns' (1996) 15(2) *Conflict Management and Peace Science* 163.

Kahgan, Carin, '*Jus Cogens* and the Inherent Right to Self-Defense' (1996) 3 *ISLA Journal of International & Comparative Law* 767.

Kegley, Charles W and Gregory A Raymond, 'Normative Constraints on the Use of Force Short of War' (1986) 23(3) *Journal of Peace Research* 213.

Keyuan, Zou, 'Maritime Enforcement of United Nations Security Council Resolutions: Use of Force and Coercive Measures' (2011) 26(2) *The International Journal of Marine and Coastal Law* 235.

King, Matthew T, 'Sovereignty's Gray Area: The Delimitation of Air and Space in the Context of Aerospace Vehicles and the Use of Force' (2016) 81 *Journal of Air Law and Commerce* 377.

Kolb, Robert, 'Le droit contre la guerre' (2014) 1(2) *Journal on the Use of Force and International Law* 395.

Kono, Keiko, 'A Japanese Perspective on Deterrence in Cyberspace Gray Zone Contingencies and the Role of the Japan-U.S. Alliance' in Scott W Harold et al (eds), *The U.S.-Japan Alliance and Deterring Gray Zone Coercion in the Maritime, Cyber, and Space Domains* (RAND Corporation, 2017) 62.

Kretzmer, David, 'The Inherent Right to Self-Defence and Proportionality in *Jus Ad Bellum*' (2013) 24(1) *European Journal of International Law* 235.

Kwast, Patricia Jimenez, 'Maritime Law Enforcement and the Use of Force: Reflections on the Categorisation of Forcible Action at Sea in the Light of the Guyana/Suriname Award' (2008) 13(1) *Journal of Conflict and Security Law* 49.

Larson, David L, 'Security Issues and the Law of the Sea: A General Framework' (1985) 15(2) *Ocean Development & International Law* 99.

Linderfalk, Ulf, 'The Effect of *Jus Cogens Norms*: Whoever Opened Pandora's Box, Did You Ever Think about the Consequences?' (2007) 18(5) *European Journal of International Law* 853.

Lubell, Noam, 'Fragmented Wars: Multi-Territorial Military Operations against Armed Groups' (2017) 93(1) *International Law Studies* 213.

Luke, Ivan T, 'Naval Operations in Peacetime: Not Just "Warfare Lite"' (2013) 66(2) *Naval War College Review* 11.

McDermott, Helen, 'Extraterritorial Kidnapping and the Rules on Interstate Force' (2014) 1(2) *Journal on the Use of Force and International Law* 299.

McLaughlin, Rob, 'United Nations Mandated Naval Interdiction Operations in the Territorial Sea?' (2002) 51 *International and Comparative Law Quarterly* 249.

Mikanagi, Tomohiro, 'Establishing a Military Presence in a Disputed Territory: Interpretation of Article 2(3) and (4) of the UN Charter' (2018) 67(4) *International & Comparative Law Quarterly* 1021.

'The Legal Basis of Missile Defence – An Examination of the Japanese Situation' (2005) 48 *The Japanese Annual of International Law* 65.

Mikanagi, Tomohiro and Hirohito Ogi, 'The Japanese View on Legal Issues Related to Security' (2016) 59 *Japanese Yearbook of International Law* 360.

Morgernstern, Felice, 'Jurisdiction in Seizures Effected in Violation of International Law' (1952) 29 *British Yearbook of International Law* 265.

Murphy, Sean D, 'Protean *Jus Ad Bellum*' (2009) 27 *Berkeley Journal of International Law* 22.

Nakagawa, Yoshiaki, 'Using Land Forces to Deter Maritime Gray Zone Coercion: The Role of the Japan Ground Self-Defense Forces in the Nansei (Ryukyu) Islands' in Scott W Harold et al (eds), *The U.S.-Japan Alliance and Deterring Gray Zone Coercion in the Maritime, Cyber, and Space Domains* (RAND Corporation, 2017) 11.

Neff, Stephen C, 'Towards a Law of Unarmed Conflict: A Proposal for a New International Law of Hostility' (1995) 28(1) *Cornell International Law Journal* 1.

O'Connell, Mary Ellen, 'Twenty-first Century Arms Control Challenges: Drones, Cyber Weapons, Killer Robots, and WMDs' (2015) 13(3) *Washington University Global Studies Law Review* 515.

'Cyber Security without Cyber War' (2012) 17(2) *Journal of Conflict and Security Law* 187.

O'Higgins, Paul, 'Unlawful Seizure and Irregular Extradition' (1960) 36 *British Yearbook of International Law* 319.

Orakhelashvili, Alexander, 'Undesired, Yet Omnipresent: *Jus Ad Bellum* in Its Relation to Other Areas of International Law' (2015) *Journal on the Use of Force and International Law* 1.

Paddeu, Federica I, 'Military Assistance on Request and General Reasons against Force: Consent as a Defence to the Prohibition of the Use of Force' (2020) 7 (2) *Journal on the Use of Force and International Law* 227.

'Self-Defence as a Circumstance Precluding Wrongfulness: Understanding Article 21 of the Articles on State Responsibility' (2015) 85(1) *British Yearbook of International Law* 90.

Palmer, Glenn, Vito D'Orazio, Michael Kenwick and Mathew Lane, 'The Mid4 Dataset, 2002–2010: Procedures, Coding Rules and Description' (2015) 32 *Conflict Management and Peace Science* 222.

Paulus, Andreas, '*Jus Cogens* in a Time of Hegemony and Fragmentation – An Attempt at a Reappraisal' (2005) 74(3) *Nordic Journal of International Law* 297.

'Realism and International Law: Two Optics in Need of Each Other' (2002) 96 *Proceedings of the Annual Meeting (American Society of International Law)* 269.

Rayfuse, Rosemary, 'Countermeasures and High Seas Fisheries Enforcement' (2004) 51(1) *Netherlands International Law Review* 41.

Reisman, Michael, 'Criteria for the Lawful Use of Force in International Law' (1985) 10 *Yale Journal of International Law* 279.

'International Incidents: Introduction to a New Genre in the Study of International Law' (1984) 10 *Yale Journal of International Law* 1.
Roberts, Anthea Elizabeth, 'Traditional and Modern Approaches to Customary International Law: A Reconciliation' (2001) 95(4) *American Journal of International Law* 757.
Roxin, Claus, 'Verwerflichkeit und Sittenwidrigkeit als unrechtsbegründende Merkmale im Strafrecht' (1964) *JuS* 373.
Ruys, Tom, 'The Meaning of "Force" and the Boundaries of the *Jus Ad Bellum*: Are "Minimal" Uses of Force Excluded from UN Charter Article 2 (4)?' (2014) 108(2) *American Journal of International Law* 159.
'The "Protection of Nationals" Doctrine Revisited' (2008) 13(2) *Journal of Conflict and Security Law* 233.
Ruys, Tom and Felipe Rodríguez Silvestre, 'Illegal: The Recourse to Force to Recover Occupied Territory and the Second Nagorno-Karabakh War' (2021) 32(4) *European Journal of International Law* 1287.
Sadurska, Romana, 'Foreign Submarines in Swedish Waters: The Erosion of an International Norm' (1984) 10 *Yale Journal of International Law* 34.
'Threats of Force' (1988) 82(2) *American Journal of International Law* 239.
Schachter, Oscar, 'The Right of States to Use Armed Force' (1984) 82(5/6) *Michigan Law Review* 1620.
Scharf, Michael P, 'On the Relation between Unlawful Use of Force and the War Crime of Disproportionate Force Not Justified by Military Necessity, Benjamin B. Ferencz Essay Competition, Second Edition: Introduction' (2016) 48 *Case Western Reserve Journal of International Law* 213.
Schmitt, Michael N, 'Classification of Cyber Conflict' (2012) 17(2) *Journal of Conflict and Security Law* 245.
'Computer Network Attack and the Use of Force in International Law: Thoughts on a Normative Framework' (1999) 37 *Columbia Journal of Transnational Law* 1998.
'Cyber Operations in International Law: The Use of Force, Collective Security, Self-Defense, and Armed Attack' in *Proceedings of a Workshop on Deterring Cyberattacks: Informing Strategies and Developing Options for U.S. Policy* (2010) 155.
Slaughter, Anne-Marie and William W Burke-White, 'An International Constitutional Moment' (2002) 43 *Harvard International Law Journal* 1.
Spiermann, Ole, 'Humanitarian Intervention as a Necessity and the Threat or Use of *Jus Cogens*' (2002) 71(4) *Nordic Journal of International Law* 523.
Steenberghe, Raphaël van, 'State Practice and the Evolution of the Law of Self-Defence: Clarifying the Methodological Debate' (2015) 2(1) *Journal on the Use of Force and International Law* 81.
Stephens, Dale, 'Rules of Engagement and the Concept of Unit Self Defense' (1998) 45 *Naval Law Review* 126.
Suzuki, Kazuto, 'A Japanese Perspective on Space Deterrence and the Role of the U.S.-Japan Alliance and Deterrence in Outer Space' in Scott W Harold et al (eds), *The U.S.-Japan Alliance and Deterring Gray Zone Coercion in the Maritime, Cyber, and Space Domains* (RAND Corporation, 2017) 91.
Talmon, Stefan, 'Determining Customary International Law: The ICJ's Methodology between Induction, Deduction and Assertion' (2015) 26(2) *European Journal of International Law* 417.

Tams, Christian J, 'Meta-Custom and the Court: A Study in Judicial Law-Making' (2015) 14(1) *The Law and Practice of International Courts and Tribunals* 51.

Thirlway, Hugh WA, 'Professor Baxter's Legacy: Still Paradoxical?' (2017) 6(3) *ESIL Reflection* 1.

Tomka, Peter, 'Custom and the International Court of Justice' (2013) 12(2) *The Law & Practice of International Courts and Tribunals* 195.

Tondini, Matteo, 'The Use of Force in the Course of Maritime Law Enforcement Operations' (2017) 4(2) *Journal on the Use of Force and International Law* 253.

Treves, Tullio, 'Piracy, Law of the Sea, and Use of Force: Developments off the Coast of Somalia' (2009) 20(2) *European Journal of International Law* 399.

Trumbull IV, Charles P, 'The Basis of Unit Self-Defense and Implications for the Use of Force' (2012) 23 *Duke Journal of Comparative & International Law* 121.

Tuffi Saliba, Aziz, Dawisson Belém Lopes and Pedro Vieira, 'Brazil's Rendition of the "Responsibility to Protect" Doctrine' (2015) 3(2) *Brasiliana – Journal for Brazilian Studies* 32.

Tzanakopoulos, Antonios, 'The Right to Be Free from Economic Coercion' (2015) 4 *Cambridge Journal of International and Comparative Law* 616.

Van Logchem, Youri, 'Submarine Telecommunication Cables in Disputed Maritime Areas' (2014) 45(1) *Ocean Development & International Law* 107.

Vasilogeorgi, Isavella Maria, 'Military Uses of Outer Space: Legal Limitations, Contemporary Perspectives' (2014) 39(2) *Journal of Space Law* 379.

Verdebout, Agatha, 'The Contemporary Discourse on the Use of Force in the Nineteenth Century: A Diachronic and Critical Analysis' (2014) 1(2) *Journal on the Use of Force and International Law* 223.

Walker, Neil, 'Beyond Boundary Disputes and Basic Grids: Mapping the Global Disorder of Normative Orders' (2008) 6(3–4) *International Journal of Constitutional Law* 373.

Waxman, Matthew C, 'Cyber-Attacks and the Use of Force: Back to the Future of Article 2 (4)' (2011) 36 *Yale Journal of International Law* 421.

de Wet, Erika, 'Military Assistance Based on Ex-Ante Consent: A Violation of Article 2 (4) of the UN Charter?' (2020) 93(3–4) *Die Friedens-Warte* 413.

Willard, Andrew R, 'Incidents: An Essay in Method' (1984) 10 *Yale Journal of International Law* 21.

Wood, Michael, 'The Law on the Use of Force: Current Challenges' (2007) 11 *Singapore Year Book of International Law* 1.

Yahn Filho, Armando Gallo, 'Environmental Aggression in the Context of Contemporary International Law' (2016) 4(25) *Environmental Quality Management* 5.

Zwanenburg, Marten, Michael Bothe and Marco Sassòli, 'Is the Law of Occupation Applicable to the Invasion Phase?' (2012) 94 *International Review of the Red Cross* 29.

BLOG POSTS

Akande, Dapo, 'The Use of Nerve Agents in Salisbury: Why Does It Matter Whether It Amounts to a Use of Force in International Law?', *EJIL: Talk!* (17 March 2018), www.ejiltalk.org/the-use-of-nerve-agents-in-salisbury-why-does-it-matter-whether-it-amounts-to-a-use-of-force-in-international-law/.

Bodansky, Daniel, 'Does Custom Have a Source?', *AJIL Unbound* (23 December 2014), www.cambridge.org/core/journals/american-journal-of-international-law/article/does-custom-have-a-source/FA9588611B2C214F602CE7FFC40C663B.

Cohen, Harlan G, 'Methodology and Misdirection: Custom and the ICJ', *EJIL: Talk!* (1 December 2015), www.ejiltalk.org/methodology-and-misdirection-a-response-to-stefan-talmon-on-custom-and-the-icj/.

Guilfoyle, Douglas, 'A New Twist in the South China Sea Arbitration: The Chinese Society of International Law's Critical Study', *EJIL: Talk!* (25 May 2018), www.ejiltalk.org/a-new-twist-in-the-south-china-sea-arbitration-the-chinese-society-of-international-laws-critical-study/#more-16226.

Henderson, Ian and Bryan Cavanagh, 'Guest Post: Military Members Claiming Self-Defence during Armed Conflict-Often Misguided and Unhelpful', *Opinio Juris* (8 July 2014), http://opiniojuris.org/2014/07/08/guest-post-military-members-claiming-self-defence-armed-conflict-often-misguided-unhelpful/.

'Guest Post: Unit Self-Defence', *Opinio Juris* (11 July 2014), http://opiniojuris.org/2014/07/11/guest-post-unit-self-defence/.

Lusa Bordin, Fernando, 'Induction, Assertion and the Limits of the Existing Methodologies to Identify Customary International Law', *EJIL: Talk!* (2 December 2015), www.ejiltalk.org/induction-assertion-and-the-limits-of-the-existing-methodologies-to-identify-customary-international-law/.

Mačák, Kubo, 'Was the Downing of the Russian Jet by Turkey Illegal?', *EJIL: Talk!* (26 November 2015), www.ejiltalk.org/was-the-downing-of-the-russian-jet-by-turkey-illegal/.

O'Connell, Mary Ellen, 'The True Meaning of Force', *AJIL Unbound* (4 August 2014), www.cambridge.org/core/journals/american-journal-of-international-law/article/true-meaning-of-force/0D138765D49FF766167A479AB081BD27.

'The True Meaning of Force: A Further Response to Tom Ruys in the Interest of Peace', *AJIL Unbound* (4 September 2014), www.cambridge.org/core/journals/american-journal-of-international-law/article/true-meaning-of-force-a-further-response-to-tom-ruys-in-the-interest-of-peace/F7C06C746AF3764F1E8E832C7E42EEB2.

Ohlin, Jens David, 'Guest Post: Henderson & Cavanagh on Self-Defense & The Privilege of Combatancy', *Opinio Juris* (8 July 2014), http://opiniojuris.org/2014/07/08/guest-post-henderson-cavanagh-self-defense-privilege-combatancy/.

Ruys, Tom, '"License to Kill" in Salisbury: State-Sponsored Assassinations and the *Jus Ad Bellum*', *Just Security* (15 March 2018), www.justsecurity.org/53924/license-kill-salisbury-state-sponsored-assassinations-jus-ad-bellum/.

'The True Meaning of Force – A Reply to Mary Ellen O'Connell', *AJIL Unbound* (3 September 2014), www.cambridge.org/core/journals/american-journal-of-international-law/article/true-meaning-of-forcea-reply-to-mary-ellen-oconnell/51D11D4211279058578434DD6A936BE9.

Sender, Omri and Michael Wood, 'The International Court of Justice and Customary International Law: A Reply to Stefan Talmon', *EJIL: Talk!* (30 November 2015), www.ejiltalk.org/the-international-court-of-justice-and-customary-international-law-a-reply-to-stefan-talmon/.

Talmon, Stefan, 'Determining Customary International Law: The ICJ's Methodology between Induction, Deduction and Assertion', *EJIL: Talk!* (27 November 2015), www.ejiltalk.org/determining-customary-international-law-the-icjs-methodology-between-induction-deduction-and-assertion/.

'Determining Customary International Law: The ICJ's Methodology and the Idyllic World of the ILC', *EJIL: Talk!* (3 December 2015), www.ejiltalk.org/determining-customary-international-law-the-icjs-methodology-and-the-idyllic-world-of-the-ilc/.

Weller, Marc, 'An International Use of Force in Salisbury?', *EJIL: Talk!* (14 March 2018), www.ejiltalk.org/an-international-use-of-force-in-salisbury/.

'Striking ISIL: Aspects of the Law on the Use of Force', *ASIL Insights* (11 March 2015), www.asil.org/insights/volume/19/issue/5/striking-isil-aspects-law-use-force.

CASES

Alleged Violations of Sovereign Rights and Maritime Spaces in the Caribbean Sea (Nicaragua v Colombia), Preliminary Objections, Judgment (2016) ICJ Reports 3

Arbitral Tribunal Constituted Pursuant to Article 287, and in Accordance with Annex VII of the UN Convention on the Law of the Sea (Guyana and Suriname), 17 September 2007

Armed Activities on the Territory of the Congo (Democratic Republic of the Congo v Uganda) (2005) ICJ Reports 168

BayObLG, NJW 1993, 213

BGH, NJW 1993, 1869

BGHSt 19, 263

BGHSt 23, 46

BGHSt 37, 350

BVerfGE 92, 1

Case concerning Application of the Convention on the Prevention and Punishment of the Crime of Genocide (Bosnia and Herzegovina v Serbia and Montenegro), Judgment (2007) ICJ Reports 43

Case concerning Military and Paramilitary Activities in and against Nicaragua (Nicaragua v United States of America), Jurisdiction and Admissibility, Judgment (1984) ICJ Reports 392

Case concerning Military and Paramilitary Activities in and against Nicaragua (Nicaragua v United States of America), Merits, Judgment (1986) ICJ Reports 14

Case concerning the Differences between New Zealand and France Arising from the Rainbow Warrior Affair Ruling of 6 July 1986 by the Secretary-General of the United Nations (1990) 19 Reports of International Arbitral Awards 197

Certain Activities Carried Out by Nicaragua in the Border Area (Costa Rica v Nicaragua) and Construction of a Road in Costa Rica along the San Juan River (Nicaragua v Costa Rica) (2015) ICJ Reports 665

Certain Expenses of the United Nations (Article 17, Paragraph 2 of the Charter), Advisory Opinion (1962) ICJ Reports 151

Continental Shelf (Libyan Arab Jamahiriya/Malta), Judgment (1985) ICJ Reports 13

Continental Shelf (Tunisia/Libyan Arab Jamahiriya), Judgment (1982) ICJ Reports 18

Corfu Channel Case (UK v Albania), Merits, Judgment (1949) ICJ Reports 4

Decision Number 7: Guidance Regarding Jus Ad Bellum Liability (2007) 46(6) International Legal Materials 1121
Fisheries Jurisdiction (UK v Iceland), Jurisdiction (1973) ICJ Reports 3
Fisheries Jurisdiction (UK v Iceland), Merits, Judgment (1974) ICJ Reports 3
Fisheries Jurisdiction Case (Federal Republic of Germany v Iceland), Merits, Judgment (1974) ICJ Reports 175
Fisheries Jurisdiction Case (Spain v Canada), Jurisdiction, Judgment (1998) ICJ Reports 432
Governing Council Decision 1: Criteria for Expedited Processing of Urgent Claims [1991] United Nations Compensation Commission S/AC.26/1991/1
Guyana v Suriname, Award (Permanent Court of Arbitration, 17 September 2007)
Investigation of Certain Incidents Affecting the British Trawler Red Crusader: Report of 23 March 1962 of the Commission of Enquiry Established by the Government of the United Kingdom of Great Britain and Northern Ireland and the Government of the Kingdom of Denmark on 15 November 1961 (1962) 29 ILR 521
Legal Consequences of the Construction of a Wall in the Occupied Palestinian Territory (Advisory Opinion) (2004) ICJ Reports 136
Legality of the Threat or Use of Nuclear Weapons, Advisory Opinion (1996) ICJ Reports 226
M/V 'Saiga' (No 2) (St Vincent v Guinea), ITLOS Case No 2, Merits (ITLOS, 1 July 1999)
North Sea Continental Shelf (Federal Republic of Germany/Denmark; Federal Republic of Germany/Netherlands) Judgment (1969) ICJ Reports 3
Oil Platforms (Islamic Republic of Iran v United States of America), Judgment (2003) ICJ Reports 161
OLG Hamm, NJW 1983, 1505
Prosecutor v Duško Tadic, ICTY Appeals Chamber Judgment of 15 July 1999
Red Crusader, Judgment of 23 May 1962 (1967) 35 International Law Reports 499
South China Sea Arbitration (Republic of the Philippines and PRC) [2016] Permanent Court of Arbitration PCA Case No 2013–19 (12 July 2016)
SS 'I'm Alone' (UK (for Canada) v USA) (1933) 3 International Law Reports 1609
SS Lotus Case (France v Turkey) [1927] PCIJ Series A No 10 (7 September) 25
Temple of Preah Vihear, Application Instituting Proceedings, 30 September 1959, Pleadings, Oral Arguments, Documents (1962) ICJ Reports 15
United States Diplomatic and Consular Staff in Tehran (USA v Iran), Judgment (1980) ICJ Reports 3

TREATIES AND DECLARATIONS

Agreement between the Government of the United States of America and the Government of the Union of Soviet Socialist Republics on the Prevention of Incidents on and over the High Seas (signed 25 May 1972, entered into force 25 May 1972), www.state.gov/t/isn/4791.htm
Agreement Governing the Activities of States on the Moon and Other Celestial Bodies 1979 (opened for signature 18 December 1979, entered into force 11 July 1984), 1636 UNTS 3

Charter of Paris for a New Europe 1990, Organization for Security and Co-operation in Europe (21 November 1990)

Charter of the United Nations 1945 (adopted 26 June 1945, entered into force 24 October 1945), 1 UNTS 16

Conference on Security and Co-operation in Europe: 1975 Helsinki Final Act

Constitutive Act of the African Union, Organisation of African Unity 2000 (adopted 1 July 2000, entered into force 26 May 2001) and *Protocol on the Amendments to the Constitutive Act of the African Union* (adopted 11 July 2003, not yet entered into force)

Convention on Intervention on the High Seas in Cases of Oil Pollution Casualties 1969 (adopted 29 November 1969, entered into force 6 May 1975), 970 UNTS 221

Convention on Registration of Objects Launched into Outer Space 1975 (opened for signature 14 January 1975, entered into force 15 September 1976), 1023 UNTS 15

Covenant of the League of Nations 1919 (adopted 28 April 1919, entered into force 10 January 1920)

Déclaration relative au droit de la guerre maritime [Declaration concerning the Laws of Naval War] (26 February 1909, not entered into force) (1909), 208 CTS 338

Declaration respecting Maritime Law between Austria, France, Great Britain, Prussia, Russia, Sardinia and Turkey (signed and entered into force 16 April 1856) (1856), 115 CTS 1

Elements of Crimes of the International Criminal Court, Reproduced from the Official Records of the Assembly of States Parties to the Rome Statute of the International Criminal Court, First Session, New York, 3–10 September 2002, part II.B and Official Records of the Review Conference of the Rome Statute of the International Criminal Court, Kampala, 31 May–11 June 2010

Geneva Convention (IV) Relative to the Protection of Civilian Persons in Time of War 1949 (adopted 12 August 1949, entered into force 21 October 1950), 75 UNTS 287

Montevideo Convention on the Rights and Duties of States 1933 (adopted 26 December 1933, entered into force 26 December 1934), 165 LNTS 19

Regulations Respecting the Laws and Customs of War on Land, Annex to Hague Convention Respecting the Laws and Customs of War on Land 1907 (adopted 18 October 1907, entered into force 26 January 1910)

Treaty between the United States and Other Powers Providing for the Renunciation of War as an Instrument of National Policy 1929 (adopted 27 August 1929, entered into Force 24 July 1929), 94 LNTS 57

Treaty of Peace with Japan (signed at San San Francisco on 8 September 1951, entered into force 28 April 1952), 1952 UNTS 46

Treaty on Principles Governing the Activities of States in the Exploration and Use of Outer Space, Including the Moon and Other Celestial Bodies 1967 (adopted 27 January 1967, entered into force 10 October 1967), 610 UNTS 205

Treaty on the Basis of Relations between the Federal Republic of Germany and the German Democratic Republic (Grundlagenvertrag) and Supplementary Documents (signed at Berlin on 21 December 1972)

United Nations Agreement for the Implementation of the Provisions of the United Nations Convention on the Law of the Sea of 10 December 1982 Relating to the Conservation and Management of Straddling Fish Stocks and Highly Migratory Fish Stocks 1995 (adopted 4 August 1995, entered into force 11 December 2001), 2167 UNTS 3

United Nations Convention on the Law of the Sea 1982 (adopted 10 December 1982, entered into force 16 November 1994), 1833 UNTS 397

Vienna Convention on the Law of Treaties 1969 (adopted 22 May 1969, entered into force 27 January 1980), 1155 UNTS 331

UN RESOLUTIONS AND OFFICIAL RECORDS

Letter Dated 10 December 2015 from the Chargé d'affairs a.i. of the Permanent Mission of Germany to the United Nations Addressed to the President of the Security Council (10 December 2015) UN Doc S/2015/946

Letter Dated 14 May 1975 from the Permanent Representative of the United States of America to the United Nations Addressed to the President of the Security Council (15 May 1975) UN Doc S/11689

Letter Dated 19 August 2008 from the Permanent Representative of the United States of America Addressed to the Secretary-General of the Conference Transmitting Comments on the Draft Treaty on Prevention of the Placement of Weapons in Outer Space and of the Threat or Use of Force against Outer Space Objects (PPWT) as Contained in Document CD/1839 of 29 February 2008 (26 August 2008) UN Doc CD/1847

Letter Dated 20 June 2002 from the President and the Chancellor of the Swiss Confederation on Behalf of the Swiss Federal Council Addressed to the Secretary-General (24 July 2002) UN Doc A/56/1009–S/2002/801

Letter Dated 25 April 1980 from the Permanent Representative of the United States of America to the United Nations Addressed to the President of the Security Council (25 April 1980) UN Doc S/13908

Letter Dated 24 November 2015 from the Permanent Representative of Turkey to the United Nations Addressed to the President of the Security Council (24 November 2015)

Letter Dated 26 June 1993 from the Permanent Representative of the United States of America to the UN Addressed to the President of the Security Council (26 June 1993) UN Doc S/26003

Letter Dated 3 September 1964 from Representative of Malaysia to the President of the Security Council (17 September 1964) UN Doc S/5930

Letter Dated 5 April 2016 from the Permanent Representative of the Republic of Korea to the United Nations addressed to the President of the Security Council (5 April 2016) UN Doc S/2016/315

Memorandum of the Government of New Zealand to the Secretary-General of the United Nations (6 July 1986) 11 Reports of International Arbitral Awards 201

Note Verbale Dated 28 April 1980 from the Permanent Representative of Iran to the United Nations Addressed to the Secretary-General (29 April 1980) UN Doc S/13915

Report of the Group of Governmental Experts on Further Practical Measures for the Prevention of an Arms Race in Outer Space (19 April 2019) UN Doc A/74/77

UNCIO, 'First Session of Commission I, June 14, 1945', vol. VI (15 June 1945) UN Doc 1006 I/6

UNCIO, 'Report of the Rapporteur of Committee 1 to Commission I' vol. VI (5 June 1945) UN Doc 784/I/1/27

UNCIO, 'Report of the Rapporteur of Committee 1 to Commission I' vol. VI p400 (9 June 1945) UN Doc 885/I/1/34

UN General Assembly, 2005 *World Summit Outcome* (24 October 2005) UN Doc A/RES/60/1

UN General Assembly, *Convention on the Law of the Sea*, 1994 UNTS 397 (concluded 10 December 1982, entered into force 16 November 1994)

UN General Assembly, *Resolution 2625: Declaration on Principles of International Law Concerning Friendly Relations and Cooperation among States in Accordance with the Charter of the United Nations* (24 October 1970) UN Doc A/Res/2625 (XXV)

UN General Assembly, *Resolution 3314: Definition of Aggression* (14 December 1974) UN Doc A/Res/29/3314

UN General Assembly, *Resolution 42/22: Declaration on the Enhancement of the Effectiveness of the Principle of Refraining from the Threat or Use of Force in International Relations* (18 November 1987) UN Doc A/Res/42/22

UN General Assembly, *Resolution* 75/36 (16 December 2020) UN Doc A/RES/75/36

UN General Assembly, *Resolution on Aggression against Ukraine* (2 March 2022) UN Doc A/RES/ES-11/1

UN General Assembly, *Verbatim Record of Plenary Meeting No. 1860* (6 October 1970) UN Doc A/PV.1860

UN Security Council, *Provisional Verbatim Record of the 3245th Meeting* (27 June 1993) UN Doc S/PV.3245

UN Security Council, *Resolution* 2087 (22 January 2013) UN Doc S/Res/2087

UN Security Council, *Resolution* 611 (25 April 1988) UN Doc S/Res/611

UN Security Council Debates, *1606th Meeting* (4 December 1971)

REPORTS

'Articles on State Responsibility', Yearbook of the International Law Commission (2001), vol. II.

Crawford, James, Second Report on State Responsibility (30 April 1999) UN Doc A/CN.4/498/Add.2.

Fifth Report of the Special Committee on Principles of International Law concerning Friendly Relations and Co-operation among States (October 1969) UN Doc A/7619.

First Report of the Special Committee on Principles of International Law concerning Friendly Relations and Co-operation among States (16 November 1964) UN Doc A/5746.

Fourth Report of the Special Committee on Principles of International Law concerning Friendly Relations and Co-operation among States (November 1968) UN Doc A/7326.

'Independent International Fact-Finding Mission on the Conflict on Georgia, Report' (2009), available at www.mpil.de/en/pub/publications/archive/independent_international_fact.cfm.

International Law Association Committee on Formation of Customary (General) International Law, 'Final Report of the Committee: Statement of Principles Applicable to the Formation of General Customary International Law' (2000).

International Law Association Committee on the Use of Force, 'Final Report on Aggression and the Use of Force' (2018).

International Law Commission, 'Draft Articles on Responsibility of States for Internationally Wrongful Acts, with Commentaries, in Report of the International Law Commission on the Work of Its Fifty-Third Session' (2001) UN Doc A/56/10.

'Draft Conclusions on Identification and Legal Consequences of Peremptory Norms of General International Law (*Jus Cogens*)', *Yearbook of the International Law Commission* (2022), vol. II, Part Two.

'Draft Conclusions on Identification of Customary International Law, with Commentaries', UN Doc A/73/10, *Yearbook of the International Law Commission* (2018), vol. II, Part Two.

'Draft Conclusions on Subsequent Agreements and Subsequent Practice in Relation to the Interpretation of Treaties', Annexed to UN GA Resolution 73/202 (A/RES/73/202, 3 January 2019).

'Formation and Evidence of Customary International Law – Elements in the Previous Work of the International Law Commission That Could Be Particularly Relevant to the Topic – Memorandum by the Secretariat' (14 March 2013) UN Doc A/CN.4/659.

'Fourth Report on Peremptory Norms of General International Law (*Jus cogens*) by Dire Tladi, Special Rapporteur' UN Doc A/CN.4/727 (31 January 2019).

'Identification of Customary International Law: Statement of the Chair of the Drafting Committee, Mr. Gilberto Saboia' (7 August 2014).

'Identification of Customary International Law: Statement of the Chair of the Drafting Committee, Mr. Mathias Forteau' (29 July 2015).

'Identification of Customary International Law: Text of the Draft Conclusions Provisionally Adopted by the Drafting Committee' (14 July 2015) UN Doc A/CN.4/L.869.

'Identification of Customary International Law: The Role of Decisions of National Courts in the Case Law of International Courts and Tribunals of a Universal Character for the Purpose of the Determination of Customary International Law – Memorandum by the Secretariat' (9 February 2016) UN Doc A/CN.4/691.

'Report of the Commission to the General Assembly on the Work of Its Thirty-Second Session', *Yearbook of the International Law Commission* (1980), vol. II(2), 1.

'Report of the International Law Commission on the Work of Its Eighteenth Session, 4 May–19 July 1966, Official Records of the General Assembly,

Twenty-First Session, Supplement No. 9 (A/6309/Rev.1)' (1966) UN Doc A/CN.4/191.

'Subsequent Agreements and Subsequent Practice in Relation to the Interpretation of Treaties: Text of Draft Conclusions 1–5 Provisionally Adopted by the Drafting Committee at the Sixty-Fifth Session of the International Law Commission' (24 May 2013) UN Doc A/CN.4/L.813.

'Subsequent Agreements and Subsequent Practice in Relation to the Interpretation of Treaties: Texts and Titles of Draft Conclusions 6 to 10 Provisionally Adopted by the Drafting Committee on 27 and 28 May and on 2 and 3 June 2014' (3 June 2014) UN Doc A/CN.4/L.833.

'Subsequent Agreements and Subsequent Practice in Relation to the Interpretation of Treaties Text and Title of Draft Conclusion 11 Provisionally Adopted by the Drafting Committee on 4 June 2015' (19 June 2015) UN Doc A/CN.4/L.854.

'Subsequent Agreements and Subsequent Practice in Relation to the Interpretation of Treaties: Statement of the Chair of the Drafting Committee, Mr. Dire Tladi' (31 May 2013).

'Subsequent Agreements and Subsequent Practice in Relation to the Interpretation of Treaties: Statement of the Chair of the Drafting Committee, Mr. Gilberto Vergne Saboia' (5 June 2014).

'Subsequent Agreements and Subsequent Practice in Relation to the Interpretation of Treaties: Statement of the Chair of the Drafting Committee, Mr. Mathias Forteau' (8 July 2015).

'Yearbook of the International Law Commission 1966, Vol. II' (1966) UN Doc A/CN.4/SER.A/1966/Add.l.

1950 *Yearbook of the International Law Commission, Vol. II* (6 June 1957) UN Doc A/CN.4/Ser.A/1950/Add.1.

Nolte, Georg, 'First Report on Subsequent Agreements and Subsequent Practice in Relation to Treaty Interpretation' (19 March 2013) UN Doc A/CN.4/660.

'Second Report on Subsequent Agreements and Subsequent Practice in Relation to the Interpretation of Treaties', (International Law Commission, 26 March 2014) UN Doc A/CN.4/671.

'Third Report on Subsequent Agreements and Subsequent Practice in Relation to the Interpretation of Treaties', (International Law Commission, 7 April 2015) UN Doc A/CN.4/683.

Second Report of the 1966 Special Committee on Principles of International Law concerning Friendly Relations and Co-operation among States) (27 June 1966) UN Doc A/6230.

Sixth Report of the Special Committee on Principles of International Law concerning Friendly Relations and Co-operation among States (31 March to 1 May 1970) UN Doc A/8018.

Third Report of the Special Committee on Principles of International Law concerning Friendly Relations and Co-operation among States (26 September 1967) UN Doc A/6799.

United Nations Institute for Disarmament Research (UNIDIR), *Existing Legal and Regulatory Frameworks concerning Threats Arising from State Behaviours with Respect to Outer Space (Advance Unedited Version)* (No A/AC.294/2022/WP.1, 5 May 2022).

US White House, 'Report on the Legal and Policy Frameworks Guiding the United States' Use of Military Force and Related National Security Operations' (December 2016)

Weedon, Brian and Victoria Samson (eds), *Secure World Foundation Global Counterspace Capabilities Report* (Secure World Foundation, April 2022) https://swfound.org/media/207350/swf_global_counterspace_capabilities_2022_rev2.pdf.

Wood, Michael, 'First Report on Formation and Evidence of Customary International Law' (International Law Commission, 17 May 2013) UN Doc A/CN.4/663.

'Formation and Evidence of Customary International Law – Note by Michael Wood, Special Rapporteur' (30 May 2012) UN Doc A/CN.4/653.

'Fourth Report on Identification of Customary International Law' (6 March 2016) UN Doc A/CN.4/695.

'Second Report on Identification of Customary International Law' (22 May 2014) UN Doc A/CN.4/672.

'Third Report on Identification of Customary International Law' (International Law Commission, 27 March 2015) UN Doc A/CN.4/682.

NEWS REPORTS

Associated Press in Stockholm, 'Sweden Confirms Submarine Violation', *The Guardian* (14 November 2014) www.theguardian.com/world/2014/nov/14/sweden-confirms-submarine-violation.

Barnes, Julian E, 'U.S. Cyberattack Hurt Iran's Ability to Target Oil Tankers, Officials Say', *New York Times* (28 August 2019) www.nytimes.com/2019/08/28/us/politics/us-iran-cyber-attack.html.

Brent, Laura, 'NATO's Role in Cyberspace', *NATO Review* (12 February 2019) www.nato.int/docu/review/2019/Also-in-2019/natos-role-in-cyberspace-alliance-defence/EN/index.htm.

Chappell, Bill, 'Former Spy Sergei Skripal Released from Hospital, Recovering from Exotic Nerve Agent', *NPR* (18 May 2018) www.npr.org/sections/thetwo-way/2018/05/18/612259535/former-spy-sergei-skripal-released-from-hospital-recovering-from-exotic-nerve-ag.

Corera, Gordon, 'Salisbury Poisoning: What Did the Attack Mean for the UK and Russia?' *BBC News* (4 March 2020), www.bbc.com/news/uk-51722301.

Coskun, Orhan, 'Turkish Military Enters Syria to Evacuate Soldiers, Relocate Tomb', *Reuters* (22 February 2015) www.reuters.com/article/2015/02/22/us-syria-crisis-turkey-idUSKBN0LQ03U20150222.

Kraska, James, 'China's Maritime Militia Upends Rules on Naval Warfare', *The Diplomat* (10 August 2015) https://thediplomat.com/2015/08/chinas-maritime-militia-upends-rules-on-naval-warfare/.

Langbroek, Marco, 'A NEMESIS in the Sky: PAN, MENTOR 4, and Close Encounters of the SIGINT Kind', *The Space Review* (31 October 2016) www.thespacereview.com/article/3095/1.

'MIDEAST – Turkey Shoots down Russian Jet for Airspace Violation near Syrian Border', *The Hurriyet Daily News* (24 November 2015) www.hurriyetdailynews

.com/turkey-shoots-down-russian-jet-for-airspace-violation-near-syrian-border.aspx?pageID=238&nID=91580&NewsCatID=352.

Murphy, Simon, 'Met Confirms Second Police Officer Was Victim of Salisbury Attack', *The Guardian* (15 August 2019) www.theguardian.com/uk-news/2019/aug/15/met-confirms-second-police-officer-was-victim-of-salisbury-attack.

Reuters, 'Turkish Prime Minister's Visit to Tomb in Syria Likely to Anger Damascus', *The Guardian* (11 May 2015) www.theguardian.com/world/2015/may/11/turkish-prime-ministers-visit-to-tomb-in-syria-likely-to-anger-damascus.

Roulette, Joey, 'Debris from Test of Russian Antisatellite Weapon Forces Astronauts to Shelter', *The New York Times* (16 November 2021) www.nytimes.com/2021/11/15/science/russia-anti-satellite-missile-test-debris.html.

'Russian Spy: What Are Nerve Agents and What Do They Do?', *BBC News* (12 March 2018), www.bbc.com/news/health-43328976.

'Russian Spy: What Happened to the Skripals?', *BBC News* (18 April 2018) www.bbc.com/news/uk-43643025.

'Sergei Skripal: Who Is the Former Russian Intelligence Officer?' *BBC News* (29 March 2018), www.bbc.com/news/world-europe-43291394.

Shaheen, Kareem et al, 'Putin Condemns Turkey after Russian Warplane Downed near Syria Border' *The Guardian* (24 November 2015) www.theguardian.com/world/2015/nov/24/turkey-shoots-down-jet-near-border-with-syria?CMP=Share_iOSApp_Other.

Stamm, Peter, 'Switzerland Invades Liechtenstein', *The New York Times* (13 March 2007) www.nytimes.com/2007/03/13/opinion/13iht-edstamm.4893796.html.

Wikileaks, 'Turkey's Statement: Claims Russia Violated Airspace for Just "17 Seconds" with Very Slow 243 Miles/Hour http://Jet.Pic.Twitter.Com/KnhdyoRWIA', *@wikileaks* (24 November 2015) https://twitter.com/wikileaks/status/669204928984915968/photo/1.

Worley, Mark, 'Turkey Downs Russian Jet', *Al Jazeera* (24 November 2015) http://live.aljazeera.com/Event/Turkey_downs_Russian_jet/207503335.

OTHER MATERIALS

38 North, 'A Quick Technical Analysis of the Hwasong-12' (19 May 2017), www.38north.org/2017/05/hwasong051917/.

Arms Control Association, 'Chronology of US-North Korean Nuclear and Missile Diplomacy' (2018), www.armscontrol.org/factsheets/dprkchron.

Australian Government, '2017 Foreign Policy White Paper' (2017) www.fpwhitepaper.gov.au.

Australia Advances Responsible Action in Space: Joint Media Release of the Minister for Foreign Affairs, Minister for Defence and Minister for Industry and Science (27 October 2022) www.foreignminister.gov.au/minister/penny-wong/media-release/australia-advances-responsible-action-space?utm_source=nationaltribune&utm_medium=nationaltribune&utm_campaign=news.

'Statement for Plenary Session on International Peace and Security, Speech by Australian Minister for Foreign Affairs, The Hon Julie Bishop MP', (17 April 2015) www.foreignminister.gov.au/speeches/Pages/2015/jb_sp_150417.aspx.

Canada's Views on Reducing Space Threats through Norms, Rules and Principles of Responsible Behaviour (Advanced Unedited Version) (2022) UN Doc A/AC.294/2022/WP.7.

Canadian Space Agency, 'CubeSats in a Nutshell' (6 May 2022) www.asc-csa.gc.ca/eng/satellites/cubesat/what-is-a-cubesat.asp.

Correlates of War Project, *Militarized Interstate Disputes (MID 4)*, www.correlatesofwar.org/data-sets/MIDs.

Duhaime's Law Dictionary, *De Minimis Non Curat Lex Definition*, www.duhaime.org/LegalDictionary/D/DeMinimisNonCuratLex.aspx.

German Government, *Antrag der Bundesregierung: Einsatz bewaffneter deutscher Streitkräfte zur Verhütung und Unterbindung terroristischer Handlungen durch die Terrororganisation IS auf Grundlage von Artikel 51 der Satzung der Vereinten Nationen in Verbindung mit Artikel 42 Absatz 7 des Vertrages über die Europäische Union sowie den Resolutionen 2170 (2014), 2199 (2015), 2249 (2015) des Sicherheitsrates der Vereinten Nationen* (1 December 2015) Drucksache 18/6866.

German Government, Criminal Code in the Version Promulgated on 13 November 1998, Federal Law Gazette [Bundesgesetzblatt] I p. 3322, Last Amended by Article 1 of the Law of 24 September 2013, Federal Law Gazette I p. 3671 and with the Text of Article 6(18) of the Law of 10 October 2013, Federal Law Gazette I p. 3799.

von Heinegg, Wolff Heintschel, 'Blockade', *Max Planck Encyclopedia of Public International Law* (Oxford University Press, October 2015) http://opil.ouplaw.com/view/10.1093/law:epil/9780199231690/law-9780199231690-e252.

Hobe, Stephan, 'Airspace', *Max Planck Encyclopedia of Public International Law* (Oxford University Press, May 2008) http://opil.ouplaw.com/view/10.1093/law:epil/9780199231690/law-9780199231690-e1138.

International Committee for the Red Cross, *Commentary to the Geneva Convention I for the Amelioration of the Condition of the Wounded and Sick in the Armed Forces in the Field* (2nd ed, 2016).

Customary IHL Database, https://ihl-databases.icrc.org/customary-ihl/eng/docs/v1_rul.

The Potential Human Cost of the Use of Weapons in Outer Space and the Protection Afforded by International Humanitarian Law (9 April 2021).

Japanese Ministry of Foreign Affairs, 'Japan-North Korea Relations' (18 January 2019) www.mofa.go.jp/region/asia-paci/n_korea/index.html.

'North Korea's Missile Launch' (23 December 2017) www.mofa.go.jp/a_o/na/kp/page4e_000714.html.

McLaughlin, Rob, 'Some Contributions from Asia to the Development of LOAC', Speech Delivered at International Law Association Meeting, South Africa (2016) (on file with author).

Merriam Webster Dictionary, 'De Minimis', www.merriam-webster.com/dictionary/de minimis.

Ministry of Foreign Affairs of Japan, *Decision Not to Conduct Destructive, Direct-Ascent Anti-Satellite Missile Testing* (13 September 2022) www.mofa.go.jp/press/release/press3e_000451.html.

New Zealand Foreign Minister Nanaia Mahuta, 'Otago Foreign Policy School, Opening Address', New Zealand Government (1 July 2022) www.beehive.govt.nz/speech/otago-foreign-policy-school-opening-address.

North Atlantic Treaty Organization, *Brussels Summit Communiqué Issued by NATO Heads of State and Government (2021)* (14 June 2021) www.nato.int/cps/en/natohq/news_185000.htm.

'NATO's Approach to Space' (2 December 2021) www.nato.int/cps/en/natohq/topics_175419.htm.

'Statement by the North Atlantic Council on the Use of a Nerve Agent in Salisbury' (14 March 2018) www.nato.int/cps/en/natohq/news_152787.htm.

OED Online, 'Force, n.1' (Oxford University Press, December 2018) www.oed.com/view/Entry/72847#eid4006249.

'Kinetic, Adj. and N.' (Oxford University Press, December 2018) www.oed.com/view/Entry/103498.

'Use, N.' (Oxford University Press, December 2018) www.oed.com/view/Entry/220635.

Outer Space Institute, 'International Open Letter Re: Kinetic ASAT Test Ban Treaty' (2 September 2021) https://outerspaceinstitute.ca/docs/OSI_International_Open_Letter_ASATs_PUBLIC.pdf.

Permanent Mission of Canada to the United Nations in Geneva, Tweet posted 9 May 2022 at 4:25 PM, https://twitter.com/CanadaGeneva/status/1523685496399966209.

Remarks by Harold Hongju Koh, 'International Law in Cyberspace' (at the USCYBERCOM Inter-Agency Legal Conference, Ft. Meade, MD, 18 September 2012) https://2009–2017.state.gov/s/l/releases/remarks/197924.htm.

Space Security Index, *Electromagnetic Interference with Space Systems* (November 2020), https://spacesecurityindex.org/2020/11/electromagnetic-interference-with-space-systems/.

Statement by Germany in the Open-Ended Working Group on Reducing Space Threats through Norms, Rules and Principles of Responsible Behaviours (13 September 2022) https://documents.unoda.org/wp-content/uploads/2022/09/220913-Statement-by-Germany-on-13-September.pdf.

UK Foreign, Commonwealth & Development Office and UK Space Agency, *Responsible Space Behaviours: The UK Commits Not to Destructively Test Direct Ascent Anti-Satellite Missiles* (3 October 2022) www.gov.uk/government/news/responsible-space-behaviours-the-uk-commits-not-to-destructively-test-direct-ascent-anti-satellite-missiles.

UK Government, 'Foreign Secretary's Remarks on the Use of a Nerve Agent in Salisbury' (13 March 2018) www.gov.uk/government/speeches/foreign-secretarys-remarks-on-the-use-of-a-nerve-agent-in-salisbury-13-march-2018.

'PM Commons Statement on Salisbury Incident Response: A Statement to the House of Commons by Prime Minister Theresa May following the Salisbury Incident' (14 March 2018) www.gov.uk/government/speeches/pm-commons-statement-on-salisbury-incident-response-14-march-2018.

'The Russian State Was Responsible for the Attempted Murder … and for Threatening the Lives of Other British Citizens in Salisbury: Statement by Ambassador Jonathan Allen, Chargé d'Affaires, at a UN Security Council Briefing on a Nerve Agent attack in Salisbury' (14 March 2018) www.gov.uk/government/speeches/the-russian-state-was-responsible-for-the-attempted-murder and-for-threatening-the-lives-of-other-british-citizens-in-salisbury.

United States and Defense Intelligence Agency, *Challenges to Security in Space: Space Reliance in an Era of Competition and Expansion* (2022) www.dia.mil/Portals/110/Documents/News/Military_Power_Publications/Challenges_Security_Space_2022.pdf.

Uppsala Conflict Data Program, *UCDP/PRIO Armed Conflict Dataset*, www.prio.org/Data/Armed-Conflict/UCDP-PRIO/.

US Government, 'Fact Sheet: Presidential Memorandum – "Legal and Policy Transparency Concerning United States' Use of Military Force and Related National Security Operations" and Accompanying Report on Transparency in Legal and Policy Frameworks' (5 December 2016) https://obamawhitehouse.archives.gov/the-press-office/2016/12/05/fact-sheet-presidential-memorandum-legal-and-policy-transparency.

US White House, *Vice President Harris Advances National Security Norms in Space* (19 April 2022) www.whitehouse.gov/briefing-room/statements-releases/2022/04/18/fact-sheet-vice-president-harris-advances-national-security-norms-in-space/.

Index

aggression, 1, 4, 23, 71, 98, 130, 133, 174, *See also* Definition of Aggression
  crime of, 4, 11
  indirect, See *Definition of Aggression, articles 3(f) and (g)*
aircraft, 164
  aerial incursion, *See* Incusion, aerial
  air fleets, 93
  civil, 5, 166, 177
Algeria, 118
Al-Wazir, Khalil, 174
Antarctica, 144, 220
Argentina, 120
Armistice lines, 94, 109, 113
article 2(4), 1, *See also* Use of force, Threat of force
  all members, 85–7
  history of, 22
  international relations, 133, 137, 142, 155, 197, 204, 227
  relationship with customary rule, 16, 17, 56–70, 77
  subsequent agreements, 106–15
  against the territorial integrity..., 101
article 51, 6, 10, 57, 61, 136, 170, 178
  armed attack, 4, 6, 145
assassination, *See* targeted killing
Australia, 120, 220

blockade, 164, See also *Definition of Aggression, article 3(c)*
Brazil, 117
Briand–Kellogg Pact, *See* Kellogg–Briand Pact
Brownlie, Ian, 3, 23, 97, 102, 125, 129, 139, 140, 149, 162, 165
Burma, 118
Bush, George, 137

Cambodia, 174, 206
Cameroon, 118
Canada, 120, 185, 219, 223
Chile, 118, 119
China, 182, 218, 225
consent, 75, 103, 168
Corten, Olivier, 15, 63, 65, 77, 79, 98, 103, 117, 125, 140, 148, 149, 151, 152, 156, 177, 184, 210
countermeasures, 7, 9, 10
Crimea, 168
custom, 9
  Baxter's paradox, 11, 30–51
  conduct referable to treaty, 20, 35–6
  crystallisation, 29
  own impact, 51–6
  silence and inaction, 44–51
  treaty ratification and, 36
  two-element approach, 30–51
  verbal acts, 44
cyber operations, 2, 7, 8, 9, 126, 129, 130, 134, 135, 141, 195
Czechoslovakia, 118, 123, 162

de minimis, 4, 99, 138, 140–3, 185
Definition of Aggression, 106, 111, 123, 151, 161, 187, 199
  article 3(a) invasion or attack, occupation, annexation, 162, 200
  article 3(b) bombardment, 126
  article 3(c) blockade, 164, 200
  article 3(e) SOFA, 167, 200
  article 3(f) indirect aggression, 169, 201

Definition of Aggression (cont.)
article 3(g) substantial involvement, 93, 171, 201
Democratic Republic of the Congo, 168
Denmark, 207
disputed territory, 94

economic coercion, 116–25
effects, 5, 130, 138, 197
direct, 134
gravity, 197
physical, 130, 132, 164, 167, 174, 176, 195
potential, 136, 202, 214
temporary, 135
embassy, 94, 144
Entebbe incident, 93, 152
erga omnes, 10

France, 120, 210
Friendly Relations Declaration, 38, 42–4, 89, 106, 109
travaux préparatoires, 92, 96, 102, 116–25, 133

Georgia, 156
Germany, 162, 169, 208, 219
Federal Republic of, 33
German Democratic Republic, 33
Ghana, 118
Green, James, 56, 61, 63, 72–4
grey zone operations, 7
Guatemala, 120
Guinea, 207
Gulf War, 165, 216
Guyana v Suriname, 208

Henderson, Christian, 99, 125, 127, 130, 133, 137, 142, 149, 153
hot pursuit, 141, 207

Iceland, 208
incursion, 5, 150
aerial, 5, 97, 141, 151, 175, 176, 200
maritime, 141, 181, 182
response to, 97, 141, 176
territorial (small-scale), 5
India, 118, 218, 222
individuals, 58, 86, 93, 132, 150, *See also* Aggression, crime of
Indonesia, 174
intent, 4, 5, 94, 140, 145–57, 204, 227
accident, 150, 196
coercive, 152
hostile, 197
mistake, 150
international armed conflict and 'use of force', 211
International Court of Justice, 3
Armed Activities case, 3, 19, 142, 163, 168, 172
Certain Expenses advisory opinion, 91
Corfu Channel case, 3, 142, 144, 146
Fisheries Jurisdiction (Federal Republic of Germany v Iceland), 3
Fisheries Jurisdiction (Germany v Iceland), 208
Fisheries Jurisdiction (Spain v Canada), 3, 185
Fisheries Jurisdiction (UK v Iceland), 10, 75
Namibia advisory opinion, 108
Nicaragua case, 3, 6, 17–18, 25, 34, 37, 39, 42, 55, 61, 67, 71, 86, 98, 110, 138, 142, 153, 171, 175
North Sea Continental Shelf Cases, 31, 33, 35, 47, 51–6, 154
Nuclear Weapons advisory opinion, 3, 42, 96, 126, 148
Oil Platforms case, 3, 142
Statute of the, 26
Tehran Hostages case, 3
Temple of Preah Vihear, 174
Wall advisory opinion, 3, 142
International Criminal Court
crime of aggression, 11
Rome Statute, 4
war crimes, 11, 191
international humanitarian law, 163, 166
classification of conflict, 10, 211
International Law Association, 6
Committee on Formation of Customary (General) International Law, 40, 47, 52
International Law Commission
Articles on State Responsibility, *See* State responsibility
Committee on Peremptory Norms of General International Law (*jus cogens*), 71
Committee on Subsequent Agreement and Subsequent Practice, 68
Committee on the Identification of Customary International Law, 31, 37, 48
international organisations
practice of, 107
use of force by, 57, 86

international peace and security, 90–2
international relations, 87–101, 133, 137, 142, 155, 197, 204, 220, 227
inter-war period, 22
Iran, 2, 8, 142, 165, 175
Iraq, 142, 170, 175, 202
Israel, 93, 174
Italy, 120

Japan, 2, 33, 127, 182, 220
jus cogens, 5, 9, 70–7
jus in bello, *See* international humanitarian law

Kellogg–Briand Pact, 22, 87
Kelsen, Hans, 23, 24, 28, 53, 88, 125
Kenya, 118
Kreß, Claus, 19, 88, 95, 97, 103, 168, 169, 171, 172
Kuwait, 137, 202

law enforcement, 5, 97, 99, 141, 177, 185
  maritime, 93, 141, 155, 180, 204
  UN Basic Principles on the Use of Force and Firearms by Law Enforcement Officials, 100
law of armed conflict, *See* international humanitarian law
law of the sea, 99, 144
  Convention on the Law of the Sea, 36, 166, 180, 207
  EEZ (Exclusive Economic Zone), 26, 144, 180, 199, 205, 207, 208
  high seas, 89, 96, 144, 183, 184, 199, 209
  innocent passage, 181
  interdiction, 9
  internal waters, 144, 180, 210
  territorial sea, 5, 103, 141, 144, 180, 181, 182, 206, 207, 208, 210
League of Nations Covenant, 22
Lebanon, 120, 175
Liberia, 152, 184, 209
Libya, 142, 175
Liechtenstein, 94, 151
Litvinenko, Alexander, 137
Lotus case, 47, 183

M/V Saiga (No. 2), 207
Madagascar, 118
Malaysia, 137, 174
Mayaguez, 152, 206
merchant vessels, 5, 93, 165, 205
mere presence, 5, 167, 195
Mexico, 119
military occupation, 95, 162, 195, *See also* Definition of Aggression, article 3(a)

NATO, 2, 57, 216
Netherlands, 25, 120, 210
neutrality, 165
New Zealand, 210, 219
Nicaragua, 18
Nigeria, 118, 122
non-intervention principle, 10, 116, 133, 153
non-State armed groups, 58, 63, 86, 98, 130, 171, 201
North Korea, 2, 127, 135, 137, 142
Nötigung, 191

O'Connell, Mary Ellen, 98, 140, 141, 165
outer space, 2, 89, 96, 144, 190, 199, 216–28
  PAROS, 217
  satellites, 126, 129, 135, 136, 216
  space debris, 219
  space law, 217

peremptory norm, *See jus cogens*
Poland, 118
police measures, *See* law enforcement

Rainbow Warrior, 152, 210
Red Crusader, 207
rescue of nationals, 152, 175
Romania, 118, 123
Russia, 1, 168, 178, 203, 212, 218, 225
Ruys, Tom, 45, 98, 99, 141, 142, 150, 156, 177, 205

self-defence, *See* Article 51
Serbia, 142
silence and inaction, 44–51
Skripal, Sergei, 2, 137, 190, 202, 212–28
South Africa, 151
South China Sea, 8, 93, 199, 205
South Korea, 135
sovereignty, 90
space law, 217
Spain, 185
St Vincent and the Grenadines, 207
State
  extraterritorial manifestation, 94, 144
State responsibility, 9, 74, 86, 145
  attribution, 169, 172, 218
  circumstances precluding wrongfulness, 10, 177

Status of Forces Agreement, 165, See also *Definition of Aggression, article 3(e)*
submarines, 5, 141, 142, 144, 181, 182
Suriname, 208
Sweden, 120, 142, 182
Switzerland, 33, 94, 151
Syria, 118, 133, 170, 178

Tadic case, 87, 172
Tallinn Manual, 130, 134, 135
targeted killing, 2, 152, 174, 202, 212–28
terra nullius, 88, 199, 220
Thailand, 174
threat of force, 72, 165, 196, 209
  coercion, and, 147
  relationship with use of force, 147
Torrey Canyon, 184, 209
treaty interpretation, 78, 81–3, *See also* Vienna Convention on the Law of Treaties
  evolutive, 66
  modification, 64, 70, 76
Tunis, 174
Turkey, 133, 178
type theory, 12, 14, 189

Uganda, 93, 163, 168
Ukraine, 1, 168
UN Basic Principles on the Use of Force and Firearms by Law Enforcement Officials, 100
UN Charter
  article 1, 91
  article 2(3), 155
  article 2(4), *See* Article 2(4)
  article 2(6), 28, 53
  article 2(7), 147
  article 27(3), 108
  article 41, 8
  article 42, 8, 125
  article 51, *See* Article 51
  article 103, 69, 76
  article 108, 68
  article 109, 68
  chapter VII, 8, 10
  object and purpose, 89–92
  Preamble, 91
  travaux préparatoires, 102, 117
UN General Assembly resolutions
  as evidence of *opinio juris*, 20, 41–4
  Resolution 2625, *See* Friendly Relations Declaration
  Resolution 3314, *See* Definition of Aggression
  Resolution 42/22, 38, 89, 106, 111
  as subsequent agreement, 107
  World Summit Outcome Document, 90, 106, 112
UN Security Council, 4, 8
  resolutions as subsequent agreement, 107
United Arab Republic, 118
United Kingdom, 2, 120, 137, 142, 165, 184, 203, 207, 209, 210, 212, 219
USA, 2, 6, 8, 18, 25, 120, 142, 175, 202, 206, 218, 219, 225
use of force
  armed attack, relationship with, 6
  armed force, 5, 114, 116–25, 162, 188, 195
  customary prohibition, 17–29
  effects, *See* Effects
  gap, 6–7, 99, 138
  gravity, 4, 5, 94, 98, 145, 156, 185, 196, 204
  indirect, 86, 110, 130, 201
  intent, *See* Intent
  international relations, 220
  lower threshold, 7, 10
  nexus, 197, 203
  object, 197, 202
  ordinary meaning, 115
  against own population, 96
  within own territory, 63, 95–100, 150
  political context, 93, 198
USSR, 118

Venezuela, 120
Vienna Convention on the Law of Treaties
  1966 draft, 64
  article 5, 81
  article 31, 60, 78, 82, 106, 231
  article 32, 82, 107, 124
  article 40, 69
  article 41, 68
  article 52, 10, 75
  article 53, 70, 75
  draft article 36, 25
Vietnam, 206

war, 24–6, 27, 117
warship, 144, 165, 181
weapons, 5, 125–30, 176, 198
  ASAT, 218
  ballistic missile, 2

biological and chemical, 128, 137, 204, 212
cyber, *See* Cyber operations
dazzling, 129, 135, 218
jamming, 129, 135, 218
kinetic, 5, 128, 161
nuclear, 97, 129, 134
spoofing, 129, 135
use of environment as, 129

Yugoslavia, 118

www.ingramcontent.com/pod-product-compliance
Ingram Content Group Australia Pty Ltd
76 Discovery Rd, Dandenong South VIC 3175, AU
AUHW010327230226
423717AU00006B/54

9 781316 516973